MW00777005

Partisan Supremacy

Partisan Supremacy

How the GOP Enlisted
Courts to Rig America's
Election Rules

Terri Jennings Peretti

University Press of Kansas

Published by the University Press of Kansas (Lawrence, Kansas 66045), which was organized by the Kansas Board of Regents and is operated and funded by Emporia State University, Fort Hays State University, Kansas State University, Pittsburg State University, the University of Kansas, and Wichita State University.

Library of Congress Cataloging-in-Publication Data

Names: Peretti, Terri Jennings, 1956– author.
Title: Partisan supremacy : how the GOP enlisted courts to rig America's election rules / Terri Jennings Peretti.
Description: Lawrence : University Press of Kansas, 2020. | Includes bibliographical references and index.
Identifiers: LCCN 2020013713
  ISBN 9780700630196 (cloth)
  ISBN 9780700630202 (epub)
Subjects: LCSH: Political questions and judicial power—United States. | United States. Supreme Court. | Judicial process—United States. | Voter registration—United States. | Apportionment (Election law)—United States. | Partisanship—Political aspects—United States. | Campaign funds—Law and legislation—United States. | Republican Party (U.S. : 1854–) | United States—Politics and government.
Classification: LCC KF8748 .P387 2020 | DDC 342.73/07—dc23
LC record available at https://lccn.loc.gov/2020013713.

British Library Cataloguing-in-Publication Data is available.

Printed in the United States of America

10 9 8 7 6 5 4 3 2 1

To my granddaughters, who fill my heart

Contents

Figures and Tables

Figures

Tables

Acknowledgments

This book took longer to write than I would like to admit, and I accumulated many debts along the way. For generously reviewing individual chapters, including some rather rough early drafts, I wish to thank Larry Baum, Rick Hasen, Jim Cottrill, and Kyle Kopko. Larry was especially helpful with the theory chapter, with which I struggled. I am also grateful for the helpful feedback I received from my departmental colleagues, who were willing to interrupt their own work to help me with the latest "urgent" challenge with which I was wrestling; thank you, Anne Baker, Matt Harrigan, Naomi Levy, and Peter Minowitz. There are multiple scholars who generously shared their expertise, whether at academic conferences or as a result of my personal outreach (in alphabetical order): Paul Chen, Tao Lotus Dumas, Nicholas Goedert, Mark Graber, Mark McKenzie, Mark Rush, Ann Southworth, Isaac Unah, and Michael Zilis. Finally, this book is much better for the helpful feedback of the two scholars who reviewed the manuscript for University Press of Kansas. I especially appreciate being forced to revisit the redistricting and campaign finance chapters and develop arguments that were more careful and persuasive.

I offer my gratitude as well to Rachel Pietron, Rachel Sargent, and Evan Sargent for their outstanding research assistance. I am also indebted to David Congdon, the acquisitions editor for political science and law at University Press of Kansas, for his encouragement and helpful advice. My experiences working with other staff members at the press were uniformly excellent; I have appreciated their expertise and professionalism. Some components of the book have previously appeared in print, particularly the empirical research on voter identification reported in chapter 3. I am grateful to *Election Law Journal* and *Utah Law Review* for granting permission to reprint.

Finally, thanks go to my family, and especially my husband, Jimmy, for their love, support, and patience. I am certain that they wondered (along with me) if I would ever finish. I now have more time to devote to my granddaughters—Quinn, Luzciana, and Greer—to whom this book is dedicated.

Partisan Supremacy

Introduction

On April 6, 2020, the US Supreme Court decided *Republican National Committee v. Democratic National Committee,* reversing a lower court ruling that had extended the absentee ballot deadline for a Wisconsin election occurring the next day amid the COVID-19 pandemic and a statewide stay-at-home order.[1] The Court split strictly along partisan lines. The five Republican justices ruled in favor of the Republican National Committee, holding that a federal judge lacked the authority to change the state's deadline for voters to cast and mail an absentee ballot, as doing so would "fundamentally alter the nature of the election."[2] The four Democratic justices sided with the Democratic National Committee and rejected the majority's "narrow, technical" framing of the question, warning of the "massive disenfranchisement" of tens of thousands of citizens forced either to forfeit their right to vote or to "brave the polls, endangering their own and others' safety." In a separate case decided the same day, the Wisconsin Supreme Court blocked the governor's executive order that would have suspended in-person voting and postponed the election for two months.[3] It, too, divided sharply. The court's conservative majority ruled that the governor had no authority to suspend or rewrite the state's election laws, while the liberal dissenters criticized the decision as "another example of this court's unmitigated support of efforts to disenfranchise voters."[4] Much was at stake in this election. Conservative justice Daniel Kelly was on the ballot, seeking—with President Donald Trump's endorsement—to retain a critical seat on a court that would be deciding a challenge to the purge of over 200,000 citizens from the voting rolls.[5] Heightening the drama was the expectation that Wisconsin would play a critical role in the 2020 presidential election, as it did in 2016 when Trump won the state by fewer than 23,000 votes.

The striking political divisions on these two high courts perfectly matched the battle lines being drawn between the parties in heated debates over how safely to hold elections during the pandemic. It was, for example, Wisconsin's Democratic governor, Tony Evers, who had urged the Republican-majority legislature to postpone the April election to June and, when it refused, did so by executive order, which Republican legislators immediately challenged in court. Similar partisan clashes have occurred in other jurisdictions, including battleground states like Ohio, Michigan, and Pennsylvania and the nation's capital.[6] Republican president Trump has, for instance, vehemently opposed Democratic proposals to expand mail-in balloting in the 2020 election as it presented, in his words, "tremendous potential for voter fraud" and "doesn't work out well for Republicans."[7]

Trump's opposition was unsurprising, given the GOP's ongoing crusade to clean up America's elections and reduce voter fraud through a variety of questionable "reform" methods. Examples abound of recent voter-suppression efforts in Republican states that have been advanced in the name of electoral integrity. North Carolina mandated strict voter ID requirements, reduced early voting, and eliminated same-day registration, out-of-precinct voting, and preregistration of sixteen- and seventeen-year olds; Wisconsin, Georgia, Ohio, and Texas conducted large-scale voter purges; North Dakota tightened its voter identification rules by requiring a residential street address that Native Americans disproportionately lack; Dodge City, Kansas, moved its only polling place out of town, beyond the reach of public transportation and its large and impoverished Latino population; and the state of Tennessee imposed jail time and substantial fines for incomplete registration applications, likely ending voter registration drives that historically serve students and people of color. President Trump has also advanced the GOP's voter fraud narrative by falsely claiming that he, and not Hillary Clinton, actually won the popular vote in the 2016 election "if you deduct the millions of people who voted illegally," a charge he used to justify the creation of a Presidential Advisory Commission on Electoral Integrity, chaired by Vice President Mike Pence and voter-fraud crusader Kris Kobach.[8] Democrats condemn such claims as phony and a cover for a cynical Republican campaign to suppress minority votes.

A related charge, and this book's focus, is that the Republican-majority Supreme Court has assisted the GOP with its election reform agenda and helped Republicans win control of the White House, Congress, and multiple state governments.[9] It has done so, critics claim, by

- Stopping the Florida recount in the 2000 election in *Bush v. Gore* (2000).

- Disabling preclearance under the Voting Rights Act in *Shelby County v. Holder* (2013).
- Upholding voter identification requirements in *Crawford v. Marion County Election Board* (2008).
- Permitting partisan gerrymandering in *Vieth v. Jubelirer* (2004) and *Rucho v. Common Cause* (2019).
- Striking down limits on corporate campaign spending in *Citizens United v. FEC* (2010).
- Ending state-mandated "fair share" union fees for public sector employees in *Janus v. AFSCME* (2018).
- Upholding Ohio's voter purge policy in *Husted v. A. Philip Randolph Institute* (2018).[10]

This allegation might, in the Trump era, be characterized as "collusion" between Republican politicians and Republican judges to tilt democracy in the GOP's favor. It is reminiscent of a famous (or infamous) conversation between President Grover Cleveland and a fellow Democrat, Congressman Timothy Campbell. In response to President Cleveland's reluctance to support a bill because of its doubtful constitutionality, the congressman reportedly quipped, "What's the Constitution between friends?"[11] This suggestion of interbranch partisan cooperation in constitutional decision-making violates core normative beliefs about the law, including the expectation that judges should serve as neutral arbiters rather than biased partisans. Supreme Court justice Neil Gorsuch expressed this norm during his Senate confirmation hearing, asserting that "there is no such thing as a Republican judge or a Democratic judge. We just have judges in this country."[12]

Challenges to normative expectations of judicial neutrality deserve close scrutiny. There is, in fact, a growing scholarly literature on partisan influences in judicial decision-making.[13] I seek to add to it by examining the GOP's recent efforts to enlist judicial aid for its highly partisan election reform agenda. I examine four election law topics—the Voting Rights Act, voter identification, redistricting, and campaign finance—and ask whether courts have acted as neutral arbiters or friendly partisans.

How judges decide election law cases is neither an idle question nor a sterile intellectual inquiry. US courts "regularly decide a plethora of election-related legal issues" from voter eligibility and ballot access to vote counting and campaign finance.[14] How judges resolve these election disputes affects the fortunes of candidates and parties and the course of public policy. Election law litigation has, furthermore, substantially increased in recent decades in both the state and federal courts. From 1996 to 1999, election challenges averaged ninety-four per year; over the thirteen-year span after *Bush v. Gore*, there were 245 per year—2.6 times as many.[15] The US Supreme Court's election law docket has grown considerably since 1960. The Court decided an average of 10.3 election-related cases in each of the first six decades of the twentieth century, with those cases comprising 0.7 percent of cases decided by written opinion; the average number of election law cases jumped to sixty per decade over the next forty years, with 5.3 percent of cases decided by written opinion.[16] Charles Smith and Christopher Shortell documented a sizable increase in lawsuits involving presidential elections from 1992 to 2004; these cases, for example, more than doubled from 2000 to 2004, with increases disproportionately occurring in states that were competitive and "rich in electoral votes."[17] The 2020 election is, furthermore, expected to produce "a record level of election-related litigation."[18]

It is clear that parties and candidates "use litigation both more frequently and more strategically than in the past."[19] This increase in the number of election disputes gives courts greater influence over more election outcomes, putting them "in the position of 'kingmaker.'"[20] The "judicialization of elections" may also increase the incentives for politicians to pack the courts with "loyal partisans," further politicizing the courts and putting the judiciary's reputation and legitimacy at risk.[21]

It is important to know how courts have responded to these increasingly frequent opportunities for and pressures in deciding election disputes. Have they offered a neutral forum for assessing competing partisan claims? Have they enhanced democracy by promoting electoral competition and thwarting "partisan lockups" that entrench those in power, as some scholars advise?[22] Alternatively, are judges deciding, consciously or not, in ways that favor their partisan allies? This might not be surprising given that "partisanship is . . . ubiquitous . . . in election law."[23] State legislatures have considered a multitude of election reform measures in recent years on topics ranging from voter identification and early voting to same-day registration and felon eligibility, with Democrats and Republicans disagreeing sharply and consistently.[24] Partisanship exists not only in the crafting of election policy but also in its implementation by state and local officials who enjoy considerable discretion and are typically elected by partisan ballot.[25] The power of partisan officials to administer elections may even extend to contests in which they appear on the ballot, as was the case in 2018 when Republicans Brian Kemp and Kris Kobach each served as secretary of state while running for governor in Georgia and Kansas, respectively; both were additionally accused of voter purges intended to aid their chances of victory.[26] Partisanship might influence judicial decisions as well, given that most state and federal judges are selected through a partisan process involving either election or appointment by elected officials.

Bush v. Gore (2000) is an unfortunate reminder that partisan judging is not just a potential phenomenon. The outcome of the 2000 presidential race between Al Gore and George W. Bush ultimately rested on the popular vote result in Florida, which was so close that it triggered a recount. Multiple lawsuits followed involving how that recount should proceed. Courts would indeed become kingmakers. The Supreme Court surprised most observers, first, by its willingness to intervene in the dispute and, second, with its decision to stop the recount and thereby guarantee a GOP victory. In the end, it was five Republican justices—O'Connor, Kennedy, Rehnquist, Scalia, and Thomas—who effectively handed Bush the White House. They did so on the basis of a liberal equal protection principle that they had never before employed and that they forbade lower court judges to apply in the future, making the decision "lawless all the way down."[27] In so transparently and insincerely manipulating legal doctrine to put George W. Bush in the White House, the justices "showed their partisan stripes."[28] There are multiple lessons from *Bush v. Gore*, but the most obvious is that judges may be unable to resist the temptation of partisan judging when the stakes are great. This is true even at the highest level of the judiciary and with the glare of public and media scrutiny.

This book explores whether a partisan label can also be attached to recent election law decisions like *Shelby County v. Holder* (2013), which invalidated the Voting Rights Act's preclearance coverage formula, and *Citizens United* (2010), which struck down federal limits on corporate spending in election campaigns. In this introduction, I lay the foundation for this inquiry, focusing on the New Right Republican regime, its electoral challenges, and its conscription of courts to address those challenges.

The Regime Politics Approach

Assessing whether judges decide election law cases neutrally or in ways that assist their political allies requires more than a mere partisan tally of judicial votes, the typical approach employed by researchers in this field of study, as I explain in chapter 1. This traditional analysis must be supplanted by a broader inquiry that looks beyond judicial votes to the partisan regimes that construct and populate courts in their pursuit of electoral and policy success.[29]

Regime politics theory is a foundational idea shaping this study. This intellectual perspective focuses on the relationship between courts and broader political currents and structures, particularly the partisan coalitions that, in cyclical fashion, tend to dominate American politics. It thus complements and extends the partisan realignment literature that focuses on the regular and "durable shifts in partisan allegiance by voting blocs large enough to bring about a long term change in the balance of party fortunes."[30] In the 1930s, for example, Franklin Roosevelt profoundly altered party politics in the United States by building a broad and long-lasting "New Deal" Democratic coalition that included workers, Southern whites, the poor, and racial, ethnic, and religious minorities; in a more recent example, the GOP transformed in the final decades of the twentieth century into a party advancing economic and racial conservatism and drawing support from white, rural, and religious voters, especially in the South.[31] Regime politics scholars connect these party transformations to courts and judges. They examine how coalition leaders empower and staff courts to be allies who support the party's interests and how doctrinal developments then reflect and are tied to electoral politics. Cornell Clayton and Mitchell Pickerill, for example, explain how jurisprudential changes by the Rehnquist Court in the federalism and criminal justice fields were "directly linked to the electoral ascendancy of the New Right . . . just as the Warren Court's 'fundamental liberties' jurisprudence was prefigured by the New Deal–Great Society political regime."[32] Although the causal mechanism is neither simple nor direct, regimists accept the premise of Mr. Dooley's famous aphorism that "th' Supreme Court follows th' iliction returns."[33]

Multiple historical accounts confirm that politicians have often succeeded in shaping judicial review to be helpful to the current regime. The Marshall Court, for example, was constructed by the Federalists to assist them in their nationalizing efforts; success came in cases like *Mc-*

Culloch v. Maryland (1819), which prevented the states from taxing and thereby undermining the Bank of the US, and *Martin v. Hunter's Lessee* (1816), which held federal law, and federal judicial interpretations of it, supreme over contrary state law and state court rulings.[34] In the post-Reconstruction period, an electorally vulnerable Republican Party employed a judicial strategy as part of its efforts to promote national economic development; it successfully entrenched its economic policy preferences by expanding federal court jurisdiction over economic matters and appointing conservatives to the bench.[35] The New Deal Court, composed of FDR appointees, abandoned existing doctrines that limited the government's economic regulatory power, thereby withdrawing its assistance from the regime's business opponents; it did not, however, abdicate its policy role, developing a "rights-centered liberalism" that favored New Deal allies like racial minorities and labor unions.[36] The Warren Court was a part and product of the liberal Kennedy-Johnson regime, assisting in its pursuit of civil rights and the Great Society and its battles against the South on issues of race, religion, and criminal justice.[37] This interbranch cooperation can be seen, for example, in doctrinal changes in the state action field where the Constitution was traditionally restricted to governmental, and not private, action. Collaborating with Democratic Party leaders in the executive branch, the Court broadened the meaning of state action in cases like *Shelley v. Kraemer* (1948) and empowered judges to reach the private race discrimination that Congress was unable to address due to the stranglehold of its Southern members.[38]

Regime politics scholarship often, and for good reason, focuses on the president since he acts as the leader of his political party, can profoundly alter the federal courts with his appointment power, and possesses the greatest potential for "disruption" in American politics.[39] Not all presidents, however, are similarly situated in "political time" with respect to this capacity for political disruption and policy transformation. According to Stephen Skowronek, the president's authority is determined, first, by whether he is "affiliated with or opposed to the dominant ideological and programmatic commitments of the era" and, second, whether those commitments are "resilient" or "vulnerable."[40] Presidents like Franklin Roosevelt and Ronald Reagan came to power as the previous regime was collapsing and were thus best situated to initiate sweeping change and lead during a "politics of reconstruction." Their successors—Harry Truman and George H. W. Bush, respectively—were affiliated with the new and still resilient regime and acted to extend its commitments during a "politics of articulation." Leaders with considerably weaker authority are "disjunctive" presidents like Herbert Hoover and Jimmy Carter, who are regime-affiliated but serve during its decline, and "preemptive" presidents like Richard Nixon and Bill Clinton, who belong to a party that is opposed to the still-resilient regime. Skowronek alerts us to the importance of where presidents find themselves in "the regime structure of American political history," which affects their capacity to direct constitutional policy and shape constitutional politics.[41] Most scholars regard Donald Trump as a "late-regime affiliate" like Jimmy Carter,[42] which has important consequences for his actions with respect to election law, a theme to which I return in the conclusion.

Partisan regimes typically use courts not only to achieve their policy objectives but also to advance their electoral interests. Franklin Roosevelt used Justice Department litigation and Supreme Court appointments to protect key coalition members like union workers and racial minorities whose ability to vote, organize, and participate politically was critical to insuring the Democratic Party's future electoral success. FDR's Justice Department accordingly sought to "subvert the state and local parties' supremacy over the electoral process" and "disrupt southern politics" by attacking tools of black disenfranchisement like poll taxes and the white primary; his judicial appointees additionally advanced a rights-oriented approach that supported these policies.[43] Because these administrative and judicial strategies were less visible, Roosevelt avoided a confrontation with a Southern-dominated Congress and was better able to manage a discordant party coalition that included both African Americans and Southern whites. In a "politics of articulation," President John F. Kennedy elaborated and extended New Deal commitments, which included efforts to insure the regime's electoral viability. For example, he continued his campaign, begun as a US senator, against the malapportionment that advantaged the Republican Party by overrepresenting conservative whites residing in rural areas.[44] As I discuss in chapter 4, JFK's Supreme Court appointments and his Justice Department's litigation strategies led to *Baker v. Carr* (1962)[45] and the Court's egalitarian one-person, one-vote rule. This "reapportionment revolution"[46] greatly aided Democrats in their desire to translate a numerical advantage in voter support into a seat advantage in the House of Representatives and state legislatures. The Warren Court thus helped the Democratic Party as much as it helped democracy.

History demonstrates that with broad and enduring electoral success, a political party is able to dominate public policy as a result of influence that spans all branches of government, including the judiciary. Such supremacy may extend to the very election rules that help determine whether the party will stay in power. While the interbranch conflict expected in a system of separation of powers and checks and balances does not disappear, cooperation becomes more likely as partisan allies across the branches pursue policies that serve their mutual interests. Regime politics theory, in this way, offers an alternative to the traditional framing of courts as independent and powerful, even to the point of illegitimacy. Instead of the traditional concern with *judicial* supremacy, which Barry Friedman has labeled an "academic obsession," regimists suggest that *partisan* supremacy is a more realistic outcome and, thus, a more logical focus of scholarly inquiry.[47] Importantly, however, the "partisan supremacy" language should not imply that courts and judges are subordinate to the regime. Rather, they are members of and partners in the partisan regimes that often dominate American democracy and policy making through legitimate electoral means.

The New Right Republican Regime

Post-1960s politics saw the rise of "the New Right Republican regime,"[48] sometimes referred to more simply as the Reagan regime.[49] The GOP won the White House in five of six elections from 1968 to 1988 and, in the 1980s and 1990s, finally broke the Democrats' monopoly as the majority party in Congress. Like the New Deal–Great Society regime before it, the Reagan regime sought to achieve its objectives not only legislatively and administratively but also judicially. Coalition leaders deliberately employed courts as part of their strategy to tilt electoral politics and public policy in the party's favor. This included trying to undermine the federal government's role in elections and dismantle the liberalized election rules established by the previous regime.

Richard Nixon's 1968 campaign attacked the Warren Court and blamed its liberal excesses for rising crime and urban unrest, seeking to destabilize the New Deal coalition and construct a new Republican majority that included conservative Southern whites and working-class Catholics in the urban North; once in the White House, Nixon sought to shift the Court to the right, but mostly on issues with an electoral payoff, like school desegregation and law and order.[50] His chances for success were greatly enhanced by the four Supreme Court vacancies that he received in his first term, both by luck and design.[51]

Ronald Reagan also enjoyed considerable opportunities to reshape constitutional policy as a result of the collapsing New Deal coalition, his 1980 landslide, and multiple vacancies on the Court. Furthermore, he had a clear constitutional vision and a strong commitment to pursuing it. A key priority was altering the balance of power between the federal and state governments, mostly by limiting Congress's power under the commerce clause and the Reconstruction amendments. An originalist approach to constitutional interpretation would additionally serve to empower judges to overturn precedents, even enduring ones, that stood in the way. This agenda was carefully laid out in multiple documents prepared at the request of attorney general Edwin Meese by the Justice Department's Office of Legal Policy, including "Guidelines on Constitutional Litigation," "The Constitution in the Year 2000," "Wrong Turns on the Road to Judicial Activism," and "Original Meaning Jurisprudence." Meese additionally used public speeches, Justice Department seminars, and the recruitment of young conservative lawyers to nurture a nascent conservative legal movement that would serve as a counterweight to the long-standing liberal legal establishment.[52] Republican appointments to the Court, particularly the so-called Federalist Five (Justices O'Connor, Rehnquist, Scalia, Kennedy, and Thomas), accomplished significant—and some say revolutionary—change in the federalism field.[53] The Court's conservative shift, strengthened by additional Republican appointments like Roberts, Alito, Gorsuch, and Kavanaugh, has had major consequences for civil rights and election law. This is seen most starkly in the *Shelby County* decision, discussed in chapter 2, which effectively ended the Voting Rights Act's preclearance regime on newly discovered "equal state sovereignty" grounds.

Challenges Facing the New Right Regime

All partisan regimes, even those as dominant as the New Deal coalition, experience electoral and policy challenges. Keith Whittington identifies "three common barriers" that party coalitions confront as they pursue their policy agendas: "federalism, entrenched interests and coalitional heterogeneity." Policy resistance, in other words, is likely from opposing-party officials at the state and local level, holdovers from the previous regime, and the regime's own members given that political parties are often "fractious coalitions."[54] The New Right regime is certainly no exception, with the ultraconservative Tea Party, the Trump populist wing, and more moderate establishment members at odds on a variety of issues including trade, immigration, and the debt ceiling. Such intraparty disagreements were sufficient to derail the efforts of President Trump and GOP congressional leaders in 2017 to repeal and replace the Affordable Care Act, a high-priority legislative goal.

The Reagan regime has, in recent years, faced considerable electoral challenges. It is not nearly as dominant electorally as might be suggested by its 2010 rout of the Democrats in elections across the nation and its 2016 victory that produced unified control of Congress and the White House. There has, in fact, been a close competitive balance between the parties in recent years, beginning with the fact that in 2019 a larger proportion of Americans identified with or leaned toward the Democratic Party (47 percent) compared to the Republican Party (42 percent).[55] Additionally, in the seven presidential contests from 1992 to 2016, the Republican candidate lost the Electoral College vote four times and the popular vote six times. In the ten elections from 2000 to 2018, the GOP secured control of the House seven times and the Senate five times. House GOP candidates, furthermore, won a majority of the nationwide two-party vote in only half of the ten elections from 2000 to 2018 and only 29 percent of the seven elections from 2006 to 2018. This pales in comparison to the electorally dominant performance of the New Deal regime from 1932 to 1964, when Democrats won the White House in seven of nine elections and both houses of Congress in sixteen of eighteen elections.

In addition to facing a highly competitive Democratic Party, the GOP is confronted with demographic trends that are not hospitable to its future electoral success. Republican voters are more likely to be white, male, rural, older, and religiously affiliated, especially evangelical Christian.[56] Reflecting these patterns, Donald Trump won majority voter support in his 2016 victory from men (52 percent), whites (57 percent), rural residents (66 percent), regular church-goers (56 percent), Protestants (58 percent), white Catholics (60 percent), evangelical Christians (81 percent), and those age forty-five or older (52 percent).[57] Like other recent GOP presidential candidates, Trump received the votes of only a minority of nonwhites (8 percent of African Americans, 28 percent of

Latinos, and 27 percent of Asian Americans), eighteen- to twenty-nine-year-olds (36 percent), and the religiously unaffiliated (26 percent).[58]

The biggest challenge for the GOP is that the groups dominating its voter base are declining as a proportion of the US population. For example, the percentage of adults affiliated with a religion dropped from 83 percent in 2007 to 77 percent in 2014; from 2009 to 2019, the share of religiously unaffiliated adults grew from 17 to 26 percent, primarily due to an older cohort of religious Americans being replaced by a younger cohort of less religious Americans.[59] With regard to rural areas, two-thirds of US counties with fewer than 50,000 residents experienced yearly population losses from 2010 to 2016, and counties with fewer than 25,000 residents lost 2 percent of their population over this time period;[60] in contrast, urban counties have grown at roughly the overall national growth rate of 13 percent from 2000 to 2018.[61] Whites are also shrinking as a percentage of the US electorate, from 88 percent in 1980, to 70 percent in 2016, and down to 67 percent in 2020.[62] According to census projections offered by William Frey, the United States will become "minority white" by 2045, when whites will constitute 49.9 percent of the population. Significant growth is expected for Asian Americans, who in 2045 will comprise 7.8 percent of the population, and Latinos, who will reach 24.6 percent.[63] Compounding the GOP's difficulties, the "minority white tipping point" for young people comes even sooner, with minorities outnumbering whites by 2020 for those under age eighteen and by 2027 for those ages eighteen to twenty-nine. Clearly, the biggest challenge for the GOP comes from explosive growth in the Latino population, which is expected to increase by 85 percent over the next four decades and will constitute a quarter of all Americans by 2045.[64] Nonwhite Hispanics, furthermore, represented only 2 percent of voters in 1980, 7 percent in 2000, 11 percent in 2016, and over 13 percent in 2020, a figure that could double by the midpoint of the twenty-first century.[65] A reasonable expectation is that the GOP's poor electoral performance—only three in ten Hispanic voters supported Mitt Romney in 2012 and Trump in 2016—will worsen, given the party's tough stance on immigration and President Trump's harsh rhetoric and policies, particularly with respect to family separation at the border and Deferred Action for Childhood Arrivals (DACA).

Another distinctive feature of the Reagan regime that poses an electoral challenge is the party's strong rightward shift, particularly among Republican elites.[66] This can be seen in Keith Poole and Howard Rosenthal's NOMINATE scores, which measure congressional ideology based on the roll-call voting history of each member over time. According to their liberal-conservative continuum, where 1.0 is very conservative and −1.0 is very liberal, the GOP mean in the House grew from approximately 0.2 in 1979 to 0.7 in 2015.[67] The growing conservatism of congressional Republicans has extended across multiple issues, including racial issues in the 1960s and cultural and social welfare issues in the 1980s and 1990s.[68] Ideological polarization between the congressional parties has increased substantially, with Poole and Rosenthal characterizing it as "at the highest level since the end of Reconstruction."[69] Less commonly observed is the disproportionate contribution to this sizable gap of congressional Republicans who from 1979 to 2015 moved substantially to the right (from 0.2 to 0.7) while congressional Democrats moved only modestly to the left (from −0.3 to −0.4).[70] In addition, recent public opinion surveys indicate that more Americans support the policy positions of the Democratic Party compared to those of the radicalized Republican Party on a broad range of issues such as climate change, health care, minimum wage, immigration, abortion, and gun control.[71]

As Matt Grossman and David Hopkins explain, the parties diverge in other "foundational" ways, beyond their increasingly distant locations on an ideological scale; while the Democratic Party is "fundamentally a group coalition," the Republican Party is "the vehicle of an ideological movement."[72] This "asymmetric configuration" includes different "governing styles," with Democrats "responsive to a set of social constituencies prizing incremental policy goals" and "Republican officeholders . . . increasingly embrac[ing] a highly confrontational approach that eschews . . . compromise in favor of maximizing partisan conflict," with government shutdowns and the Clinton impeachment serving as examples.[73] As Thomas Mann and Norman Ornstein more provocatively state the matter, when it comes to political challenges in the United States like polarization, ideological extremism, and gridlock, "Republicans are the problem."[74]

Given these weaknesses in its electoral base and limited voter support for its increasingly extreme policy positions, how has the Republican Party succeeded electorally and maintained its considerable political power? How, for example, did the GOP in 2018 enjoy unified control of the elective branches of the national government and majority status on the Supreme Court? There are multiple reasons, but the most important are elections that are geographically based and winner-take-all, equal state representation in the Senate, and life tenure for Supreme Court justices.

Instead of large, multi-member districts with seats awarded through proportional representation, the United States uses single-member districts with each seat for a district or state awarded to the plurality winner. This greatly increases the likelihood of having a two-party rather than a multi-party system, though it does not inherently favor one party over another. That has changed with the trend of geographic polarization that began in the mid-1970s. As Jonathan Rodden explains, the correlation between population density and Democratic voting has greatly increased, with the Democrats on their way to becoming "an exclusively urban party."[75] Many (though not all) political scientists believe that this contributes to their underrepresentation in legislative bodies as Democratic candidates tend to win by larger vote margins in heavily Democratic urban areas.[76] For example, in 2016 victorious House Democrats won an average of 67.4 percent of the two-party vote in their districts, compared to 63.8 percent for victorious Republicans.[77] This explains why Democrats must win a sizable majority of the nationwide popular vote—by as much as a 6- or 7-percent margin—in order to win a majority of seats in the House.[78]

Equal state representation in the Senate has also aided the GOP as it gives disproportionate voter influence and political power to sparsely populated rural states where Republican support is strong.[79] Benjamin Highton illustrates this advantage by pointing out that although Obama won the national popular vote in 2012 by nearly four percentage points, the average state vote margin favored Romney by nearly 2 percent.[80] Especially significant, in the twenty-five most populous states containing 258 million people, Obama won by an average of 2.3 percent, but in the twenty-five least populous states, containing only 50.4 million people, Romney won by an average of 6 percent. This helps to explain how, in the 2012, 2014, and 2016 elections that produced the GOP-majority Senate in 2017 (albeit by a slim one-vote margin), Republican candidates actually earned fifteen million fewer votes than Democratic candidates—102.3 million compared to 117.4 million;[81] in the 2018 election, Democratic Senate candidates earned twelve million more votes than the Republican candidates, though the GOP retained its majority and gained two seats.[82] The Republicans' advantage in the Senate is expected to grow due to a population trend that actually favors the GOP: by 2040, 69 percent of the US population will live in sixteen states controlling thirty-two Senate seats, with the remaining 31 percent of Americans—who are "older, whiter, more rural, [and] more male"—choosing a supermajority of sixty-eight senators.[83]

Because of the Senate's role both in granting two additional electoral votes to each state and in confirming Supreme Court nominees, this pro-Republican bias extends further to these additional sites of electoral influence and political power. State-based representation in the Senate has, for example, aided the Republicans in their efforts to place conservative copartisans on the Supreme Court. Clarence Thomas, for instance, would not have been confirmed if Senate seats were apportioned on the basis of population.[84] Representational distortions in both the Senate and Electoral College have, furthermore, created a new phenomenon that Kevin McMahon calls "minority justices": Supreme Court justices who have been confirmed by a majority of US senators who do not represent a majority of voters nationwide.[85] The only minority justices over the past century, during which senators have been directly elected, are all recent Republican nominees: Clarence Thomas, Samuel Alito, Neil Gorsuch, and Brett Kavanaugh. Gorsuch, for example, was confirmed by fifty-one Republicans and three Democrats who had won 54.1 million votes in their elections—nearly twenty million fewer votes than those earned by the forty-five Democrats who voted against confirmation. Justices Gorsuch and Kavanaugh, furthermore, were nominated by a minority president, Donald Trump, who lost the popular vote in 2016 by over 2.8 million votes. This may explain why these justices—or at least the three included in Stephen Jessee and Neil Malhotra's study (Thomas, Alito, and Gorsuch)—are more conservative than most Americans and more conservative even than most Republicans.[86]

Life tenure for Supreme Court justices is a final constitutional feature that has worked to the GOP's advantage in the modern era, through both luck and strategic retirements. Because the justices face neither term limits nor a mandatory retirement age, they can stay on the bench as long as they like and time their departures when a copartisan president is in office. Turnover on the Court is inevitably erratic, and the distribution of vacancies across presidential terms has been quite uneven. Richard Nixon, for example, enjoyed four appointment opportunities in his first three years in office, while Jimmy Carter received none in his four-year term; Donald Trump filled two Supreme Court vacancies in his first two years in office, while Barack Obama filled two in his entire eight years as president. It is a simple fact that the GOP has been quite fortunate in recent decades when it comes to the timing of Supreme Court vacancies. For example, in the ten presidential elections spanning the 1980 to 2018 period, the Republican Party won the popular vote four times (40 percent) and the Electoral College six times (60 percent), but filled ten out of fourteen vacancies (71 percent). In the thirteen presidential elections from 1968 to 2018, Republicans won the popular vote six times (46 percent) and the Electoral College eight times (62 percent) but filled fifteen of nineteen vacancies (79 percent). This advantage in appointment opportunities—aided by timely retirements like those of Republican justices Potter Stewart, Warren Burger, Sandra Day O'Connor, and Anthony Kennedy—has helped the party secure a majority on the Supreme Court for the past half century.

Multiple factors such as geographic polarization, representational distortions in America's elective institutions, and the irregular departures of life-tenured Supreme Court justices have enabled the Republican Party to enjoy electoral success and political power beyond what its voter support would predict. Some commentators even contend that "we are living in an age of minority rule."[87] This is not to claim that the GOP does not deserve the power that it holds. It has wisely taken advantage of the electoral rules that currently exist and has, like most parties in US history, sought to manipulate those rules even further in order to preserve its power.

The GOP's Response to Its Electoral Challenges

The Republican Party has responded to its electoral challenges and desire for political survival with, first, a distinctive election reform agenda and, second, a fierce commitment to conservative judicial appointments. With regard to the former, the GOP has been forced to address the challenge of a dwindling voter base and the reality that "youthful minorities" who strongly support the Democratic Party "are the engine of future growth" in the American electorate.[88] Party elites are also well aware of "the crucial role turnout plays in Republican victories," with Democrats overrepresented among "non-voters and presidential-year-only voters" and underrepresented among "core voters," who regularly participate and are "disproportionately white, wealthier and older."[89] An unsurprising result is a Republican reform agenda that restricts access to the ballot in ways that are expected to affect young, poor, and minority voters disproportionately; such measures include voter identification requirements, shorter early-voting periods, reductions in polling places, and tighter registration rules that include regular voter purges.

The party's growing commitment to restrictive voter reforms can be seen both in its national platforms and in the hundreds of state legislative proposals that it has introduced since 2000. With regard to the former, Table I.1 provides multiple statements pertaining to voting rights, presidential elections, and redistricting that are found in each party's national platforms from 1968 to 2016.[90] (The extensive comments that both parties provided over the years regarding campaign finance are covered in chapter 5.) Looking first at the Republican National Committee (RNC) platforms, there has not been until recently a strong concern by the Republican Party with election security and reform. Instead, it has for most of this period offered general statements affirming the importance of expanded citizen participation. It additionally recommended in 1968 that states "remove unreasonable requirements . . . for voting in Presidential elections"; praised in 1972 President Nixon's approval of amendments to the Voting Rights Act; and expressed in 2004 its commitment to "free and fair elections" and its concern that minorities might fear the loss of their voting rights due to "inaccurate or insecure technology or because of a rolling back in the gains made by the passage of civil rights legislation." The party sometimes advanced specific positions on election reform issues, such as favoring Electoral College reform in 1968, opposing "postcard voter registration" in 1980, and supporting independent redistricting commissions in 1992. A concern for electoral integrity and state autonomy in safeguarding it appears here and there but plays a much more prominent role in the 2008, 2012, and 2016 platforms. In these three documents, the GOP endorses a number of seemingly antidemocratic (and anti-Democratic) policies: for example, opposing Electoral College reform (2008, 2012) and the restoration of voting rights to felons (2008); supporting photo identification requirements and the states' freedom to adopt them without federal interference (2008, 2012, 2016); and favoring proof of citizenship for voter registration, the Interstate Voter Registration Crosscheck Program (Kris Kobach's pet project), and the use of citizenship rather than residency as the basis for representation (2016).

The GOP's commitment to election reform has also appeared in state legislatures, which have seen a dramatic increase in proposals to restrict voting access. An average of 107 such bills were introduced each

Table I.1. National Party Platform Statements Regarding Election Reform, 1968–2016

Year	Election Law Topic	Republican Party	Democratic Party
1968	Voting rights		"Because of the Voting Rights Act of 1965, the right to the ballot box—the right on which all other rights depend—has been reinforced by law."
	Presidential elections	"The strengthening of citizen influence on government requires a number of improvements in political areas. For instance, we propose to reform the electoral college system, establish a nation-wide, uniform voting period for Presidential elections, and recommend that the states remove unreasonable requirements, residence and otherwise, for voting in Presidential elections."	"We fully recognize the principle of one man, one vote in all elections. We urge that due consideration be given to the question of presidential primaries throughout the nation. We urge reform of the electoral college and election procedures to assure that the votes of the people are fully reflected. . . . We urge all levels of our Party to assume leadership in removing all remaining barriers to voter registration. . . . We will also seek to eliminate disenfranchisement of voters who change residence during an election year."
	Redistricting		"We fully recognize the principle of one man, one vote."
1972	Voting rights	"In 1970 President Nixon approved strong new amendments to the Voting Rights Act of 1965, and we pledge continued vigilance to ensure that the rights affirmed by this act are upheld."	"We . . . call for full and uniform enforcement of the Voting Rights Act of 1965. But further steps are needed to end all barriers to participation in the political process: Universal voter registration by post card;

Bilingual means of registration and voting; Bilingual voter education programs; Liberalized absentee voting; Minimum residency requirements of 30 days for all elections, including primaries; Student voting where they attend schools; Study and review of the Hatch Act, to see what can be done to encourage good citizenship and reasonable participation by government employees."

Presidential elections

"We favor a Constitutional change to abolish the Electoral College and to give every voter a direct and equal voice in Presidential elections. The amendment should provide for a run-off election, if no candidate received more than 40 percent of the popular vote. . . . The Presidential primary system today is an unacceptable patchwork. The Democratic Party supports federal laws that will embody the following principles: Protect the opportunity for less-known candidates to build support; Establish uniform ground rules; Reduce the cost of primary campaigns; Promote maximum voter turnout."

1976   Voting rights

"We support . . . vigorous enforcement of voting rights legislation to assure the constitutional rights of minority and

(continued on the next page)

Table I.1. *Continued*

Year	Election Law Topic	Republican Party	Democratic Party
			language-minority citizens; the passage of legislation providing for registration by mail in federal elections to erase existing barriers to voter participation."
1980	Voting rights	"The Republican Party has consistently encouraged full participation in our electoral processes and is disturbed by the steady decline in voter participation in the United States in recent years. . . . Republicans support public policies that will promote electoral participation without compromising ballot-box security. We strongly oppose national postcard voter registration schemes because they are an open invitation to fraud."	"In the 1980s we need to enact reforms which will . . . encourage voter participation in elections through use of simplified procedures for registration in states that lack mail or election day registration procedures, and by resisting efforts to reduce access to bilingual ballots; and Increase opportunities for full participation in all areas of party and government affairs by the low and moderate income majority of Americans."
	Presidential elections	"We prefer the present system of having the states and party rules determine the presidential nominating process to the concept of a uniform national primary which would only add to the already high costs of, and excessive federal intrusion into, presidential campaigns."	
1984	Voting rights	"Free individuals must have unrestricted access to the process of self-government. We deplore the growing labyrinth of bewildering regulations and	"Although the statute protecting voting rights has been extended through a massive bipartisan effort, opposed by the Reagan

Year	Topic	(Republican)	(Democratic)
		obstacles which have increased the power of political professionals and discouraged the participation of average Americans. Even well-intentioned restrictions on campaign activity stifle free speech and have a chilling effect on spontaneous political involvement by our citizens."	Administration, a Reagan Supreme Court could still effectively nullify it simply by erecting impossible standards of proof."
1988	Voting rights	"Republicans want to broaden involvement in the political process. We oppose government controls that make it harder for average citizens to be politically active."	"We believe that this country's democratic processes must be revitalized: by securing universal, same day and mail-in voter registration . . . by preventing the misuse of at-large elections, the abuse of election day challenges and registration roll purges . . . by assuring and pledging the full and equal access of women and minorities to elective office and party endorsement.
	Redistricting		"We believe that this country's democratic processes must be revitalized: by . . . preventing . . . any undercounting in the national census, and any dilution of the one-person, one-vote principle."
1992	Voting rights	"We support State efforts to increase voter participation but condemn Democrat attempts to perpetrate voter fraud through schemes that override the States' safeguards of orderly voter registration. And it is critical that the States retain the authority to tailor voter registration	"We support . . . stronger protection of voting rights for racial and ethnic minorities, including language access to voting; and continued resistance to discriminatory English-only pressure groups. . . . We need new voter registration laws that expand the

(continued on the next page)

Table I.1. *Continued*

Year	Election Law Topic	Republican Party	Democratic Party
		procedures to unique local circumstances."	electorate, such as universal same-day registration."
	Redistricting	"Throughout the 1980s, voters were cheated out of dozens of seats in the House of Representatives and in State legislatures because of Democrats. districts were oddly shaped to guarantee election It was swindle by law. We support State-level appointment of non-partisan redistricting commissions to apply clear standards for compactness of districts, competitiveness between the parties, and protection of community interests."	
1996	Voting rights		"After years of Republican delay, Democrats passed and the President signed the Motor Voter Bill to make it easier for people to participate in our democracy and exercise their civic responsibility in the voting booth. . . . We believe all Americans have a right to fair political representation—including the citizens of the District of Columbia who deserve full self-governance."
	Redistricting	"We will continue our fight against gerrymandered congressional districts designed to thwart majority rule."	

Year	Category	
2000	Redistricting	"Gerrymandered congressional districts are an affront to democracy and an insult to the voters. We oppose that and any other attempt to rig the electoral process."
2004	Voting rights	"The foundation of our democratic republic is our commitment to conducting free and fair elections. Unfortunately, in November 2000, too many people believed they were denied the right to vote. Many African Americans, Hispanics, and others fear they may lose the right to vote because of inaccurate or insecure technology or because of a rolling back in the gains made by the passage of civil rights legislation. Our national commitment to a voting process that has integrity was underscored in 2002 when Congress passed and the President signed the Help America Vote Act (HAVA). We will continue to do all we can to ensure that every lawful vote counts for all Americans." "We will call for legislative action that will fully protect and enforce the fundamental Constitutional right of every American to vote—to ensure . . . that, in disputed elections, every vote is counted fully and fairly . . . it is the priority of the Democratic Party to fulfill the promise of election reform, reauthorize the expiring provisions of the Voting Rights act, and vigorously enforce all our voting rights laws."
2008	Redistricting	"We support moving toward a census that duly counts every American."
	Voting rights	"We will fully fund the Help America Vote Act and work to fulfill the promise of election reform, including fighting to end long lines at voting booths and ensuring that all registration materials, voting materials, polling places, and voting machines are truly accessible "We oppose attempts to distort the electoral process by wholesale restoration of the franchise to convicted felons. . . . Preventing voting fraud is a civil rights issue. We support the right of states to require an official government-issued photo identification for voting and call upon the

(continued on the next page)

Table I.1. *Continued*

Year	Election Law Topic	Republican Party	Democratic Party
		Department of Justice to deploy its resources to prevent ballot tampering in the November elections. We support efforts by state and local election officials to ensure integrity in the voting process and to prevent voter fraud and abuse, particular as it relates to voter registration and absentee ballots."	to seniors, Americans with disabilities, and citizens with limited English proficiency.... We will vigorously enforce our voting rights laws instead of making them tools of partisan political agendas; we oppose laws that require identification in order to vote or register to vote, which create discriminatory barriers to the right to vote and disenfranchise many eligible voters; and we oppose tactics which purge eligible voters from voter rolls."
2012	Voting rights	"We ... applaud legislation to require photo identification for voting and to prevent election fraud.... We support State laws that require proof of citizenship at the time of registration to protect our electoral system against a significant and growing form of voter fraud. ... We call on every citizen, elected official, and member of the judiciary to preserve the integrity of the vote.... With a Republican Administration, the Department [of Justice] will stop suing States for exercising those powers reserved to the States, will stop abusing its preclearance authority to block photo-ID voting laws."	"We believe the right to vote ... is an essential American freedom, and we oppose laws that place unnecessary restrictions on those seeking to exercise that freedom. ... During the Obama administration, the Justice Department has initiated careful, thorough, and independent reviews of proposed voting changes, and it has prevented states from implementing voter identification laws that would be harmful to minority voters. Democrats know that voter identification laws can disproportionately burden young voters, people of color, low-income families, people

		with disabilities, and the elderly, and we refuse to allow the use of political pretexts to disenfranchise American citizens."
	Presidential elections	"We oppose the National Popular Vote Interstate Compact or any other scheme to abolish or distort the procedures of the Electoral College . . . as every ballot box in every state would become a chance to steal the presidency."
	Redistricting	"We support changing the way that the decennial census is conducted, so that citizens are distinguished from lawfully present aliens and illegal aliens. . . . In order to preserve the principle of one-person, one-vote, the apportionment of representatives among the States should be according to the number of citizens."
2016	Voting rights	"We support . . . legislation to require proof of citizenship when registering to vote and secure photo ID when voting. We strongly oppose litigation against states exercising their sovereign authority to enact such laws. . . . We urge every state to join the Interstate Voter Registration Cross Check Program to keep voter rolls accurate and to prevent people from voting in more than one state in the same election."	"We must rectify the Supreme Court decision gutting the Voting Rights Act, which is a profound injustice. . . . We will stop efforts by Republican governors and legislatures to disenfranchise people of color, low-income people, and young people, and prevent these voters from exercising their right to vote through onerous restrictions. We will ensure that election officials comply with voting protections, including provisions mandating bilingual materials and voter assistance. We will bring our democracy into the . . . 21st

(continued on the next page)

Table I.1. *Continued*

Year	Election Law Topic	Republican Party	Democratic Party
			century by expanding early voting and vote-by-mail, implementing universal automatic voter registration and same day voter registration, . . . and making Election Day a national holiday. We will restore voting rights for those who have served their sentences. And we will continue to fight against discriminatory voter identification laws, which disproportionately burden young voters, diverse communities, people of color, low-income families, people with disabilities, the elderly, and women. We support fully funding the Help America Vote Act and will work to fulfill the promise of election reform, including fighting to end long lines at voting booths."
	Presidential elections	"We oppose the National Popular Vote Interstate Compact and any other scheme to abolish or distort the procedures of the Electoral College. . . . We urge state legislatures that have voted for this proposal to rescind their approval."	
	Redistricting	"In order to preserve the principle of one person, one vote, we urge our elected representatives to ensure that citizenship, rather than mere residency, be made the basis for the apportionment of representatives among the states."	"We will bring our democracy into the 21st century by . . . ending partisan and racial gerrymandaring."

year from 2006 to 2011, with these proposals disproportionately found in Southern states (with Texas, Mississippi, Tennessee, and Florida leading the way) and after the 2010 election in which the GOP gained 675 state legislative seats.[91] From 2006 to 2013, eighty-seven restrictive voter-access laws were adopted by states, with the greatest likelihood of adoption occurring in states with Republican control of the government, swing-state status in presidential elections, a larger African American population, and growing minority turnout in presidential elections.[92] From 2012 to 2017, 569 voter-access restrictions were proposed and eighty-four were adopted[93] and, in 2017 alone, ninety-nine bills that would reduce voter access were introduced in thirty-one state legislatures.[94] Of course, the Court's *Shelby County* decision looms large here, as it freed states from the Voting Rights Act's preclearance requirement of federal review and approval of electoral changes.

The GOP justifies its election-reform proposals as essential to prevent voter fraud and insure public confidence in the integrity of the electoral process. There are, however, some rare moments of candor from Republican politicians and party operatives regarding their true motivations. For example, according to a 2012 *Palm Beach Post* report, former Republican governor Charlie Christ, former GOP state chairman Jim Greer, and two GOP consultants admitted that the impetus for Florida's restrictions on early voting, including the elimination of the Sunday before election day that has been heavily used by black churches, was not—as the party had publicly claimed—to save money and inhibit voter fraud; rather, their purpose was to suppress Democratic votes, which were substantially overrepresented in the 2008 early voting process.[95] More recently, President Trump explained his opposition to Democratic proposals for mail-in balloting for elections held during the COVID-19 pandemic by stating that "if you ever agreed to it, you'd never have a Republican elected in this country again."[96] The Republican Speaker of the Georgia House, David Ralston, similarly warned that legislative proposals to expand absentee voting in 2020 would be "extremely devastating to Republicans and conservatives in Georgia."[97]

The Republican Party has rationally, though not commendably, pursued voting restrictions in order to reshape the electorate and enhance its electoral prospects and political power. It is not, of course, the only party to have done so. The Democratic Party has a particularly sordid history when it comes to manipulating election rules to disenfranchise African Americans, out of both racial prejudice and partisan self-interest; Democrats, after all, were responsible for the white primary, the poll tax, literacy tests, and the grandfather clause. In the modern era, in contrast, the party's electoral interests have coincided with "small d" democratic ideals of expansive and inclusive voter turnout. Supporting voting-rights protections for racial and ethnic minorities, while nobly advancing civil rights and democracy, simultaneously serves the party's self-interests by boosting turnout by a loyal and growing constituency. Referring back to Table I.1, the Democratic Party platforms from 1968 to 2016 consistently advocate "maximum voter turnout" and "stronger protection of voting rights for racial and ethnic minorities." Across the 2008, 2012, and 2016 platforms, Democrats favored making election day a national holiday, restoring voting rights to felons, expanding early voting and vote-by-mail, adopting "universal automatic voter registration," reforming the Electoral College, and "restor[ing] . . . the full protections of the Voting Rights Act." The importance the party places on election reform is also evident in the first bill introduced in the House in 2019 by the new Democratic majority: the For the People Act that proposed sweeping voting, campaign finance, and ethics reforms. H.R. 1, which Mark Graber has referred to as "the shadow constitution of the Democratic Party should they gain power,"[98] restored voting rights to felons, mandated same-day voter registration, required states to establish independent redistricting commissions, weakened voter ID requirements, and made Election Day a federal holiday. The Senate's Republican majority leader, Mitch McConnell, characterized the bill as a "power grab" and refused to permit a vote on what he derisively called the "Democrat Politician Protection Act." Although neither party acts altruistically when it comes to election reform, their current composition leads to very different strategies. Democrats are able to promote both their self-interests and democratic ideals by expanding access to the ballot. Republicans, by rejecting the RNC's suggestion of minority outreach in its post-mortem analysis of the 2012 election,[99] have left themselves with little choice but to limit voter access and turnout, especially among minorities, a strategy that also threatens civil rights and weakens democracy.

Experience has taught politicians that even minor modifications to election rules can have a significant impact on electoral outcomes. A well-known example is the felon purge conducted by the state of Florida prior to the 2000 election. The company contracted to manage voter rolls employed an approach, at the state's insistence, that did not re-

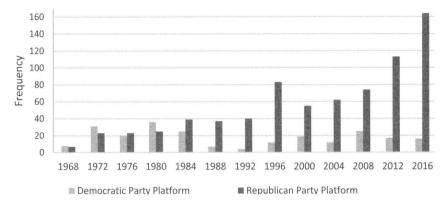

Figure I.1. Use of Judicial/Constitutional Terms in National Party Platforms, 1968–2016. Each bar indicates the number of times a national party platform employs a term referencing judges or the Constitution. *Source:* Author's analysis of party platforms.

quire an especially close and careful match between the names of felons and those of registered voters, producing many false positives that disproportionately targeted African Americans for removal.[100] The US Civil Rights Commission estimated that these errors likely cost Al Gore black votes that far exceeded Bush's 537-vote margin in the state.[101] The clear lesson is that election procedures can be quite consequential. The 2000 election—particularly the experiences in Florida with ballot irregularities, the felon purge, and the recount—"taught political operatives the benefits of manipulating the rules"[102] and "kicked off a new wave of GOP-led voter disenfranchisement efforts."[103]

The Republican Party's response to its electoral vulnerabilities has included a focus not only on election law but also on judicial appointments. GOP leaders like Ronald Reagan, Ed Meese, George W. Bush, Donald Trump, and Mitch McConnell have invested considerable effort in placing conservatives on the federal bench. In fact, this has become a central component of the Republican Party brand. It has in recent years aligned itself quite closely with conservative legal groups like the Federalist Society and the Heritage Foundation, granting them a key role in suggesting and vetting Supreme Court nominees. Donald Trump, for example, announced a list of candidates to fill the seat vacated by Justice Kennedy's retirement that was developed entirely by the Federalist Society.[104]

The GOP's intensive focus on judicial appointments and constitutional doctrine is especially evident in its national platforms. I reviewed each party's platform statements from 1968 to 2016, counting the number of terms pertaining to judges, judicial appointments, the Supreme Court, and the Constitution, including references to interpretive methods and constitutional provisions. This review uncovered two clear developments: first, enormous differences between the two parties in recent years and, second, dramatic change over time in the Republican Party's platforms.

As illustrated in Figure I.1, prior to 1996 the parties were not all that different in terms of the frequency with which they employed words like *constitution, judge, judicial, amendment,* or *Supreme Court.* For example, from 1968 to 1992 the RNC platforms used those terms an average of 27.7 times, while the DNC platforms did so an average of 18.7 times. Of course, the content of those references was quite different. In 1980, for instance, the GOP expressed concerns about federalism and the desire to appoint judges "who respect traditional family values and the sanctity of innocent human life." Democrats, in contrast, emphasized the need to appoint women and racial and ethnic minorities to the bench and lent support to abortion rights, school desegregation, and affirmative action. From 1996 to 2016 the platforms diverge significantly not only with respect to their substantive positions on issues like same-sex marriage and abortion but also regarding the average number of mentions of "constitutional" and "judicial" topics. While the Democrats employed these terms an average of 16.8 times in each platform, Republicans did so an average of 91.8 times. The RNC platforms also began supplementing their specific policy positions on issues like abortion with multiple statements evoking broader themes like the dangers of judicial activism, the importance of an originalist approach to discerning constitutional meaning, and the need to appoint "restrained," "originalist," or "constitutionalist" judges.[105] The most dramatic differences between the parties appear in their 2008, 2012, and 2016 platforms. While the three Democratic platforms employed terms like *Constitution, judges, amendments,* or *Supreme Court* an average of nineteen times, the GOP did so an average of 117 times—over six times as much. In fact, the 2012 and 2016 RNC platforms reference the Constitution so frequently throughout the document[106] that it becomes difficult to distinguish between policy discussions and constitutional discussions. It is clear that, as its 2016 platform proclaims, the GOP is "the party of the Constitution." This, then, is another foundational difference that has recently emerged between the two parties.

As with its focus on election reform, it is not surprising that the Republican Party would employ a judicial strategy to preserve its dwindling electoral prospects and its precarious hold on political power. Such an approach has been used by outgoing parties throughout history, as regime politics scholars have observed. For example, as the Federalists' electoral vulnerability grew and their control over elective institutions diminished after the 1800 election, they too sought to entrench their power in the judiciary.

Chapter Overview

The GOP has been both lucky and smart in the modern era. Compared to the Democratic Party, its base of supporters is modest and shrinking. It has, nonetheless, succeeded electorally with the help of political features like geographical representation that magnify the influence of its white, rural base. The Republican Party has not, however, been merely a passive beneficiary. It has consciously adopted a "peculiar fixation with election security,"[107] advancing election rule changes that limit voter access in order to help boost its electoral prospects and preserve its power. It has also sought to enable its wealthy and corporate supporters to donate and spend unlimited sums of money in election campaigns. The question this book addresses is whether Republican politicians have also pursued and secured judicial assistance as part of these endeavors. In other words, is election law a doctrinal area that has been forged "between friends?"

I have structured the book's argument in the following way: In chapter 1 I seek to clear some of the conceptual and methodological underbrush in the study of partisan influence on judicial decision-making. I first review the judicial behavior literature and identify several problems with the traditional treatment of judicial partisanship, including using the party affiliation of the judge or the appointing president as a proxy for judicial ideology. Not only are these measures crude, they inhibit our ability to detect the independent role of partisanship in shaping judicial choice. Another problem is that scholars tend to ignore the sources of judicial partisanship, failing to acknowledge the partisan backstory of how courts have been constructed and populated by partisan regimes. I then discuss how we might improve the study of judicial partisanship by more carefully distinguishing partisan behavior from policy-oriented behavior, both conceptually and methodologically. One important take-away is a recommendation to focus on election law cases, as this book does, which better enables partisan favoritism to be disentangled from ideologically motivated behavior. Election law cases also provide an especially effective test of the regime politics model, assessing whether judges support their regime partners when the electoral stakes are high.

In chapter 2 I turn to *Shelby County v. Holder*, a 2013 Supreme Court ruling that disabled the preclearance regime of the Voting Rights Act by invalidating its coverage formula. After reviewing doctrinal developments in this area, I address the claim that *Shelby County* is the result of partisan collaboration between Republican judges and Republican politicians. Evidence includes a five-member majority that consisted exclusively of Republican justices; their suspicious reliance on both faulty factual evidence and a novel "equal state sovereignty" principle; and an easily foreseen partisan impact in which Republican-controlled states adopted a slew of new voting restrictions targeting minorities. Especially important, however, *Shelby County* represents the successful culmination of a long-standing Republican project led by multiple GOP presidents, beginning with Richard Nixon, to weaken the Voting Rights Act and end federal control over election rules. This objective was accomplished not legislatively, but judicially, with the doctrinal groundwork effectively laid by the Reagan Justice Department and Republican Supreme Court appointees who advanced their party's views on federalism. The chapter concludes by observing the act's continued vulnerability to the Court's Republican majority, which was significantly strengthened when Trump filled Anthony Kennedy's seat with Brett Kavanaugh.

As I explain in chapter 3, the recent explosion in voter identification restrictions is, at least in part, an unsurprising result of the freedom the Court afforded states after *Shelby County*. Their adoption is chiefly a function of partisanship: they can be found almost exclusively in states that are Republican-controlled, and they are rarely enacted with any Democratic votes. Little is known, however, about whether partisanship has also affected *judicial* decisions involving voter identification. I test this question with original data from voter ID cases decided in the state and federal courts from 2005 to 2015 and find a strongly partisan pattern, with Republican judges far more likely than Democratic judges to vote in favor of such policies, although this partisan gap is not as large as for legislators. Additionally, after the Supreme Court's 2008 *Crawford* decision upholding Indiana's strict photo ID law, Democratic judges became significantly more supportive of voter ID laws. Some might consequently argue that judges after *Crawford* acted more as neutral arbiters than friendly partisans and mostly upheld voter ID policies. This, however, overlooks how legal and political factors are inextricably intertwined, with *Crawford* itself a partisan decision that reflects the GOP's strong commitment to voter identification requirements, both in its national platforms and its extensive policy efforts across multiple states.

In the next case study in chapter 4, I ask whether the New Right Court has aided the GOP with its reapportionment and redistricting decisions. The evidence in this area is rather mixed, and the story is more complicated. The Roberts Court did not, for example, advance Republican preferences and interests in *Department of Commerce v. New York* and *Evenwel v. Abbott*. In the former, the Court blocked the GOP's efforts to add a citizenship question to the census, and in the latter, it ruled against Republican efforts to require the state of Texas to use voter-eligible population rather than total population in drawing legislative districts.[108] When it comes to the proper standard for judging partisan gerrymanders, the Court has been deeply divided, more often along ideological than partisan lines. The lack of agreement on a definitive standard, in practical effect, empowered *both* Republican and Democratic politicians to gerrymander, with no clear advantage to either party—at least not until recently. The Court's 2019 *Rucho* decision, however, represents a turning point and a clearer sign of Republican collaboration across the branches as this new precedent of judicial noninterference was endorsed exclusively by the Court's five Republican justices, matches a growing doctrinal consensus among GOP leaders, and could very well continue their party's recent advantages in the redistricting process. A final complication comes from the racial gerrymandering cases that show the Republican Court refusing to support the Republican strategy of creating majority-minority districts that disadvantage Democrats in House and state legislative races. The commitment of the conservative justices to the constitutional principle of color blindness, one ironically fostered by the Reagan regime, proved to be more powerful than any temporary or strategic impulse toward partisan favoritism. The Warren Court's "reapportionment revolution" offers, in contrast, a far better historical example of a partisan regime, in this case a Democratic one, constructing and benefiting from court-imposed redistricting rules.

In chapter 5 I examine whether "friendly" judicial review has occurred in the campaign finance field, observing three noteworthy trends that support this claim. The first, which greatly accelerated after John Roberts and Samuel Alito joined the Court, is growing opposition to government regulation, a high-priority GOP objective in the campaign finance field. The second development is a heightened level of activism in the Roberts Court's approach to campaign finance, seen in cases like *Citizens United* and *Janus*. The Republican majority has shown a willingness to abandon long-standing precedent and depart from traditional legal norms and practices in creatively constructing a path for major doctrinal change. The third trend is the emergence of a sharply partisan pattern of decision-making that represents a substantial shift from the last quarter of the twentieth century when bipartisan coalitions were common. These dramatic changes in the area of campaign finance can be traced to broader developments in US politics, including partisan polarization and a more extreme view of the First Amendment advanced by Republican elites and conservative legal groups. Nonetheless, how exactly campaign finance fits into the GOP's electoral strategy is neither simple nor obvious, particularly in light of the uncertain partisan impact of ending regulatory restrictions in election financing. The impact of *Janus*, in comparison, is more obviously partisan, as ending mandatory agency fees was intended, and has great potential, to harm public sector unions and the Democratic causes and candidates that they support.

In the conclusion, I take a step back and review what has been learned about the relationship between parties and courts when it comes to contemporary election law controversies. The evidence reveals an impressive record of success for the GOP in securing judicial aid for its election reform agenda. Nonetheless, that success varies by election law topic. The contrast is especially pronounced when comparing voter identification and campaign finance, where friendly judicial review is quite evident, to redistricting, where it is less obvious. After exploring the likely causes of both Republican Party success and variation in that success, the conclusion poses two questions. The first is normative, focusing on the threats posed to court legitimacy and democracy itself when election law is the product of interbranch partisan cooperation. The second question ponders the future of election law and party politics in light of what appears to be a disjunctive Trump presidency. I arrive at a somewhat optimistic place that sees popular mobilization and "more politics" as the best remedy.

1 | Understanding Judicial Partisanship

The central question I address in this book is whether judges have acted as neutral arbiters or friendly partisans in the field of election law. More specifically, I investigate the recent efforts of the New Right Republican regime to secure judicial aid in transforming election law in order to sustain its power in American politics. These lines of inquiry require a theory of judicial partisanship that does not exist, a deficiency that this chapter seeks to address. I first review the existing literature that seeks to explain judicial behavior. I then look specifically at how political party influence on that behavior has been traditionally treated in this literature, identifying both theoretical and methodological challenges. Finally, I discuss how we might productively move forward in untangling the mystery of how, when, and why partisanship shapes judicial choice. In the chapter's conclusion, I explain how the book's election-law focus and case study approach are designed to enhance our understanding of judicial partisanship.

The Study of Judicial Behavior: The Attitudinal Model and Beyond

Scholars studying law and courts seek to answer a simple question: how do judges decide? What factors influence their votes and opinions? Great strides have been made in how researchers study and understand judicial behavior. Today, there is a deep appreciation by scholars in both law and political science that "influences on judicial decision-making . . . are complex and multifaceted," with a variety of factors—legal, attitudinal, strategic, and psychological—"inextricably interwoven."[1] The precise role of partisanship, however, remains understudied, undertheorized, and, consequently, poorly understood. This will be explained following a brief historical tour of the judicial behavior literature.

The appropriate place to begin this tour is with the formalist perspective on law, dominant for much of the nineteenth century. This view characterized legal decision-making as a mechanical, apolitical, and even scientific enterprise; properly trained judges employing appropriate methods of logical reasoning could find clear and certain answers in the law.[2] Toward the end of the nineteenth century and into the twentieth, Progressive judges[3] and scholars[4] challenged this "mechanical jurisprudence" model and aimed for a more realistic understanding. Legal Realists argued that judicial decisions required discretionary judgments, even "inarticulate and unconscious" ones that were inevitably influenced by the judge's personal characteristics, experiences, and beliefs.[5] The Realists further invited scholars to dispense with the sterile and technical study of law as a body of rules and precedents and instead examine what judges actually do.

This invitation to study judicial behavior was given a boost by the Supreme Court itself as its members, beginning around 1940, broke with long-standing tradition and began expressing their disagreements in case votes and opinions.[6] In fact, whereas 90 percent of the Court's opinions between 1801 and 1940 were unanimous, nearly half of the decisions of the Stone Court (1941–1946) contained at least one dissent, with that proportion increasing to more than two-thirds over the next seven years spanning the Vinson Court.[7] Suddenly, "after 1941, there were huge variations in judicial voting behavior begging to be explained."[8]

Scholars like C. Herman Pritchett took up the Realist cause. His groundbreaking study of the Roosevelt Court used statistical methods to analyze a large sample of case data, concluding that the justices' policy preferences could explain their decision-making behavior, particularly their voting alignments.[9] Pritchett's research inspired a generation of scholars to examine case votes quantitatively and to look for patterns rooted in judicial "attitudes."[10] The most influential account of such ideology-based decision-making was provided by Jeffrey Segal and Harold Spaeth in *The Attitudinal Model*.[11] Their empirical tests failed to support the "legal model" in which "the decisions of the Court are substantially influenced by the facts of the case in light of the plain meaning of statutes and the Constitution, the intent of the Framers, and/or precedent."[12] Segal and Spaeth advanced instead, as a more persuasive and empirically grounded account, the "attitudinal model" in which "the Supreme Court decides disputes in light of the facts of the case vis-a-vis the ideological attitudes and values of the justices. Simply put, Rehnquist votes the way he does because he is extremely conservative; Marshall voted the way he did because he is extremely liberal."[13]

The attitudinal model has long dominated the judicial behavior field, no doubt a product of its power and simplicity, as well as continued improvements in the measurement of judicial ideology.[14] Decades of empirical studies have confirmed the attitudinal model's central tenet that "viewing justices as policy seekers provides enormous leverage in understanding their behavior."[15] Such behavior includes their votes on the merits,[16] case selection,[17] oral argument,[18] and opinion assignment and writing.[19] Empirical evidence also confirms that membership change on the Court plays a significant role in historical changes in the Court's ideological direction.[20] Studies have demonstrated that ideology also influences judicial decision-making in both the state courts and lower federal courts, though to a lesser extent.[21]

The attitudinal model's simplicity is both its strength and its weakness. While it effectively explains considerable variation in a broad range of judicial behavior, critics complain that it is *too* simple, failing to acknowledge other influences on judicial behavior. For example, some scholars note that judges who truly wish to accomplish their policy goals must do more than merely vote their sincere preferences. They must act strategically in the face of real-world constraints and consider the preferences of other actors who can help or hinder the achievement of the judge's policy goals.[22] This strategic, rational-choice account of judicial decision-making does not dispute the prominent role of policy motivation; rather, it insists that policy goals cannot be accomplished simply by straightforward "value-voting." A Supreme Court justice wishing to set or change a legal precedent, for example, must marshal the votes of other justices to secure a majority, which often requires doctrinal adjustments and compromise.[23] Ensuring that her preferences become policy that is faithfully implemented requires a justice to think about and strategically accommodate the views of the president, members of Congress, and state and local officials who have discretionary authority to promote or impede judicial decisions and, in some cases, harm the Court itself.[24] State court judges who must periodically face voters necessarily consider the popular reaction to their decisions and the possibility of electoral reprisal.[25]

The most common criticism of the attitudinal model is its dismissal of legal factors as inconsequential, a complaint advanced primarily by law professors[26] and judges.[27] Attitudinalism must be regarded as incomplete, if not false, they argue, if it regards legal norms like *stare decisis* as irrelevant to case outcomes. Judges, after all, take those norms seriously and make honest efforts to reason correctly and persuasively to the right legal result. Critics additionally point to the attitudinal model's inability to account for consensual behavior among appellate court judges who are ideologically dissimilar. Even on the US Supreme Court, unanimity is not uncommon; one-third of its decisions from 1953 to 2004 did not include a dissenting opinion, and half offered either no dissent or only one dissent.[28]

Increasingly sophisticated empirical studies have successfully tested the influence of legal factors on judicial decisions. They persuasively conclude that "law matters"[29] and that judges "take law seriously."[30] Dozens of empirical studies have demonstrated that judicial decision-making is influenced by legal factors like precedent;[31] interpretive methodology;[32] legal doctrine;[33] legal clarity;[34] the quality of lawyers' oral arguments;[35] and deference to Congress,[36] lower court judgments,[37] and "courts of equal authority."[38] Additionally, judicial decision-making is shaped by legal norms acquired in law school and reinforced in the professional legal community, including a shared commitment to making good law and interpreting law well.[39]

Largely because of this growing evidence, there is now a consensus that regards the long-standing "law-politics dichotomy as false" and unhelpful.[40] Law professors and political scientists alike doubt that a "unicausal explanation can account for all the choices" that judges make; instead, "political and legal explanations weave together in a complex knot."[41] More scholars today are testing "hybrid" or "integrated" models, employing multidimensional measures, and concluding that legal and political factors interact in complicated ways to influence judicial decisions.[42]

Another noteworthy development in this field is a resurgence in the use of psychology knowledge and methods to help explain significant gaps in our understanding of judicial behavior. As Eileen Braman and Thomas Nelson explain, while scholars "have succeeded in demonstrating a link between preferences and decisions, they are less able to reveal the precise mechanisms by which the former guides the latter. Judicial decision-making therefore remains locked in the proverbial 'black box,' concealing the cognitive processes that underlie the relationship between preference and decision."[43] Early studies from scholars like

Pritchett, Spaeth and Glendon Schubert in fact employed psychological concepts in their approach to studying Supreme Court decision-making, but this practice largely disappeared as strategic-choice models rooted in economics took hold.[44] Scholars simply assumed that judges single-mindedly pursued their policy preferences with no concern for why that would be the case or how that motive operated in a legalistic framework that includes norms like stare decisis. Especially problematic is the fact that the assumption of a predominant policy motivation is "wholly at odds with how judges view themselves."[45] Lawrence Baum has wisely counseled researchers to acknowledge the greater likelihood that judges possess mixed motives, which should be analyzed "more broadly and deeply . . . [to] gain a richer sense of the bases for judicial choice."[46] While judges want to make good policy, they also want to make good law,[47] dispose of cases,[48] maximize their leisure,[49] and enhance their prestige.[50] Not only do non–policy goals influence judicial behavior, so do a judge's psychological traits. New empirical studies document how traits like extraversion, conscientiousness, and openness affect a variety of decision-making behaviors on the Court, including voting to grant cert, casting a dissenting vote, assigning the majority opinion, and writing a separate opinion.[51]

Instead of "assuming away the judicial reasoning process," new psychology-inspired research explores the cognitive processes by which judges try to reach accurate legal conclusions while, nonetheless, often making decisions that match their policy preferences.[52] "Motivated reasoning" is a central concept from the psychology field that Eileen Braman has employed to explain the subconscious impact of ideology on judicial decision-making. Borrowing from Ziva Kunda, she explains how judges can be motivated by both "accuracy" goals and "directional" goals.[53] By virtue of their legal training and professional socialization, judges "come to internalize legal norms and 'accuracy' goals consistent with idealized notions of decision making";[54] nonetheless, their directional (i.e., policy) goals subtly influence their reasoning process. For example, experiments by Braman and Nelson demonstrated that both undergraduates and law school students perceived precedents differently depending on whether a case advanced their policy views, particularly when the target case and precedent were moderately similar rather than extremely similar or extremely dissimilar.[55] As Dan Kahan aptly states this idea, ideology is not "a *self-conscious motive* for decision making" but "a *subconscious influence on cognition*."[56]

The main thrust of these various critiques of the attitudinal model is that ideology takes us far, but not far enough, in our mission to understand judicial behavior. Many factors—legal and political, internal and external—operate and interact in complex ways to affect judicial choice.

What About Judicial Partisanship?

The treatment of partisanship in this extensive literature on judicial behavior has been both incomplete and muddled. A judge's partisan affiliation has most often been treated as a proxy for ideology, though it can and should be treated as much more than that. Insufficient attention has been given both to the independent role of partisanship in influencing judicial decision-making and to the ways in which courts are constructed by partisan regimes. Partisanship is, in any case, a flawed measure of judicial ideology. The need to address these multiple deficiencies is great, as will be explained in the paragraphs that follow.

The attitudinal and strategic models that dominate the study of judicial behavior assume that judges, or at least appellate court judges, are motivated predominantly by their policy desires. They seek to vindicate those preferences through their decisions, whether consciously or subconsciously. Segal and Spaeth note that it is Supreme Court justices who enjoy the greatest freedom to do so given that they need not worry about reversal by a higher court, electoral retribution, or promotion to higher office.[57] As previously noted, multiple studies spanning multiple decades have successfully documented such policy-oriented behavior in the voting patterns of individual judges, blocs of like-minded judges, and appellate courts undergoing membership change. Many of these studies employed partisanship as a proxy for a judge's policy preferences. In fact, political scientists in the mid- and late twentieth century consistently found a significant link between a judge's party affiliation and her case votes across a variety of issue areas.[58] Highlighting only a few of these important studies, Stuart Nagel found significant partisan differences in the voting behavior of state and federal supreme court justices, with Democratic judges displaying "a general affinity for the 'liberal' . . . position" when it came to criminal law, administrative law, tax law, personal injury cases, and landlord-tenant disputes.[59] Glendon Schubert and S. Sydney Ulmer studied workmen's compensation cases decided by the Michigan Supreme Court in the 1950s and also found significant partisan differences, with Democratic justices considerably more likely to accept such claims.[60] C. Neal Tate's "personal attribute model" that included partisan affiliation successfully predicted over half of the variation in the liberalism of US Supreme Court justices in civil liberties and economics cases from 1946 to 1979.[61] Melinda Hall and Paul Brace studied the imposition of the death penalty on six state supreme courts from 1980 through 1988 and found that Republican justices were significantly more likely to uphold death sentences than Democratic justices.[62] Finally, Daniel Pinello's meta-analysis of eighty-four empirical studies from 1959 to 1998 confirmed the "conventional wisdom among students of judicial behavior that party is a dependable yardstick for ideology: Democratic judges are more liberal on the bench than Republican judges."[63]

Following these early political science studies, entreaties by Brian Tamanaha and Frank Cross that law professors pay more attention to social science research on courts and employ its methods led to an empirical legal studies movement and a "flowering of 'large-scale quantitative studies of facts and outcome.'"[64] One of the best known is a 2006 study by Cass Sunstein, David Schkade, Lisa Ellman, and Andres Sawicki.[65] Their analysis of 6,000 federal appellate court decisions revealed that 52 percent of the votes of Democratic judges were liberal, compared to 40 percent of the votes of Republican judges. This modest but significant partisan gap varied across circuits (a 10-point gap on the DC Circuit, compared to a 22-point gap on the Sixth) and issues (a negligible gap on criminal appeals, federalism, and takings cases and very large gaps on affirmative action, capital punishment, and gay rights). A key finding was that partisan differences were especially pronounced on panels that were unified in terms of their partisan composition: 62 percent of the decisions rendered by all-Democratic (DDD) panels were liberal, compared to 36 percent of all-Republican (RRR) panels. In contrast, mixed panels produced a smaller partisan divide, with 52 percent of DDR-panel decisions and 41 percent of DRR-panel decisions characterized as liberal. The authors reasoned that an opposite-party judge served as a "whistle-blowing" dissenter, which dampened the other judges' ideological tendencies; a unified panel, in contrast, amplified those tendencies.[66] Finally, Thomas Keck's 2014 study of federal appellate court decisions from 1993 to 2013 on four culture war issues—abortion, affirmative action, gay rights, and gun rights—found a sizable partisan gap: 51 percent of liberal votes were cast by Republican judges, compared to 84 percent for Democratic judges.[67] These findings of significant partisan differences in the votes of federal appellate court judges have been so consistently confirmed[68] that Thomas Miles and Cass Sunstein label them "the Standard Pattern of Judicial Voting"; in their characterization of this pattern, "Democratic appointees cast liberal votes more often than Republican appointees" and "liberal voting . . . increases with the number of co-panelists who are Democratic appointees . . . and correspondingly falls with the number of Republican appointees."[69]

It is not, of course, unreasonable for students of judicial behavior to employ "party labels as surrogates for ideological orientation," as party and ideology are "inextricably intertwined."[70] As Nagel explains, judges "rely on their personal standards of value in reaching a decision, and these same personal standards also frequently account for their party affiliation"; thus, "party affiliation and decisional propensity for the liberal or conservative position correlate with each other because they are frequently effects of the same cause" rather than independent influences.[71] This "behavioral equivalence" should, in fact, be even stronger in the twenty-first century as the Democratic and Republican parties have become both more internally unified and more distant from each other ideologically.[72] Such partisan polarization has had a clear effect on the Supreme Court, with Neal Devins and Lawrence Baum recording a growing ideological gap when comparing the votes of Democratic justices and Republican justices and a shrinking one when comparing co-partisan justices.[73] Furthermore, since 2010, following Justice John Paul Stevens's retirement, "for the first time in its history, the Court has had liberal and conservative blocks that fall perfectly along party lines."[74]

Another obvious reason for researchers to employ party affiliation in their studies is that it is extraordinarily easy to use and measure. There are, nonetheless, several problems with using a judge's political party as an indicator of her policy preferences. As Lee Epstein and Gary King explain, party affiliation is a crude and sometimes inaccurate measure of judicial ideology.[75] Political parties in the United States have not, after all, always been ideologically distinctive and internally unified. In the mid-twentieth century, for example, each of the major parties was quite diverse ideologically. Southern Democrats were far more conservative than Northern Democrats, and Eastern Republicans were more liberal than other Republicans and even more liberal than Southern

Democrats. These regional differences inevitably affected judicial partisanship. Earl Warren, for example, chose to align with the Republican Party, not because of a strong ideological affinity but as a necessity for advancing his career in California politics.[76] Even in recent years when both major parties have become more nationally unified in ideological terms, the Republican Party remains internally divided between the right-wing Tea Party, its more moderate "establishment" element, and its new economic-nationalist and populist Trump wing. Party affiliation will, thus, fail to distinguish among copartisans who are quite different ideologically. The policy preferences of Earl Warren, John Paul Stevens, and David Souter vary considerably from those of fellow Republicans Antonin Scalia, Clarence Thomas, and Samuel Alito, and it is sloppy if not nonsensical to treat similarly Democratic justices as diverse ideologically as McReynolds, Frankfurter, Douglas, Brennan, and Powell. This applies with equal force to lower federal court judges and state court judges.

Using the party of the appointing president as an indicator of judicial ideology is, of course, problematic for the same reasons. Copartisan presidents can differ significantly in terms of their policy preferences. Dwight Eisenhower and Ronald Reagan are not ideological clones, nor are Lyndon Johnson and Jimmy Carter.[77] Additionally, though it is rare, presidents have nominated opposite-party judges, such as Richard Nixon selecting Lewis Powell and Eisenhower choosing William Brennan; in the latter case, President Eisenhower's party affiliation is a very poor indicator of Brennan's ideology and voting behavior and, of course, a contrary indicator of Brennan's partisanship. The appointing-president measure, furthermore, ignores reality by failing to acknowledge the Senate's confirmation power, which can force presidents to moderate their ideological preferences in selecting judicial nominees.[78] The moderately conservative Anthony Kennedy was not, after all, Ronald Reagan's first choice. Additionally, the Senate's influence in judicial selection is far greater when it comes to appointees to the lower federal courts. Senatorial courtesy, for example, required Democratic presidents like Harry Truman and John Kennedy to accede to the wishes of Southern senators and place conservative, racist judges on the federal bench; the ideological preferences of these judges do not match those of their appointing president.

Adam Cox and Thomas Miles's study of voting rights cases highlights these various problems. In justifying their focus on ideology and race as potential explanatory factors, the authors correctly observe that judicial ideology strongly correlates with judicial votes, the minority plaintiffs in voting rights cases overwhelmingly support the Democratic Party, and voting rights cases have clear partisan consequences that can alter the balance of power in government and future policy outcomes.[79] Problems quickly emerge, however, with their assertion that "we must first pick a measure of judicial partisanship or ideology," a failure at the outset to decide whether it is a judge's ideology or partisanship that is being tested.[80] After pointing out that political scientists tend to use continuous measures of ideology while legal scholars "typically code judicial ideology as a binary variable . . . using the political party of the appointing President," the authors acknowledge "a lively debate" over how best to measure judicial ideology and multiple criticisms by Epstein and King of the poor statistical practices employed in many judicial behavior studies.[81] They nevertheless concede that they will make "no attempt to resolve" these controversies and forge ahead in using the appointing president's party as the key independent variable.[82] They defend it as "a particularly appropriate measure" since they are interested not only "in judicial ideology [but also] in the possibility that a judge's affiliation with a particular party itself, rather than just her ideology, might influence her actions."[83] This single variable, thus, ends up pulling double duty, serving to indicate both partisan and ideological influence. If it proves statistically significant, as it does—Democratic appointees are significantly more likely than Republican appointees to vote for liability under Section 2—we have no way of learning whether this indicates the existence of partisan influence, ideological influence, or both.

The Cox and Miles study is not, of course, unique. All of the studies that use party as an ideological measure inherently restrict our ability to detect the separate and distinctive influences of party and ideology on judicial choice. A judge's party affiliation may have significant effects that are independent of ideology, but those "unique contributions" cannot be uncovered.[84]

Another weakness that too often accompanies researchers' use of party affiliation to study judicial behavior is the failure to explore the *source* of that partisan identity. A judge's partisan affiliation is typically treated as a given rather than itself an important area of inquiry. As Kevin McMahon puts it, studies of judicial voting behavior are often caught in "an attitudinal bubble" that "gives far too much credit to the individual views of the Justices themselves" and far too little to "the larger political regime from which they emerged."[85] The critical question that is ignored when scholars focus narrowly on judicial votes is how particular judges with particular policy views and partisan attachments get placed on the bench at particular times in history. This question requires attention to regime politics theory.

Robert Dahl observed in his famous 1957 article that presidents fill a vacancy on the high bench on average every two years, ensuring that "the policy views dominant on the Court are never for long out of line with the policy views dominant among the law making majorities of the United States."[86] His finding that the Court was more likely to invalidate older laws enacted by the previous regime compared to newer laws enacted by the current regime helped to support his claim that "the Supreme Court is inevitably a part of the dominant national alliance."[87] Dahl's insights inspired the regime politics movement that emphasizes the power of successful partisan coalitions to construct and populate courts and thereby create a judiciary that is "friendly"[88] and "collaborative."[89] According to the multiple scholars advancing this perspective, courts are inevitably a part and product of the partisan regimes that typically dominate American politics.[90]

As these scholars explain, partisan regimes have a variety of tools that enable them to construct friendly courts, supplying them with power, personnel, and policy guidance. Most importantly, politicians seek to appoint right-thinking, copartisan judges through "a self-consciously partisan appointment process."[91] This includes efforts to secure judges with the right jurisprudential commitments, such as FDR's insistence on deference to the elected branches[92] and the GOP's recent emphasis on originalism.[93] Judicial appointments can be used not only to advance the party's favored policy goals but also to help it build and sustain a winning electoral coalition. McMahon, for example, describes Richard Nixon's appointment strategy as partisan and electoral rather than ideological.[94] The president focused on only a few issues, like busing and law and order, and chose nominees who could help him exploit the crumbling New Deal coalition and build a "New American Majority" by attracting white Southerners and northern ethnic Catholics to the Republican Party.

Regime leaders, furthermore, do not patiently wait for judicial vacancies to occur but seek actively to create appointment opportunities. During periods of unified government, Congress has expanded the size of the federal judiciary, as it did by over a quarter with the Omnibus Judgeship Act of 1978, which provided copartisan president Jimmy Carter with 152 new judicial vacancies.[95] In the nineteenth century, Congress periodically used its power to alter the size of the Supreme Court, expanding it when a copartisan won the White House and reducing it, as each vacancy occurred, when an opposite-party president was in office. Although this particular tool of Court design and control has fallen into disuse, Senate Majority Leader Mitch McConnell accomplished the same result in 2016 by refusing to act on President Barack Obama's nomination of Merrick Garland to fill the vacancy created by Antonin Scalia's death. McConnell handed his party and its new president the chance to retain the Court's Republican majority and conservative tilt, an objective effectively achieved with the successful appointment of Neil Gorsuch. Of course, the justices can themselves assist these efforts by timing their retirements strategically. They might choose to retire while a copartisan president is in office, as Justices O'Connor and Kennedy did, or to delay their departures during the term of an opposite-party president, a charge leveled at Justices Ginsburg and Breyer.

Politicians also do not merely sit on the sidelines waiting for the right legal questions to appear before their right-thinking judges. Regime members and supporters craft litigation strategies designed to achieve legal outcomes that advance the party's policy and electoral aims. For instance, Republican attorneys general in over half of the states challenged the Affordable Care Act, President Obama's signature legislative achievement; they were joined in this effort by several prominent members of the Federalist Society, a powerful network of conservative and libertarian lawyers and academics closely aligned with the GOP. While FDR used his Justice Department to launch legal attacks on Southern institutions like the white primary and poll tax and enhance federal power over voting rights, recent Republican administrations have employed judicial strategies to reduce the federal role in elections and restore autonomy to the states. Of course, the commitment of Republican presidents to state autonomy in Justice Department litigation in the electoral arena has been selective; they have promoted it with respect to voter access and redistricting, but not campaign finance.

The regime politics perspective reminds us that the broader partisan and institutional context cannot be overlooked in studying judicial behavior. A fuller understanding requires that researchers look beyond—or, more accurately, behind—formal votes to the partisan regimes that constituted those courts.[96] It is not enough simply to observe that Democratic and Republican judges vote differently on a variety of issues. Scholars must additionally investigate whether politicians deliberately constructed that partisan bias as a product of the regime's policy desires and electoral needs. The regime politics model is not, of course, without its weaknesses. It remains undertheorized,[97] insufficiently tested,[98] and incapable of explaining the specific doctrinal choices that the Court makes, including some that the regime would oppose.[99] The justices are, after all, "not minions who simply do the bidding of party leaders. They are allies of coalition leaders, not their agents."[100]

The multiple problems accompanying the traditional treatment of judicial partisanship—equating party and ideology, ignoring uniquely partisan influences, and overlooking the partisan-regime context—need attention. Otherwise, this research will remain atheoretical and incomplete, with scholars merely "piling up facts."[101] We must think more carefully about how to conceptualize, observe, and evaluate partisan judicial behavior and especially how to distinguish it from policy-oriented judicial behavior. This requires thinking through *conceptually* the different motivations that exist for both types of behaviors and exploring *methodologically* how different types of cases affect our ability to discern partisan judicial behavior.

Understanding Partisan Judicial Behavior Conceptually

Bush v. Gore (2000) is nearly universally regarded as the most partisan decision in Supreme Court in history, inspiring extensive discussions of the role of partisanship in judicial decision-making.[102] Critics begin with the fact that the justices who ended Florida's ballot recount and insured George W. Bush's victory were all Republican. There is more, however, as Howard Gillman explains: "the five justices in the *Bush v. Gore* majority . . . fall uniquely within the category that is most indicative of partisan justice: they made a decision that was consistent with their political preferences but inconsistent with precedent and inconsistent with what would have been predicted given their views in other cases. Moreover, their decision received no support from any judge with presumably different partisan loyalties."[103] As Lawrence Solum simply states the matter, the majority's five conservative members acted "contrary to the law . . . on the basis of an equal protection theory they didn't believe . . . in order to favor their own party."[104] This characterization of *Bush v. Gore* as a partisan decision is further buttressed by the majority's unwillingness to apply its equal protection rule to future cases, making the decision "nearly irrelevant as a doctrinal matter . . . in spite of its historical magnitude."[105] Michael Klarman additionally points out that it is inconceivable that the justices would have voted the same way had the identities of the parties been switched—a claim, he says, that cannot be credibly made about any other Supreme Court decision.[106]

The most prominent framework that emerged in the wake of *Bush v. Gore* is the distinction between high politics and low politics. As described by Jack Balkin and Sanford Levinson, "'high politics' . . . involves struggles over competing values and ideologies, and 'low politics' . . . involves struggles over which group or party will hold power.[107] This distinction is not, however, entirely new. Harold Spaeth, in multiple studies, distinguished between "attitudes toward situations" and "attitudes toward objects."[108] The former refers to a judge's views regarding the particular legal issue presented in a case, such as civil rights, the First Amendment, or criminal justice, while the latter refers to a judge's attitude toward the particular litigant engaged in that issue, whether the NAACP or the Republican Party. A broader and more accurate characterization of the attitudinal model is that a judge's decision results from the interaction of her attitudes regarding both the object (i.e., litigant) and the situation (i.e., "the legal constitutional context in which the attitude object is acting");[109] most scholars expect that the latter will be the more powerful influence. *Bush v. Gore*, however, presents a case in which judicial preferences regarding the object—Republican candidate George W. Bush—outweighed judicial preferences regarding the situation—the question of federal judicial interference in a state's vote-counting process in a presidential election under the equal protection clause.

The "high politics–low politics" framework has been helpful in moving scholarship beyond the reflexive rejection of partisan influence as illegitimate, a normative distortion that Charles Geyh attributes to the dominance of the rule of law paradigm.[110] Instead, "it depends" is the correct answer to whether partisan behavior by judges is legitimate or illegitimate. It depends on the particular form that the partisan behavior takes.[111] Judges might crassly and without principled reasons favor same-party candidates in deciding election disputes. Judges might alternatively make decisions that advance their party's constitutional vision that has been convincingly validated by voters. This latter type of partisan behavior obviously has a much stronger claim to legitimacy than the former.[112] Without paying attention to the various types of partisan judicial behavior, ideological and nonideological, our normative analysis will remain rigid and narrow.[113] While the high politics–low politics framework is an improvement over the reflexive denigration of all partisan judicial behavior, it is only a beginning.

We must think more rigorously and systematically about how partisan behavior by judges differs from policy-oriented behavior and how to distinguish them conceptually, methodologically, and normatively. A starting point is to examine the variety of possible motives or incentives, apart from policy concerns, for judges to be affected in their decisions by their party affiliation. As Kyle Kopko suggests, there exist both psychological and instrumental motivations.[114] With regard to the former, judges are human, despite being idealized as "sainted genius-heroes."[115] As such, they develop psychological attachments to various reference groups, including political parties, as part of their social identity.[116] These in-groups serve as a source of self-esteem and pride. Judges' identification with a particular political party likely begins in early childhood and reflects their parents' partisan identity. This attachment acts as a perceptual lens that shapes how they view candidates, groups, political events, and policy issues.[117] Judges believe in their party, its candidates, and its policy positions, and they surely have "rooting interests" in electoral and policy contests.[118] Judges may, furthermore, derive psychological satisfaction, though perhaps subconsciously, from deciding in ways that help and protect their Democratic or Republican in-group. Kopko suggests, for example, how "out-group bias" in the form of "aversion for an opposing political party" might help explain why US district court judges were more likely to rule against opposite-party redistricting plans[119] and opposite-party plaintiffs in campaign finance cases.[120]

The internal psychological satisfaction that judges gain by helping their in-group or refusing to help an out-group can be reinforced, as Baum explains, by the normal human desire to please and gain respect from "salient audiences" such as friends, lawyers, judges, and party elites.[121] Legal peers may, for example, write favorably or critically about a justice's decisions and reasoning in highly respected scholarly and journalistic venues, which might influence their decision-making "in a subtle, but significant way."[122] A key method by which the Federalist Society exerts influence in constitutional policy making, according to Amanda Hollis-Brusky, is by acting as a "judicial audience": members applaud or boo judges' decisions and help to insure that Republican appointees stay faithful to conservative principles and do not drift ideologically, as did Justices Blackmun, Souter, and Stevens.[123] Conservative justices like Scalia, Thomas, Alito, Gorsuch, and Kavanaugh have additionally been featured speakers at the annual meetings of the Federalist Society, where they are applauded and celebrated. These interactions are both professional and social, formal and informal. An important change in this mechanism of elite influence on the justices is, as Devins and Baum observe, increasing polarization in the Court's elite environments. In the past, that environment "leaned to the left, especially on civil rights and liberties issues, and their influence likely helped to move moderately conservative Justices to the left"; today, "with the rise of conservative legal networks . . . liberal and conservative Justices both live . . . in worlds that reinforce . . . their ideological positions."[124]

Another way that partisan favoritism by judges may be expressed is in terms of bias for and against the groups that align with their party. After all, a political party is more than a collection of policy positions; it is also, and perhaps centrally, a coalition of interests. Groups frequently participate in litigation containing high-policy stakes, either as a direct party or amicus. Even when they do not participate, the impact of judicial decisions on particular groups is often quite obvious. Evidence suggests that this group context matters. Baum convincingly argues that Supreme Court justices have developed positions on particular issues not simply from "reason[ing] deductively from broad ideological values" but, in significant part, as a product of "group affect" toward particular types of claimants.[125] Pro-claimant votes in takings cases, for example, consistently came from the more liberal justices on the Court—*except* in cases brought by companies rather than individuals. Pro-claimant justices in free speech cases were consistently more liberal than anticlaimant justices but mostly when those claimants were "on the left," such as labor unions, government employees, and news media; when free speech claims were brought by business or pro-life groups, which was increasingly the case after the 1993 term, the traditional ideological polarity—"liberal justices favor free speech more than conservative justices"—disappeared, a finding also supported by Lee Epstein, Andrew Martin, and Kevin Quinn.[126] The Warren Court's decisions in a variety of areas including state action[127] and criminal justice[128] were affected by the presence of African American claimants, reflecting the Court's "clientele relationship" with a key constituency of the New Deal Democratic regime.[129] This may not be a pure form of partisan favoritism in which judges vote for their political party's interests in particular cases. It is nonetheless a type of group affect, which Baum regards as an "intermediate case," in which the justices respond favorably to the particular groups that make up the party's electoral coalition.[130]

There are not only psychological but also instrumental reasons why judges might engage in partisan behavior. Individuals who aspire to a successful judicial career must go beyond a mere sidelines rooting role. It is simply a fact that judges wishing to be recruited, selected, promoted, and retained in office must engage in partisan activity. Three-quarters of states require judges to win an election either to attain office or to stay there after being appointed. These elections are often explicitly partisan and, thus, require the party's support. Even when elections are formally nonpartisan, however, judicial candidates may need and would certainly appreciate their party's campaign assistance.[131] When judges are appointed by elected officials, successful candidates in nearly all cases must have been active politically, with partisan activities especially likely to bring potential nominees to the attention of politicians such as governors, presidents, and senators. Of course, this provides yet another reason for a judge to hope that her preferred party wins control of these offices.

When it comes to Supreme Court appointments in particular, "political activism of a rather intense kind" has been a "virtual precondition" for most of its history.[132] A snapshot of the Warren Court in 1954, for example, includes a former governor of California (Warren), three US senators (Black, Burton, and Minton), two US attorneys general (Jackson and Clark), two high-ranking executive branch officials (Reed and Douglas), and a law professor (Frankfurter) who had also served in the executive branch and as an informal presidential advisor. While the norm of prominent political experience, particularly elective office, has substantially weakened as a prerequisite for a Supreme Court appointment,[133] nearly all of the justices serving in the 2019 term had some form of political experience in their backgrounds. Breyer was a staffer for Senate Democrats on the Judiciary Committee; Ginsburg was a prominent women's rights litigator before the US Supreme Court; Kagan was White House counsel for President Clinton and solicitor general for President Obama; Thomas worked for John Danforth both when he served as Missouri's attorney general and as a US senator; several justices—Roberts, Thomas, Alito, and Gorsuch—served in the Justice Department under

Republican presidents; and Kavanaugh worked in George W. Bush's White House and on Ken Starr's independent counsel team investigating President Bill Clinton. It is, of course, no coincidence that Supreme Court nominees have historically been drawn from the president's own party well over 90 percent of the time. Following the trend of partisan polarization that began in the mid-1970s, it is unthinkable today that a president would select a nominee to the high bench who belonged to the opposite party. In fact, the last time this happened was in 1971 with Nixon's appointment of Lewis Powell, a Southern Democrat.

Ideological, psychological, and instrumental incentives for partisan behavior can, of course, overlap. A judge might, for instance, favor her party's interests in an election law case for multiple reasons. She might derive psychological satisfaction from seeing and helping her team succeed in an electoral contest. She might receive the continued support and approval of her social group that includes other judges and party elites. Assisting her party electorally may also increase professional opportunities for advancement. Enhancing her party's chance of victory could also produce policy outcomes that she prefers. Thus, whether for psychological satisfaction, social support, professional success, or policy achievements, judges may favor their party's interests in their decisions. An additional complication, as Baum observes, is that judges are certain to vary in their "motivational profiles."[134] Judges who experience different systems of selection, reappointment, and promotion would logically develop different motivations as a result. For example, a judge facing reelection in which partisan ballots are employed should have stronger instrumental reasons to support her party compared to a judge facing a nonpartisan retention election or a federal judge with no continuing need for party support to stay in office, although such support would be necessary if she desired a higher position within the federal bench. As this suggests, the incentives for judges to assure that they have ongoing party support may vary, not only by selection method but also by court level. Supreme Court justices, for instance, should no longer have instrumental reasons to favor their party's interests since they no longer need party support to stay in office or secure promotion. To the degree that the justices' votes continue to be affected by partisan considerations, as appeared to be the case in Bush v. Gore, it must be due to reasons other than instrumental ones, such as the continuation of strong psychic ties and loyalties to their preferred party.

We know surprisingly little about these potential motivations for partisan behavior. The key reason is the dearth of research devoted to exploring, specifying, and testing the causal mechanisms of judicial decision-making behavior, both generally and with regard to partisan behavior more specifically. I include my own research in this criticism. My 2016 study found substantial differences between Republican and Democratic judges in their propensity to support voter identification policies; while my conclusion of "widespread partisan behavior" was defensible, I devoted only one paragraph to exploring why that might be the case, briefly speculating it could be the result of motivated reasoning or the selective consumption of media stories favoring their party's views regarding the incidence of voter fraud.[135] This relative inattention to causation is not unusual. With few exceptions, studies simply report partisan differences in judicial votes without identifying or testing the specific causal mechanism that might have produced them.[136] More research is clearly needed on the psychology of partisan bias with respect to judicial decision-making.[137] Scholars must test whether partisan differences are a product of motivated reasoning in which judges subconsciously favor their party's policy positions, a type of group affect in which judges are moved by their feelings toward the particular groups with significant stakes in the case, or some other cognitive or emotional mechanism that we do not yet understand.

Discerning Partisan Judicial Behavior Methodologically

Understanding causality is, of course, made more problematic by the measurement issues that were previously discussed. Partisanship and ideology are not identical factors. They can be independent forces that do not always exert a uniform, unidirectional influence on judicial decisions.[138] It can be rather difficult, however, to identify partisan favoritism that is distinct from policy-motivated behavior. For example, a Democratic judge upholding a redistricting plan crafted by a Democratic legislature might look like a partisan decision, but we cannot be certain about such an inference. Perhaps the judge was indeed seeking, as a simple act of partisan loyalty, to confer an electoral advantage on her party and help it to win more seats. What, however, if the judge is upholding the redistricting plan because she believes it will increase the likelihood of the government adopting superior policies? Does this transform an illegitimate form of tribal partisanship into a more defensible policy pursuit? Additionally, does it matter if the judge honestly believes that she is following the law? What if a Republican judge who upholds a Republican redistricting plan is an elected state court judge who received campaign donations from the Republican Party and Republican-affiliated interest groups? What, however, if this Republican judge rarely invalidates redistricting plans, whether Republican or Democratic, because of a principled commitment to minimizing judicial interference in a highly partisan process? What if the redistricting decisions of Democratic judges are found to enhance electoral competition; do we praise this seemingly nonpartisan behavior? Not if, as Jordan Peterson discovered, Democratic judges improve the competitiveness of House elections primarily in districts whose seats are held by Republicans.[139] What if a Democratic judge votes to uphold a Republican redistricting plan in order to insure party support for a subsequent reelection campaign under a new GOP affiliation, an allegation publicly lodged against Justice Joseph Cunningham by a fellow justice in a 1992 Illinois Supreme Court redistricting case?[140] These multiple questions are meant as a reminder that labeling a judicial decision as partisan or nonpartisan is not so simple since that single vote can be motivated by multiple factors that are often hidden and sometimes conflict.

One approach to sorting this out is to explore how ideology and partisanship might interact and present themselves in different types of cases. There are, in fact, several distinct possibilities, with key factors focused on whether partisanship and ideology are relevant to the outcome and whether they lead in the same or in different directions. Our ability to detect partisan behavior will be easier in some of these situations compared to others.

First, there may be cases in which both partisan and policy interests are weak or nonexistent. Perhaps a lawsuit raises a simple issue that generates virtually no legal or political conflict. There are certainly many of these kinds of cases in trial courts and specialized lower courts, such as traffic and family law courts. Even at the higher levels of the judiciary, however, there may be cases that lack a strong partisan or ideological component. They might involve a narrow or technical question possessing a high degree of legal certainty, for example, whether income tax refunds are property under the Consumer Credit Protection Act, a question answered unanimously by the Supreme Court in *Kokoska v. Belford* (1974).[141] Cases presenting complex legal questions where the answers are not so certain permit alternative influences such as ideology or partisanship to enter the decision-making process. Kopko et al., for example, found in their experimental test of motivated reasoning that ballot counters were more likely to favor their party's candidates when provided with ambiguous rather than specific instructions for determining voter intent.[142] Mark McKenzie similarly found evidence of "constrained partisanship" in redistricting cases: judges favored their party's interests when ambiguous precedents provided them with the opportunity to do so.[143]

Some cases, furthermore, may contain an issue with clear policy implications but nonexistent or uncertain partisan implications. Perhaps the issue has failed to interest or affect either party or has produced no clear partisan divide. This was actually the case for the abortion issue in the 1960s and early 1970s. In 1972, sizable majorities in both parties supported abortion rights, and the GOP platform did not mention abortion until 1976 and did not oppose it until 1980. As a consequence, there would not be a particular party position that judges could support in the 1973 *Roe v. Wade* case.[144] Obviously, when partisan considerations are not present to influence judges' decisions, partisan judicial behavior cannot exist or be detected.

Alternatively, some cases might present judges with the opportunity to help their party but without also advancing their policy preferences. In these cases, partisan judicial behavior can in fact be tested and discerned. Michael Kang and Joanna Shepherd's study of judicial partisanship provides an excellent example. The authors deliberately focused on "candidate-litigated election disputes" that raised "arcane questions of law [lacking a] . . . clear ideological valence" but that had a "short-run partisan payoff in the current election."[145] Examples included disputes over a candidate's eligibility due to residency requirements, the validity of an incomplete ballot, and the process for filling a vacated office. Kang and Shepherd credibly claimed that this combination of case characteristics—strong partisan stakes but low policy stakes—enabled a "clean test of partisan loyalty" that "isolates the raw partisan motivations of judges."[146] Kopko's study of ballot access litigation involving Ralph Nader's candidacy in 2004 presented a similar situation.[147] The partisan context of these cases for judges was obvious. The Democratic Party devoted considerable resources to challenging Nader's candidacy while the Republican Party sought to aid it; additionally, both parties were involved in all of the cases either directly or indirectly. Presumably, this litigation also presented little in the way of obvious policy gains or long-term advantage for one party over another with respect to ballot access rules. In both studies, careful case selection enabled an effective test of whether judges exhibited partisan favoritism in their decisions.

Yet another scenario exists in which both partisan and policy concerns are present and lead judges in the same decisional direction. This is the likely focus of typical studies of judicial behavior: politically salient appellate court cases where legal certainty is low and outcomes are disputed. As we know, research has frequently found pronounced differences in case votes between judges belonging to different parties and, inferentially, having different policy views; this is particularly true on divisive culture-war issues like abortion, LGBT rights, and affirmative action.[148] When partisanship and ideology lead in the same direction and favor the same outcome, it is obviously difficult to distinguish between the two influences, particularly when the dependent variable is a single dichotomous vote. In an example suggested by Kopko, a Republican judge could favor a same-party litigant challenging a campaign finance regulation; that decision need not be regarded as partisan, however, if it is based on policy grounds as confirmed by other cases in which she invalidates such regulations when challenged by Democratic or nonpartisan claimants.[149]

In contrast, there are cases in which partisanship and ideology conflict and act as independent forces pulling a judge in different and even opposing directions. In *Bush v. Gore*, for example, a conservative decision deferring to state court judgments and rejecting federal judicial interference in elections on equal protection grounds would harm the Republican candidate, George W. Bush. As a result, conservative justices who embraced liberal doctrines in order to favor their party's candidate can credibly be accused of partisan favoritism, particularly when they tell lower court judges to ignore their newly adopted rule. In a similar example, Baum points to the criminal appeals of Oliver North and Lyn Nofziger in which conservative Republican judges voted to overturn the Reagan aides' convictions, while liberal Democratic judges voted to affirm; because these judges deviated from their typical ideological position, partisan favoritism is a reasonable inference.[150] The racial gerrymandering cases, discussed in chapter 4, present another example. A liberal decision that sanctioned majority-minority districts would aid the election of minority candidates but would also harm the Democratic Party since drawing heavily minority districts in a state inevitably leaves behind more white-majority districts favoring the GOP. In cases like

Shaw v. Reno (1993), both Republican and Democratic justices voted against the electoral interests of their preferred party and in accordance with their sincere policy beliefs regarding the government's use of racial preferences.[151] This leads us away from an inference of partisan judicial behavior. These instances where partisan and ideological considerations diverge and favor different outcomes enable judicial partisanship to be detected.

To summarize, discerning partisan influence in judicial choice is challenging, but its difficulty varies across case categories. When party interests are not clear or strong, they obviously cannot influence judicial choice. Additionally, when party and ideology lead the judge in the same direction, it is difficult to discern whether one factor or both factors are influencing the outcome and to what degree. Alternatively, when party and ideology lead in different directions, identifying the existence of partisan influence is more easily accomplished. This suggests several ways in which research on judicial partisanship can be improved.

Moving Forward

One important step forward in studying judicial partisanship is to exercise greater care in the selection of cases, given their varied capacity for enabling partisan judicial behavior to be tested. Election law cases, in fact, present a subset of cases that are extremely well-suited to this task. They quite remarkably present judges with the opportunity to have a direct and significant impact on their party's electoral interests. Deciding whether a candidate gets on the ballot, permitting a redistricting plan to go into effect, invalidating the rules by which candidates raise campaign funds, or accepting a claim under the Voting Rights Act have partisan impacts on election outcomes that are distinct, foreseeable, and often immediate. The value of these cases from a research perspective is that they can help disentangle partisan favoritism from ideologically motivated behavior. This is particularly true for election law questions that possess "ideological banality . . . coupled with uncertainty about their political consequences over the long term," as in Kang and Shepherd's study of candidate-litigated election disputes.[152]

Election law cases additionally enable an effective test of the regime politics model. Obviously, party elites and officeholders care very deeply about case outcomes in the election law field, as their electoral fortunes are directly affected. A logical expectation flowing from the regime politics perspective is that judges, as regime partners, would make election law decisions that support their partisan allies. Put another way, if judges fail to help their regime partners when the party's electoral fate is centrally at stake, a major blow has been struck against this model.

Multiple studies of election law cases are, in fact, already generating new findings with respect to partisan influence in judicial decision-making. Kang and Shepherd, for example, found strong evidence of "an asymmetrical pattern of judicial partisanship" as Republican justices on state supreme courts were much more likely than Democratic justices to favor their own party in candidate-focused election disputes.[153] In contrast, Kopko found that neither Republican nor Democratic state court judges systematically favored their party's interests when given the chance to do so in ballot access cases involving Ralph Nader's candidacy in the 2004 presidential race.[154] In contrast, Scott Graves found significant partisan differences in how supreme court justices in twenty-four states decided ballot access cases.[155] Judges who were elected to office or appointed by the governor were significantly more likely to vote to limit access if they were affiliated with the state's dominant party; judges who were the product of a merit selection process displayed no such partisan bias. Jackson Williams's study of a small number of cases involving party or candidate litigants found that justices on the Illinois Supreme Court were much more likely to vote for, rather than against, their own political party.[156] Empirical analysis of redistricting cases in the US district courts spanning two distinct periods—1964 to 1983 for Randall Lloyd and 1982 to 2007 for Mark McKenzie—found that judges were more likely to strike down redistricting plans created by the opposing party compared to those crafted by the same party.[157] Gary Cox and Jonathan Katz similarly found that "hostile" courts whose party identity did not match the majority party of the legislature were significantly more likely to reject those legislatures' redistricting plans compared to "friendly" courts; the authors also credit Democratic dominance on the federal bench in the 1960s with helping to eliminate a pro-Republican bias in non-Southern congressional elections.[158] Kopko's study of campaign finance cases from 1971 to 2007 found that US district court judges were less likely to rule in favor of opposite-party plaintiffs, although no partisan difference emerged in the treatment of same-party plaintiffs.[159] Additionally, Kopko's dissertation research found that judicial partisanship had uneven effects that depended on the type of election law case.[160]

For example, the party affiliation of federal judges significantly affected outcomes in campaign finance cases but not right of association cases; moreover, judges were more likely to favor their party's interests in redistricting cases as the percentage of same-party judges on the panel increased. As previously noted, Cox and Miles examined challenges under Section 2 of the Voting Rights Act from 1982 to 2004 and found that judges appointed by Democratic presidents voted for liability significantly more often (36 percent of the time) than Republican appointees (21 percent of the time); there was also evidence of partisan-based panel effects as the pro-claimant tendency of Democratic appointees was greater on panels that included other Democratic appointees.[161]

There remains in some of these studies, such as the one by Cox and Miles, the challenge of inferring that partisan favoritism rather than policy motivation was responsible for the partisan differences in judicial voting patterns. An obvious solution is to try to control for judicial ideology when testing for distinctively partisan effects, as both Kopko and McKenzie have done.[162] Controlling for ideology is not, however, always possible. When both state and federal judges are included in the data set, as was the case in my study of voter identification litigation, it is not feasible as there currently exists no common ideology measure available for both sets of judges.[163]

Clearly, when the goal is to discern partisan judicial behavior as distinct from policy-oriented judicial behavior, care and innovation in research design is needed. Corey Yung, for example, developed a measure of judicial partisanship that is deliberately independent of ideology.[164] He examined whether federal appellate court judges were more likely to employ a deferential standard in reviewing the decisions of same-party judges as compared to those of opposite-party judges. Using this approach, he found that Republican appointees were significantly more partisan, particularly the appointees of the two Bush presidents and those who previously worked in the Department of Justice. Thomas Keck provided another helpful contribution in his 2014 study.[165] He insisted that we clarify our baseline or referent when assessing partisan judicial behavior. Do we, he asked, expect judges to be "nonpartisan umpires" or "partisan zealots" and to be substantially, or only modestly, less partisan than elected politicians?[166] Keck's comparison of the behavior of voters, legislators, and federal appellate judges on culture war issues found that judges were significantly less polarized than legislators but just as polarized as voters. This perspective enabled him to move beyond merely reporting partisan gaps in judicial votes to exploring why judges might be more willing and able to cross party lines compared to legislators. Keck, furthermore, did not simply implore judges to be more restrained after finding partisan differences in their voting patterns. He instead recommended "bipartisan judicial activism" since a "politically balanced" bench would be more likely than a judiciary dominated by a single party to protect a variety of rights, such as same-sex marriage *and* the Second Amendment.[167] These innovative approaches to testing and assessing partisan judicial behavior must be applauded and encouraged.

Another important way to advance our scholarship in this area is to investigate partisan regimes as a likely source of judicial partisanship. Instead of a narrow focus on judicial votes, scholars must look beyond those votes to the partisan regimes that may have engineered them. Such an inquiry asks whether the issue raised in particular cases has been an explicit focus of regime leaders, for example, in the party's national platform, presidential speeches, and its judicial policies that include appointment and litigation strategies. This helps to reveal whether court decisions are the result of deliberate interbranch strategies adopted by parties to attain electoral and policy success. This in turn affects how those court decisions are assessed normatively. Additionally, we need not restrict those assessments to the binary framework of high and low politics. As Justin Levitt notes, partisanship is not "a single phenomenon" but "a spectrum," with "ideological partisanship" quite different from "tribal partisanship."[168] In talking about judicial partisanship, a continuum[169] or more "fine-grained" multidimensional scale[170] may be more productive.

To conclude, there are several steps that scholars can take to improve the study and understanding of judicial partisanship. We must devote more effort to distinguishing conceptually between partisan motivations and policy motivations. We should additionally explore how those motivations play out in the internal cognitive processes of judicial choice, particularly as judges strive to follow the law. Scholars must also take greater care in research design, for example, controlling for judicial ideology where possible and selecting cases that help to isolate partisan behavior from policy-oriented behavior, with election law cases particularly appropriate for this endeavor. New and innovative approaches, such as those of Yung (2012) and Kang and Shepherd (2016), should be commended and replicated.[171] Finally, scholars must be sure to investigate whether partisan judicial behavior is a part and product of the interbranch strategies adopted by partisan regimes; the partisan back-story can illuminate the historical and political context shaping judicial choice and may produce a different normative assessment.

The Book's Approach: Four Election Law Case Studies

In the remainder of this book I seek to add to our knowledge of parti-san judicial behavior by focusing on four election law areas: the Voting Rights Act, voter identification, redistricting, and campaign finance. These four topics share several important characteristics. First, policy outcomes in each area, including decisions by courts, can affect each party's electoral prospects. Additionally, those effects are typically dis-tinctive for each party. Voter identification requirements, for example, are expected to have a disproportionate impact on the poor, racial and ethnic minorities, and young people, all of whom tend to vote Demo-cratic. Partisan disagreement on all four issues has also intensified in recent years, increasing their contemporary relevance and, thus, their importance for researchers. A highly relevant fact, however, is that the parties have not always developed distinctive and well-publicized posi-tions on each issue with, for example, far more national party platform statements devoted to voter identification and campaign finance com-pared to redistricting. Quite importantly, the GOP has recently devoted considerable attention—sometimes publicly, sometimes not so pub-licly—to each of these election law topics as it seeks to preserve its power in the face of a declining electoral base and close competition with its Democratic rivals.

In the chapters that follow, I explore the role of judicial partisanship in several key election law areas. I ask whether the Supreme Court's Republican majority aided its partisan allies electorally through its deci-sions on the Voting Rights Act, voter identification, redistricting, and campaign finance. Analysis includes, but goes beyond simply reporting partisan differences in judicial voting patterns. There may, for example, be significant doctrinal deficiencies that support an inference of parti-san motive. Each case study also appraises the efforts of regime leaders, successful and unsuccessful, to construct favorable judicial outcomes on each issue, with evidence found both in national party platforms and case briefs. I also assess the potential partisan impacts flowing from those case outcomes. Although the primary focus is the US Supreme Court, research findings with regard to other courts, state and federal, are sometimes reported. Chapter 3, for example, includes original data and analysis of voter identification cases in both the state and federal courts.

I now turn to the first election law topic: the Voting Rights Act and the partisan battle over Section 5's preclearance regime. Did the Supreme Court neutrally call balls and strikes when presented with this issue, or did the justices vote with their partisan team?

2 | Courts, Parties, and the Voting Rights Act

Have courts exercised friendly judicial review with respect to the Voting Rights Act? Did the Republican Party, as regime politics theory predicts, both cause and benefit from the Supreme Court's 2013 Shelby County ruling ending preclearance and its growing conservatism in voting rights cases?

On June 25, 2013, in *Shelby County v. Holder*,[1] the Supreme Court invalidated the Section 4(b) coverage formula of the Voting Rights Act (VRA), rendering inoperable Section 5's preclearance regime that is widely regarded as the act's "crown jewel."[2] After *Shelby County*, federal preapproval of election rule changes in covered jurisdictions, many in the South, would no longer be required. Reactions to this "blockbuster" ruling were voluminous and mostly negative, claiming that the Court's "conservative majority . . . washed its hands of a half century of voting rights jurisprudence,"[3] "cut the heart out of the most important civil rights statute since Reconstruction,"[4] and took "a shameful step backward."[5] A prominent narrative is that the Republican justices in *Shelby County* aided the GOP's election reform agenda, eliminating federal oversight and giving a green light to Republican legislatures seeking to suppress minority votes for electoral gain.[6]

This chapter finds considerable evidence to support the claim of partisan collaboration in which members of the *Shelby County* majority acted more as friendly partisans than neutral arbiters. Not only were the five justices striking down the VRA's coverage formula exclusively Republican, they curiously relied on a novel "equal state sovereignty" principle and ignored the Court's long-standing practice of deference to Congress in the exercise of its enforcement powers under the Fourteenth and Fifteenth Amendments. Additionally, the factual evidence on which they relied was weak and unpersuasive. The ruling, furthermore, had an easily foreseen partisan impact: a flurry of new voting restrictions adopted in Republican states with large minority populations.

These disparate pieces of evidence are effectively tied together by a broader partisan-regime narrative. The New Right regime has long sought to undermine the liberal election-law policies adopted by its New Deal–Great Society predecessor. The GOP's highly strategic approach to the Voting Rights Act has produced support that is symbolic and selective and opposition that is substantial and veiled. Congressional Republicans, for example, repeatedly and overwhelmingly voted to reauthorize the act, though only in the final and highly public stages when the electoral risks of opposition were greatest.[7] The GOP has also favored the Voting Rights Act when it required majority-minority districts that advantage Republican candidates, but not when it prevented at-large elections and voter ID policies. Republican presidents have, furthermore, sought to weaken the act in less visible ways, including lax enforcement by the Justice Department and conservative Supreme Court appointments, with Section 2's intent requirement and Section 5's preclearance regime serving as key targets. Thus, when the Supreme Court effectively ended preclearance in *Shelby County*, it handed the GOP an extraordinary victory whose importance cannot be overstated. The Court's five Republican justices, led by Chief Justice Roberts, accomplished what their copartisans in the other branches wished to but could not: eliminate federal control over state and local election rules.[8] They liberated Republican officials across the nation to pursue the restrictive election policies their party sees as vital to preserving their power.

It is also true, however, that the GOP had to wait a very long time for this victory. After all, President Nixon targeted preclearance as early as 1970, in the first VRA reauthorization process. Additionally, conservatives both in the White House and on the Supreme Court repeatedly tried to restrict the reach and impact of the Voting Rights Act but were often rebuffed by Congress. Civil rights groups effectively countermobilized and worked with Democrats and moderate Republicans in Congress to overturn conservative measures adopted by the executive and judicial branches.

I begin this chapter by describing the history of the Voting Rights Act, its key provisions, and its powerful impact in advancing minority voting rights. I next describe Supreme Court doctrine with respect to the VRA, culminating in the *Shelby County* decision. In the remainder of the chapter I discuss the varied evidence with respect to the "*Shelby*

County as partisan collusion" claim. I conclude by noting the ongoing vulnerability of the Voting Rights Act to an increasingly conservative Court skeptical of the need for federal protection of voting rights.

The Voting Rights Act

The Fifteenth Amendment, adopted after the Civil War, prohibited the federal and state governments from denying or abridging the right to vote "on account of race, color, or previous condition of servitude." It additionally empowered Congress to enforce this prohibition "by appropriate legislation." The history of official compliance with the amendment's command has been checkered, to put it mildly, although some initial successes included the election of sixteen black Southerners to Congress. The collapse of Reconstruction, however, and Supreme Court rulings like *U.S. v. Cruikshank* (1876),[9] *U.S. v. Reese* (1876),[10] and the *Civil Rights Cases* (1883)[11] enabled Southern states both to erect their Jim Crow system of apartheid and to adopt literacy tests, poll taxes, and other devices that effectively disenfranchised black voters,[12] particularly when reinforced by intimidation and violence.

After decades of neglect by the federal government, meaningful efforts to protect the voting rights of blacks resumed in the twentieth century. The Supreme Court, for example, struck down the grandfather clause in *Guinn v. U.S.* (1915) and the white primary in *Smith v. Allwright* (1944),[13] and Congress adopted some modest voting rights protections in the Civil Rights Acts of 1957 and 1960. Voter registration among African Americans in the South, however, remained "dismally low," at 6.7 percent in Mississippi and averaging only 22.5 percent in the five Southern states with the largest black populations (Alabama, Georgia, Mississippi, North Carolina, and South Carolina).[14]

Revolutionary change was on the horizon, however. Spurred by the violent police assault on peaceful civil rights marchers on Bloody Sunday on the Edmund Pettus Bridge in Selma, Alabama, President Lyndon Johnson called on Congress to adopt expansive voting rights protections. It responded by passing the Voting Rights Act of 1965, though only after a contentious legislative battle lasting five months.[15] The act regulated elections and voting in a variety of ways. Section 2, incorporating language from the Fifteenth Amendment, prohibited any jurisdiction from employing "a voting qualification . . . , practice, or procedure . . . which results in a denial or abridgment of the right . . . to vote on account of race or color."[16] In addition to this nationwide ban, the act included, for certain jurisdictions with egregious histories of voting discrimination, specific provisions such as temporarily suspending literacy tests,[17] permitting federal examiners to register voters and federal observers to monitor elections, and requiring preclearance with the federal government of any election modifications. This latter provision, Section 5, was no doubt the act's most radical. It required "covered" jurisdictions to prove either to the US attorney general or the US District Court for the District of Columbia that proposed voting changes would not have a racially discriminatory purpose or effect.[18] Section 4(b) provided the coverage formula for determining which jurisdictions had to comply with Section 5's preclearance requirements. Covered jurisdictions were those that, on November 1, 1964, used a test or device, such as a literacy test,[19] to restrict registration and voting and in which less than half of those eligible were either registered to vote or did vote in that year's election; this trigger date was later expanded by Congress to include 1968 and 1972, and the coverage formula was amended in 1975 to encompass "language minority" groups. Under Section 3, federal courts also had the power to "bail in" additional jurisdictions or, under Section 4, to grant requests by a covered jurisdiction to "bail out" of coverage if it had not used a discriminatory test or device in the previous five years. The initial set of covered jurisdictions included six Southern states (Alabama, Georgia, Louisiana, Mississippi, South Carolina, and Virginia) and multiple counties in North Carolina. Alaska, Arizona, and Texas were later added to the list, along with particular counties in California, Florida, Michigan, New Hampshire, New York, and South Dakota.

The Voting Rights Act is rightly regarded as "the most important piece of civil rights legislation in the twentieth century and one of the most transformational laws ever passed by Congress."[20] Guy-Uriel Charles and Luis Fuentes-Rohwer label it a "superstatute," indicating that it is landmark legislation addressing "the big, fundamental questions of the day" in a way that "renegotiates . . . our constitutional or first-order principles" and "compels the cooperation of all branches of government."[21] With this united federal effort, the VRA had a swift and substantial impact.[22] Nearly 250,000 black voters were registered in the first year, with at least a third being registered by federal examiners.[23] By 1968 the percentage of African Americans registered to vote in the South doubled, from 31 to 62 percent,[24] and turnout increased from

46 to 60 percent.[25] Gains were especially pronounced in Mississippi and Alabama.[26] Minority office holding also grew dramatically. From 1965 to 1985 the number of black state legislators in the eleven former Confederate states increased from three to 176 and, from 1965 to 2005, the number of African American elected officials nationwide increased twenty-fold, from less than 500 to over 10,000, with the ranks of black congressional representatives growing from five to 43.[27]

Congress has continued to offer strong bipartisan support for the Voting Rights Act, renewing it by huge margins in 1970, 1975, 1982, and 2006. In the most recent reauthorization, preclearance was extended for twenty-five years by a vote of 390–33 in the House and 98–0 in the Senate, with Republican president George W. Bush signing the bill into law. What exactly the act requires has, of course, evolved over time, through congressional amendment, Department of Justice implementation, and, quite importantly, judicial interpretation.

Supreme Court Doctrine: From *Katzenbach* to *Shelby County*

In this cooperative policy venture, the Supreme Court—at least initially—"willingly partnered with Congress and the executive branch to give effect to the Act" and interpreted it "pragmatically" and "expansively."[28] On the one-year anniversary of Bloody Sunday and after seven hours of arguments spanning two days, the Warren Court rejected the first legal challenge to the Voting Rights Act in *South Carolina v. Katzenbach* (1966).[29] It showed great deference to Congress, arguing that it did not exceed its broad remedial power to enforce the Fifteenth Amendment and instead employed valid measures for addressing the "insidious and pervasive evil" of race discrimination in voting and the considerable enforcement challenge that lay ahead, given the strong likelihood of continued Southern evasion.[30] Only Justice Black dissented, objecting on federalism grounds to what he saw as Sections 5's extraordinary intrusion into state prerogatives. Three months later, in *Katzenbach v. Morgan* (1966), the Court upheld another provision that had preempted New York's literacy requirement for voting, despite the absence of evidence of racially discriminatory intent.[31] Justice Brennan's majority opinion was notable for granting considerable deference to Congress, recognizing its discretionary power to create statutory protections of voting rights beyond what courts might constitutionally require. Brennan advanced, in footnote ten, a "one-way 'ratchet theory' of constitutional law," asserting that Congress could use its enforcement powers under Section 5 of the Fourteenth Amendment to expand ("ratchet up") but not restrict ("ratchet down") judicially recognized constitutional rights.[32]

With all three branches aligned behind the VRA, the system of mass disenfranchisement that Southern states had erected quickly crumbled. Blacks could no longer be denied the ability to register and vote, and long-standing tools like literacy tests and poll taxes were now forbidden. There remained, though, alternative methods that diluted minority votes, such as annexation of white areas and at-large elections, which could insure that black voters were outnumbered and less influential. The Court would soon have to develop legal rules for this "second generation" of VRA enforcement challenges.

As the following summary suggests, the Court's record in interpreting the Voting Rights Act is mixed. It has sometimes adopted expansive interpretations and broadly empowered the Justice Department and federal courts in their enforcement efforts. The overall trajectory in the half-century since the VRA's enactment is conservative, however, as more and more Republican appointees joined the Court—thirteen from GOP presidents in the five decades from 1965 to 2015, compared to six from Democratic presidents.[33] Another distinctive and recurring pattern that can be discerned is a conservative Court offering a restrictive interpretation of Section 2 or Section 5, the VRA's two key provisions, followed by congressional reversal in its periodic reauthorizations.

Section 2 imposed a nationwide ban on the denial or abridgement of the right to vote on the basis of race; both vote denial and vote dilution were forbidden. The burden of proof and litigation costs, however, lay on the plaintiff challenging a law as discriminatory. In contrast, Section 5 placed the burden on covered jurisdictions to prove to the government that its proposed electoral changes were not racially discriminatory, with preclearance seeking "to interrupt discriminatory laws *before* they were enacted."[34] As a result, Section 2 was initially the less potent of the two provisions. That changed, as will be explained, after Congress mandated a "results" or "effects" test in 1982, a response to and reversal of the Court's decision in *City of Mobile v. Bolden* (1980) that required proof of a racially discriminatory purpose.[35]

In developing a legal standard for evaluating vote dilution claims under Section 2, the Court in both *Whitcomb v. Chavis* (1971) and *White v.*

Regester (1973) held that multimember districts were not per se unconstitutional.[36] In *White*, however, the Court invalidated multimember districts in Texas because, based on "the totality of the circumstances" they systematically diluted minority voting strength by providing racial minorities with "less opportunity than . . . other residents to participate in the political processes and to elect legislators of their choice."[37] Whether proof of racially discriminatory purpose was required would remain an open question until 1980, when the Court provided an affirmative answer in the *Bolden* case. Justice Stewart's plurality opinion reasoned that, since Section 2 simply restated protections afforded by the Fifteenth Amendment, the city's long-standing at-large system for electing city commissioners would be sustained in the absence of clear proof of a racially discriminatory purpose. This appeared to raise the bar significantly above *White*'s totality-of-circumstances standard and was, at the time, widely regarded as "the most significant setback for the VRA since 1965."[38] In 1982, in direct response, Congress amended Section 2 to clarify that a violation required proof only of racially discriminatory effects, succeeding against the Reagan administration's campaign to retain the Court's intent requirement. Nonetheless, to allay concerns expressed by Republicans (including a young Justice Department lawyer named John Roberts) that an effects test would lead to quotas and proportional representation, the amendment expressly stated that it would not be construed as a mandate for protected minorities to be represented proportionally.

With the 1982 reauthorization and the Court's application of the new effects test in *Thornburg v. Gingles* (1986),[39] vote dilution claims became central in redistricting litigation, and the number of successful Section 2 cases increased dramatically, from three in 1981 to 175 in 1988.[40] The Court in *Gingles* struck down North Carolina's redistricting plan on vote dilution grounds and fleshed out what would constitute a racially discriminatory result under Section 2. Justice Brennan's opinion (some, but not all, of which commanded a majority) stated that "the essence" of a successful Section 2 claim was that a law or practice "interacts with social and historical conditions to cause an inequality in the opportunities enjoyed by black and white voters to elect their preferred representatives."[41] The Court went on to establish three specific threshold conditions—that the minority group is large and compact enough to constitute a majority in a district, that it has a history of political cohesiveness in voting, and that the white majority also votes cohesively as a group sufficiently to defeat the minority group's preferred candidate.

This approach focused the judicial inquiry on racial polarization and the potential for drawing majority-minority districts. Once the *Gingles* factors of compactness and racially polarized voting were satisfied, a court additionally had to consider whether, in light of "the totality of circumstances," the minority group has less opportunity than others to influence the electoral process and elect its preferred candidates.[42]

States at the time felt pressured by these doctrinal rules and by the Justice Department to draw majority-minority districts where possible as protection against legal challenges. The Supreme Court began pushing back against these efforts in the 1990s, however. As I explain more thoroughly in chapter 4, the Court in *Shaw v. Reno* (1993) and *Miller v. Johnson* (1995) cautioned that strict scrutiny would apply when race became the "predominant factor" in drawing district lines.[43] Daniel Tokaji aptly characterizes the challenge presented by these two doctrinal lines as the "Goldilocks" problem: race must be taken into account in drawing district lines to avoid a minority vote dilution challenge under Section 2 of the Voting Rights Act, but not so much as to violate equal protection under *Shaw* and *Miller.*[44]

When it comes to the preclearance regime, the Supreme Court's initial treatment was quite generous in cases like *South Carolina v. Katzenbach* (1966) and *Allen v. State Board of Elections* (1969).[45] The former upheld Section 5 as within Congress's broad remedial powers under the Fifteenth Amendment (with only Justice Black dissenting), and the latter ruled 7–2 (with Harlan and Black dissenting) that preclearance could reach "subtle, as well as the obvious, state regulations that have the effect of denying citizens their right to vote because of their race."[46] The Court, furthermore, acknowledged in *Allen* that "voting includes 'all action necessary to make a vote effective.'"[47] Thus, the many second-generation barriers to African Americans exercising their vote and attaining political power that Southern states were quickly enacting in the face of rising black registration rates, such as at-large elections and county consolidation, would not be beyond the purview of the federal government. The Court's broad interpretation thus insured that vote dilution by a variety of means would be within the federal government's reach under Section 5. *Allen* had a powerful and immediate impact. Although "very few jurisdictions sought preclearance . . . between 1965 and 1969,"[48] the number of Section 5 submissions jumped to 110 in 1970, 333 in 1972, and 1359 in 1972, while objections grew from three to 71 over that same time period.[49] Preclearance requests continued to "skyrocket . . . reaching an average of 17,000 preclearance submissions per year."[50] The Court supported the imposition of preclearance requirements for redistricting in *Georgia v. United States* (1973), candidate eligibility rules in *Dougherty County Board of Education v. White* (1978), and relocation of polling places and city boundaries in *Perkins v. Matthews* (1971).[51] It additionally upheld the 1975 reauthorization of Section 5 in *City of Rome v. United States* (1980) highlighting the persistence of race discrimination in the covered jurisdictions and emphasizing Congress's broad power to enforce the Fifteenth Amendment.[52]

Under Section 5 of the Voting Rights Act, covered jurisdictions are required to prove that their proposed electoral changes neither have a racially discriminatory effect nor are motivated by a racially discriminatory purpose. Regarding the "effects" prong, the Court held in *City of Rome* (1980) that the attorney general could indeed reject a proposed electoral change solely because of its racially discriminatory impact. Even though the Fifteenth Amendment only prohibited purposefully discriminatory voting practices, the Court reasoned, Congress might have rationally concluded that practices with discriminatory effects should also be prohibited. Justice Rehnquist dissented, objecting to Congress usurping judicial power to define the substantive rights protected by the Reconstruction amendments.

Rehnquist's concerns were increasingly embraced by Republican justices like Kennedy, Scalia, and Thomas, and reflected in the Court's "new federalism" rulings that restricted congressional power to define and enforce constitutional rights. Especially significant, the Court rejected *Katzenbach*'s ratchet theory in *City of Boerne v. Flores* (1997) as it would enable Congress to "define its own powers by altering the Fourteenth Amendment's meaning."[53] The Court additionally imposed a new and tougher standard requiring "congruence and proportionality" between the constitutional right and the means employed by Congress to enforce it. The congruence and proportionality test did, in fact, result in the invalidation of some federal statutes, including in *Boerne* the application of the Religious Freedom and Restoration Act to states and localities. The Court, however, often distinguished such laws from those remedying discrimination against a suspect class (*Nevada Department of Human Resources v. Hibbs*, 2003) or protecting a fundamental right (*Tennessee v. Lane*, 2004).[54] It seemed, at least for the time, that Section 5 would be safe from *Boerne*'s more demanding standard.

Another line of cases more clearly and directly restricted Section 5.

In *Beer v. United States* (1976), a five-member majority consisting of the Court's more conservative justices (Stewart, Blackmun, Powell, Burger, and Rehnquist) adopted what is known as the "retrogression" standard.[55] The Court ruled that New Orleans's reapportionment plan did not violate Section 5 since it did not worsen the existing representation of African Americans on the city council, even though it would not produce or approximate proportional representation. In other words, preclearance required that a voting change was not retrogressive, meaning that it did not render minorities worse off in terms of the effectiveness of their vote. If, for example, a redistricting plan reduced the number of majority-minority districts, it would be considered retrogressive and would fail preclearance. According to Jesse Rhodes, the *Beer* standard "gravely limited the potential of Section 5 to promote African American voting power" and perversely "reward[ed] jurisdictions that had discriminated most egregiously prior to enactment of the VRA by allowing them to receive preclearance for new submissions so long as these did not further diminish black voting power."[56] Its practical consequence was a 50 percent drop in Section 5 objections by 1981.[57]

In a 5–4 ruling in *Georgia v Ashcroft* (2003), an exclusively Republican majority went further and loosened the retrogression standard by holding that a reduction in the number of majority-minority districts did not alone indicate a retrogressive effect.[58] Other factors could be considered, including substantive representation (whether minorities' policy interests were effectively achieved) and the presence of coalitional or influence districts (where minorities could still play a substantial role in an election with the help of voters of another race in the former or without such help in the latter). Under the Court's new rule, states gained both flexibility in redistricting and a greater likelihood of securing preclearance. Congress, however, was not pleased with this doctrinal shift and included in its 2006 reauthorization an amendment referred to as "the *Georgia v. Ashcroft* fix" which reinstated the previous understanding that any voting change reducing the ability of a racial minority group to elect their preferred candidates of choice would be considered retrogressive and would not be precleared.

With regard to Section 5's discriminatory purpose requirement, a slim Court majority in *City of Richmond v. U.S.* (1975) upheld an annexation plan that would have reduced the city's black population from 52 to 42 percent.[59] Because the plan also switched from at-large to district-based elections, which would boost the electoral power of minorities, the Court appeared to be less concerned that a racially discriminatory purpose had initially "infected" the annexation. In another restrictive move, a Court majority consisting only of Republican justices held in *Reno v. Bossier Parish School Board* (*Bossier II*) (2000) that Section 5 only prohibited election changes that were purposefully retrogressive rather than—more broadly—purposefully discriminatory.[60] This "contributed to the precipitous decline in the rate of objections to proposed voting changes in the 2000s."[61] As with *Bolden* and *Georgia,* Congress expressly overruled this conservative doctrinal change, reimposing in 2006 the previous understanding that "any discriminatory purpose" would be grounds for rejection under preclearance.

Of course, the issue raised by *Bossier II* would soon be moot. In 2009, in *Northwest Austin Municipal Utility District No. 1 v. Holder,*[62] the Court expressed clear "signs of discontent" with the preclearance system that Congress had just reauthorized.[63] The Court ruled against the Obama administration and reversed a lower court ruling that only political subdivisions like counties that register voters could bail out of the VRA's preclearance requirement. More significantly, the Court offered what many regarded as "unnecessary dictum"[64] in signaling its concern that the preclearance provisions renewed by Congress in 2006 "raise serious constitutional questions" to the degree that they are not "justified by current needs."[65] The conservative Project on Fair Representation, which had sponsored the litigation, called the ruling "an excellent first chop on the log."[66] Unsurprisingly, multiple lawsuits challenging Sections 4(b) and 5 ensued.

Four years later, in *Shelby County v. Holder,* a closely divided Supreme Court ruled that the Section 4(b) coverage formula was unconstitutional as it was "based on decades-old data and eradicated practices" and "unchanged for 40 years" was not "grounded in current conditions."[67] The Court observed parity in the covered jurisdictions in white and nonwhite rates of voter registration and turnout and "unprecedented levels" of minority office-holding.[68] Speaking for the five-member Republican majority, Chief Justice Roberts instructed Congress that "history did not end in 1965" and that Section 5 could not be extended for another twenty-five years using an outdated formula that "no longer made sense."[69] The extraordinary "blight of racial discrimination in voting" that the nation faced in 1965 had permitted traditional federalism principles to be overridden.[70] In the absence of similarly compelling circumstances in current times, however, Congress would not be permitted to depart from the Tenth Amendment's "fundamental principle of equal sovereignty" among the states.[71] Justice Thomas joined the majority opinion but argued in his concurrence that the Court should take the additional step of ruling Section 5 unconstitutional.

Justice Ginsburg's dissent, joined by Justices Breyer, Sotomayor, and Kagan, argued that race discrimination in voting had "evol[ved] . . . into more subtle second-generation barriers" such as racial gerrymandering and at-large voting, which makes preclearance "vital to protect minority voting rights and prevent backsliding."[72] She argued, in sharp contrast to the majority opinion, that Congress had "amassed a sizable record" of 15,000 pages of evidence developed in twenty-one hearings at which over ninety witnesses testified.[73] That evidence led Congress to conclude that "intentional race discrimination in voting remains so serious and widespread in covered jurisdictions that section 5 preclearance is still needed."[74] After all, the opinion noted, the Justice Department objected to 626 proposed changes to voting laws between 1982 and 2004, with an additional 800 potential changes withdrawn or altered as a result of requests for more information. The covered jurisdictions, furthermore, had four times as many successful Section 2 lawsuits per capita as noncovered jurisdictions, with Alabama leading the pack. Finally, Ginsburg accused the majority of "hubris" in its "demolition of the VRA," accomplished by abandoning the Court's long-standing practice of "substantial deference" to Congress in the exercise of its Fourteenth and Fifteenth Amendment enforcement powers.[75]

As this doctrinal survey conveys, the Supreme Court has played a significant role, first, in supporting the ambitious legislative aims and tools of the Voting Rights Act and, second, in shaping their use in the ensuing years. It not only upheld but broadly interpreted the powerful preclearance provisions, enabling federal supervision over redistricting and many other important electoral changes being pursued by states and localities mostly in the South. The Court, furthermore, supported the VRA being used against vote dilution in addition to vote denial, with only a few justices—Scalia, Thomas, and Gorsuch—expressing opposition. It is also clear, however, that an increasingly conservative Court dominated by Republican justices sought to push doctrine to the right in cases like *Beer, Bolden, Ashcroft, Bossier II*, and *Shelby County*. The strong hostility of civil rights groups and congressional Democrats to these changes typically produced legislative reversals. Congress has not, however, responded to *Shelby County* by updating the coverage formula and restoring preclearance, allowing this most aggressive act of the Court's Republican majority to stand.

Shelby County as Partisan Collaboration?

In the remainder of this chapter I explore the claim that *Shelby County* is an example of interbranch collaboration among regime members. I look at several types of evidence: Republican Party goals with respect to the Voting Rights Act, partisan patterns in judicial votes, the persuasiveness of the Court's reasoning, and the ruling's impact.

Judicial Voting Patterns

An obvious place to begin is with the voting alignment in the case. The justices in *Shelby County* divided strictly along party lines and exclusively favored the rights claims of their affiliated party. All five of the Republican justices—Roberts, Scalia, Alito, Thomas, and Kennedy—voted to strike down the VRA's preclearance coverage formula, while all four Democratic justices—Ginsburg, Breyer, Sotomayor, and Kagan—voted to uphold it. Interestingly, the voting pattern on the Supreme Court was more sharply partisan than on the lower courts, where two of the three judges who upheld Section 4(b) were Republicans. It is nonetheless striking that in the *Shelby County* litigation, no Democratic judge voted against the coverage formula and all six judges who ruled it unconstitutional—five on the Supreme Court and one on the District of Columbia Circuit Court—were Republican.

Additionally, the Court's significant shift to the right in interpreting the Voting Rights Act is overwhelmingly due to the votes of its Republican members. For example, the *Bolden* plurality advancing an intent requirement for Section 2 and the *Beer* majority establishing the retrogression standard consisted entirely of the appointees of Republican presidents (with Justice Powell the only Democratic justice, though a Nixon appointee). Four of the five justices in the *City of Richmond* majority permitting an annexation plan that reduced the city's black population were Republican. Additionally, the five-justice majority in the *Ashcroft* and *Bossier II* decisions that eased preclearance requirements was exclusively Republican.

It is important to acknowledge, however, that many of these voting patterns can also be explained by ideology. For example, while the voting alignment in *Shelby County* is perfectly partisan, it is also perfectly ideological: the five most conservative justices voted to invalidate the preclearance formula, and the four most liberal justices voted to uphold it. This perfect overlap is not surprising, given that "the liberal-conservative division on the Supreme Court since 2010 falls along party lines, with all the justices appointed by Republican presidents on one side and all the Democratic appointees on the other side."[76] Additionally, *Shelby County* is not the type of case in which partisan motivation can be easily distinguished since, first, policy concerns are present and, second, partisan and policy considerations push the justices in the same direction. In other words, the case did not present a clean test of partisan loyalty as did *Bush v. Gore*. It did indeed provide to the Republican justices the opportunity to support their party's election reform agenda and boost its electoral prospects; after all, eliminating preclearance would enable Republican states to adopt policies like voter identification that are expected to hurt minority voters and Democratic candidates. *Shelby County*, however, also involved broader issues of federalism and civil rights. Any decision regarding preclearance affects the balance of power between the federal and state governments and the degree of autonomy states enjoy in election administration. *Shelby County*, thus, aided both a partisan end and an ideological one, enabling conservative justices to advance the "new federalism" championed by the Reagan administration aimed, in part, at reducing congressional enforcement powers under the Reconstruction amendments. VRA litigation, additionally, directly affects racial and ethnic minorities and their ability to participate and exercise power in the political process and, thus, constitutes a critical civil rights issue. This civil rights issue, moreover, carries strong partisan and electoral implications given the overwhelming support minority voters provide to the Democratic Party. As I discussed in the previous chapter, Cox and Miles found that Democratic judges were significantly more likely than Republican judges to vote for liability in Section 2 cases, but the authors' empirical measures did not permit partisan influences to be distinguished from ideological ones.[77]

A final complication is that even if a justice's ideological beliefs strongly influenced her vote in *Shelby County*, those beliefs—whether about civil rights or congressional powers under the Reconstruction amendments—have likely been intentionally planted on the Court by the ruling regime. Ideological influences are, thus, closely tied to a partisan agenda. The fact that ideological and partisan considerations in *Shelby County* are numerous, intertwined, and unidirectional, of course, increases the challenge of detecting the independent influence of judicial partisanship. One interesting exception, however, is Justice Black, who broke with his party in *Katzenbach* and voted in his solo dissent against Section 5 based on his federalism concerns; for Black, ideology won out over party.

The Court's Reasoning in Shelby County

A partisan voting alignment is, in any case, only the beginning rather than the end of any inquiry regarding the influence of judicial partisanship. Further exploration is required to confirm a suspicion of partisan voting. One line of inquiry involves the role of the law and the facts in influencing a justice's vote. If neither influenced the outcome in a clear or logical way—for example, if the Court employed a new, unusual, or unpersuasive doctrinal rationale—this might support an inference of partisan motivation. In fact, critiques of the reasoning in *Shelby County* abound. Richard Hasen calls the majority opinion "audacious" and "sloppy," Richard Posner claims the ruling "rests on air," and Scott Lemieux observes "spectacular shoddiness" in its reasoning that makes *Shelby County* "the worst Supreme Court decision of the last 20 years."[78]

The two primary complaints of critics are the Court's reliance on the novel "equal state sovereignty" principle and its unexplained break from precedent with respect to congressional powers to enforce the Reconstruction amendments. With regard to the former, Roberts's majority opinion emphasized that under the Tenth Amendment, states retain broad authority to regulate their elections, which implicitly includes the "fundamental principle of *equal* sovereignty" among the states.[79] The preclearance provisions of the Voting Rights Act represented an "extraordinary departure" from this federalism principle by subjecting covered jurisdictions to substantially different treatment.[80] *South Carolina v. Katzenbach* ruled that this departure was justified by "exceptional conditions," most notably "the blight of racial discrimination in voting" that had "infected the electoral process in parts of our country for nearly a century."[81] Given that "nearly 50 years later, things have changed dramatically" and race discrimination in voting is no longer "pervasive" and "flagrant," this exceptional justification is no longer available.[82] Roberts's citation of authority for the equal state sovereignty principle was extremely limited, with the majority opinion referencing *Northwest Austin* and *Coyle v. Smith*, a 1911 case that allowed Oklahoma to move its capital city from Guthrie to Oklahoma City.[83] This central "equal state sovereignty" holding has been widely panned by a broad range of scholars, including conservatives like Michael McConnell, who regards the principle as "made up,"[84] and Richard Posner, who flatly states that "there is no such principle."[85] Litman's careful analysis concludes that the equal sovereignty principle "is not articulated in the constitutional text, its historical roots are thin, and it potentially undermines other [constitutional] principles."[86]

The Court majority has also been criticized for failing to identify the true roots of this principle: the infamous *Dred Scott* decision, in which Chief Justice Roger Taney argued that blacks could not be recognized as US citizens without violating the equal sovereignty of the slave states.[87] *Shelby County*, however, is "the first decision since *Dred Scott* to invoke the doctrine of equal sovereignty where the right to vote was involved."[88] Invoking this "nebulous concept"[89] is also blatantly "ahistorical"; it ignores that the core purpose of the post–Civil War amendments was to alter the balance of power between the federal and state governments when it comes to the rights of blacks.[90] As Justice Ginsburg's dissent additionally points out, the equal sovereignty principle has traditionally been limited to the admission of new states, with its "unprecedented extension" in the voting rights field "capable of much mischief."[91] It places at risk a plethora of federal statutes that routinely treat states differently, including laws that allocate funds according to population and exempt particular states from regulatory requirements ranging from sports betting to nuclear waste disposal.

In addition to this odd resurrection of the notion of equal state sovereignty from "the darkest chapter of American history,"[92] the majority "abrogat[ed] *Katzenbach*" and departed from "long-standing precedent" that the Court should "defer to Congress's decisions regarding the enforcement" of the Fourteenth and Fifteenth Amendments.[93] The Court disregarded its traditional use of the rational basis test in this area and appeared to employ a stricter standard, but without acknowledging that it was doing so. In fact, the majority opinion sidestepped the issue of the appropriate standard of review, ignoring doctrinal developments like *City of Boerne* and holding that the coverage formula would fail even the weakest standard.[94] This, to Hasen, was the majority's worst sin: its brief and "falsely modest" opinion "seeks to mask major doctrinal and jurisprudential change" and "hide the . . . jurisprudential hurdles it jumped to reach a political decision."[95] Finally, the majority ingeniously struck down only the coverage formula and not preclearance itself, employing a "shrewd political maneuver" that supported its pretense of minimalism.[96]

The majority's reduced deference to Congress is seen not only in the stricter standard of review it seemed to employ but also in how it "barely engaged" with the "massive" 15,000-page congressional record.[97] Ginsburg's dissent, in fact, accused the majority of ignoring that record, with Roberts responding that it was irrelevant since it "played no role in shaping the statutory formula before us today."[98] The majority relied instead on its own evidence in judging whether the coverage formula was justified by "current needs."[99] Roberts observed, first, increases in minority registration and voting rates and minority office holding and, second, a reduction in the number of Justice Department objections in the covered jurisdictions. Since Congress did not revise the coverage formula to reflect these changed conditions, it no longer "made sense" and was unconstitutional.[100]

This "central message" of Roberts's opinion—that "'the era of big racism' is over"[101]—in fact, rests on evidence that is "crude"[102] and "misleading,"[103] For example, Roberts only used presidential elections when comparing white and nonwhite turnout, even though racial disparities are more sizable in midterm and primary elections.[104] He additionally relied on self-reported registration and voting, which is known to be inaccurate, particularly in the Deep South.[105] Finally, the observation that the percentage of Justice Department objections declined from 1995 to 2005 compared to the 1965 to 1975 period badly misses the mark, according to Morgan Kousser.[106] After all, the number of submissions in the initial period was quite small as the guidelines were just being developed. Additionally, "bureaucratic regularity" and clear expectations had been achieved by the latter period, and Section 5 became very effective in deterring discriminatory election changes.[107] The reduced rate of objections that Roberts identifies actually indicates the routinization and growing effectiveness of the preclearance process, not an independent decline in race discrimination.[108] Finally, Ian Vanderwalker and Keith Bentele find that restrictive voting laws adopted after *Shelby County* were more likely in jurisdictions that experienced higher minority turnout;

thus, they argue, in pointing to higher rates of black registration and voting, Roberts is actually identifying potent "risk factors for potentially discriminatory voting laws."[109]

The majority opinion relied not only on misleading data but "a narrow slice of available evidence" as well.[110] It ignored substantial social science evidence in the congressional record and amici briefs showing, in the covered jurisdictions, higher rates of racially polarized voting, greater racial resentment among whites, more Section 2 cases, and a larger number of successful Section 2 cases.[111] Kousser's study, though published after *Shelby County*, is especially effective in challenging Roberts's claim that voting rights violations are neither more frequent nor no longer concentrated in the covered jurisdictions. He found that over 90 percent of the 4,000 "legal events" involving voting rights from 1957 to 2014 occurred in the covered jurisdictions, including 83 percent of successful Section 2 cases.[112] It thus appears that the coverage formula is quite accurate in locating the vast majority of potential and actual voting rights violations. Kousser, furthermore, documents how the frequency of voting rights events rise and fall with congressional actions such as reversing *Mobile* and imposing an effects test, and Supreme Court rulings like *Allen, Beer, Gingles,* and *Shaw;* Roberts's simplistic approach ignores these important causal factors.

The Impact of Shelby County

Additional evidence that supports an inference of partisan motivation concerns the impact of *Shelby County*. The Court claimed that it had no choice but to invalidate the coverage formula given Congress's failure to revise it, despite *Northwest Austin*'s clear warning. The majority insisted that it was not overreaching; after all, it was only invalidating Section 4(b) and issuing no holding with respect to Section 5. Congress, Roberts noted, "may draft another formula based on current conditions."[113] The likelihood of Congress doing so, as everyone knows, however, is infinitesimally small. The justices "are not politically naive. They must have known that pressing a virulently polarized Congress to amend the law would probably leave a crippled VRA unaltered for years to come."[114]

There have been a variety of suggestions for how Congress could respond to the Court's concerns, perhaps by creating a new trigger and restoring the preclearance regime or by moving voting rights protection in a new direction.[115] As could have been easily predicted, however, Congress has failed to act. The Voting Rights Amendment Act, introduced in 2014 by Senator Patrick Leahy (D-VT) and Representatives John Lewis (D-GA), John Conyers (D-MI), and James Sensenbrenner (R-WI), would have reinstated preclearance with a new coverage formula based on a pattern of recent voting rights violations. Unsurprisingly, the bill was cosponsored by very few Republicans (eleven in the House and none in the Senate), received no support from Republican Speaker of the House John Boehner or Republican Senate Minority Leader Mitch McConnell, and quickly stalled at the committee hearing stage.[116] Another bill was introduced in 2015 after Republicans increased their majority in the House and won control of the Senate. The Republican leadership quickly made clear that the bill would not be considered, with Senator Leahy noting that a "decision has been made within the Republican Party that we're not going to do anything."[117] Representative Terry Sewell (D-AL) has introduced in multiple congressional sessions since 2015 the Voting Rights Advancement Act that would subject to federal preclearance any state with fifteen or more voting rights violations in the past twenty-five years or ten or more violations, one of which was committed by the state; this formula would result in eleven mostly Southern states being subject to preclearance.[118] No Republican members have signed on to Sewell's bill. As long as Congress remains sharply polarized and Republican-controlled, the chance of a successful legislative fix to the coverage formula is remote. There exists "no path forward for reform."[119]

Even if Congress was somehow able to agree on a revised formula, most legal experts are not optimistic that the Court would uphold it.[120] The *Shelby County* majority explicitly warned Congress that any revised formula would need to prove the current existence of "exceptional conditions" that justify an "extraordinary departure from the traditional course of relations between the States and Federal Government."[121] The result, given that "a regulatory scheme at the intersection of what Congress can pass and what the Court can accept . . . may well be a null set," is that the preclearance regime that *Shelby County* rendered inoperable is unlikely to be resurrected any time soon.[122]

The impact of both the Court's decision in *Shelby County* and Congress's failure to reinstate preclearance has been substantial, partisan, and predictable. With preclearance disabled, states became free to enact discriminatory laws that could take effect without federal review and approval, even while lengthy legal challenges are underway. The state of Texas, on the day that *Shelby County* was decided, announced the immediate implementation of its strict voter identification law. Alabama and Mississippi similarly began enforcing voter ID requirements that had previously been barred. Within a month of *Shelby County*, North Carolina adopted what has been called "the most sweeping anti-voter law in at least decades," which imposed voter identification requirements, reduced early voting, and eliminated same-day registration, out-of-precinct voting, and preregistration for sixteen- and seventeen-year-olds.[123] This is the law that a federal court struck down because it "targeted African Americans with almost surgical precision."[124]

The NAACP's Legal Defense Fund has documented dozens of state and local voting changes that were adopted from 2013 to 2016 in the wake of *Shelby County*.[125] The Brennan Center for Justice found that in "2013 and 2014, at least 10 of the 15 states that had been covered in whole or in part by Section 5 introduced new restrictive legislation that would make it harder for minority voters to cast a ballot."[126] Fourteen states, all but one controlled by Republicans, implemented new voter restrictions for the 2016 presidential election,[127] and the 2018 midterm elections saw eight states with more stringent voting regulations compared to 2016.[128] A 2018 report from the US Commission on Civil Rights found that, since *Shelby County*, twenty-three states have adopted voting restrictions like strict voter ID rules, proof of citizenship for voter registration, reductions in polling locations and early voting, and voter purges.[129] The Leadership Conference Education Fund found that in the three years after *Shelby County*, 868 polling places were closed in counties previously covered by Section 5, a 16 percent reduction.[130] Additionally, nearly sixteen million voters were removed from the rolls via purges between 2014 and 2016, a 33 percent increase over the 2006 to 2008 period; furthermore, the median purge rate in counties previously subject to preclearance was 40 percent higher than the purge rate in other jurisdictions.[131] Finally, empirical studies have demonstrated that partisanship and race are the most powerful explanatory factors for why some states and not others have proposed and adopted restrictive election regulations like voter identification; such policies are substantially more likely in states with larger African American populations and where the government is controlled by the Republican Party.[132]

The evidence is clear that following *Shelby County*, many states—nearly all controlled by Republicans—adopted more restrictive election rules that are predicted to affect minority voters disproportionately and, thus, presumably disadvantage Democratic candidates. There is little doubt that the Court's Republican justices were unaware of this extraordinarily likely impact of invalidating the coverage formula.

The GOP Project to Weaken the Voting Rights Act

The argument that the Republican justices in *Shelby County* helped their party by ending preclearance in *Shelby County* must confront the central question of whether there existed a GOP mission to do just that. After all, skeptics would point out that all four extensions of the Voting Rights Act—in 1970, 1975, 1982, and 2006—received overwhelming numbers of votes from congressional Republicans and were signed by four different Republican presidents. While it is true that in the 2006 reauthorization, the only opposing votes—thirty-three in the House—came from the GOP, 85 percent of House Republicans and 100 percent of Senate Republicans who voted supported renewing the VRA, including extending preclearance for another twenty-five years.[133] During oral argument in *Shelby County,* Justice Antonin Scalia famously attributed this lopsided vote to the "perpetuation of racial entitlement. . . . Whenever a society adopts racial entitlements, it is very difficult to get out of them through the normal political processes."[134] Richard Pildes also regards "unanimous legislation" with suspicion as it likely indicates that Congress is avoiding making tough choices on serious issues and engaging instead in "credit-claiming, symbolic legislation";[135] it may indicate "a political system . . . frozen in place on issues concerning race."[136] Regardless of the true cause, the huge vote margins are indeed misleading in suggesting an overwhelming bipartisan consensus supporting the Voting Rights Act. In fact, "within the strikingly brief space of a decade," the initial policy consensus had "imploded."[137]

THE GOP'S LEGISLATIVE STRATEGIES

The story of the Republicans' curious relationship with the Voting Rights Act since its passage has been effectively told by journalists,[138] historians,[139] law professors,[140] and political scientists.[141] They advance a common narrative indicating significant Republican opposition to the act, always from the conservative wing of the party and often from the leadership as well. GOP resistance has appeared at every renewal, including from each Republican president serving at the time. Such opposition, however, typically appears behind the scenes and in the early stages of the legislative process—though not on the final votes, which are more visible and electorally risky.[142] When it comes to Republican presidents, they not only fought against clean legislative extensions of the VRA but also "employed subterranean administrative practices to shift . . . voting rights enforcement within the DOJ to the right . . . [and] accelerated the rightward march of the Supreme Court on voting rights issues through their judicial appointments."[143] Nonetheless, officially and publicly—for example, on final reauthorization votes—the GOP supported the Voting Rights Act, likely fearing electoral reprisals for not doing so.

Consistent with this explanation, the Republican Party has been rather quiet regarding the Voting Rights Act in its national party platforms. A review of platform statements with respect to the VRA from 1968 to 2016 reveals that the GOP mentioned the act only twice. In 1972 it took credit for President Nixon approving "strong new amendments" to the Voting Rights Act and "pledge[d] continued vigilance to ensure that the rights affirmed by this act are upheld." In 2012 the Republican platform criticized the Obama Justice Department for "abusing its preclearance authority to block photo ID voting laws." In contrast to this inattention from the GOP, the Democratic Party highlights the Voting Rights Act in nearly every platform spanning the 1968–2016 period. It strongly affirms the act's importance, acknowledges reauthorization as a high priority, pledges vigorous enforcement, criticizes lax enforcement by Republican administrations, and, in 2016, supported efforts to "rectify the Supreme Court decision gutting the Voting Rights Act, which is a profound injustice."

Hiding behind the GOP's relative silence on the Voting Rights Act in its national platforms is a "Republican countermovement of ideologues and partisan operatives . . . [that] from the moment the Voting Rights Act became law, methodically set out to undercut or dismantle its most important requirements."[144] These "counter-revolutionaries"[145] hoped to eliminate Section 5, require proof of intent for Section 2 violations, and block Justice Department efforts to increase minority representation by eliminating at-large election systems. Journalistic accounts tend to emphasize the importance of activists like Hans von Spakovsky, Ed Blum, Abigail Thernstrom, and Roger Clegg.[146] These individuals have indeed been quite active in trying to shape voting rights policy, often participating as amici in important Voting Rights Act cases. Ed Blum's Project on Fair Representation, furthermore, sponsored the *Northwest Austin* and *Shelby County* litigation. Nonetheless, a persistent campaign against the VRA was also carried out by GOP insiders.

Republican presidents have consistently sought to weaken the Voting Rights Act through legislative, administrative, and judicial means. Their legislative strategies are apparent when examining each of the four VRA renewal efforts, beginning with President Nixon. His Southern strategy to win the White House included assurances to Southern delegates at the 1968 Republican National Convention that he "would amend the VRA so that it no longer singled out southern states."[147] With the act set to expire in 1970, Nixon sent to Congress a bill that would eliminate preclearance, which the House approved, with 85 percent of the Republicans who voted supporting the change. Democrats and moderate Republicans in the Senate refused to cooperate and restored Section 5, however, with the House later adopting the Senate's version. It did so with the support of 69 of the 169 Republican members who had previously voted for Nixon's measure to strip preclearance from the VRA but who apparently no longer felt electorally safe in doing so.[148] In the end, Nixon signed the bill, though he seriously considered a veto.

In 1975, President Gerald Ford initially supported a strong bill that not only renewed the Voting Rights Act but expanded it by adding protection for minority-language speakers. That changed, however, with Ford's belated support for a proposal by Mississippi Democrat John Stennis to "nationalize" preclearance and impose it on every state. Rhodes describes this as a strategic move motivated by concerns about a possible primary challenge from the right by Ronald Reagan.[149] This and other Republican attempts to water down the act, for example, by allowing Southern states to bail out of preclearance more easily, were defeated due to the vigorous efforts of civil rights organizations and the strong support of Democrats and moderate Republicans. In the end, an expansive renewal bill was adopted by Congress and signed by President Ford.

Ronald Reagan, who had opposed the Voting Rights Act in 1965, would later criticize its "vindictive, selective application" to Southern states as unconstitutional in his 1980 presidential campaign.[150] Unlike Nixon, however, Reagan did not follow through with a proposal to eliminate Section 5 during the 1982 congressional reauthorization, as the administration believed this to be "a hopeless battle."[151] It instead focused on preventing the adoption of an effects test for assessing Section 2 claims. Assistance in this cause came from John Roberts, later chief justice and then serving as special assistant to the attorney general, who became "a zealot" on the issue, writing "over 25 memos" and drafting speeches and talking points for attorney general William French Smith and assistant attorney general for civil rights William Bradford Reynolds.[152] As Rhodes explains, the House considered several Republican proposals to weaken the act, for example, by making it easier to bail out of preclearance.[153] A majority of Republicans (55 percent) voted for these proposals, compared to only 8 percent of Democrats.[154] In the end, however, the House fully reauthorized the act, though nearly half of the House Republicans who voted affirmatively had previously voted to weaken it. Congressional Democrats and moderate Republicans successfully resisted the administration's push for an intent requirement, with Senator Robert Dole's compromise including an effects test but specifying that it would not mandate proportional representation. The Voting Rights Act, in the end, was reauthorized for another twenty-five years, with 94 percent of congressional votes and President Reagan's signature.

The Voting Rights Act was renewed in 2006 by enormous margins in both chambers, with George W. Bush signing the bill in a formal Rose Garden ceremony. Once again, however, this falsely conveys an image of strong unity both within and across the parties. In fact, President Bush and White House advisors like Karl Rove were "dubious" about preclearance, some Justice Department officials were clear in their opposition to Section 5, and Bush shockingly professed ignorance and ambivalence about renewing the act in a meeting with members of the Congressional Black Caucus.[155] Internal divisions within the GOP became clear as reauthorization proceeded through Congress. Republican leaders had hoped for a quick and clean extension to help insure that the party would retain control of Congress in the midterm elections. A handful of upstart House Republicans foiled these plans, however, and forced the leadership to allow consideration of four proposals that would have eliminated the minority language provisions, altered the triggers for Section 5 preclearance (leaving Hawaii as the only covered state), limited reauthorization to ten years rather than twenty-five, and eased the bailout process. Although these amendments were all defeated, support for them came overwhelmingly from Republicans and representatives from covered jurisdictions.[156] In fact, three of the four amendments commanded majority support within the GOP conference.[157] Ultimately, thirty-three House members voted against renewal of the act, all of them Republicans and most (twenty-six) from Section 5 states.[158] Republican leaders fared better in the Senate, keeping opposition to a minimum and securing unanimous support for a twenty-five-year extension of preclearance. Nonetheless, Republicans on the Senate Judiciary Committee, all of whom had voted for reauthorization, published a lengthy minority report criticizing the legislation and the process that produced it and expressing regret that preclearance had not been sufficiently reviewed. The report included data drawn from a study by Ed Blum's Project on Fair Representation that emphasized the great progress made both across the United States and in covered states with respect to African American registration, turnout, and office holding; these claims laid the groundwork for and found their way into *Shelby County*'s majority opinion.

A final interesting note regarding the 2006 reauthorization concerns the Court's *Georgia v. Ashcroft* ruling. As previously explained, in 2003 a Court majority consisting of five Republican justices loosened the requirement that redistricting plans would not be precleared if they diminished the ability of minority voters to elect a candidate of their choice. In response, Congress included in the 2006 renewal a provision reversing *Georgia v. Ashcroft*. Republican legislators were not at all reluctant to support this change. After all, doing so would insure continued pressure on legislatures to draw majority-minority districts whenever possible, which helps Republicans since more minority districts also means more white districts favoring GOP candidates. As I discuss in chapter 4, partisan and ideological concerns diverge in the case of majority-minority redistricting, creating crosscutting decisional pressures. This dynamic was apparent with congressional Republicans, many of whom favored weakening the Voting Rights Act, *except* when it came to majority-minority redistricting. The Court's Republicans, however, have not been so willing to sacrifice their principled opposition to race-conscious government policies in order to favor their party's electoral self-interests.

THE GOP'S ADMINISTRATIVE STRATEGIES

Although conservative Republicans failed to damage the Voting Rights Act legislatively, they have been quite successful in narrowing its scope and impact through administrative and judicial means.[159] Richard Nixon, Ronald Reagan, and George W. Bush were particularly effective in using these highly potent, but less transparent, policy tools. Nixon, for example, appointed his campaign manager, John Mitchell, as attorney general, providing a "clear indication that [he] . . . intended to employ administrative maneuvers as a means to align civil and voting rights enforcement with his conservative ideological commitments, the demands of core constituencies, and the administration's strategy of allying white southerners with the GOP."[160] Under Mitchell's leadership, the Justice Department limited the use of federal registrars, despite their great effectiveness, and chose to "soft-pedal federal preclearance" in a variety of ways.[161] The department, for example, drafted new guidelines that would have reversed the standard of proof required under preclearance; rather than a jurisdiction having to prove that its electoral changes were not racially discriminatory, the attorney general would only object if he concluded that they were racially discriminatory. The administration abandoned this effort only after both Congress and Civil Rights Division (CRD) lawyers strongly objected. In another sign of its "lax implementation of the law,"[162] the Justice Department gave its approval to two controversial voting changes adopted by the state of Mississippi: a dual registration system that posed an additional obstacle to potential black voters, and a requirement that candidates win a majority of the vote that made it more difficult to elect black candidates.

During the Reagan administration, the CRD experienced a "rightward lurch on civil rights matters."[163] The president appointed William Bradford Reynolds to head the CRD, and under his leadership, Section 5 objections and Section 2 lawsuits "fell to a new low."[164] Career attorneys saw their work being closely monitored and their decisions frequently overturned, several of which were later reversed by courts.[165] Reynolds actually sided with covered jurisdictions in several key VRA cases, including favoring North Carolina in the *Gingles* case and trying but failing to get the Court to limit Section 2's new effects test. The CRD was no longer regarded as an advocate for minority rights, with many career attorneys leaving the division in protest and the NAACP actually asking Congress to abolish it.[166]

Under George W. Bush, "VRA enforcement came to a standstill"[167] as attorney general John Ashcroft turned his department's attention from ballot access and minority rights to voter integrity and fraud prevention. As a result of this shift in CRD priorities, Section 2 cases and preclearance objections both "fell precipitously"; in fact, Bush's first term saw only forty-eight Justice Department objections out of 81,000 submissions, a rate ten times lower than during Reagan's first term.[168] This dramatic change was accomplished in part by CRD leaders like Bradley Schlozman assigning important voting rights cases to administration loyalists rather than career attorneys and making "routine . . . [the] practice of overruling staff attorney recommendations on voting rights matters, particularly when Republican Party interests were at stake";[169] the latter included Georgia's voter identification proposal and Texas's controversial redistricting plan that the Supreme Court partially struck down in *LULAC v. Perry* (2006).[170] President Bush additionally enlisted several high-profile VRA critics to serve in his administration, appointing Hans von Spakovsky to the voting section of the Civil Rights Division and Abigail Thernstrom to the Commission on Civil Rights. Thernstrom had long criticized majority-minority redistricting and the extension of preclearance to vote-dilution claims. Von Spakovsky argued against preclearance during the 2006 reauthorization, claiming that the Voting Rights Act had been used to "help . . . only minority voters and . . . one political party.[171] Von Spakovsky is regarded as a major contributor to the partisan "corruption of the Bush Civil Rights Division" that triggered a mass "exodus" of over half of its lawyers."[172] As experienced career civil-rights litigators left the Justice Department "in droves," including the chief of the voting section,[173] Schlozman brought in "a new cadre of lawyers who lacked experience litigating civil rights matters but were overwhelmingly affiliated with conservative groups like the Federalist Society, the Heritage Foundation, or the Republican National Lawyers Association."[174] "An ideological fervor . . . pervaded the entire department."[175] It is worth noting that many of these officials who served in Republican administrations and fought to limit the Voting Rights Act filed an amicus brief supporting Shelby County and emphasizing Section 5's "constitutional flaws."[176] This included Hans von Spakovsky, Clint Bolick, Roger Clegg, Charles Cooper, William Bradford Reynolds, and Bradley Schlozman.

THE GOP'S JUDICIAL STRATEGIES

Weak Justice Department enforcement offered a highly effective tool for limiting the Voting Rights Act. Another was appointing conservative Supreme Court justices who adopted rules that narrowed the act's scope and impact. This can be seen in specific doctrinal developments in cases like *Beer, Bolden,* and *Bossier II.* It is also evident in the more conservative voting record that GOP appointees have compiled in voting rights cases. Table 2.1 informs this analysis by reporting the proportion of liberal votes cast in voting rights cases by both the thirteen justices appointed by recent Republican presidents who joined the Court from 1969 to 2017 and the justices who each appointee replaced. This information was drawn from the US Supreme Court Database and includes both VRA cases and a broader category that includes both VRA and non-VRA voting rights cases.[177]

Nixon fortuitously enjoyed four vacancies in his first term, and, while voting rights were not his primary concern in filling them, his appointees—Burger, Blackmun, Rehnquist, and Powell—largely compiled a more conservative record in voting rights cases than their predecessors, as Table 2.1 demonstrates. Chief Justice Warren Burger, for example, cast a liberal vote in voting rights cases 53 percent of the time, substantially less than Chief Justice Earl Warren, who did so 86 percent of the time. William Rehnquist was also considerably more conservative in voting rights cases (35 percent) compared to his predecessor, John Harlan (52 percent). President Nixon was certainly aware of Rehnquist's extraordinary conservatism on civil rights generally and voting rights more particularly. After all, as assistant attorney general, Rehnquist had advised Nixon to veto the 1970 reauthorization of the Voting Rights Act. Additionally, although Nixon may not have been aware of it, Rehnquist had been in charge of the GOP's ballot security effort in Phoenix, Arizona, in the 1960s, called "Operation Eagle Eye," that challenged the eligibility of minority voters in Democratic precincts. The one exception to this strong trend of Nixon's justices voting more conservatively in voting rights cases than the justices they replaced is Lewis Powell, who voted the liberal position more frequently than Hugo Black in VRA cases—55 percent versus 17 percent, although the number of cases for Black (six) is small. When it comes to voting rights doctrine, Nixon's four appointees to the Supreme Court played a critical role in the Court's conservative shift. For example, three Nixon appointees voted for the intent requirement in *Bolden* and with the majority in *City of Richmond,* which upheld an annexation plan that reduced the electoral power of black voters. Additionally, all four Nixon justices voted for the retrogression standard in *Beer.*

The appointments of President Reagan and the two Bush presidents definitely shifted the Court to the right, both generally and with respect to voting rights. President Reagan appointed two moderately conserva-

Table 2.1. Percentage of Liberal Votes in Voting Rights Cases by Recent GOP Supreme Court Appointees and Their Predecessors

GOP President	Successor Justice	% Liberal Votes (VRA)	% Liberal Votes (voting rights)	Predecessor Justice	% Liberal Votes (VRA)	% Liberal Votes (voting rights)	Δ VRA	Δ voting rights
Nixon	Burger	66.7 (N=21)	52.8 (N=36)	Warren	83.3 (N=6)	85.7 (N=21)	-16.6	-32.9
	Blackmun	89.3 (N=28)	70.7 (N=41)	Fortas	100 (N=5)	87.5 (N=8)	-10.7	-16.8
	Powell	55.0 (N=20)	48.3 (N=29)	Black	16.7 (N=6)	62.1 (N=29)	+38.3	-13.8
	Rehnquist	36.8 (N=38)	34.6 (N=52)	Harlan	57.1 (N=7)	51.9 (N=27)	-20.3	-17.3
Ford	Stevens	86.5 (N=37)	77.6 (N=49)	Douglas	100 (N=16)	92.1 (N=38)	-13.5	-14.5
Reagan	O'Connor	56.0 (N=25)	56.3 (N=32)	Stewart	50 (N=20)	50 (N=48)	+6.0	+6.3
	Scalia[a]	34.8 (N=23)	38.7 (N=31)	Burger	66.7 (N=21)	52.8 (N=36)	-31.9	-14.1
	Kennedy	39.1 (N=23)	45.7 (N=35)	Powell	55.0 (N=20)	48.3 (N=29)	-15.9	-2.6
H. W. Bush	Souter	95.2 (N=21)	92.6 (N=27)	Brennan	92.9 (N=28)	91.5 (N=59)	+2.3	+1.1
	Thomas	20.0 (N=20)	31.3 (N=32)	Marshall	100 (N=27)	93.3 (N=45)	-80.0	-62.0

(continued on the next page)

Table 2.1. *Continued*

GOP President	Successor Justice	% Liberal Votes (VRA)	% Liberal Votes (voting rights)	Predecessor Justice	% Liberal Votes (VRA)	% Liberal Votes (voting rights)	Δ VRA	Δ voting rights
W. Bush	Roberts	16.7 (N=6)	42.9 (N=14)	Rehnquist	36.8 (N=38)	34.6 (N=52)	-20.1	+8.3
	Alito	16.7 (N=6)	35.7 (N=14)	O'Connor	56.0 (N=25)	56.3 (N=32)	-39.3	-20.6
Trump	Gorsuch	0 (N=1)	0 (N=2)	Scalia	34.8 (N=23)	38.7 (N=31)	-34.8	-38.7

Sources: Harold J. Spaeth, Lee Epstein, Andrew D. Martin, Jeffrey A. Segal, Theodore J. Ruger, and Sara C. Benesh. 2018 Supreme Court Database, Version 2018, Release 01, http://supremecourtdatabase.org (Justice-Centered Data: Cases Organized by Supreme Court Citation"; http://scdb.wustl.edu./data/php.

Notes: Data are reported for two categories: cases involving only the Voting Rights Act and a broader category of "all voting rights cases." The data concludes with the 2017 term.

[a] Because the focus here is *replacement* on the Court, I treat Scalia as Burger's replacement. Although Rehnquist technically replaced Burger as chief justice and Scalia filled Rehnquist's vacancy, the impact on voting rights decision-making comes from Burger leaving the Court and Scalia joining the Court.

tive Republicans (O'Connor and Kennedy) and two very conservative Republicans (Scalia and Rehnquist, whom he elevated to the chief justice seat). As Table 2.1 reports, Justice Sandra Day O'Connor decided voting rights cases in a liberal direction at a similar rate (56 percent) compared to her predecessor, Potter Stewart (50 percent). Justice Anthony Kennedy (at 39 percent liberal votes) was significantly more conservative in VRA cases than the justice he replaced (Powell, at 55 percent liberal votes), though they decided voting rights cases at a similar rate. As indicated in the table, I treat Scalia as Burger's replacement, as any impact on voting rights decision-making would come from Burger leaving and Scalia joining the Court, rather than from Burger "replacing" Rehnquist in the chief justice seat; looking at the data, I find that Justice Scalia cast significantly fewer liberal votes in VRA cases (−32 percent) and voting rights cases (−14 percent) than Chief Justice Burger. George H. W. Bush added two more Republicans, Clarence Thomas and David Souter, although only the former would prove to be a reliably conservative vote both generally and on voting rights more particularly. When it comes to the Voting Rights Act, for example, Justice Thomas has filed concurrences to express his opposition to vote dilution claims in *Holder v. Hall* (1994)[178] and Section 5 in both *Northwest Austin* (2009) and *Shelby County* (2013). Furthermore, as Table 2.1 shows, Clarence Thomas and his predecessor, Thurgood Marshall, are the pair with the most starkly different record in terms of their voting-rights liberalism; for example, 20 percent of Thomas's votes in VRA cases were liberal, compared to 100 percent of Marshall's. Finally, President George W. Bush appointed two conservative Republicans, John Roberts and Samuel Alito, to the high bench. Chief Justice Roberts was a more reliable conservative vote in VRA cases compared to his predecessor, Chief Justice Rehnquist, although the number of cases (six) is small; additionally, Roberts was somewhat more likely to vote the liberal position in all voting rights cases. Justice Alito, in contrast, has been significantly less likely to cast a liberal vote in both categories of voting rights cases compared to Justice O'Connor, although he had, prior to the 2018 term, decided only six VRA cases.[179]

The Reagan appointees have played an important role in several conservative VRA rulings, although Justices Thomas, Roberts, and Alito certainly added their support once on the Court. The four Reagan appointees, for example, were joined by Justice Thomas in the 5–4 rulings in *Shaw v. Reno* (1993) and *Miller v. Johnson* (1995) that erected constitutional barriers to the majority-minority redistricting that the VRA encouraged. This same group of Republican justices comprised the majority in both *Georgia v. Ashcroft* (2003), which made it more difficult to prove retrogression, and *Bossier II* (2000), which permitted preclearance of intentionally discriminatory election rules if they were not also retrogressive. Finally, in *Shelby County*, the five-member Republican majority invalidating the coverage formula and ending preclearance consisted of two Reagan appointees (Kennedy and Scalia), one H. W. Bush appointee (Thomas), and both W. Bush appointees (Roberts and Alito).

A few final observations can be drawn from Table 2.1. First, out of the twenty-six cells comparing a GOP appointee with a predecessor, over three-quarters (twenty) indicate a decline in the proportion of liberal votes. Second, many of those reductions in liberal voting between predecessor and successor justices are quite sizable, with drops of 14 percentage points or more occurring for nine of the thirteen pairs of justices. Finally, because the question being addressed is whether the GOP has sought to weaken the Voting Rights Act through its judicial strategies, Table 2.1 deliberately excluded the six justices appointed by Democratic presidents since the adoption of the Voting Rights Act in 1965. Nonetheless, it is worth noting that not only did Democratic presidents appoint far fewer justices—only six over the 1965–2017 period—but those appointees did not render significantly more liberal decisions in voting rights cases. This is because all of the Democratic appointees (Fortas, Marshall, Ginsburg, Breyer, Kagan, and Sotomayor) and all of their predecessors (Goldberg, Clark, White, Blackmun, Stevens, and Souter) posted very high rates of liberal voting in voting rights cases, nearly always above 80 percent and never below 70 percent. In other words, the ideological gap in voting rights cases is much smaller for Democratic appointees and their predecessors, all of whom posted strongly liberal voting records. For example, 81 percent of Justice Byron White's votes in voting rights cases were liberal, compared to 87 percent for his replacement, Justice Ginsburg; 93 percent of Justice Souter's votes were liberal in voting rights cases, compared to 88 percent for his replacement, Justice Sonia Sotomayor. It is fair to conclude that while a small number of Democratic appointees (six) continued the liberal voting pattern of their predecessors, a large proportion (three-quarters) of a much larger number of Republican appointees (thirteen) voted significantly more conservatively than the justice they replaced.

The Court's conservative shift in voting rights cases can also be understood as part of the broader efforts of the New Right regime to revolutionize constitutional doctrine in the federalism field. As many scholars have explained, the Reagan administration had a clear constitutional philosophy that focused on reducing federal power and enhancing state and local authority, with direct policy implications when it came to criminal justice and race.[180] A key concern was judicial reinstatement of constitutional limits on congressional power derived from the commerce clause, the Tenth Amendment, and the enforcement provisions of the Reconstruction amendments. The administration believed that careful litigation strategies and judicial appointments could revitalize these important constitutional restraints and properly restore autonomy to the states. The administration's views were laid out in Justice Department documents, like the Office of Legal Policy's "Guidelines on Constitutional Litigation" and "The Constitution in the Year 2000." With respect to voting rights, the "Guidelines" report identified *Bolden* and its intent requirement as a Supreme Court decision that was correctly decided. *Katzenbach v. Morgan* and *City of Rome v. U.S.* were viewed as incorrectly decided as they permitted Congress to usurp judicial authority, not only in enforcing the Reconstruction amendments but in defining and expanding the substantive rights embodied in them. Originalism was also advanced, most famously by attorney general Ed Meese, as an interpretive approach that empowered judges to reverse precedents, even historic ones, if they did not reflect a provision's originally intended meaning. The Reagan administration, thus, laid the intellectual groundwork for the new federalism that the Court would develop over the next several decades. For example, it invoked the Tenth Amendment and the commerce clause to impose new limits on congressional power in cases like *New York v U.S.* (1992), *Printz v. U.S.* (1997), *U.S. v. Lopez* (1995), and *U.S. v. Morrison* (2000).[181] Especially significant, *City of Boerne* fashioned a stricter standard requiring that remedial measures adopted by Congress under the Fourteenth Amendment would need to be congruent and proportional to the constitutional violations, which themselves would need to be proven with strong evidence. Civil rights advocates rightly feared that *Boerne* could end up restricting congressional power in the voting rights field, with the Court abandoning in *Shelby County* its long-standing view that the egregious history of Southern disenfranchisement of African Americans was sufficient to justify preclearance.[182]

CONCLUSION

The evidence is clear that, from the start, the GOP opposed and sought to weaken the Voting Rights Act. It has persistently opposed preclearance, minority-language protections, lengthy renewal periods, and the Section 2 effects test. It has not succeeded legislatively, however, as Republicans both in Congress and the White House could not overcome the mobilization efforts of civil rights groups that were supported by Democrats and moderate Republicans. In each instance, congressional Republicans ended up voting overwhelmingly for reauthorization and a Republican president signed the resulting legislation, fearing the electoral consequences of failing to do so.[183] GOP success in weakening the act has come, nonetheless, through less visible and, thus, less risky administrative and judicial measures.[184] Justice Department enforcement of the VRA became more centralized, partisan, and lax under GOP leadership. Republican presidents also succeeded in shifting both voting rights and federalism doctrines to the right with multiple appointments to the Supreme Court, culminating in *Shelby County*. As Desmond King and Rogers Smith note, "because of the efficacy and prestige of the Voting Rights Act, probably *only* the Supreme Court could have openly sought to restrict it."[185]

Shelby County represents the most noteworthy and consequential achievement of a persistent Republican campaign against the Voting Rights Act. It is, furthermore, "the culmination of Chief Justice John Roberts's career-long antipathy for major parts of the VRA, including its preclearance requirements.[186] The Court's Republican majority not only ended preclearance but additionally created a policy dynamic that makes congressional restoration nearly impossible. Since 2013, GOP lawmakers have no longer had to face the electoral consequences of opposing the VRA and preclearance, since all they need to do is *not* act. The new "programmatic status quo" created by *Shelby County* "finally freed Republicans to fully express their opposition to the coverage formula and preclearance."[187] They can now quietly resist legislative efforts to revise the coverage formula and restore preclearance and endure no electoral risk.

Finally, two developments have helped to solidify GOP opposition to the Voting Rights Act. During the 1980s and 1990s, the VRA presented a strategic opportunity to the party by enhancing pressure for majority-minority districts that elect both more minorities and more Republicans.

When, ironically, a Republican Supreme Court restricted that strategy with rulings like *Shaw* and *Miller*, the act became less valuable electorally and opposition increased. GOP hostility grew as well when the Obama Justice Department used the Voting Rights Act to block voter identification policies adopted by Republican states.[188]

The Future of the Voting Rights Act

There is considerable evidence that the *Shelby County* decision invalidating the preclearance requirement of the Voting Rights Act is the result of interbranch partisan collaboration. Votes to strike down the preclearance formula came exclusively from Republican justices who employed an unusual federalism principle and ignored long-standing precedent regarding congressional power to enforce the Reconstruction amendments. The ruling also had an easily foreseen partisan impact with predominantly Republican states and localities adopting voting restrictions in its aftermath and Republican opposition in Congress sufficient to insure that the coverage formula would not be updated. Finally, the justices' votes are consistent with and a product of an unwavering GOP campaign, one in which every Republican president participated, to limit the Voting Rights Act and reduce federal power in the civil rights field. The Court's Republican majority did precisely what GOP officials desired: it eliminated federal supervision of electoral changes affecting minority voting that Republican politicians wish freely to adopt. Although *Shelby County* might have been a long time coming in the view of Republican leaders, it most definitely represents judicial support for and participation in the GOP's demobilization strategy that has become critical to maintaining its power.

Several things are certain when it comes to the future of the Voting Rights Act. First, it will remain a flashpoint between the parties as long as certain conditions hold. These include sharp differences between the parties in their racial composition, the persistence of racially polarized voting, and a declining voter base for the Republican Party. These factors ensure that the GOP will continue to perceive the Voting Rights Act as an obstacle to maintaining its hold on political power. Another certainty is bitter partisan fights both within and across the government institutions involved in voting rights policy—Congress, the Justice Department, and the courts. The easiest prediction is that courts will continue to play a substantial role in shaping voting rights policy. Although the path has been somewhat uneven, the Supreme Court has since the 1970s mostly tried to steer VRA doctrine in a conservative direction. In some cases, this was reversed by a Democratic Congress moved to act by both electoral self-interest and the strong mobilization activities of civil rights groups. In other instances, most notably *Shelby County*, the Court has had its way. This momentous decision has additionally served as "an accelerant" to new constitutional challenges to Section 2.[189] A continued conservative path for VRA doctrine is assured by the increasingly solid Republican majority on the Court that was secured by Donald Trump's 2016 election.

President Trump has continued, and further amplified, the GOP's campaign against voter fraud, a concern that scholars uniformly dismiss as unfounded. He has advanced a variety of baseless claims, including millions of votes being illegally cast against him in 2016, high rates of noncitizen voting, and multiple voting in the 2018 midterm elections by individuals who changed clothes in their cars and returned to the polling place in disguise. The president's more significant and enduring impact on voting rights law, however, will come from his conservative Supreme Court appointments. His first, Justice Neil Gorsuch, joined the Republican majority in *Abbott v. Perez* (2018), which reversed a lower federal court decision and upheld Texas's redistricting plan, with the Court insisting that voters must prove that they were harmed, and intentionally so, by the state legislature.[190] As Richard Hasen notes, *Abbott* demonstrates the difficulty of winning a voting rights case after *Shelby County*.[191] Justice Gorsuch additionally joined Justice Thomas's concurrence in *Abbott* that would have gone even further than the majority in ruling that the Voting Rights Act should not be applicable to redistricting claims. Election law experts regard President Trump's selection of Brett Kavanaugh to replace Anthony Kennedy as "terrible news for voting rights."[192] Michael Waldman, Brennan Center for Justice president, claims that Kavanaugh's appointment will reinforce the Roberts Court's "active, relentless, and destructive" path when it comes to "the law of democracy."[193] Kavanaugh, after all, wrote the lower court opinion upholding South Carolina's voter identification law that the Obama Justice Department had blocked because of its racially discriminatory impact.[194] He may also support the views of justices like Scalia and Thomas, expressed in *LULAC v. Perry* (2006) and *Holder v. Hall* (1994), regarding the limited reach of other parts of the Voting Rights Act, including

Section 2. With that, the Court "could vote to kill off what's left of the act."[195] Finally, with Kavanaugh replacing Kennedy, Chief Justice Roberts has become the new median justice, and his long-standing hostility to the Voting Rights Act is incontrovertible.

3 | Courts, Parties, and Voter Identification

Have courts exercised friendly judicial review with respect to voter identification policies? Did the GOP, as regime politics theory predicts, both cause and benefit from the Supreme Court's 2008 Crawford decision upholding Indiana's voter ID law?

Voter identification resides at the top of the GOP's election reform agenda. This policy seeks to reduce fraud and enhance public confidence in elections by requiring voters to provide identification documents (ID) before casting a ballot in person at the polls. The strictest regulations require a government-issued photo ID that is valid, meaning that it is unexpired and contains a correct address; individuals lacking such documentation may be permitted to cast a provisional ballot, which is then counted only if the voter visits an election office soon after election day and provides the proper identification. Voter ID is a hotly debated and intensely partisan issue. Democrats and Republicans have taken sharply opposed positions in their national platforms; the adoption of new voter ID requirements occurs nearly exclusively in states under Republican control; and legislative voting patterns are strictly partisan, with voter ID measures often adopted without a single Democratic vote.

Much less is known about whether judges have also sharply divided along partisan lines, acting more as friendly partisans than neutral arbiters in deciding voter ID cases. In this chapter I seek to fill this gap in our knowledge in two ways. First, I examine *Crawford v. Marion County Election Board*, the 2008 Supreme Court decision that upheld Indiana's strict photo ID law, observing both the role of partisanship and the conservative shift in voting rights doctrine that enabled it.[1] Second, and setting this chapter apart from the others, I analyze my original data set of voter ID cases in the state and federal courts from 2005 through 2015. The data reveal a substantial partisan disparity: over three-quarters of Republican judicial votes favored voter identification requirements whereas less than a third of Democratic judicial votes did so. While this partisan gap shrunk following the Court's 2008 *Crawford* decision, an inference of neutral or legalistic behavior by judges does not necessarily follow. After all, *Crawford* is itself a partisan decision. A Republican Court supported its team's crusade for voter ID policies and did so rather effortlessly—it merely followed the weakened judicial standards that Republican justices had already put into place in the voting rights field. The Reagan regime's successful mission to weaken federal control and enhance state authority over election rules has continued to bear fruit.

The Partisan War over Voter Identification

The history of voter identification laws begins with South Carolina becoming, in 1950, the first state to enact legislation requesting voters to provide identification at the polls; any document with the voter's name was permitted, and a photo ID was not required.[2] Several other states—Texas, Florida, and Alaska—passed similar legislation in the 1970s, and by 2000, fourteen states had voter identification laws on the books. Interestingly, the legislatures enacting these statutes contained both Democratic and Republican majorities. Voter ID was not yet a partisan issue. The twenty-first century witnessed an explosion of voter ID measures on the state legislative scene. According to the National Conference of State Legislatures, nearly a thousand bills were proposed in forty-six states from 2001 to 2012, and twenty-eight states from 2002 to 2014 either enacted new voter identification laws or tightened their existing laws, typically by adding a photo ID requirement.[3] The most intense period of legislative activity followed the GOP's dominant electoral performance in 2010 that gave them full control of twenty-six state legislatures (with a net gain of eleven) and twenty-nine governorships (with a net gain of six). Voter ID proposals were considered by thirty-four states in 2011, thirty-two states in 2012, thirty states in 2013, and twenty-four states in 2014.[4] By 2018, thirty-four states had voter identification laws in effect.[5]

The conventional wisdom is that, in *Shelby County v. Holder* (2013),[6] the Supreme Court freed Republican states, mostly in the South, to adopt restrictive policies like voter identification that disproportionately hinder minorities who lean Democratic. This view is simplistic and incomplete, however. After all, the voter ID movement was well under way and seeing significant success prior to the 2013 *Shelby County* ruling, and the Supreme Court had, by 2008, already upheld Indiana's photo ID law in *Crawford*. Nonetheless, after *Shelby County*, covered jurisdictions were no longer constrained by the need for federal approval and could both adopt stricter identification requirements and implement them immediately. That is no small gift to Republican-controlled states seeking to fulfill a high-priority policy goal.

The Republican National Committee's amicus brief in the *Crawford* case claimed that voter identification laws are not motivated by a selfish desire for partisan gain but instead command bipartisan support.[7] There is considerable evidence to the contrary regarding the strongly partisan character of this policy endeavor. The parties have, for example, expressed diametrically opposed positions in recent national party platforms. In 2008, the first year in which voter identification is mentioned, the GOP pledged its support for "the right of states to require an official government-issued photo identification for voting" whereas the Democrats "oppose[d] laws that require identification in order to vote or register to vote, which create discriminatory barriers . . . and disenfranchise many eligible voters." The 2012 platforms reiterated those distinctive positions, with Democrats also highlighting the efforts of Obama's Justice Department to "prevent . . . states from implementing voter identification laws that would be harmful to minority voters" and Republicans urging "every citizen, elected official, and *member of the judiciary* to preserve the integrity of the vote" (emphasis added). In 2016 the Democrats again pledged "to fight against discriminatory voter identification laws" whereas the GOP platform favored "legislation to require . . . secure photo ID when voting" and "oppose[d] litigation against states exercising their sovereign authority to enact such laws." These competing statements include an important federalism subtext. Democrats expressed their commitment to using the Justice Department's preclearance power against states adopting voter identification requirements; in contrast, Republicans insisted that states have the sovereign authority to pursue such policies, free from federal interference and intrusive litigation. Of course, the Court's Republican majority definitively resolved this partisan dispute in the GOP's favor in 2013 in *Shelby County*.

The parties' distinctive positions on the voter ID issue are also seen in profoundly partisan patterns of legislative activity. For example, in the nine states that considered new documentation requirements for in-person voting between 2005 and 2007,[8] legislative support has been aptly described as "a one-party affair," with 95 percent of Republican legislators and only 2 percent of Democratic legislators voting in favor of those bills; in the eight states where the legislature approved its voter ID proposal, three Democratic governors vetoed their states' bills and five Republican governors signed theirs into law.[9] In the twenty-eight states that adopted restrictive voter ID laws or placed such a measure on the ballot from 2005 to 2013, William Hicks et al. found "massive partisan polarization . . . with more than 97% of Republicans voting 'yea' and more than 88% of Democrats voting 'nay.'"[10] Applying their polarization measure, in which 100 is a perfect score (i.e., no legislator voted with the opposing party), twenty-one of those twenty-eight states scored above 90 and three additional states scored over 80.[11] North Carolina earned a perfect score in 2013, as its restrictive voter ID law did not receive a single Democratic vote and no Republican voted to oppose it.

Partisan patterns of legislative voting are not restricted to the states. At the federal level, congressional Republicans have proposed amendments to the Help America Vote Act that would require voters in federal elections to provide valid photo identification and proof of citizenship. For example, the Federal Election Integrity Act of 2006 was introduced by Republican congressman Henry Hyde, cosponsored by eleven other Republicans, and passed in the House on a nearly straight party-line vote, with 99 percent of the affirmative votes coming from Republicans and 98 percent of the negative votes coming from Democrats.[12]

Partisan behavior on the voter identification issue extends beyond legislatures to the executive branch. For example, political appointees in George W. Bush's Justice Department disregarded the recommendation of career attorneys and precleared Georgia's voter identification law in 2005.[13] It also responded to Republican complaints regarding a draft report of the US Election Assistance Commission by delaying its release and then revising a key sentence; the original sentence— "allegations of fraud through voter impersonation at polling places are greatly exaggerated"—was altered to state that there is "a great deal of debate on the pervasiveness of fraud."[14] US Attorneys were additionally pressured to pursue voter fraud cases, and at least two, David Iglesias and John McKay, were fired for not doing so aggressively enough.[15] Justice Department participation in voter identification issues did not stop under President Obama, but it did change direction. The department, for example, refused to preclear voter ID laws from Texas and South Carolina, no doubt strengthening GOP opposition to the Voting Rights Act. It also, after *Shelby County* was decided in 2013, challenged voter ID laws from both North Carolina and Texas, urging the courts to find racially discriminatory intent and bail in both states, thereby reinstating preclearance requirements. Under President Trump and his first attorney general, Jeff Sessions, the Justice Department again reversed course. For example, within six weeks of Trump's inauguration, its ongoing objection to Texas's voter ID law was dropped.

In another sign of the importance of partisanship on this issue, multiple studies have found that Republican electoral gains in a state substantially increase the likelihood that it will adopt new voter identification requirements.[16] According to my analysis of data provided by Lorraine Minnite, of the twenty-five states enacting new voter ID requirements from 2003 to 2012, nearly 90 percent had Republican legislatures and over three-quarters had unified Republican control of the government.[17] Republican control of both the legislative and executive branches additionally leads to more restrictive types of voter identification laws being adopted, including photo ID requirements and stricter provisional balloting rules.[18] Finally, Rene Rocha and Tetsuya Matsubayashi found that the likelihood of a unified Republican government approving a new photo ID law over the 1980 to 2011 period was sixteen times greater than for governments with shared party control or Democratic control.[19]

Research has additionally found that partisanship interacts with race and electoral competitiveness to help explain why some states and not others propose or adopt voter ID policies. For example, Hicks and his coauthors found that partisan polarization in legislative voting on voter ID bills was less sharp where electoral competition was reduced and the district's African American population was smaller.[20] Seth McKee similarly found that as the size of the district's black population increased, Democratic votes against and Republican votes for voter ID laws increased.[21] According to Daniel Biggers and Michael Hanmer, new voter identification requirements are especially likely to be adopted by states when partisan control of the legislature and governor's office has switched to the Republican Party, with increases in the size of the African American and Latino populations further enhancing the likelihood of adoption.[22] Kathleen Hale and Ramona McNeal similarly found that both Republican control of the state government and greater racial and ethnic diversity increased the likelihood that a state would enact more stringent forms of voter identification.[23] An exception to the consensus of a significant racial effect comes from Rocha and Matsubayashi, who found that the influence of Republican legislative control on the adoption of photo identification weakened as the minority population increased.[24] When it comes to electoral competition, Hicks et al. found that the relationship between the prevalence of Republican legislators and the likelihood of a state considering and adopting restrictive voter ID laws was stronger in electorally competitive states.[25] Finally, according to studies by Keith Bentele and Erin O'Brien and by Ian Vandewalker and Bentele, states that were more likely to propose and pass restrictive voting laws, including voter identification requirements, were controlled by the Republican Party, had a larger African American and noncitizen population, and experienced recent increases in minority registration and turnout.[26]

This varied evidence supports a strategic explanation: Republicans facing a competitive Democratic Party and a large minority population use their legislative power to try to reshape the electorate and boost their electoral prospects, with strict voter ID rules seen as an effective means to that end. The GOP campaign for voter identification laws is, thus, "indicative of the larger struggle for electoral advantage between two highly polarized and demographically differentiated parties trying to maintain their coalitions with an eye on electoral success"; this is, furthermore, "merely history repeated" and little different from white Southern Democrats employing literacy tests and poll taxes to shrink the black electorate and upper-class Progressive reformers enacting voter registration requirements that inhibit the mobilization of poor immigrants.[27]

Like politicians, the American people divide along partisan lines when it comes to voter identification requirements at the polls, although surveys typically convey strong support overall. In fact, in recent years, nearly four in five Americans have expressed their approval of voter ID policies.[28] Nonetheless, there are considerable differences in the views of Republicans and Democrats. For example, a 2016 Gallup poll reported that 95 percent of Republicans and 63 percent of Democrats favored voter ID laws, with a national survey by David Wilson and Paul Brewer also finding a thirty-two-point partisan gap.[29] Public support for voter identification requirements appears to be slipping in recent years, however. A 2018 Rasmussen poll found that 67 percent of likely voters believed that voters should be required to show photo identification at the polls, declining from 70 percent in 2017 and 82 percent in 2010.[30] Charles Stewart et al. also report a decrease in public support for strict photo ID requirements, from 76 percent in 2008 to 70.4 percent in 2014, a significant drop that is due entirely to declining Democratic support.[31] While Republican support for photo ID laws has remained strong and stable—90 percent in 2008 and 91 percent in 2014—Democratic support dropped from 65 percent to 52 percent, increasing the partisan gap from twenty-five to nearly forty percentage points.[32] Especially interesting, partisan differences are significantly larger for those who follow the news closely, suggesting that exposure to media coverage and elite cues helps to polarize public opinion. Supporting this connection is Wilson and Brewer's finding that Fox News viewers are especially likely to favor voter ID laws.[33] Finally and unsurprisingly, Republicans are more likely than Democrats to believe that voter fraud is a major problem; a slight majority of Republicans expressed that view in a 2016 Gallup poll, compared to only a quarter of Democrats.[34]

Another source of evidence for partisanship serving as the primary motivation for voter ID laws is the dearth of evidence of in-person voter impersonation, the particular type of fraud to which voter ID laws are directed.[35] Studies consistently find voter impersonation to be the least frequent type of voter fraud, no doubt because it the type that is most difficult to commit, the least efficient, and the most easily discovered.[36] Furthermore, the risks are considerable, given that a single act of voter fraud in a federal election can be punished with a five-year prison term and a $10,000 fine. With respect to the evidence of voter fraud, a nonpartisan investigative team commissioned by the Carnegie and Knight Foundations found 2,068 allegations of voting fraud from 2000 through 2008, a tiny percentage of the hundreds of millions of votes cast in the three presidential elections covered by the study; additionally, only ten cases of in-person voter fraud were found during that time period.[37] Justin Levitt found only thirty-one credible claims of impersonation fraud out of the one billion ballots cast from 2000 to 2014.[38] A 2007 Brennan Center report estimated that the incident rate for impersonation at the polls ranged from 0.0003 to 0.0025 percent, suggesting that an American is more likely to be struck by lightning than commit this particular type of voter fraud.[39] Stephen Ansolabehere and his coauthors have also firmly refuted research by Jesse Richman et al. reporting a significant rate of noncitizen voting in recent elections, a study that President Trump has frequently referenced.[40] Finally, David Cottrell et al. studied the 2016 presidential election and found no evidence to support Donald Trump's claim of voter fraud, whether by noncitizens, dead people, or hostile election officials.[41] It appears that voter ID laws are, as Richard Hasen simply puts it, "an unnecessary solution to a non-existent problem."[42]

Even when the government is tasked with investigating voter fraud, usually by Republican presidents or governors, little evidence is uncovered. For example, a five-year effort by the US Justice Department to crack down on voter fraud at the direction of George W. Bush produced only eighty-six convictions, with over half of those against campaign workers or government officials rather than individual voters.[43] Additionally, the individual voters who were convicted were honestly mistaken about their eligibility rather than deliberately trying to cast a fraudulent vote.[44] A two-year investigation by the state of Texas managed to indict only eight individuals out of over four million voters from its 2006 general election; furthermore, none of those charged involved the type of in-person fraud that its strict photo ID law seeks to prevent.[45] A two-year investigation by Iowa's Republican secretary of state produced 117 possibly fraudulent votes and only six criminal convictions.[46] The South Carolina attorney general examined allegations that 207 dead people had voted in the 2010 general election, but his staff was unable to confirm a single instance of voter impersonation and found instead that nearly every case of alleged voter fraud was attributable to "human error," mostly clerical mistakes.[47] Finally, Kris Kobach's two-year investigation of voter fraud in Kansas elections as secretary of state led to only nine convictions, only one against a noncitizen and most against older individuals who had misunderstood their voting rights.[48]

In defending its photo ID law in the *Crawford* case, the state of Indiana conceded that it could not identify a single case of in-person voter impersonation fraud in the state's entire history. Even Supreme Court justice Stevens, in his opinion upholding Indiana's photo ID law, only cited two historical examples: one voter committed in-person fraud in a 2004 Washington gubernatorial election, and a member of Boss Tweed's machine alleged that he engineered multiple voting in an 1868 New York City election.[49] Following Occam's razor, the simplest inference for why "voter impersonation fraud is never prosecuted is that it almost never happens,"[50] supporting Minnite's conclusion that "the push for voter ID laws [is] part of a party-motivated political strategy and not simply a good government concern for electoral integrity."[51]

Republicans are not alone in ignoring evidence that contradicts their party's position on voter identification. Democrats have often exaggerated the effects of identification requirements on voter turnout. Social scientists, in fact, find this impact question to be very challenging to answer. Analysis is confounded, first, by the considerable variation across states in the details of their identification requirements and provisional balloting rules. Additionally, voter ID laws are often a part of a broader package of reforms that include other restrictions, such as limits on early voting and the elimination of same-day registration, making it more difficult to attribute changes in turnout to a single voter-ID provision. Probably the biggest challenge for researchers is that voter turnout can be affected by many different factors in particular elections, including candidate quality, the level of competition, the existence of salient ballot measures, voter mobilization efforts, and even weather conditions. For example, some journalists pointed out that minority turnout was lower in 2016 compared to 2012, particularly in strict voter-ID states like Wisconsin, and prematurely attributed this decline to new voter identification requirements without exploring whether the absence of Obama or another minority candidate from the ballot played a more important role. A final consideration is that even a small negative impact on turnout can be mitigated with increased mobilization efforts and enhanced voter education efforts by state election officials.[52]

Scholars addressing this challenging research question agree that voter ID laws do not significantly affect aggregate turnout levels; many, but not all, also agree that they have a disparate racial impact when individual-level effects are examined. We certainly would expect voter identification requirements to affect turnout as they raise the costs of voting relative to the rather modest benefits of voting.[53] Even "free" government ID cards, on average, cost from $75 to $175 when calculations include time, travel, and the costs of procuring supporting documents.[54] Nonetheless, as Benjamin Highton's careful review of the literature finds, "to date, there is little convincing evidence that voter identification laws influence turnout substantially."[55] Multiple studies have found that voter ID laws have either no impact or a negligible impact on voter turnout.[56] Only a few studies report a significant decline in voter turnout, in the 2 to 4 percent range.[57] These findings that identification requirements do not substantially affect voter turnout are perhaps not surprising given that most adults, probably the vast majority, possess the requisite identification, and many of those who do not are neither registered nor likely to vote. While Stewart estimates that 9 percent of registered voters nationwide do not possess a driver's license, which most voter ID laws require, Stephen Ansolabehere and Eitan Hersch found that in Texas, only 4.5 percent of registered voters lacked acceptable photo identification and only 1.5 percent of those present at the polls did so.[58] A survey by Mark Jones et al. found that over 97 percent of Texans in Harris County and Congressional District 23 who failed to vote in 2016 possessed valid identification required under law.[59] This may help to explain why, at least initially, groups challenging voter ID laws had a difficult time finding plaintiffs who were actually prevented from voting because they lacked proper identification. It, furthermore, supports Minnite's view that voter ID laws are unlikely to deter significant numbers of existing voters from showing up at the polls, but may serve as "surge protection" for the GOP, preventing the "kind of mobilization of new, first-time voters who very likely handed Obama his election" in 2008.[60]

The absence of evidence of both voter impersonation fraud and reduced voter turnout suggests that the intense partisan fights over voter ID are rather like, as Ethan Bronner aptly puts it, "a fight between two bald men over a comb."[61] There are several valid reasons for concern, however, including the fact that even a very small dip in voter turnout can be problematic in democratic terms. As Levitt notes, a conservative estimate of only 1.2 percent of registered voters being unable to meet new identification requirements could translate in a national election to two million otherwise eligible voters being unable to vote.[62] Additionally, the type of laws that are likely to have the most significant impact are strict photo ID laws, and they are relatively new—with more limited turnout data available as a result. We thus may not yet have the final verdict with respect to the impact of voter identification policies.

Most importantly, many studies suggest that voter ID laws have a disproportionate racial impact. African Americans and Latinos are significantly less likely to possess the identifying documents required by law.[63] They are additionally more likely to be asked to show identification at the polls compared to whites.[64] Though there are some exceptions,[65] many studies have found that voter ID laws have a disproportionately negative effect on nonwhite turnout compared to white turnout, especially for African Americans and Latinos and for the strictest identification requirements.[66] This evidence—that "the racial gap in turnout increases when strict ID laws are implemented" and, thus, that "strict voter ID laws discriminate"—constitutes the strongest reason for concern over the continued potency of this Republican reform movement.[67] Voter identification requirements, furthermore, do not have a positive effect on public confidence in elections, a claim advanced by GOP leaders and accepted by the six justices upholding Indiana's photo ID law in *Crawford*.[68]

Fights over voter identification have been intensely partisan and extremely toxic, as illustrated by the Texas experience. As Hasen describes the legislative battle, Republicans held the governorship and majorities in both the house and senate in 2007 and introduced a photo ID bill.[69] The Texas senate's rule that two-thirds of those present must agree to take up a bill was the Democrats' only chance of defeating the proposal. This required Democratic representative Mario Gallegos, suffering complications from a liver transplant, to lie in a hospital bed installed near the senate sergeant's office in order to cast the critical vote to prevent consideration of the voter ID bill, earning him a standing ovation from his Democratic colleagues. After Democrats gained an additional senate seat in the 2008 elections, Republicans enacted a special rule exempting voter identification bills—and only voter identification bills—from the senate's two-thirds rule, a clear sign of the importance they attached to this legislation. Democrats still managed to prevent the bill's passage in 2008 and 2009. In 2011, Republican governor Rick Perry deemed voter identification an "emergency item" that could be considered immediately rather than waiting for the first sixty days of the legislative session to pass. With the Democrats' delaying tactics finally overcome, Texas successfully adopted S.B. 14, which was described as "the toughest voter identification law in the nation"[70] and as particularly partisan in permitting as valid identification concealed-handgun licenses and military IDs but not state university IDs.

The partisan battle did not end there. Participation simply broadened to include the Justice Department and the federal courts. Under President Obama, the Department of Justice refused to preclear Texas's voter identification statute, a decision that was upheld in August 2012 by a three-judge federal court.[71] In June 2013 the Supreme Court vacated that ruling, however,[72] following its invalidation in *Shelby County* of the Voting Rights Act's preclearance coverage formula. Texas officials quickly acted to implement its voter ID law. Efforts by US Attorney General Eric Holder to bail in Texas to a preclearance requirement under Section 3 of the Voting Rights Act triggered angry complaints from both

Governor Perry and Attorney General (and later governor) Greg Abbott. In October 2014, US District Judge Nelva Gonzales Ramos held that S.B. 14 violated both the US Constitution and the Voting Rights Act.[73] A Fifth Circuit panel stayed that judgment, however,[74] with the US Supreme Court refusing to vacate the stay without comment, except for a dissent by Justices Ginsburg, Sotomayor, and Kagan that warned of the grave risk of allowing a potentially unconstitutional poll tax and purposefully discriminatory law to disenfranchise hundreds of thousands of eligible voters.[75] The portion of the district court decision holding that S.B. 14 violated Section 2 of the VRA was affirmed by a three-judge Fifth Circuit panel in 2015[76] and by the entire Fifth Circuit in 2016.[77] While the district court, at the Fifth Circuit's request, was reconsidering its earlier finding of racially discriminatory intent, the state enacted a new voter ID law, S.B. 5, which softened the rules along the lines of an earlier order by Judge Ramos that provided an affidavit option for voters lacking the required photo identification. This new and more lenient voter ID law passed only after Governor Abbott issued an emergency declaration that moved the legislation onto the state's house calendar and only after strong pushback by Democrats and a heated and lengthy debate. In late May 2017, the Texas house and senate both approved the bill on a nearly perfect party-line vote. President Trump's Justice Department shortly thereafter dropped the Obama-era objection to the law's racially discriminatory intent and has since "essentially abandoned the case altogether,"[78] arguing in its July 2017 brief that the state's revised voter identification requirements have no discriminatory effect and advance a legitimate state objective. In a 2–1 partisan split, the Fifth Circuit upheld the law in April 2018 and allowed it to be enforced in the 2018 midterm elections.[79]

The vicious and protracted fight in Texas over voter ID is not unique. Many bitter and intensely partisan policy contests have occurred in multiple political arenas at both the federal and state levels. I will now turn to the question of whether partisanship has also affected how judges have addressed this polarizing issue.

Judicial Partisanship and Voter Identification

There is no doubt about the willingness of politicians, whether Republican or Democratic, to advance their party's position aggressively in clashes over voter identification policies. An important question is whether this partisan pattern also occurs in judicial decision-making. Have judges been able to rise above the partisan fray and neutrally police the election process, a role that many see as critically important given the "pervasive partisanship" of lawmakers and election administrators?[80] Alternatively, does the polarized political environment in which the voter identification issue resides include the courts and not just the political branches? Most relevant to this book's focus, has the Republican Party effectively enlisted judges in this highly partisan cause?

Regimists, of course, would expect partisanship to influence judicial decisions in election law cases generally and voter identification cases more specifically. After all, the assistance of partisan allies in the courts would be especially important when the party's electoral fortunes are directly at stake. Additionally, voter identification is a highly salient partisan issue. This is especially true for the Republican Party, which has made its advocacy of electoral integrity and voter ID laws a prominent component of its party brand. In examining whether judges, like their copartisans in the other branches, are advancing their party's position in voter identification cases, I focus, first, on the 2008 *Crawford* decision and, second, on voter ID cases from 2005 to 2015.

Crawford *and the* Anderson-Burdick *Approach to Voting Rights*

Given that there are few formal guarantees in the US Constitution with respect to voting and elections, it is not surprising that the Court rarely addressed voting rights issues for most of its history. That changed, however, in the second half of the twentieth century. The Warren Court began hearing more voting rights cases and also became more skeptical of state election regulations affecting the right to vote, although it did not invariably use strict scrutiny or invalidate them. For example, it upheld a literacy test in *Lassiter v. Northampton County Board of Elections* (1959) but struck down an "understanding test" in *Louisiana v. U.S.* (1965) that permitted election officials to refuse to register applicants who did not sufficiently understand the US and Louisiana constitutions.[81] The Court also invalidated Virginia's poll tax in *Harper v. Virginia Board of Elections* (1966), a property requirement for school district elections in *Kramer v. Union Free School District No. 15* (1969), and Tennessee's one-year residency requirement to vote in state elections in *Dunn v. Blumstein* (1972).[82] Finally, the Court permitted Congress to enfranchise eighteen- to twenty-year-olds in federal, though not state, elections in *Oregon v. Mitchell* (1970).[83]

Many believed, given some of the language in *Harper* and *Kramer*,[84] that the Warren Court would establish voting as a fundamental right, thereby rendering all laws affecting the franchise presumptively uncon- stitutional. This expectation was short-lived, however, with the Burger Court backing away from treating voting as either a fundamental right or as core political speech. *Richardson v. Ramirez* (1974), for example, up- held felon disenfranchisement laws, and *Holt Civic Club v. City of Tuscalo- osa* (1978) allowed a city to impose criminal regulations against residents of an unincorporated area who could not vote in municipal elections.[85]

A fundamental rights approach was most clearly rejected with the Court's adoption of a flexible, balancing test in *Anderson v. Celebrezze* (1983) and *Burdick v. Takushi* (1992).[86] In *Anderson*, the Court struck down an early filing deadline in Ohio that was challenged by independent presi- dential candidate John Anderson, although it did not employ strict scru- tiny in doing so. The majority reasoned that subjecting all regulations that burden voters in some way to this stringent test would hamper the state's ability to enact the "comprehensive" and "complex" regulations neces- sary for an orderly, equitable, and efficient election process.[87] Instead of a "litmus paper test," the Court advanced a flexible approach that balanced "the character and magnitude" of the burden imposed on voters against the "precise interests put forward by the State" to justify that burden.[88] *Burdick* (1992), which upheld Hawaii's ban on write-in voting against a challenge based on the First and Fourteenth Amendments, offered ad- ditional guidance. The Court established what has been described as a two-track approach: strict scrutiny would be used for regulations impos- ing a "severe" burden on constitutional rights involving expression and voting, while "reasonable" and "nondiscriminatory" restrictions imposing "nonsevere" burdens would not trigger strict scrutiny and could be justi- fied by the state's "important regulatory interests."[89]

Against this doctrinal backdrop, the Court decided *Crawford v. Mar- ion County Election Board* in 2008, upholding Indiana's strict photo ID law against a facial challenge.[90] Although six justices voted to uphold the law, no single opinion united them and set precedent. Both of the three-justice plurality opinions, one by Stevens and the other by Sca- lia, agreed that the *Anderson-Burdick* balancing approach should be followed and that the law's slight burden on voters outweighed the state's legitimate interests in "deterring and detecting voter fraud" and "safeguarding voter confidence."[91] The two opinions diverged, however, on whether evidence could have been provided to prove a harmful effect on specific individuals or sub-groups of voters, thereby invalidating the law. For Stevens, who was joined by Roberts and Kennedy, the record was insufficient for determining and quantifying that burden, leaving no grounds for invalidating the law under the "heavy burden of persuasion" accompanying a facial challenge.[92] In contrast, Scalia's opinion, joined by Thomas and Alito, rejected that possibility entirely, arguing that "our precedents refute the view that individual impacts are relevant"; these justices instead evaluated the law based on its "reasonably foreseeable effect on voters generally."[93] Under that assessment, "the burden of acquiring, possessing, and showing a free photo identification is simply not severe . . . and the State's interests are sufficient to sustain that minimal burden. That should end the matter."[94] Justices Souter, Breyer, and Ginsburg dissented and also employed a balancing approach; in contrast, however, they found that the "nontrivial" burden on voters was not adequately justified by the state's asserted interests, particularly given the lack of evidence of in-person voter impersonation fraud in Indiana elections.[95] To summarize, all of the justices in *Crawford* employed a balancing approach in line with *Anderson* and *Burdick*; six justices (Stevens, Roberts, Kennedy, Scalia, Alito, and Thomas) rejected the facial challenge to Indiana's photo ID requirement; a different set of six justices (Stevens, Roberts, Kennedy, Souter, Breyer, and Ginsburg) left open the possibility of a successful as-applied challenge to voter ID laws in the future; and three justices (Souter, Breyer, and Ginsburg) voted to accept the facial challenge and strike down the law.

When it comes to the voting patterns in *Crawford*, they are strongly partisan. First, all six justices upholding Indiana's voter ID requirement and giving a significant boost to the GOP's campaign for voter identification were Republican. Additionally, both Democratic justices voted to strike down the law. An exception to this partisan pattern, however, is Justice Souter, the sole Republican on the Court to rule against the voter ID law. Among the four lower federal court judges participating, all three Republican judges voted to uphold Indiana's law and the one Democratic judge voted to strike it down. Furthermore, three of the four judges dissenting from the Seventh Circuit's refusal to grant an en banc hearing were Democratic.[96]

There was also a strongly partisan cast to the groups participating as parties and amici in the *Crawford* litigation. Baum has persuasively argued that the justices' positive or negative attitudes toward particular groups, whether the NAACP or the Chamber of Commerce, affects the way they react to cases in which those groups participate.[97] Looking at *Crawford*, the lead plaintiff was William Crawford, a Democratic member of the Indiana House of Representatives; his case was later joined with another lawsuit, *Indiana Democratic Party v. Rokita*, that was brought by the Indiana Democratic Party, the Marion County Democratic Central Committee, and several organizational plaintiffs like the Indiana branch of the NAACP and the Indiana Coalition on Housing and Homeless Issues.[98] Participating as amici on behalf of Rep. Crawford were several congressional Democrats (such as Senator Dianne Feinstein and Representatives Zoe Lofgren, Robert Brady, and Keith Ellison) and a variety of Democratic-leaning groups (like the Mexican American Legal Defense and Educational Fund; People for the American Way; the American Federation of State, County and Municipal Employees; and Service Employees International Union). Briefs supporting the state of Indiana and the Marion County Election Board came from the Republican National Committee; George W. Bush's solicitor general; Senator Mitch McConnell; a number of (mostly) red states, including Texas, Alabama, Florida, and South Dakota; and conservative legal groups like the Pacific Legal Foundation and Mountain States Legal Foundation. The participation of these varied groups, who are either political parties themselves or closely tied to a party, could very well have played a role in shaping a partisan response and voting alignment.

This is not, however, to say that the justice's votes were a simple matter of crass partisan favoritism. After all, the voting alignment in *Crawford* is strongly ideological in addition to being strongly partisan. The five most conservative members on the Court (Kennedy, Roberts, Scalia, Alito, and Thomas) all voted in favor of the voter ID law, and three of the four most liberal members (Ginsburg, Souter, and Breyer) voted against it. Additionally, the three justices (Thomas, Scalia, and Alito) rejecting the possibility of a future as-applied challenge were the Court's most conservative members. Justice Stevens represents an exception and disruption to this perfect ideological array, however. After all, he rejected the facial challenge and upheld the law despite being, at that time, the Court's most liberal member. Might this be evidence that Stevens's partisan affiliation won out over his ideological preferences? Or might his

116 | CHAPTER 3

vote have been strategic in nature? Perhaps Justice Stevens crafted a middle-ground position that rejected the facial challenge while retaining the option of an as-applied challenge as a way to attract the votes of the more moderately conservative justices like Roberts and Kennedy. Stevens later acknowledged discomfort with his decision, expressing both regret over weaknesses in the record that limited his decisional choices and concern over the recent proliferation of voter ID laws.[99]

A final point regarding the interplay of ideology and partisanship in the *Crawford* decision looks to the conservative doctrinal shift in voting rights that enabled it and that resulted from multiple Supreme Court appointments by Republican presidents. *Crawford* was not a significant deviation from existing doctrine as were *Shelby County* and *Citizens United v. Federal Election Commission* (2010), which I discuss in chapter 5.[100] Instead, as the New Deal Court became the New Right Court, it established an increasingly lax standard of review in the voting rights field, ultimately enabling a conservative outcome and a GOP victory in *Crawford*. The Warren Court had strongly hinted in *Harper* and *Kramer* that voting would be treated as a fundamental right. This view was supported by liberal and nearly exclusively Democratic justices like Douglas, Brennan, Warren, White, Fortas, and Marshall (with Warren as the notable Republican exception). As Nixon appointees joined the Court, this commitment to a fundamental rights approach "died at a very young age."[101] In *Oregon v. Mitchell*, for example, the five-member majority that rejected congressional authority to grant voting rights in state elections to eighteen- to twenty-year-olds consisted of four Republican justices, including Burger and Blackmun, the two new Nixon appointees. It is also notable that all four Nixon appointees (Burger, Blackmun, Rehnquist, and Powell) joined the six-justice majority upholding voting restrictions in both *Richardson* and *Holt Civic Club*. *Burdick*, however, marked a key turning point, establishing an approach that restricted strict scrutiny for discriminatory restrictions that severely burdened voters, with eight of the nine justices endorsing this more lenient standard.

On closer examination, however, this partisan account is not so straightforward. After all, the six justices in the *Burdick* majority and the three dissenters all endorsed the new two-track approach, disagreeing only with respect to its application to the write-in ballot restriction that the majority upheld. Furthermore, the *Anderson* ruling that initiated this doctrinal transition presented an unusual voting alignment. Remember that the Court in *Anderson* cautioned against a rigid "litmus paper test"[102] that would leave states with insufficient discretion to enact necessary election rules, leading the majority to suggest instead a somewhat vague balancing test. The majority's application of that test led it to invalidate Ohio's early filing deadline. Voting with the majority were three Republicans (Stevens, Blackmun, and Burger) and two Democrats (Marshall and Brennan). Two Democratic justices (White and Powell) and two Republican justices (O'Connor and Rehnquist) dissented and advocated for even greater deference to the states. This odd partisan split also divided the Nixon appointees, with Blackmun and Burger in the majority and Powell and Rehnquist dissenting. While voting rights doctrine moved in a somewhat more conservative direction with *Anderson*'s balancing standard, this may not have been clear at the time, particularly given the case's liberal outcome. It was not until *Burdick* that *Anderson*'s balancing approach would become "more formal and categorical," restricting the use of strict scrutiny more definitively and substantially.[103]

Although the role of partisanship in these doctrinal developments is not so straightforward, it is easy to conclude that the Warren Court would neither have treated voting rights in the same way as the New Right Court that replaced it nor decided *Crawford* in the same way. *Crawford* is an unsurprising result of the lax standard of review that (mostly) Republican justices put into place after stopping the Warren Court's march toward declaring voting a fundamental right. These conservative changes in voting rights doctrine would not have occurred without the rise to power of, and conservative judicial appointments by, a Republican regime focused on returning control of elections and voting to the states. Nonetheless, a partisan regime account cannot explain the specific doctrinal path nor the odd voting alignment in the *Anderson* case that opened the door to *Burdick*. This remains a major shortcoming of regime politics theory: its defense of a whole range of choices by the Court as consistent with regime preferences without explaining the specific doctrinal choices that the Court in fact made.[104]

Empirical Analysis of Judicial Partisanship
in Voter ID Litigation, 2005–2015

An additional angle on whether the GOP has succeeded in enlisting judicial support for its voter ID campaign looks at the large number of cases that have been decided in the state and federal courts. As Daniel

Tokaji notes, "voter identification has been the most hotly contested—and one of the most heavily litigated—election administration issue since *Bush v. Gore*."[105] Judicial votes in these cases provide a rich source of information for exploring whether Democratic judges and Republican judges have decided differently and in support of their party's position on the voter ID issue. There is, in fact, surprisingly little research on this question. The political science literature primarily focuses on the determinants of voter ID laws and their impact on turnout, while most of the legal scholarship analyzes and mostly criticizes the Court's reasoning in *Crawford*.[106] A few studies document statistically significant differences between Republican and Democratic judges in deciding voting rights cases, but they do not specifically focus on voter identification.[107]

With regard to the latter, the literature is quite thin. Hasen claims that "on issues such as the constitutionality of voter ID laws, many courts have divided along Democratic-Republican lines," but he offers only anecdotal evidence.[108] Christopher Elmendorf's examination of judicial decisions involving photo ID laws from 2005 through 2007 revealed a sharp partisan divide, with fifteen of the eighteen votes of Republican judges supporting their validity, compared to only three of the seventeen votes of Democratic judges.[109] Joshua Douglas's survey of recent voting rights decisions by state courts concluded that "most (although not all) of the state judges ruling on voter ID laws in the past decade . . . followed their ideological predilections," with conservative judges more likely to support voter ID laws than liberal judges;[110] although purportedly about ideology rather than partisanship, Douglas determined a judge's ideology by the partisan identity of the judge or governor appointing the judge. Douglas and Elmendorf both regard their studies' conclusions as limited and tentative, given the small sample size and the absence of statistical analysis.

DATA AND METHODS

In seeking to address these weaknesses in the literature, I developed an original data set of judicial votes in voter ID litigation from 2005 to 2015. These various lawsuits present a variety of factual situations and legal claims—statutory and constitutional, federal and state, substantive and procedural. My data collection efforts began with reading every judicial opinion emerging from a voter ID lawsuit from 2005 through

2015, while also devising a set of selection and coding rules to enable meaningful patterns to emerge from this tangle of state and federal judicial opinions.[111] An initial choice was to exclude lawsuits involving identification requirements for voter registration, relying instead on the conventional understanding of voter ID laws as polling place regulations requiring identification for in-person voting.[112] I further distinguished between rulings on the merits and those relating to jurisdictional or procedural matters. Even though the latter can be partisan and consequential, I excluded decisions that did not express a judge's assessment of the merits of at least one of the substantive legal claims raised by a plaintiff. For example, I did not include the Georgia Supreme Court's 2007 decision in *Perdue v. Lake* vacating a lower court injunction on grounds of standing. Rulings with respect to requests for temporary injunctive relief were included only if the opinion offered a substantive assessment of a legal claim. While this could be considered a controversial selection criterion, I did not want to exclude relevant data, including the significant variation among judges even at this preliminary stage.

Applying these selection rules, I ended up with 145 votes from 126 judges in twenty-two voter identification cases.[113] These cases arose in fourteen states—Arizona, Arkansas, Colorado, Georgia, Indiana, Michigan, Missouri, New Mexico,[114] North Carolina, Pennsylvania, South Carolina, Tennessee, Texas, and Wisconsin. Twelve of the lawsuits were filed in state court and ten in federal court. Seventeen of the 126 judges contributed two votes, and one judge contributed three votes. Although those votes were typically consistent, there were a few exceptions. For example, Seventh Circuit Court of Appeals Judge Richard Posner offered a positive assessment of Indiana's strict photo identification law in the 2007 *Crawford* case[115] but had a well-publicized change of heart by 2014, offering a scathing thirty-page critique of voter identification policies in his dissent from the Seventh Circuit's denial of a request for en banc rehearing in *Frank v. Walker*.[116]

After reading each case, I recorded several pieces of information. I first determined whether a judge's opinion expressed a positive or negative view of the legality of the voter identification statute at issue. In many cases, this was a simple and straightforward process. For example, the Michigan Supreme Court, in an advisory opinion requested by the Michigan House of Representatives, ruled 5–2 that the state's photo identification requirement was facially valid under both the state and federal Constitutions.[117] For the dependent *Vote* variable, I thus coded the votes of the five justices in the majority as "positive" (assigning a 1) and those of the two dissenting justices as "negative" (assigning a 0).

There were a few opinions that were challenging to code. For example, a Tennessee court of appeals unanimously ruled for the state in upholding its voter identification law but against the state in holding that the Memphis City Library's new photo ID cards were acceptable under that law.[118] I coded these votes as positive in their view of the state's voter ID law, even though they were negative with respect to the subsidiary library card issue. In another example, a three-judge panel of the US District Court for the District of Columbia unanimously reversed the Department of Justice and precleared South Carolina's photo identification law.[119] It did so, however, based on state officials promising in their testimony that they would interpret a key provision liberally, resolve any doubts in favor of the right to vote, and seek federal approval for any deviation from that implementation approach. Although the court upheld the law under the Voting Rights Act, it did so, some claim, by allowing the state to rewrite its law. I coded these three judicial votes as positive, even though this was concededly not as simple and straightforward as the coding might suggest. Finally, the Pennsylvania Supreme Court, in a 4–2 ruling, vacated a trial court's refusal to enjoin temporarily the implementation of the state's voter ID law and remanded the case with instructions that the lower court judge take another, more skeptical look at the law's capacity for voter disenfranchisement.[120] The two dissenters favored outright reversal rather than remand, leading me to code these votes as negative. The four judges in the majority were not, however, so easily categorized since the decision did not straightforwardly affirm or reverse the lower court's denial of injunctive relief. I ultimately coded these four votes as providing a negative assessment because they did not simply affirm the lower court decision and also because they advanced a strong concern with voter disenfranchisement. To reiterate, the vast majority of the coding decisions were simple and straightforward, with a few cases presenting a special challenge.

To help establish the reliability of my coding of the *Vote* variable, a research assistant independently coded around 30 percent of the votes in the data set. Our coding differed in only three of the forty cases, producing a 92.5 percent agreement rate. The Kappa-statistic measure of inter-rater agreement offers a more robust measure, however, taking into account agreement that would occur simply by chance. The Kappa value in this case was 0.84, which statistician Joseph Fleiss characterizes as "excellent" and J. Richard Landis and Gary Koch regard as "almost perfect" agreement.[121]

After determining whether each judicial vote was positive or negative with respect to the voter identification law at issue, I then ascertained the judge's partisan affiliation. For federal judges, I employed the Attributes of US Federal Judges database.[122] If that database identified a judge as an Independent, I used Mark McKenzie's approach and assigned the party affiliation of the appointing president.[123] Discovering the partisan identity of state judges chosen in partisan elections was quite simple, of course. For judges selected through other means, I relied on a variety of sources, including news reports and the partisan identity of the appointing governor. In two instances, I consulted with election law experts residing in the relevant state. For judicial partisanship, I created a dummy variable—*GOP Judge*—to which a 0 was assigned for judges identified as Democratic and a 1 for judges identified as Republican.

Each vote was next coded as partisan or nonpartisan. For this dichotomous *Partisan* variable, a vote was counted as partisan and assigned a 1 if the vote was positive and issued by a Republican judge or the vote was negative and rendered by a Democratic judge; otherwise a 0 was assigned. For example, the previously mentioned advisory opinion by the Michigan Supreme Court upholding its state's voter identification statute presented a straightforward partisan vote, with five Republican justices voting for and two Democratic justices voting against the law; all seven votes were, thus, coded as partisan. In a lawsuit challenging Albuquerque's photo ID requirement for its municipal elections, Republican US District Court Judge Christina Armijo struck down the law.[124] Because her vote was inconsistent with the Republican Party position on voter identification, it was judged to be nonpartisan and coded as 0.

Exploring whether a judge's partisan affiliation influences his decisions in voter identification cases does not rule out the possibility of legal influences. As Michael Bailey and Forrest Maltzman note, "political and legal explanations weave together in a complex knot," with legal influences like adherence to precedent and legislative deference often "hidden in a thicket of seemingly ideological behavior."[125] Because judicial decision-making is not exclusively political and might also be affected by legal factors like law, facts, and precedent, I constructed three independent variables—*State Court, Strict Photo ID*, and Crawford-*constrained*. This enables more rigorous empirical testing, particularly of legally relevant factors. Whether a judicial vote issues from a state court or federal court could prove important. For example, state constitutions typically protect the right to vote more broadly and explicitly than does the US Constitution, giving state court judges more law-based opportunities to strike down voter identification policies.[126] Perhaps this is why David Schultz has argued that state courts and state constitutions offer more fertile ground for plaintiffs seeking to block voter ID laws.[127] To enable testing of this hypothesis, I created *State Court*, a variable assigning a 1 to judicial votes issuing from state courts and a 0 to the votes of federal court judges.

Strict Photo ID is another legally relevant variable categorizing the voter ID statute being challenged in terms of how strict or lenient it is. The National Conference of State Legislatures categorizes voter ID laws in two ways—according to, first, the types of identification (photo/nonphoto) that are permitted and, second, the leniency of the provisional balloting procedures (strict/nonstrict) when a voter lacks the requisite documentation.[128] With regard to the latter factor, under a nonstrict policy, a voter without proper identification might still be able to cast a ballot by signing an affidavit of identity; alternatively, a strict voter ID statute would permit and then count a provisional ballot only if the voter provided the proper documentation to an election official soon after the election. *Strict Photo ID* assigns a 1 for strict photo ID statutes from states included in the data set, such as Georgia, Indiana, Pennsylvania, Tennessee, Texas, and Wisconsin; otherwise a 0 is assigned.[129]

Crawford-*constrained* is a measure indicating whether a judge identified the US Supreme Court's *Crawford* decision as a constraining factor in her decision. It was on April 28, 2008, that the Supreme Court rejected a facial challenge to and thereby upheld Indiana's strict photo identification law. Because the six justices doing so disagreed with respect to their reasoning, *Crawford* is not a precedent. It is possible, however, that lower court judges could choose to follow the Supreme Court's lead and similarly uphold voter ID statutes via the *Anderson-Burdick* balancing approach. While a reasonable expectation for federal judges, it might also be true for state court judges. Douglas, for example, has observed that many state court judges who invalidated voter ID laws "followed *Crawford* even when interpreting their state constitutions, thereby unduly narrowing the scope of the constitutional right to vote. . . . Put differently, when state courts followed *Crawford*'s narrower interpretation of the right to vote, the courts usually upheld the laws, but when courts independently construed the broader grant of voting rights in state constitutions, they were more likely to strike down these voting restrictions."[130] In my review of voter ID cases, I too observed that some state court judges ignored *Crawford* in their decisions or explicitly stated that *Crawford* was not controlling; they would then rely exclusively on their own state constitutions. Other times, however, state court judges "volunteered" to be constrained by the federal *Crawford* ruling. For example, the six-justice majority in the Georgia Supreme Court's decision in *Democratic Party of Georgia v. Perdue* (2011) noted that the Georgia Constitution's equal protection provision was "coextensive" with and "substantially equivalent" to the equal protection clause of the US Constitution; they were, thus, "treated as one," and *Anderson, Burdick,* and *Crawford* were followed.[131]

This Crawford-*constrained* variable was coded 1 if the judge, federal or state, expressed the opinion that she was "following *Crawford.*" Thus, opinions by state court judges that relied exclusively on their state constitutions were coded as 0, as were the decisions of federal judges that rested on statutory grounds, such as Section 2 of the Voting Rights Act. Obviously, all of the votes cast in cases decided before April 28, 2008, when *Crawford* was decided, were also coded as 0.

With respect to the representativeness of the resulting data set, there are significantly more votes from state court judges (80) compared to federal court judges (65) and slightly more votes from Democratic judges (76) than Republican judges (69). Nearly a third of all judicial votes (47 of 145) come from state Democratic judges, one-quarter (36) from federal Republican judges, nearly a quarter (33) from state Republican judges, and one-fifth (29) from federal Democratic judges. The primary bias in the data is that the cases and judicial votes are unevenly distributed geographically. For example, a disproportionate number of votes come from Indiana (26) and Wisconsin (29), where there have been multiple lawsuits, protracted litigation, and court decisions at both the state and federal levels. Additionally, the data set includes only fourteen states, a majority of which are red states in the South and Midwest and nearly half of which are Southern. The simple fact is that no voter identification policies have been adopted in blue states like California, Oregon, New York, and Massachusetts; there are, thus, no legal challenges in those states and no court decisions to include. While the votes are not geographically representative, these are simply the data (i.e., cases) currently available for studying whether partisanship has played a role in judicial decisions on this highly contentious issue. Nonetheless, I included in the regression model a dummy variable—*South*—coded

1 for the thirteen states of the former Confederacy and 0 for the remaining non-Southern states. Because the more conservative political culture of the South might exert an independent influence on judicial votes, increasing the likelihood of a positive vote, I include *South* as a control variable.

RESULTS AND ANALYSIS

With these disclosures about the data now complete, I proceed to the analysis, examining whether partisanship affects judicial votes in voter ID cases. I begin with simple bivariate analysis, using Pearson's chi-square test to confirm statistical significance, followed by a regression model that includes both politically and legally relevant variables and produces greater empirical rigor.

Several noteworthy findings emerge from the data. First, as seen in Figure 3.1, judges were quite divided in their assessment of voter identification policies, with 54 percent of the votes positive and 46 percent negative. The evidence displayed in Figure 3.1 also validates the anecdotal accounts of judges sharply dividing along partisan lines in voter identification cases: 80 percent of votes from Republican judges over the 2005 to 2015 period were positive, compared to only 32 percent of Democratic judicial votes. (Pearson's chi-square test unsurprisingly confirms that this difference is statistically significant.) Analysis of the votes of federal and state court judges do not support Schultz's expectation that state courts are more receptive to voter ID challenges as there is no statistically significant difference in the percentage of positive votes issuing from state judges (53 percent) compared to federal judges (57 percent). Dividing votes by both party and court level shows that the largest differences emerge when comparing federal Republican judges, 81 percent of whose votes are positive, to those of federal Democratic judges, 28 percent of whose votes are positive.

Given this sizable partisan divide, it is not surprising to find that nearly three-quarters of all judicial votes in voter identification cases (107 out of 145) are partisan in the sense that those votes conform to the position of the party to which the judge belongs. It thus appears that partisan behavior is a widespread, though not universal, phenomenon in judicial decision-making on this particular issue. It is important to note, however, that although 68 percent of Democratic votes and 80 percent of Republican votes can be characterized as partisan, Pear-

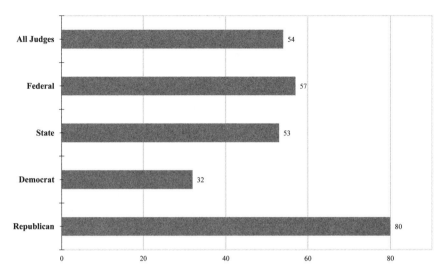

Figure 3.1. Judicial Support for Voter ID Laws, 2005–2015. Each bar indicates the percentage of judicial votes favoring the voter identification law under review.

son's chi-square test does not confirm that this difference is statistically significant. There is also no statistically significant difference between the proportion of partisan votes cast by federal judges compared to state court judges.

This finding of a close link between a judge's partisan affiliation and her decisions in voter ID cases does not necessarily mean that judges are crassly favoring their party's policy goals and electoral interests. It does not mean, for example, that Republican judges are conspiring with their copartisans to suppress Democratic votes and help elect more Republicans, or that Democratic judges are helping their copartisans fraudulently inflate the number of Democratic votes in order to help elect more Democrats to office. Rather, it may operate at a subconscious level[132] through cognitive biases such as motivated reasoning.[133] Like their copartisans, Republican judges, particularly if they watch Fox News, may believe that voter fraud is a serious problem that should be addressed with corrective legislation. Democratic judges, on the other hand, likely share the beliefs of other Democrats that voter fraud is not a significant problem. They may additionally be sensitive to the potentially negative impact of voter ID laws on allied groups such as African Americans, especially when Democratic politicians and organizations like the NAACP and American Civil Liberties Union have clearly communicated that concern.

Regardless of the particular causal dynamic, a regimist explanation would expect the evidence to show—and it does in fact show—that judges are likely to support their copartisans in the other branches on highly salient issues like voter identification. Although this political explanation of judicial behavior in voter ID cases is a reasonable one, it does not rule out the possibility of a legal explanation. The seemingly partisan behavior of judges may hide the influence of legal considerations like case facts and precedent. For example, perhaps the leniency of the statute under review is influencing case outcomes. The data, however, do not confirm this hypothesis. There is no statistically significant difference in the percentage of positive judicial votes in cases involving strict photo ID policies (53 percent) compared to cases challenging more lenient policies (58 percent). The presence of a strict photo ID statute does not significantly affect case outcomes, whether looking at all votes or those of Democratic or Republican judges. As additional though indirect confirmation, there was no statistically significant increase in negative votes in voter ID cases after 2010, when major Republican electoral gains resulted in stricter voter ID policies that would have presumably been more vulnerable to judicial invalidation.

A regression model enables these factors to be tested more rigorously. Because the dependent variable, *Vote*, is dichotomous, I used logistic regression to estimate the model coefficients. (To remind the reader, *Vote* is coded 0 for a negative vote and 1 for a positive vote.) Independent variables (where 1 = yes and 0 = no) include *GOP Judge, State Court, Strict Photo ID*, Crawford-*constrained*, and *South*. Unfortunately, I was unable to add a control for judicial ideology, in order to test whether a judge's party affiliation exerts an independent influence on his vote, because there is no common ideology measure for both federal and state judges.

Table 3.1 provides the results of this regression model. It shows that, even in the presence of other variables, *GOP Judge* has a statistically significant and, as expected, positive relationship to the dependent *Vote* variable.[134] The predicted probabilities indicate that the likelihood of a positive vote increases from 30 percent to 83 percent—nearly tripling—when the value of *GOP Judge* changes from 0 (i.e., Democrat) to 1 (Republican), holding other variables constant at their means. Crawford-*constrained* is the only other variable in the model that attains

Table 3.1. Judicial Decision-Making in Voter ID Cases

Variable	Expected Direction	Logistic Coefficient (Std. Error)
GOP Judge	+	2.41*
		(.46)
State Court	–	0.68
		(.46)
Strict Photo ID	–	–0.48
		(.45)
Crawford-constrained	+	1.64*
		(.49)
South	+	0.19
		(.44)
Constant		–1.54
		(.61)

N = 145
Log-likelihood = –75.1
R^2 = .248
*p≤.05

Note: Dependent variable is Vote. Is judicial vote on voter ID law positive (1) or negative (0)?

statistical significance.[135] As expected, the coefficient's sign is positive, indicating that judicial votes that are constrained by *Crawford* are significantly more likely to be positive than those that are not so constrained. In calculating the predicted probabilities, we see that the likelihood of a positive vote nearly doubles, increasing from 43 to 80 percent, as Crawford-*constrained* moves from 0 to 1, holding the other variables to their means. The regression results also indicate that strict photo ID laws are not more likely to be struck down, consistent with the previous bivariate analysis and as indicated by the lack of statistical significance. Nor are state court judges, as some have predicted, more likely to rule against voter identification policies than federal court judges. Finally, *South* has no independent influence on the likelihood that a voter ID statute will receive a negative or positive judicial vote.

Some final bivariate analysis will enable closer examination of how judicial treatment of voter ID policies changed after the Supreme Court's 2008 *Crawford* decision. As Figure 3.2 reports, positive votes were much more common (74 percent of the total) when judges explicitly identi-

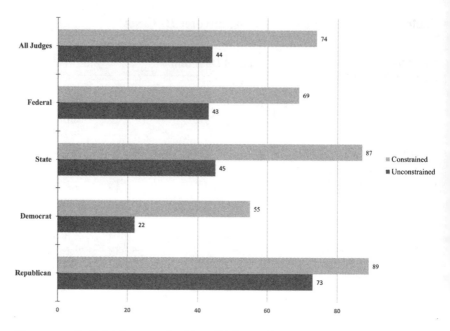

Figure 3.2. Judicial Support for Voter ID Laws, if *Crawford*-Constrained, 2005–2015. The figure indicates the percentage of judicial votes favoring the voter identification law under review, depending on whether the judge identifies *Crawford* as a constraint.

fied *Crawford* as a constraint or guide than when they did not (44 percent).[136] That pattern also exists for both federal and state judges. Sixty-nine percent of federal judicial votes were positive when *Crawford* was identified as a constraint, compared to 43 percent of votes that were not constrained by *Crawford*. Eighty-seven percent of votes from state court judges volunteering to be constrained by *Crawford* were positive, compared to 45 percent of state-court judicial votes when *Crawford* was not a guide or constraint.[137] These findings are especially surprising given that *Crawford* did not set precedent and that the *Anderson-Burdick* test it employs leaves judges with significant discretion.

These results might lead to the conclusion that judges are behaving legalistically rather than politically and are following the Supreme Court's lead in evaluating voter identification laws. In fact, the story is more complicated than what this dichotomous framing of the issue suggests. The evidence shows that the proportion of Republican judicial votes that are positive was very high before *Crawford* (79 percent), after

Crawford (80 percent), when constrained by *Crawford* (89 percent), and when not constrained by *Crawford* (73 percent); there are no statistically significant differences here. For Democratic judges, in contrast, *Crawford* matters. The proportion of Democratic judicial votes that were pro–voter ID increased from 11 percent prior to *Crawford* to 39 percent after *Crawford*, a statistically significant difference. A similar and statistically significant gap is seen in Figure 3.2 when comparing the percentage of positive votes when a Democratic judge was (55 percent) and was not (22 percent) constrained by *Crawford*.

Looking at the data in a slightly different way, the proportion of votes that can be characterized as partisan before *Crawford* was substantial for both Republican (79 percent) and Democratic (89 percent) judges. After *Crawford*, however, there is a statistically significant difference, with 80 percent of Republican votes, but only 61 percent of Democratic votes, classified as partisan. For both Republican and Democratic judges, around three-quarters of their votes were partisan when unconstrained by *Crawford*; when constrained by *Crawford*, however, a statistically significant partisan difference emerges, with 89 percent of Republican votes and only 45 percent of Democratic votes considered partisan. It thus appears that the Supreme Court's *Crawford* ruling curbed the partisan behavior of Democratic judges; they responded to the legal force exerted by a US Supreme Court ruling in the voter identification field. Republican judges, in comparison, had no reason to change their behavior; their preexisting support for voter identification laws was now consistent with *Crawford*.

A study that I have assigned to students to help them understand social science research on judicial decision-making is Jon Gottschall's study of federal appellate court decision-making, and it is helpful here as well.[138] This study rejected the common claim that President Reagan was shifting the federal courts in a radically conservative direction and found instead that he was merely continuing the conservative trend begun by Richard Nixon. Especially relevant, Gottschall found that Reagan and Carter appointees agreed in 74 percent of the cases they decided when serving on the same appellate panel. In the 26 percent of cases in which they disagreed, however, Carter's judges voted the liberal position 95 percent of the time whereas Reagan's judges did so only 5 percent of the time. This finding suggests that when the law is clear and certain, judges of different ideological and partisan stripes straightforwardly apply it and agree with one other. When the law is unclear and uncertain, however, judges disagree as their ideological differences come to the fore to "fill in the blanks" and influence their decisions. In other words, ideology matters a lot, a minority of the time.[139]

Applying this lesson to voter identification, both Republican and Democratic judges were free in the period of legal uncertainty prior to *Crawford* to vote consistently with their political views, and they did. After a majority of Supreme Court justices upheld a strict photo identification statute in 2008, however, Democratic judges may have felt cross-pressured. A ruling from the top of the judicial hierarchy dictated an outcome that was inconsistent with their political preferences, and many responded to this new legal cue.

While the data indicate that *Crawford* provided a significant legal constraint, multiple questions remain. Why, for example, is there still such a large difference in the proportion of positive assessments offered by Republican judges (89 percent) and Democratic judges (55 percent), even when both groups claim to be constrained by *Crawford?* And why do some state judges but not others choose voluntarily to follow *Crawford?* Douglas suggests that their choice to be bound by *Crawford* is closely intertwined with and perhaps a product of a narrow and preexisting view of voting rights.[140] Bailey and Maltzman similarly observe that while most Supreme Court justices are influenced by legal values, they may "choose" the legal values that best advance their policy goals.[141] For example, Justice Frankfurter chose the legal norm of deference to Congress, which also served his policy goal of protecting the New Deal. Adopting originalism allowed conservative justices like Scalia and Thomas to overrule precedent aggressively even as they claimed to be restrained by law.

An additional complication comes from the fact that *Crawford* does not represent a sudden and dramatic change in Supreme Court doctrine in the voting rights field. The Court had already weakened the standard for evaluating election regulations over two decades earlier, adopting a flexible balancing test for election regulations in *Anderson* in 1983 and allowing the lenient rational basis test to be applied to "reasonable, nondiscriminatory" restrictions in *Burdick* in 1992. *Crawford* was, thus, not a dramatic turn. The Court was already, by the 1980s and 1990s, giving lower court judges permission to avoid the typically fatal strict scrutiny test when reviewing voting restrictions. It appears, however, that Republican judges were more likely than Democratic judges to accept that invitation, at least when it came to voter identification.

The interaction of legal and political factors is further revealed when we examine the *causes* of the doctrinal transformations that enabled *Crawford*. Explaining judicial decision-making in voter ID cases as adherence to precedent ignores a critical fact (in addition to *Crawford* not actually being a precedent). *Burdick* and *Crawford* are not neutral, and they are not a static element of the legal environment. The regime politics perspective reminds us that the Republican Party's electoral success, particularly winning seven of ten presidential elections from 1968 to 2004, enabled it to adopt judicial policies that would help accomplish its partisan agenda—an agenda that recently came to include voter identification. Dominating the Supreme Court appointment process produced more conservative rulings in the voting rights field like *Burdick* and *Crawford*. To then claim that judges following *Crawford* are behaving legalistically ignores this chicken-and-egg problem and overlooks the way that legal constraints interact with and are themselves a product of partisan influences. Judges voted consistently with their party prior to *Crawford*, with Republicans supporting voter ID laws and Democrats voting against them. After a conservative Supreme Court upheld Indiana's photo identification law, Republican judges continued to support voter ID laws, and a significant number of Democratic judges altered their behavior and began also supporting voter ID laws. The more complete story, however, is that an electorally successful Republican regime created a Republican Supreme Court that constructed a favorable legal environment for voter identification laws. GOP elites were, furthermore, exceptionally united in what amounted to a nationwide campaign for voter identification policies. They adopted national platform planks in 2008, 2012, and 2016 that were devoted to voter ID advocacy, and Republican legislators across the states pushed ardently for the adoption of voter ID laws, particularly strict photo ID laws after *Shelby County* had eliminated preclearance as an obstacle.

A FINAL NOTE ON PARTISAN JUDGES:
COMPARED TO WHOM?

Thomas Keck wisely insists on a baseline or referent when assessing the significance of partisan differences in judicial voting; this assessment will vary depending on whether we expect judges to be "nonpartisan umpires" or "partisan zealots."[142] Keck, for example, compared the behavior of voters (on referenda and ballot initiatives), legislators, and federal appellate judges on culture war issues and found that the judicial rate of partisan polarization was similar to that of voters but significantly lower than that of elected legislators. This suggests, he argues, a valuable capacity on the part of judges, at least sometimes, to cross party lines in "responding to clear legal signals from SCOTUS, in rejecting extreme legal claims . . . [or] in forging doctrinal compromises."[143]

When it comes to the voter identification issue examined here, the evidence shows that over the 2005 to 2015 period, 74 percent of judicial votes were consistent with the position of the party to which the judge belongs. While strongly partisan, this voting pattern is not as starkly partisan as that of elected legislators, where over 95 percent have regularly voted with their party on voter ID bills. Clearly, there is more to judicial decision-making on voter ID cases than partisanship alone. This is certainly seen in the post-*Crawford* tendency of many Democratic judges to stray from their party's position and support voter ID policies.

Conclusion

The Republican campaign to address alleged election fraud through policies like voter identification has been very successful and remains a relevant and energetic movement. Severe partisan clashes over voter identification laws, rather than rational policy debates rooted in evidence, have occurred across the nation, particularly after 2000. It has not been known, however, whether judges have behaved like neutral arbiters or more like their copartisans in the elective branches when deciding voter ID cases. Examining twenty-two voter identification challenges in fourteen states from 2005 to 2015 revealed that nearly three-quarters of judicial votes can be characterized as partisan. In short, a strong partisan divide exists in voter identification cases, with a much larger proportion of Republican judicial votes cast in favor of such policies compared to those of Democratic judges. These differences did dissipate significantly after the Supreme Court's 2008 *Crawford* decision, which appears to have curbed the partisan behavior of many Democratic judges. A purely legal explanation, however, fails to account for sizable partisan differences both before and after *Crawford* and the "cause" of *Crawford* itself—the Republican Party's electoral success since 1968, which shifted the Supreme Court rightward and voting rights doctrine away from a fundamental rights approach and toward the flexible and deferential *Anderson-Burdick* test. The New Right Republican Court created a more favorable doctrinal environment for restrictive voting laws, upheld a strict photo ID law in *Crawford*, and eliminated the obstacle of federal preclearance in *Shelby County*. Republican judges, both federal and state, have also voted overwhelmingly in favor of voter ID laws and at a much higher rate than Democratic judges. Friendly judicial review has, in short, greatly aided the GOP's voter-ID crusade.

4 | Courts, Parties, and Redistricting

*Have courts exercised friendly judicial review with respect to redistricting?
Did the Republican Party, as regime politics theory predicts, both cause and
benefit from recent Supreme Court decisions in the redistricting field, particularly regarding partisan gerrymandering and racial gerrymandering?*

Chapters 2 and 3 demonstrate that the Republican Party has been quite
successful in enlisting judicial support for two major items on its election reform agenda: ending the Voting Rights Act's preclearance regime
and requiring voter identification at the polls. The story with respect to
redistricting, the topic of this chapter, is not so simple. The New Right
Court has not, for example, ruled in the GOP's favor on several important redistricting issues, such as including a citizenship question on
the census,[1] basing representation on voter eligibility rather than resi-
dence,[2] and promoting majority-minority districts.[3] With regard to the
latter, most Republican justices, particularly the conservative ones, have
not supported the GOP's strategy of encouraging majority-minority districts that help elect minority candidates while reducing the number of
Democratic districts. The conservative justices, rather than displaying
tribal party loyalty or crass partisan self-interest as they did in *Bush v.
Gore*, decided consistently with their philosophical commitment to color
blindness, a principle embraced by the New Right regime. The Court
was, in this sense, broadly regimist rather than narrowly partisan.

The story with respect to partisan gerrymandering is also complicated. Some claim that the Court's refusal to invalidate extreme partisan
gerrymanders in cases like *Vieth v. Jubelirer* (2004) and *Rucho v. Common Cause* (2019) has greatly aided the Republican Party.[4] Connecting
the Court's decisions to a Republican agenda is difficult, however. First,
GOP leaders have often allowed state and local affiliates to pursue their
self-interests in individual cases and only recently began advancing a
strong position against courts entertaining partisan gerrymandering
challenges. Additionally, the Court has been exceptionally divided in

these cases, and voting patterns are more ideological than partisan. Another challenge comes when examining the impact of the Court's partisan gerrymandering decisions. Political science research consistently demonstrates that one-party control of redistricting has only a marginal impact on electoral competition and partisan bias in seat allocation, and that both Democratic and Republican mapmakers face multiple constraints in their efforts to engineer substantial and durable partisan bias. Nonetheless, there is some evidence that Republican gerrymanders have since 2000 generated greater partisan advantage than Democratic gerrymanders. These careful scholarly assessments are no match, however, for the widespread belief that gerrymandering is a powerful tool for rigging elections and winning seats and that Republicans excel in employing it. It is this perception that has likely contributed to the GOP's growing commitment to judicial noninterference in this area. The Roberts Court's establishment of a new precedent in *Rucho* that partisan gerrymandering is nonjusticiable and that lower courts may no longer entertain such challenges—particularly when endorsed exclusively by the five Republican justices—looks more like the interbranch partisan cooperation that the regime politics model predicts.

An especially clear example of courts being successfully deployed by a political party to secure redistricting policies that favor its self-interests is the Warren Court's pro-Democratic reapportionment rulings and their pro-Democratic implementation in the lower courts. Such "judicial gerrymandering" would not be seen by regimists as surprising given that redistricting can affect a party's electoral prospects, including the possibility of gaining majority status in the legislature. A logical expectation is that politicians would do everything possible, including enlisting judicial aid, to secure as much partisan advantage as they can in the redistricting process. The Republicans' uneven record of success in this area thus poses an interesting puzzle and a challenge to the regimists.

I begin this chapter with a brief description of the legal framework that shapes the redistricting process and enables judicial participation in it, followed by an overview of current redistricting processes. I next analyze, particularly in the context of party preferences, the Warren Court's "reapportionment revolution"[5] and the Court's decisions with respect to partisan and racial gerrymandering. The justices' votes and doctrinal choices appear to be driven more by ideology than partisanship, although voting patterns have become more sharply partisan in recent years. I conclude with reflections on future challenges in the redistricting field, an area that is both terribly complicated and terribly consequential for democratic governance. One important question is whether the Republican Court will be content to remain on the sidelines when it comes to partisan gerrymandering or will choose to play a more active role in erecting constitutional barriers to reform efforts by voters and Democratic politicians.

The Legal Framework of Redistricting

A variety of constitutional and statutory provisions at both the federal and state levels dictate how Americans are provided with representation in the House of Representatives and their state legislatures. These provisions relate to each step of the process: the decennial count of the population, the subsequent apportionment of seats, and, finally, the determination of geographic boundaries for each district. The US Constitution's rather modest guidance begins with Article I, Section 2, which states that "the House of Representatives shall be composed of Members chosen . . . by the People of the several States" and "each State shall have at Least one Representative." It further specifies that "Representatives . . . shall be apportioned among the several States . . . according to their respective numbers"[6] with the "actual Enumeration . . . made within three Years after the first Meeting of the Congress . . . and within every subsequent Term of ten Years, in such Manner as they shall by Law direct." Article I, Section 4 additionally provides that "the Time, Places and Manner of holding Elections for Senators and Representatives, shall be prescribed in each State by the Legislature thereof; but the Congress may at any time by Law make or alter such Regulations." Thus, the Constitution grants power to both Congress and state legislatures when it comes to redistricting, though Congress has only intermittently used its authority to regulate the redistricting process. For example, it mandated the use of single-member districts initially in 1842, periodically thereafter, and permanently in 1967. The Apportionment Act of 1911 required congressional districts to be compact and contiguous and to contain equal populations. Congress also in 1911 increased the number of House representatives to 435, which it made permanent in 1929 due to fears over urban population growth that was fueled by immigration.

The Voting Rights Act has also significantly constrained the redistricting process over the past half century, with both Sections 2 and 5 enabling considerable federal involvement. As was explained in chapter 2, Section 2 forbids the denial or abridgement of the right to vote on the basis of race, color, or membership in a specified language minority group. This prohibition includes vote dilution, with mapmakers prevented from affording a racial or language minority "less opportunity than any other members of the electorate to participate in the political process and to elect representatives of their choice." Section 5 requires covered jurisdictions to submit proposed voting changes to the federal government for review and approval, prior to implementation, with the Supreme Court ruling in *Georgia v. U.S.* (1973) that preclearance extends to redistricting plans.[7]

As this suggests, the Supreme Court has significantly shaped the legal framework of redistricting through its interpretation of federal constitutional and statutory provisions. For example, in *Wesberry v. Sanders* (1964) it imposed a one-person, one-vote requirement for House districts under Article I, Section 2's mandate that representatives be "chosen by the People of the several States."[8] The Court warned mapmakers in *Thornburg v. Gingles* (1986) to consider race when redistricting in order to prevent the dilution of minority voting power and comply with the Voting Rights Act, but it also cautioned them in *Shaw v. Reno* (1993) not to rely excessively on race to avoid violating the equal protection clause.[9] (I provide more detailed descriptions of the Court's doctrinal rules regarding redistricting in the remainder of this chapter.)

As part of the legal framework shaping the redistricting process, states also impose constitutional and statutory restrictions. Many states, for example, require compact and contiguous districts that preserve political subdivisions and communities of interest.[10] Some states since 2000 have additionally required competitive districts, forbade the use of partisan data, and banned discrimination against any political party. In an interesting move, Ohio will require "proportionality" for its legislative districts in the 2020 redistricting cycle, with the statewide proportion of districts favoring each party required to correspond to statewide voter preferences.

Reflecting these various legal dictates, the redistricting process in the United States currently and generally works as follows. A census is taken every ten years to determine the population of each state. Following the census, redistricting occurs in states with more than one House district[11] that have either gained or lost at least one seat and states where population shifts necessitate the redrawing of House or state legislative districts in order to adhere to the Court's equal population standard. The redistricting process commonly follows each state's regular legislative process: both legislative chambers pass a redistricting bill by majority vote, which the governor must sign into law or veto, subject to a legislative override. There are some exceptions, however.[12] For example, in Maryland the governor presents a redistricting plan to the legislature, which can adopt the governor's plan with a majority vote or enact its own plan with a two-thirds vote. Maine also requires supermajority approval of new district lines. Five states—Connecticut, Florida, Maryland, Mississippi, and North Carolina—permit redistricting plans to be adopted by joint resolution, without a gubernatorial-veto option.

A notable trend is the growing success of reform efforts to transfer redistricting authority from legislatures to independent commissions. These independent redistricting commissions (IRCs) may be bipartisan or nonpartisan and either can have primary responsibility for drawing district boundaries or serve in an advisory or backup role in the case of legislative stalemate. As of January 2020, primary responsibility for devising a redistricting plan is assigned to a commission in eight states with respect to congressional districts and fourteen states with respect to state legislative districts; IRCs serve in an advisory role or backup role in eight states for congressional districts and eleven states for state legislative districts.[13] Iowa's approach to redistricting fits none of the traditional categories, uniquely empowering nonpartisan legislative staff to draw maps, though with no initial reliance on political or election data, which the legislature must then approve.

Another important trend spanning the past half century is the "juridification of legislative districting processes."[14] "Few redistricting plans escape court challenges," with judges intervening "in hundreds, perhaps thousands, of cases" over the past several decades.[15] A total of 249 cases were filed in the 2010 round of redistricting, with courts reviewing congressional plans in twenty-two states and state legislative plans in thirty-four states.[16] Courts, furthermore, not only review those plans and invalidate the ones found to be illegal, they "also . . . draw remedial plans to take their place. Courts are [thus] not mere referees of the redistricting process; they have become active players . . . in . . . determining winners and losers in redistricting and, therefore, elections."[17]

The content, direction, and impact of these court decisions offer evidence regarding the role of partisanship. Such evidence comes both from lower court decisions and from Supreme Court doctrine, which has undergone remarkable change over time, most notably since the early 1960s. It is here, with the Warren Court, that there exists especially striking evidence of partisan cooperation across the branches.

The Warren Court's Pro-Democracy—and Pro-Democrat—Reapportionment Revolution

For most of its history, the US Supreme Court largely abstained from the redistricting field. Until 1962 it treated malapportionment challenges as nonjusticiable as they raised political questions that were not appropriate for or amenable to judicial resolution. For example, in 1946 in *Colegrove v. Green* the Court by a 4–3 vote refused to entertain a voter challenge to severely malapportioned congressional districts in Illinois.[18] Voters in the most populous district had only one-ninth the voting power of those in the least populous district. Justice Black argued in dissent that this was "wholly indefensible discrimination" that violated equal protection and resembled the "rotten borough system" that Article I, Section 2 sought to prevent.[19] The Court, however, dismissed the complaint, with Justice Frankfurter asserting that it was "hostile to a democratic system to involve the judiciary in the politics of the people" and famously warning that courts "ought not to enter this political thicket."[20]

A revolutionary change occurred in *Baker v. Carr* (1962), which Chief Justice Earl Warren asserted was "the most important case of my tenure on the Court."[21] Memphis residents had claimed a denial of equal protection due to the failure of the Tennessee legislature to redistrict since 1901, despite major population shifts that rendered their vote one-tenth the value of that of rural residents. After a lengthy and discordant decision-making process that reportedly triggered severe health problems for Justices Whittaker and Frankfurter, the Court ruled in a 6–2 vote that reapportionment was indeed a justiciable issue, with Justice Brennan's majority opinion arguing that well-developed judicial standards were available under the equal protection clause.

Thus began decades of federal judicial involvement in the redistricting process. The Court rather quickly developed new constitutional standards to guide that process. In *Wesberry v. Sanders* (1964) the Court interpreted Article I, Section 2's requirement that representatives be "chosen by the People of the several States" to mean that "as nearly as is practicable one man's vote in a congressional election is to be worth as much as another's."[22] House districts were thus bound by the "one person, one vote" principle of equal representation. In *Reynolds v. Sims* (1964) the Court extended this principle to state legislatures, requiring districts in both houses to be "as nearly of equal population as is practicable."[23] Even when overwhelmingly approved by voters themselves, deviation from this standard was not permitted.[24] The Court has additionally required a very high degree of mathematical precision in drawing districts, at least for the House of Representatives. It upheld in 1983 a state legislative plan that had a nearly 10 percent population deviation between the largest and smallest districts[25] but rejected congressional redistricting plans with much smaller disparities, including one with a disparity of less than 1 percent in *Karcher v. Daggett* (1983).[26] Particularly with respect to the House, the Court's mandate has been clearly and strictly egalitarian.

The dominant view today of *Baker* and its progeny is that the Court properly intervened to address an entrenched democratic malfunction and correct the unfair distortions in both representation and policy that they produced. Malapportionment had been a serious problem over much of the first half of the twentieth century, one that politicians repeatedly refused to address. Massive migration had occurred from rural to urban areas, and the traditional approach of representing geographic entities, such as towns and counties, produced severe representational inequities. Legislative incumbents and their rural constituencies had no incentive to address this problem by revising district lines to reflect population shifts, despite the typical presence of legal mandates for regular redistricting. Malapportionment thus continued to worsen, with the largest interdistrict disparity in terms of representation per resident growing "from 6 to 1 in 1910 to 20 to 1 in 1950, and then to 35 to 1 in 1960."[27] As characterized by Lucas Powe, legislatures at the mid-twentieth-century mark were "ruled 'by the hog lot and the cow pasture.'"[28] The policy consequences were predictable: significantly lower per capita state spending in metropolitan areas and a nationwide failure to address pressing urban problems involving race, poverty, and housing.

The justices themselves defended their intervention and egalitarian standards in democratic terms, as seen in the Court's opinion in *Reynolds*:

> We are cautioned about the dangers of entering into political thickets and mathematical quagmires. Our answer is this: a denial of constitutionally pro-

tected rights demands judicial protection; our oath and our office require no less. . . . To the extent that a citizen's right to vote is debased, he is that much less a citizen. . . . A nation once primarily rural in character becomes predominantly urban. Representation schemes once fair and equitable become archaic and outdated. But the basic principle of representative government remains . . . the weight of a citizen's vote cannot be made to depend on where he lives. . . . This is an essential part of the concept of a government of laws and not men. This is at the heart of Lincoln's vision of "government of the people, by the people, [and] for the people."[29]

Chief Justice Warren's majority opinion additionally argued that it was only "logical" and "reasonable that a majority of the people of a State could elect a majority of that State's legislators."[30] Furthermore, given that "the right to elect legislators in a free and unimpaired fashion is a bedrock of our political system," it was "inconceivable" that a state law that in effect multiplies some citizens' votes "by two, five, or 10 . . . could be constitutionally sustainable."[31] The Court relied heavily on the irrefutable logic and power of democratic principles. Justice John Harlan II offered detailed and persuasive textual and historical analysis to the contrary in dissent, but his careful legal reasoning would not stand in the way of inexorable democratic commands.

In sharp contrast to its school desegregation and school prayer rulings, compliance with the Court's one-person, one-vote principle was surprisingly swift and broad, despite the predictable initial resistance. Senator Everett Dirksen proposed a two-year moratorium on implementing *Reynolds* and a constitutional amendment that would allow unequal state legislative districts, a position also taken by the 1964 Republican Party platform. Multiple congressional bills would have prevented federal courts either from reviewing apportionment challenges altogether or imposing an equal-population standard. Nonetheless, most states by 1967 and every state by 1970 had reorganized their legislative institutions to satisfy the Court's new equal-population standard. In the typical state in 1960, the most overrepresented county had thirty-five times as much representation in the state legislature as the most underrepresented county, but this enormous gap had closed by 1970.[32] Only nine congressional districts in 1962 were within 1 percent of the average district size in their states, compared to 385 districts by 1972.[33] According to Stephen Ansolabehere and James Snyder, this improved representational accuracy helped to bring about a more equitable distribution of state revenues and an increase in education and welfare spending in the Midwest.[34]

Legal scholars were initially critical of the Warren Court's reapportionment rulings. They accused the liberal majority of risking the Court's legitimacy with rulings rooted more in personal preference than in the Constitution's text and history.[35] Critics also argued that the Court improperly enmeshed judges in the rough and tumble of redistricting politics and forced them to police a process that is impossibly infected with partisan intrigue.[36] It is much more common today, however, to find scholars strongly praising the Warren Court's reapportionment decisions. They played a critical role in John Hart Ely's representation-reinforcing theory of judicial review, in which the Court may legitimately use its counter-majoritarian power only when correcting democratic malfunctions, with malapportionment serving as a prime example.[37] Jeffrey Rosen has similarly praised the Warren Court for being willing to "break the political logjam" and use its unique "ability to promote democracy."[38] Many other scholars have joined the chorus,[39] with Jack Balkin and Sanford Levinson including *Baker* in the modern "constitutional canon" of cases that are so obviously correct that they are now immune from scholarly challenge.[40]

This representation-reinforcing, democracy-assisting version of the Warren Court reapportionment story has limitations, however. Most importantly, it fails to help us answer a simple but important question: why did the Court choose to "break the logjam" in 1962, rather than 1952 or 1942 or 1932 or 1922?[41] After all, malapportionment was a serious nationwide problem well before 1962. In fact, Congress failed to reapportion House seats after the 1920 census, which had revealed majority status for urban residents for the first time in history. Malapportionment then worsened considerably over the next four decades and existed in the House of Representatives and nearly every state legislative house. Why, then, did the Court wait until the 1960s to intercede and perform its democracy-assisting role? Why too did it choose a strict egalitarian standard, despite the existence of "the federal analogy" (i.e., the Senate) and the absence of a clear equality mandate with regard to representation from the Fourteenth Amendment's text and history?

The Court's timing and its egalitarianism make sense when we adopt a regime-politics lens and reflect on the electoral success, policy aims, and interbranch strategies of the Democratic regime. From 1932 through 1964 the Democratic Party experienced extraordinary success in national elections, winning the White House seven out of nine times and control of both houses of Congress sixteen out of eighteen times. That success paid off handsomely in terms of partisan control of the judiciary. Why, however, do we not see the partisan deployment of courts to assist with redistricting and wrest power from rural conservatives until the 1960s? The most likely answer is found in the judicial policies pursued by the executive branch, particularly Supreme Court appointments. Especially relevant to the timing issue, President Kennedy's replacement in 1962 of Charles Whittaker with Byron White and Felix Frankfurter with Arthur Goldberg had an enormous impact on the ideological composition and direction of the Supreme Court. The percentage of conservative decisions made by the Court fell from 42 percent in the 1960 term to 22 percent in the 1962 term.[42] Using Martin-Quinn ideology scores, where negative numbers indicate a liberal orientation and positive numbers indicate a conservative orientation,[43] the ideological location and identity of the median justice changed dramatically from 0.533 (Justice Stewart) in the 1960 term to −0.046 (Justice White) in the 1961 term, to −0.808 (Justice Goldberg) in the 1962 term, and −0.874 (Justice Brennan) in the 1963 term. The Court's strong shift to the left should not be a surprise, given Democratic domination at the polls and, thus, Democratic control of judicial appointments.

The timing of the Court's intervention also makes sense when we look at the leadership and support of the Kennedy administration with respect to redistricting. President Kennedy made "the crisis of the cities" an important part of his presidential campaign, and he wooed the urban vote beginning when he was a senator in the late 1950s.[44] He claimed that the litany of ills plaguing America's cities—crime, poverty, overcrowding, scarce housing, and inferior education—were caused by "political discrimination" against and underrepresentation of the urban majority.[45] Once in power, President Kennedy lent support to the reapportionment cause. As described by Ansolabehere and Snyder, one of the lawyers in the *Baker* case knew Attorney General Robert Kennedy and had worked with Solicitor General Archibald Cox on President Kennedy's presidential campaign.[46] The *Baker* attorneys had hoped, but were unable, to discuss their case and cause with Attorney General Kennedy; they nonetheless had a lengthy meeting with Solicitor General Cox and Deputy Attorney General (and future Supreme Court justice) Byron White. After discussing the matter with the attorney general, Cox decided to file an amicus brief in the *Baker* case.

The Kennedy administration vigorously argued in *Baker* for judicial assistance in correcting the representational distortions created by legislators' refusal to redistrict and offered enthusiastic support for the ruling after the decision was made.[47] President Kennedy expressed his approval of *Baker* at his first press conference following the decision, reminding the public and press that his administration had urged the Court to do the right thing and intervene since "the right to fair representation and to have each vote counted equally is, it seems to me, basic to the successful operation of a democracy."[48] Other executive branch officials publicly praised the ruling as well, including Robert Kennedy, who stated that *Baker* was "a landmark in the development of representative government."[49] The administration stayed active in the reapportionment litigation that followed,[50] and President Kennedy's view that each vote should count equally became Court doctrine. As a final sign of Democratic Party support, its 1968 platform chose to "fully recognize the principle of one man, one vote."

The conventional view, expressed in the constitutional canon, suggests that the Warren Court acted virtuously and independently to vindicate democratic values. The partisan backstory, however, casts the reapportionment revolution in a different light. The criticism of legal scholars like Rosen that the Court need not have been so rigidly egalitarian and could have used the guarantee clause to open a dialogue with state legislatures similarly misreads the Court's policy interventions in this area.[51] By 1964 the Court consisted solidly of active and loyal members of the dominant Democratic regime. As Powe puts it, the Warren Court was a "functioning part of the Kennedy-Johnson liberalism of the mid and late 1960s."[52] Strict equality, imposed by the *judicial* members of this broad, powerful, and united Democratic coalition, should not be a surprising policy choice. As Keith Whittington points out, *Baker* is not an example of the Court "simply acting on behalf of popular majorities"; rather, it "cut . . . through the 'political thicket'" and assisted "liberal Democrats who had long chaffed [*sic*] at the legislative obstacle posed by entrenched conservatives."[53]

The alignment of the justices' votes in *Baker, Wesberry*, and *Reynolds* is, furthermore, strongly partisan. Of the twenty votes favoring the Democratic Party position in these three majority opinions, fifteen were cast by Democratic justices and only five by Republican justices, with Chief Justice Warren accounting for three of those five votes.

Finally, the implementation and impact of the Court's reapportionment decisions also had a strongly Democratic cast, lending further support to a regime-politics interpretation. As Martin Shapiro notes, "by the time of *Reynolds*, the Democrats had enjoyed a majority position among voters for state and national legislatures for over thirty years. Nothing could have more clearly favored the Democratic over the Republican party than a one-person-one-vote standard, which is, after all, the ultimate majority-serving standard and was so intended."[54] Aided by Lyndon Johnson's 1964 landslide victory, the Democratic Party in 1965 enjoyed legislative control in thirty-two states, compared to only six for the GOP, and was thus far more responsible for redistricting outcomes in the wake of *Wesberry* and *Reynolds*.[55] Cox and Katz additionally found significant partisan effects resulting from the fact that redistricting plans were being evaluated and supervised by a mostly Democratic federal judiciary, again a legacy of the party's long-standing electoral success.[56] With *Baker*, Gary Cox and Jonathan Katz argue, the Supreme Court changed the strategic redistricting game by introducing a new player: federal court judges. It was no longer the case that previous district lines would stay in place if the legislature and governor could not agree to a new plan. Now a federal judge, and most likely a Democratic judge, could impose a new plan. This "reversionary outcome" affected the negotiation process, with the legislature sometimes agreeing to a new plan to avoid a worse plan that a (probably) Democratic judge might impose.[57] In the end, three factors—the *Baker* decision, a predominantly Democratic federal judiciary, and the 1964 Democratic landslide—combined to produce "the abrupt eradication of a 6% pro-Republican bias in the translation of congressional votes into seats outside the South."[58] Cox and Katz convincingly portray judges not as neutral democracy-assisting reformers but as regime allies in a strategic partisan game.

The Warren Court's intervention and egalitarianism in the redistricting field, though justified in neutral democratic principles, is better understood in partisan terms. The revolutionary changes in Court doctrine with respect to reapportionment resulted from the judicial policies and appointments of Democratic administrations. The implementation of those new doctrinal rules by a Democratic federal judiciary further assisted this partisan cause. Finally, the primary beneficiary of the resulting redistribution of power from rural to urban areas was intended to be and was in fact the Democratic Party.

Existing Research on Judicial Partisanship
in Redistricting Cases

The finding that judicial implementation of the Warren Court's new constitutional rules had a partisan cast is, in fact, consistent with other studies of redistricting litigation. Researchers are in substantial agreement with respect to two of the three key questions they pose. First, empirical studies uniformly conclude that judges enhance competition relative to legislatures when they draw electoral districts. Second, most studies also find evidence of partisan favoritism, with judges more likely to reject plans crafted by the opposite party. Third, the evidence is mixed with regard to court-drawn redistricting plans having a partisan impact and improving the electoral performance of the judge's party.

With regard to electoral competition, studies consistently find that court-drawn plans produce more competitive elections than legislative plans, even when employing different measures and focusing on different time periods.[59] For example, Jaimie Carson and Michael Crespin looked at congressional elections in 1992 and 2002 and found that more competitive elections, as indicated by the margin of victory, occurred when redistricting was handled by courts rather than legislatures.[60] Adding the 1972, 1982, and 2012 elections to this data, Carson and his coauthors reached similar conclusions: competitive races were significantly more likely in court-drawn districts compared to legislatively drawn districts.[61] James Cottrill and I studied the five House elections following the 2000 apportionment cycle and also found that judicial maps were significantly more likely than legislative maps to enhance electoral competition by attracting experienced challengers.[62] Jordan Peterson's analysis of House elections over a three-decade period (1982 to 2002) similarly found that judicial redistricting increased competitiveness by reducing victory margins as compared to legislative redistricting.[63] Finally, Corbett Grainger studied California legislative elections from 1968 to 2006 and found that districts drawn by the legislature were less competitive than districts drawn by a panel of retired judges appointed as special masters by the California Supreme Court (after the governor and legislature failed to agree on a plan after the 1970 and 1990 censuses).[64]

Despite this impression that judges are deciding in a neutral, pro-democracy manner, multiple studies have nonetheless found that partisan affiliation affects judicial votes in redistricting cases. Kathleen

Barber's examination of the twenty-seven judges deciding thirteen redistricting cases in Ohio and Michigan found that "partisan values assume a significant role in the resolution of reapportionment controversies"; this was true for various types of judges—federal and state, appointed and elected.[65] Peterson uncovered evidence of partisan behavior in designing House districts by Democratic judges but not Republican judges.[66] Randall Lloyd looked at redistricting decisions from 1964 to 1983 in the US district courts and discovered two types of partisan effects.[67] First, judges were more skeptical of and, thus, more likely to strike down maps when a single party controlled the redistricting process. Second, judges held redistricting plans crafted by the opposing party to a stricter standard and were more likely to strike them down. Mark McKenzie looked at state supreme court justices and similarly found that they were more likely to favor their own political party by voting against the plans of the opposing party.[68] His 2012 study of federal district court redistricting decisions (1982 to 2007) produced the same results: judges were significantly less likely to approve maps drawn by the opposite party.[69] That partisan effect was conditioned by the type of case, however. Partisan favoritism was more likely in areas of redistricting law where doctrinal ambiguity was greater, such as the Voting Rights Act and racial gerrymandering, compared to cases where the law was clear, such as equal population cases. Judges, McKenzie concluded, act as "constrained partisans" in redistricting litigation: they are "more likely to favor their own party in redistricting when a lack of clarity in precedent provides them with that window of opportunity."[70] Finally, Kyle Kopko's dissertation research on federal judicial decisions in redistricting cases from 1962 to 2007 found partisan influence, but only in the form of a "panel effect": a judge was more likely to vote in her party's interests as the number of same-party judges on the panel increased.[71]

The final research question in this literature asks whether judicial redistricting decisions have a partisan impact by improving the electoral performance of the judge's copartisans. As previously mentioned, Cox and Katz found that the predominantly Democratic character of the federal bench in the 1960s was a key factor in the demise of a long-standing pro-Republican bias in non-Southern congressional elections; in fact, whether a redistricting plan had a pro-Democratic or pro-Republican bias in allocating congressional seats was determined as much by "the partisanship of the judges supervising redistricting cases . . . as which party controlled state government."[72] In contrast, my study of House elections with James Cottrill did not find a systematic partisan impact: court-drawn plans did not confer electoral advantages on the party with which the judge or judicial panel was affiliated.[73] More specifically, while the number of Democrats in the legislature that drew the redistricting plan significantly affected the likelihood of an experienced Republican challenger, the vote margin of Democratic incumbents, and the Democratic share of House seats in the state, these partisan outcomes were not affected by whether the judge or judicial panel drawing the map was Republican or Democratic. Finally, Peterson's study of congressional elections from 1982 to 2012 did find a partisan impact, though a narrow and unusual one: the redistricting decisions of Democratic judges but not Republican judges increased the vote share of copartisan challengers.[74]

These results, at least initially, appear perplexing. Most studies have found that judges' redistricting decisions increase electoral competitiveness *and* favor the party with which they affiliate. Peterson offers a "theory of judicial partisan calculation" that helps to reconcile these seemingly contrary results.[75] Judges, he argues, can act to enhance electoral competition while also, behind this "mask of neutrality," engaging in a sophisticated, calculated strategy to help their copartisans.[76] For example, while he found that judicial intervention in redistricting significantly reduced the winner's margin of victory, this was largely due to judges drawing more competitive districts for opposite-party incumbents. Surprisingly, however, it was only Democratic judges who exhibited this strategic partisan behavior. By "adding Democratic voters to Republican-held House constituencies," Democratic judges increased Democratic vote share in Republican districts—and, even more remarkably, by a larger margin than what Democratic legislatures achieved.[77] Certainly more empirical testing is needed to support this provocative finding. Nonetheless, Peterson helpfully reminds scholars that this research question need not be binary. Judges can decide redistricting cases in ways that both increase electoral competition *and* favor their partisan allies. In fact, most empirical studies support precisely that conclusion.

The New Right Court and the Challenge of Partisan Gerrymandering

The most challenging redistricting issue that courts have had to address in recent years is partisan gerrymandering. After describing this practice and the primary complaints about it, I will explain the Court's doctrinal choices and analyze whether they have been motivated by and served partisan ends.

The primary complaint about redistricting in the early- and mid-twentieth century was malapportionment resulting from the government's failure to act—a "sin of omission" as Bullock puts it; partisan gerrymandering, a "sin of commission," has been the dominant target in recent years.[78] Critics argue that politicians harm democracy by engaging in "the dark art" of manipulating legislative district boundaries to advantage their own political party, tilting the translation of votes into seats unfairly in their favor.[79] The primary aim is to waste opposition votes, mostly through the favored tactics of packing and cracking. Partisan mapmakers concentrate or "pack" the opposing party's supporters into as few districts as possible, which are then won by needlessly large margins. They then "crack" or divide the remaining opposite-party supporters into multiple districts where they constitute a minority unable to elect their preferred candidate. In cracked districts, wasted votes go to the party that loses, presumably and intentionally by a relatively small margin; in packed districts, wasted votes go toward unnecessarily large margins of victory.

Partisan gerrymandering is widely criticized by journalists,[80] legal scholars,[81] advocacy groups,[82] political scientists,[83] and even politicians. President Reagan referred to gerrymandering as "a national scandal"; Ohio governor John Kasich claimed it is "the biggest problem we have"; and President Obama, in his final State of the Union address, called for an "end [to] the practice of drawing our congressional districts so that politicians can pick their voters and not the other way around."[84] Critics claim that gerrymandering unfairly disenfranchises voters, distorts election outcomes, and subverts the will of the people. They point, for example, to the 2012 midterm election in which the GOP won control of the House of Representatives by a thirty-three-seat margin despite winning 1.4 million fewer votes nationwide than the Democrats, an outcome typically attributed to newly gained Republican control over redistricting in many states and aided by new computing technologies that give mapmakers greater precision in drawing districts.[85] An additional complaint about partisan gerrymandering is the weakened competition and inflated incumbent reelection rates that result; this, in turn, increases polarization as representatives from safe districts need only worry about winning their primaries by guarding against ideologically extreme intraparty challengers. Dysfunction and gridlock then prevail, as legislative institutions populated mostly with ideological extremists and few moderates cannot forge policy agreement.[86] It is no surprise that calls for reform are abundant. In fact, 152 bills relating to redistricting were introduced in the 2015 legislative session in thirty-four states and Puerto Rico, and, in 2019, 186 bills were introduced in thirty-nine states; most of these proposals sought to alter the process for drawing district lines or the criteria that must be used.[87]

The Development of Constitutional Doctrine Regarding Partisan Gerrymandering

Legal challenges to alleged partisan gerrymanders have also been abundant, initiated both by reformers and aggrieved politicians. Constitutional doctrine in this area, however, has been rather muddled, with the Supreme Court divided and unclear. A bare majority of justices ruled several times that partisan gerrymandering claims are justiciable, but no majority either agreed on the constitutional standard for judging them or invalidated a redistricting plan as an unconstitutional partisan gerrymander. The Court ended this confusion in 2019 with a 5–4 ruling in *Rucho v. Common Cause* that partisan gerrymandering claims are not justiciable and federal courts may no longer entertain them. It is quite interesting that the Court has not been reluctant to intrude into the election process in cases like *Wesberry v. Sanders* (1964), *Bush v. Gore* (2000), and *Shelby County v. Holder* (2013).[88] The Court's approach in partisan gerrymandering cases, however, stands apart and has conveyed a very different message, assuring politicians that they have little reason to fear this type of legal challenge to their redistricting activities.

Davis v. Bandemer (1986) offered the Court's first major pronouncement on this issue.[89] Democrats had challenged the redistricting plan enacted by the Republican-controlled Indiana legislature as an unconstitutional partisan gerrymander under the equal protection clause. A six-justice majority held that such claims were justiciable. That majority fell apart, however, on the merits of the equal protection claim. Justice White's plurality opinion, joined by Justices Blackmun, Marshall, and Brennan, held that the plaintiffs did not meet the stringent standard for invalidating partisan gerrymanders. It was not enough, these four justices argued, that a party had engineered districts to win more seats relative to their statewide vote. To prevail, plaintiffs would need to prove both discriminatory intent and discriminatory effect, demonstrating that the "electoral system is arranged in a manner that will consistently degrade a voter's or a group of voters' influence on the political process as a whole."[90] Justices Powell and Stevens, in contrast, voted to strike down the redistricting plan as unconstitutional due to its partisan purpose, the exclusion of Democrats from the redistricting process, and its disregard of existing political subdivisions. The final group of justices—O'Connor, Rehnquist, and Burger—preferred to dismiss the plaintiffs' claim as a nonjusticiable political question. To rule otherwise, O'Connor's opinion argued, would put the Court on a "slippery slope" to recognizing a "group right to an equal share of political power," a proportional representation requirement contrary to US history and traditions.[91] In a particularly interesting comment, O'Connor—the only justice with legislative experience on the Court at that time—observed that partisan gerrymandering was inherently risky and self-limiting; after all, dispersing the opposing party's supporters across many districts in order to engineer multiple narrow victories could easily backfire and put the legislative majority in jeopardy. Judicial supervision, O'Connor argued, was thus unnecessary.

After *Bandemer*, most lower courts applied to partisan gerrymandering challenges the two-prong test suggested by Justice White's plurality opinion. They have required proof that districts were intentionally drawn to disadvantage a political group and actually had a discriminatory effect, degrading the group's influence on the political process as a whole. Unsurprisingly, this very high bar—a perhaps impossible bar[92]—resulted in no federal court striking down a redistricting plan on partisan gerrymandering grounds over the next thirty years.[93] Michael Smith's assertion that in *Bandemer*, the Court "essentially found political gerrymandering to be constitutional" thus appears credible.[94]

In 2004 in *Vieth v. Jubelirer*, Democrats had challenged as an unconstitutional partisan gerrymander the congressional redistricting plan adopted by Pennsylvania's Republican legislature after the state lost two House seats following the 2000 census. Many hoped that the Court would provide greater doctrinal clarity, perhaps definitively ruling that partisan gerrymandering claims were nonjusticiable or providing a clear-cut test for determining when an alleged partisan gerrymander crossed the line and became unconstitutional.[95] Those expectations were definitely not met, however, with *Bandemer* "a model of clarity" by comparison.[96] Although a majority of the Court did not find the plan to be an unconstitutional partisan gerrymander, it again splintered, offering no majority opinion on the merits. Justice Scalia, speaking for a four-member plurality, would have reversed *Bandemer* and dismissed the plaintiffs' claim due to the lack of judicially manageable standards, a conclusion easily proven, he argued, by the divisions among *Vieth*'s dissenters and "eighteen years of essentially pointless litigation" in the lower courts.[97] The four dissenters regarded partisan gerrymandering claims as justiciable, but they agreed on little else, including the proper standard for evaluating them.[98] The deciding vote was cast by Justice Kennedy, who, though dismissing this particular challenge, was unwilling to foreclose the possibility that a proper standard for judging such claims might emerge in a future case. He thus "sat uncertainly on the fence, unwilling either to embrace a test or to conclude that no test could be devised."[99] Interpretations of *Vieth*'s meaning vary considerably. To some, *Vieth* "vacated" *Bandemer*;[100] for others, it reversed it;[101] and, for still others, *Bandemer* remained good law under "the principle that you can't replace something with nothing."[102]

In 2006 the Court once again refused to invalidate an alleged partisan gerrymander in *League of United Latin American Citizens (LULAC) v. Perry* (2006).[103] This case involved the mid-decade redrawing of Texas's congressional districts by the Republican-controlled legislature that had increased the Republican share of the state's delegation from 47 percent (i.e., fifteen seats) to 66 percent (i.e., twenty-one seats). On the question of whether partisan gerrymandering claims were justiciable, five justices (Kennedy, Souter, Ginsburg, Stevens, and Breyer) answered in the affirmative, two (Scalia and Thomas) responded negatively, and two (Roberts and Alito) sidestepped the issue. Among the five justices entertaining the plaintiffs' claim, three (Kennedy, Souter, and Ginsburg) rejected it and two (Stevens and Breyer) accepted it. The deep divisions on the Court continued.

A recent flurry of partisan gerrymandering cases in the lower courts provided the Court with new opportunities to clear up this doctrinal confusion. In *Gill v. Whitford* (2018) the Court reviewed a lower court ruling that Wisconsin's state legislative map was an unconstitutional partisan gerrymander, a notable deviation from the historical practice of federal courts rejecting such claims.[104] The Supreme Court unanimously vacated that judgment on grounds of standing, ruling that the plaintiffs had failed to demonstrate a "concrete and particularized" injury that was "district specific."[105] On the same day that *Gill* was announced, the Court refused in *Benisek v. Lamone* (2018) to reverse a district court decision rejecting a request for a temporary injunction against an alleged Democratic gerrymander in Maryland's Sixth Congressional District.[106] Its per curiam opinion did not address the merits of the partisan gerrymandering claims, relying instead on the plaintiffs' unreasonable delay in requesting a preliminary injunction. To most observers, the Court "punted" yet again on this challenging constitutional question.[107]

In 2019 the Court finally offered a clear and definitive ruling barring federal courts from reviewing partisan gerrymandering claims. *Rucho v. Common Cause* involved North Carolina's congressional districts that plaintiffs argued were unconstitutionally gerrymandered by the Republican legislature, while a companion case, *Lamone v. Benisek*, involved an alleged Democratic gerrymander of Maryland's Sixth Congressional District. Chief Justice Roberts wrote the opinion for the five-justice majority, ruling that "partisan gerrymandering claims present political questions beyond the reach of the federal courts."[108] Although not disputing that the districts crafted by the legislature were "highly partisan, by any measure," there were, he argued, "no legal standards discernible in the Constitution" for assessing the "fairness" of a particular allocation of seats and power among political parties, "let alone limited and precise standards that are clear, manageable, and politically neutral."[109] Roberts further noted that the "determinative question" with regard to unfairness—"how much is too much?"—would remain."[110] Justice Kagan's impassioned dissent, which she read from the bench, lamented the Court's willingness to tolerate practices that "imperil our system of government" and have "debased and dishonored our democracy."[111] She disputed the majority's claim regarding the absence of neutral and judicially manageable standards, arguing that "federal courts across the country . . . [have] largely converged on a standard for adjudicating partisan gerrymandering claims," one requiring evidence that state officials' "'predominant purpose' . . . was to 'entrench [their party] in power'" and that their drawing of districts additionally had "the intended effect" of "substantially diluting the votes of citizens favoring their rivals."[112] Finally, the dissent noted that North Carolina offered no "legitimate, non-partisan justification" for why it chose "a map that produces a greater partisan skew than any of 3,000 randomly generated maps" presented by the plaintiffs, leading Kagan to respond to the "majority's 'how much is too much' critique" with a simple and "first-cut answer: This much is too much."[113]

It is fair to say that for several decades, the Court's divisions yielded a doctrinal muddle with respect to partisan gerrymandering. While a slim majority of justices consistently held that these claims are justiciable, no majority either agreed on a workable constitutional standard for judging them or invalidated a redistricting plan as excessively partisan. Finally, in 2019, the Roberts Court abandoned this endeavor altogether.

Did the Republican Court Aid the GOP in Partisan Gerrymandering Cases?

Unsurprisingly, the Court's performance in this area has prompted considerable critical commentary, with Justice Kennedy the typical target.[114] He has been attacked for his "paralysis" and "odd" and "untenable" opinions[115] and accused of "blaz[ing] a new trail on the frontier of judicial irresponsibility."[116] These complaints, however valid, do not address this chapter's question of judicial partisanship and whether the Republican justices aided their copartisans through their votes and doctrinal choices.

An important study by Anthony McGann, Charles Smith, Michael Latner, and Alex Keena makes such a claim, at least with respect to *Vieth*.[117] This decision, the authors argue, granted politicians complete freedom to gerrymander for partisan gain, which Republicans used after their 2010 electoral wave[118] to engineer unprecedented bias in congressional and state legislative elections, a development that Sam Wang labels "the Great Gerrymander of 2012."[119] The analytical tool that McGann et al. employ in their study is a "partisan symmetry" measure that assumes "if the Democrats get 52% of the votes and win 60% of the seats as a result, then if the Republicans were to win 52% of the vote in the next election, they should get 60% of the seats."[120] In other words, any disproportionality in translating votes into seats should be the same for both parties. Applying that measure to the 2012 House elections reveals a sizable asymmetry score of 9.4 percent in favor of the Republican Party—which means that, for a given level of voter support between 45 and 55 percent, Republicans win 9.4 percent more seats than Democrats would win for the same level of support.[121] Especially significant, this represents a near tripling of the level of pro-Republican asymmetry (3.4 percent) that was seen in House elections after the 2000 redistricting cycle.[122] The authors bemoan this sharp increase in partisan bias as "the revenge of the Anti-Federalists": state governments, rather than the people, can now determine national election outcomes and control of Congress.[123] A minority of voters can, furthermore, elect a majority of House representatives, undermining the egalitarian intent of *Baker* and *Wesberry*. None of this could have happened, the authors argue, without *Vieth*, whose effects "were . . . momentous."[124]

Various types of evidence can help to assess whether the New Right Court's reluctance to accept partisan gerrymandering claims—in multiple cases and not just *Vieth*—resulted from a deliberate Republican strategy and aided the Republican Party electorally. With regard to the GOP's agenda, the Republican National Committee's national platforms serve as one evidentiary source. In fact, the Republican Party has said very little about redistricting over the past half-century, offering a statement on the topic in only five of its thirteen platforms from 1968 to 2016 and specifically referencing partisan gerrymandering in only three.[125] In 1992, 1996, and 2000 the GOP platform complained about, though did not offer any corrective to, pro-Democratic gerrymandering. In 2012 the party proposed changing the census to insure that "citizens are distinguished from lawfully present aliens and illegal aliens," and in 2012 and 2016 it favored citizenship over residency as the basis of representation. These two policy changes would, of course, significantly affect redistricting and hurt the Democratic Party. Requiring that the census count the number of US citizens is predicted to depress the response rate among Hispanics, Asians, urban residents, and the young, thereby undercounting residents in predominantly Democratic areas; using citizenship or voter eligibility rather than residency to determine representation would have a similar impact, advantaging the Republican Party by making districts "substantially whiter as well as older and less urban."[126]

The Trump administration's efforts to add a citizenship question to the 2020 census in advance of redistricting directly advanced this GOP objective. In defending this move in a subsequent legal challenge, the Commerce Department claimed that more accurate citizenship data would improve the enforcement of the Voting Rights Act, with the Court rejecting this rationale as "contrived" in *Department of Commerce v. New York* (2019).[127] Because this left little time to develop and secure judicial approval of an alternate rationale in advance of implementing the 2020 census, President Trump reluctantly abandoned this initiative. Nonetheless, he issued an executive order less than a month after the

Court's decision that was described as a "stealth plan to preserve white electoral power."[128] The president ordered all federal agencies to share any citizenship data they possessed with the Commerce Department, with the Department of Homeland Security quickly complying.[129] The executive order expressly offered as one of its aims permitting "states to design State and Local legislative districts based on the population of voter-eligible citizens;" this, the administration argued, would enable the Supreme Court to answer the question it left open in *Evenwel v. Abbott*: whether states are free to adopt, and not only merely protected from being forced to use, alternative population baselines such as citizenship or voter eligibility in designing its districts.[130]

Aside from a recent focus on the population basis of representation, this review of RNC platforms from 1968 through 2016 shows that the party has not consistently expressed a strong concern with redistricting generally, partisan gerrymandering more specifically, or the proper approach judges should employ in deciding challenges in this area. This stands in sharp contrast to the GOP's intense focus in its platforms on other election issues like voter identification and campaign finance.

The GOP's position on this issue can also be gleaned from the briefs it submits in partisan gerrymandering cases. Unsurprisingly, the Republican National Committee often defers to state and local party leaders, allowing them to decide how to defend their districting plans and whether and how to challenge those of the opposing party.

The RNC, nonetheless, has sometimes participated as amicus in cases like *Bandemer*, *LULAC*, *Gill*, and *Rucho*, with *Vieth* a notable exception, and its position has changed considerably over time. For example, in *Bandemer* (1986) the RNC supported the Indiana Democrats who challenged the Republican redistricting plan, arguing that partisan gerrymandering presented a justiciable issue since it burdened the First Amendment rights of parties and voters. Its 2006 *LULAC* brief claimed that although partisan gerrymandering could indeed violate the Fourteenth Amendment, the Texas plan under review would survive constitutional scrutiny. In *Gill v. Whitford* (2018), the Republican National Committee took a new tone, strongly cautioning against a broad cause of action for partisan gerrymandering and advancing a high bar for judicial invalidation of any plan on those grounds. Finally, in *Rucho* (2019) the RNC flatly stated that partisan gerrymandering claims were not justiciable. Nonetheless, it did not make that claim in a companion case, *Lamone v. Benisek*, involving an alleged Democratic gerrymander, confirming that its amicus activity has been partisan and strategic. It is also notable that in *Rucho* the RNC was joined by the National Republican Congressional Committee and the National Republican Redistricting Trust,[131] a sign of the growing importance the GOP has recently come to place on partisan gerrymandering cases.

The Republican Party's selective and strategic approach to partisan gerrymandering is similar to its approach to the Voting Rights Act. On both issues, the party has taken politically acceptable positions publicly—for example, opposing the practice of partisan gerrymandering and supporting the Voting Rights Act—while pursuing behind the scenes contradictory policies that protect its short-term self-interests. Party leaders, including Republican presidents, have publicly bemoaned the practice of partisan gerrymandering, even as Republican legislators and GOP officials engage in it and participate in litigation defending their own gerrymanders and attacking those of the opposing party. Additionally, in sharp contrast to other election issues like voter identification and campaign finance, the Republican National Committee has not taken a clear and consistent position on partisan gerrymandering in its amicus briefs. Of course, this necessarily complicates the analytical task of tying the justices' votes to party preferences.

It is, nonetheless, helpful to examine those votes for the presence of strong and distinctive partisan divisions. Such an inquiry offers mixed results, however. Looking first at the period from *Bandemer* (1986) to *LULAC* (2006), the only members of the Court who flatly concluded that partisan gerrymandering claims are not justiciable—O'Connor, Rehnquist, Burger, Scalia, and Thomas—were all Republican. Nonetheless, of the ten justices who regarded such as claims as justiciable, six (Powell, White, Marshall, Brennan, Breyer, and Ginsburg) were Democrats and four (Stevens, Blackmun, Kennedy, and Souter) were Republican. The partisan pattern is also weak when looking at the justices who at some point voted to invalidate a redistricting plan as excessively partisan: three (Powell, Breyer, and Ginsburg) were Democrats and two (Stevens and Souter) were Republican. Ideology, it seems, provides a more persuasive explanation than partisanship. After all, the Republican justices who ruled that partisan gerrymandering claims are justiciable—Blackmun, Stevens, Kennedy, and Souter—are the more moderate justices in the Republican cohort. McGann et al. make a similar argument, characterizing O'Connor's argument in *Bandemer* and Scalia's in *Vieth* as part of a long-standing philosophical dispute over congressional representation and districting practices dating back to the Warren Court's reapportionment revolution and its efforts to vindicate the Great Compromise that granted the people direct control over the House of Representatives.[132] Scalia's position in *Vieth* is "a conscious attempt to limit the effects of the reapportionment cases of the 1960s," particularly its egalitarianism, and to "turn . . . the clock back to before *Baker v. Carr.*" Overall, there is no stark pattern of partisan voting in *Bandemer, Vieth,* and *LULAC,* and an ideological explanation is more plausible. The 2019 *Rucho* case, however, offers a strictly partisan lineup of votes, with the Court's five Republican justices ruling, over the objections of the four Democratic justices, that partisan gerrymandering claims are not justiciable. This is, perhaps, not a surprising development given that the justices became strictly aligned on both partisan and ideological grounds after 2010 and that the Republican Party had recently begun advancing more clear and consistent doctrinal opposition to judicial interference with partisan gerrymanders.

The impact of the Court's reluctance to invalidate extreme partisan gerrymanders provides another possible source of evidence for the existence of friendly judicial review in this redistricting subfield. It is, first, unclear how the Republican justices could predict that a doctrine of noninterference would advantage their party. While a pro-Republican impact from upholding voter identification policies can be reasonably predicted, ruling that partisan gerrymandering is not justiciable does not inherently favor one party over the other. At least in theory, judicial abstinence frees both Republican-controlled and Democratic-controlled legislatures to gerrymander aggressively. Furthermore, the academic literature indicates that mapmakers are limited in their ability to create sizable and durable partisan bias, particularly in the face of other powerful forces like incumbency, political geography, and national election trends.

In fact, most political scientists regard redistricting and, thus, partisan gerrymandering, as "a fundamentally constrained activity."[133] Unified partisan control of state government is a necessary ingredient for successful gerrymanders, an assumption confirmed by Nicholas Stephanopoulos's study that found one-party control to be the most powerful cause of partisan bias in House and state legislative districts from 1972 to 2016.[134] Unified party control, however, has not been "the norm in the United States . . . in recent decades," thus insuring that partisan gerrymandering is "not a widespread phenomenon."[135] In the 2000 redistricting cycle, for example, only twenty-three states had unified party control, and partisan gerrymandering of congressional districts was possible in only thirteen of them, either because the state had only one House seat or because it employed nonlegislative redistricting methods.[136] The number of states capable of partisan gerrymandering increased significantly in the 2010 redistricting cycle, to twenty-two, with the GOP enjoying exclusive control over redistricting in twenty of them, a result of its remarkable success in the 2010 elections.[137] According to McGann and his coauthors, this enabled the party to craft highly advantageous maps in time for the 2012 elections, particularly in critically important states like Ohio, Pennsylvania, North Carolina, and Wisconsin.[138] The broader point remains, however. A majority of states, even after the lopsided 2010 elections, did not possess the basic elements necessary for partisan gerrymandering: multiple House seats and exclusive control of the redistricting process. Additionally, even when a single party enjoys such control, its legislators may face a reduced number of House districts to gerrymander, as well as legal challenges in both the state and federal courts. Quite significantly, however, states no longer faced the powerful constraint of preclearance after the Court's 2013 *Shelby County* decision.

Incumbency poses another significant limitation on partisan gerrymandering. John Sides and Eric McGhee, in fact, dispute the conventional wisdom that partisan redistricting caused the GOP's electoral success in 2012 and instead found incumbency to be a more potent explanation.[139] The authors point out that many Republican incumbents who first won office in 2010 were reelected in 2012, and their empirical tests taking incumbency into account eliminated any apparent effects from gerrymandering. As a general matter, conflict inevitably arises in the redistricting process between a party's incumbents, who want safer districts, and party leaders, who would rather use those wasted votes to create more marginal districts that increase the party's overall seat advantage.[140] Multiple studies have indeed found that partisan redistricting increases electoral competition relative to bipartisan redistricting, where shared power and cooperation among legislators tend to result in incumbent-protection plans that increase the number of safe districts for both parties.[141] Research has additionally shown that the recent decline in the electoral competitiveness of House elections is due not to redistricting but to the advantages of incumbency such as name recognition, constituency service, and fundraising.[142] A landmark study by

Alan Abramowitz, Brad Alexander, and Matthew Gunning, for example, rejected redistricting as a cause of the increase in safe seats in the House since the 1970s; more powerful explanatory factors included incumbency advantages like sizable campaign spending gaps between challengers and incumbents and increased district partisanship caused by geographic sorting in the electorate.[143] This conclusion is confirmed by Cottrell's recent study of safe seats in Congress, which found that "much of the variation in seat safety . . . is caused by factors other than gerrymandering, like incumbency advantage and partisan geography."[144]

This latter factor represents yet another constraint on the effectiveness of partisan gerrymandering: the number and distribution of the party's supporters within a state that impose demographic and geographic limits on how much partisan advantage can be created.[145] Sides and McGhee, for example, attribute the pro-Republican bias in House elections since the 1990s to the urban concentration of Democratic voters, which produces large numbers of wasted votes—a conclusion endorsed by some, though not all, scholars.[146] Nicholas Goedert similarly finds a "persistent pro-Republican bias" resulting from the "asymmetric geographic distribution of partisans" that is apparent "even when maps are drawn by courts or bipartisan agreement."[147] Stephanopoulos also finds that urbanization has a pro-Republican impact in generating "partisan skews" when it comes to redistricting, but he regards that effect as both modest and easily reduced by Democratic redistricting.[148]

An additional component of this geographic and demographic constraint is that district populations are not stable. As Nicholas Seabrook explains, "any electoral coalition created by targeted redistricting, especially the necessarily marginal majorities required to implement an effective partisan gerrymander, are likely to erode over time as populations and voting blocs shift and change due to migration, immigration, and generational replacement."[149] As Vladimir Kogan and Eric McGhee put it, "today's ingenious partisan gerrymander can become tomorrow's electoral disaster,"[150] a phenomenon cleverly labeled a "dummymander."[151] Goedert's study of four decades of congressional elections found such dummymanders to be "quite common."[152] McGhee agrees, noting that the "small" effects that redistricting generates with respect to partisan advantage "decay rapidly," making redistricting "at best a blunt tool for promoting partisan interests."[153] The Democrats' experience in the 1990s offers a perfect example: despite enjoying exclusive redistricting authority in nine states compared to only two for Republicans, the GOP won control of the House in the 1994 midterm elections, having gained a total of fifty-four seats, including twenty-one in the nine states that Democrats had themselves redistricted.[154] In another example, the allegedly pro-Republican congressional districts in Pennsylvania that the Court reviewed in *Vieth* produced a 12–7 Republican advantage in 2002, but a 12–7 Democratic advantage by 2008. A final observation with respect to geographic and demographic limitations comes from David Wasserman, who attributed the decline of swing seats in the House, from 164 in 1997 to seventy-two in 2016, to "natural geographic sorting" rather than changes in district boundaries; voters, he says, are "choosing sides with their feet."[155]

Not only are district populations unstable, so are electoral conditions. Cracking and packing, the traditional tools of partisan gerrymandering, involve inherent risks, as marginal districts may prove to be too competitive and can be lost due to shifting electoral tides.[156] Pro-Republican bias, for example, declined from the 2012 election to the 2014 election, reminding us that "bias is the product of the interaction of districts with the national election environment, and [is] not stable across all elections."[157] In a more recent example, national electoral currents led to a wave of Republican departures from the House in the 2018 election (forty-four total), helping Democrats gain a net total of forty-one seats and control of the House.[158] Of course, critics of partisan gerrymandering would argue that Democrats still had to win 9.6 percent more votes nationwide compared to Republicans to gain majority status and a slight advantage in House seats and that they could have won an additional sixteen seats if not for Republican gerrymanders.[159]

A final cautionary note about the supposed power of partisan gerrymandering is that a "seats bonus" is "a durable feature of U.S. congressional elections," which employ the single-member district, winner-take-all system.[160] The size of this bonus has varied considerably over the past seven decades (1946–2016), ranging from 0.5 percent to 11 percent, with an overall average of 5.6 percent; in fact, the seats bonus in 2012 after the GOP's supposed Great Gerrymander was only slightly above this average and was slightly below it in 2014 and 2016.[161]

Political science research teaches that redistricting is an exceptionally complicated endeavor involving multiple constraints and trade-offs and that it "isn't always as powerful or pernicious as its critics suggest."[162] Perhaps, then, the Court has been correct to be cautious and restrained. For those who believe that judicial review of partisan gerrymandering is inappropriate or impossible,[163] the academic literature offers support. Judicial reluctance may be further justified by the considerable disagreement over how best to measure partisan bias and how to determine when it has crossed a threshold and become excessive and thus unconstitutional.[164]

It is important, however, not to exaggerate these research findings. No political scientist claims, for example, that redistricting never has an impact on electoral competition or partisan bias in seat allocation either in the United States or elsewhere. We know, for example, that gerrymandering was "the single biggest trick that converted" Hungarian prime minister Viktor Orban's 45 percent voter support into a two-thirds supermajority in the parliament in 2014.[165] There is also no disputing that redistricting can have a significant, though generally marginal, effect in generating partisan bias. That effect can, furthermore, vary across redistricting cycles and individual states and between the parties. For example, Seabrook found that in the 1990 and 2000 cycles, the partisan advantage created through redistricting was modest and short-lived, though more likely in large states, in states gaining seats due to reapportionment, and with Republican compared to Democratic gerrymanders.[166] Michael Peress and Yangzi Zhao's study of House elections from 1942 to 2018 similarly found that partisan control over redistricting generated only a "moderate" seat advantage that, nonetheless, was greater in states with close partisan divisions and varied over time between the parties.[167] For example, the benefits of partisan control were equal for the two parties during the mid-twentieth century, mostly disappeared in the 1980s and 1990s, and have increased since for the Republican Party.

These research findings of a pro-Republican advantage in redistricting in recent years support the widespread perception among party leaders, pundits, journalists, and educated voters that the GOP has, in recent years, been extraordinarily successful in employing gerrymandering to game the system to its advantage.[168] Whether the academic literature confirms it or not, party leaders certainly *believe* that their Redistricting Majority Project (REDMAP) in 2010 was highly successful, and they have made a similar push in 2020 to prioritize state races in order to gain a redistricting advantage.[169] This confidence in both the great power of gerrymandering and its disproportionate benefit to Republicans has likely reinforced the GOP's growing commitment to judicial noninterference in redistricting. The Roberts Court now shares this commitment and has formalized it in precedent with *Rucho,* suggesting that a new era of interbranch collaboration with respect to partisan gerrymandering is underway.

The Supreme Court and Racial Gerrymandering

Another redistricting area that can be explored for evidence of collaboration between the GOP and the New Right Court is racial gerrymandering. As Donald Stokes notes, both "positive" and "negative" racial gerrymandering have been practiced in the United States.[170] "Negative" racial gerrymandering, the dominant practice in the past, was aimed at restricting the influence of African Americans voters. For example, in 1957 the Alabama legislature replaced Tuskegee's square-shaped boundary with a twenty-eight-sided figure that not so coincidentally removed nearly all of the city's African Americans, who could no longer vote in municipal elections. This obvious effort to disenfranchise blacks and deny them representation was struck down by the Court under the Fifteenth Amendment in *Gomillion v. Lightfoot* (1960).[171] In the modern-day "positive" form of racial gerrymandering, minority voters are packed into one or more districts, where they constitute a majority that is able to elect minority candidates. This "affirmative action redistricting" has an important side-effect, however: it "bleaches" the remaining districts, increasing the proportion of white voters, which helps to elect more Republican candidates overall.[172] Because of this partisan impact, Republican politicians in the 1990s, including the Republican National Committee,[173] abandoned their commitment to color-blind government policies and aggressively pursued majority-minority districts, making for unusual bedfellows. Virginia's 1990s redistricting process, for instance, brought together the minority Republican Party, the NAACP, and the ACLU, who united to pressure the majority Democratic Party to create more majority-minority districts.[174]

As will be explained, in contrast to strategic-minded Republican politicians, most Republican justices have viewed racial gerrymandering skeptically in cases like *Shaw v. Reno* (1993), voting in line with their philosophical concerns over the government's use of racial criteria instead of their party's self-interest.[175] A new and more traditional partisan pattern is emerging, however, in the so-called second generation of racial gerrymandering cases.[176] In cases like *Alabama Legislative Black Caucus v. Alabama* (2015) and *Cooper v. Harris* (2017), the Court has taken seriously the claims that Republican legislators have unnecessarily and excessively used race in creating majority-minority districts, limiting the influence of black voters.[177] Court majorities in these cases typically include all of the Democratic justices, with the dissenters consisting only of Republican justices.

Pressure on state legislatures to create majority-minority districts grew significantly in the 1980s and 1990s due to the changes made to Section 2 of the Voting Rights Act. As explained in chapter 2, Congress amended the VRA in 1982 to replace the Court's intent requirement from *City of Mobile v. Bolden* (1980) with an effects test.[178] A unanimous Court applied this congressional mandate in *Thornburg v. Gingles* (1986), invalidating six new legislative districts in North Carolina because, considering "the totality of circumstances," they diluted the power of the black vote.[179] *Gingles* required that a minority group be politically cohesive and "sufficiently large and geographically compact to constitute a majority in a single-member district" and that "the white majority votes sufficiently as a bloc to enable it . . . usually to defeat the minority's preferred candidate."[180] Although the precise meaning of these requirements for compactness and racially polarized voting would be the subject of continued litigation, the impact of *Gingles* cannot be overstated. Many state legislators felt that in order to reduce the risks of a vote-dilution challenge, they would need to create majority-minority districts in which racial or ethnic minorities constituted a majority sufficient to elect their candidates of choice. The Department of Justice—both career lawyers and appointees of Presidents George H. W. Bush and Bill Clinton—added to this pressure by quite deliberately seeking to increase minority representation in its review of redistricting plans in the preclearance process. Following the logic that a redistricting plan should not be approved under Section 5 preclearance if it could invite a Section 2 lawsuit, officials began insisting that covered jurisdictions draw additional majority-minority districts where possible, going beyond the previous requirement of merely avoiding retrogression.

These legal changes were initially supported by Democratic leaders as part of their alliance with and support for civil rights groups. Strategic-minded Republican leaders, such as Lee Atwater, Benjamin Ginsberg, and Newt Gingrich, however, saw a significant electoral opportunity. They realized that majority-minority districts had the potential to strain the relationship between civil rights leaders and Democratic politicians, whose electoral base of reliable voters would likely be weakened. This, of course, would help Republican candidates and increase the GOP advantage in House elections, particularly in the South. David Canon characterizes the Republican pursuit of majority-minority redistricting in the South in the late 1980s and early 1990s as "a campaign of guerilla warfare" that intentionally pitted African American Democrats against white Democrats; Bernard Grofman asserts that this "well-coordinated and well-financed strategy originat[ed] at the Republican National Committee."[181] Bush appointees leading the Justice Department at that time additionally supported the intensive efforts of career staff to pursue majority-minority districts, primarily in the South through its preclearance role.[182] Of course, the irony is that majority-minority districts are "the only race-based remedy the GOP has supported in the modern era."[183]

These efforts produced immediate and substantial effects. Following the 1990 census, Southern legislatures created twelve majority-black districts and three majority-Hispanic districts; New York, Illinois, and Maryland also contributed, bringing the total to twenty-five majority-minority congressional districts.[184] This directly and significantly increased minority representation in the House and state legislatures, especially in the South.[185] In fact, the number of African Americans elected to the House from Southern states rose from five in 1990 to seventeen in 1992, all of whom were elected from majority-minority districts.[186] Majority-minority redistricting also helped to elect more Republicans, though scholars disagree over the size of this increase and its role in the GOP securing majority status in the House in 1994;[187] they disagree as well over its "perverse effects" in the form of weakened substantive representation for minority constituents.[188]

A predominantly Republican Court did not stand quietly by amid these significant changes. It instead pushed back and let lawmakers know, beginning with *Shaw v. Reno* (1993), that they would not have a free hand in creating majority-minority districts. The initial *Shaw* litigation challenged two majority-black congressional districts that had been drawn by North Carolina's state legislature in order to secure preclearance from the Bush Justice Department. By a 5–4 vote, the Court reversed the lower court decision that had dismissed the case, reasoning that the districts, especially the serpentine Twelfth District, were bizarrely drawn and a departure from traditional districting principles of contiguity and compactness, thereby supporting an inference that race was a predominant consideration. This, the Court ruled, did indeed state a cause of action under the equal protection clause. Some of the provocative language in Justice O'Connor's majority opinion included a concern over the plan's "resemblance to political apartheid" and its dangerous tendency to "balkanize us into competing racial factions . . . threaten[ing] to carry us further from the goal of a political system in which race no longer matters."[189]

The same five-member and exclusively Republican majority from *Shaw I*—O'Connor, Kennedy, Rehnquist, Scalia, and Thomas—clarified in *Miller v. Johnson* (1995) that strict scrutiny would apply whenever race is the "overriding, predominant force" in the redistricting process.[190] A significant number of *Shaw* lawsuits followed over the next decade, with the justices struggling to provide clear guidance in what became an increasingly complicated doctrinal area. Questions of standing split the justices, as did the issue of whether fear of liability under the Voting Rights Act would constitute a compelling state interest. The Supreme Court often invalidated majority-minority districts, as in *Miller v. Johnson* (1995), *Shaw v. Hunt (Shaw II;* 1996), *Bush v. Vera* (1996), and *Meadows v. Moon* (1997).[191] It sometimes upheld them, however, as in *Lawyer v. Department of Justice* (1997), *King v. Illinois Board of Elections* (1998), and *Easley v. Cromartie* (2001).[192] What is clear from these cases is that the justices have been quite willing to intervene when it comes to racial gerrymandering, to apply the exacting strict-scrutiny test, and to invalidate districts that they believe rely excessively on race. This has put mapmakers in a very difficult position as Supreme Court doctrine from both *Gingles* and *Shaw* are "at war" with each other.[193] Together, they provide a very narrow path in which race must be used to avoid a challenge under the Voting Rights Act but not used so much as to trigger an equal protection challenge.

Significantly fewer *Shaw* lawsuits occurred in the 2000s redistricting cycle as a product of two developments: reduced Justice Department pressure to draw majority-minority districts and the Court's ruling in *Easley v. Cromartie*. Justice O'Connor, in an unexpected move, voted with the liberal justices in *Easley* to uphold the redrawn Twelfth Congressional District in North Carolina that had been rejected in *Shaw II*; she endorsed the majority's reasoning that politics, not race, was the predominant factor in its creation. It is, of course, quite difficult to separate partisan motives from racial ones in the presence of racially polarized voting patterns.[194] The clear effect of this confusing doctrinal development was that states could more easily defend their majority-minority districts by asserting that their motives were political and, thus, legally immune rather than racial and, thus, constitutionally vulnerable.[195]

A resurgence of *Shaw* litigation occurred after the 2010 round of redistricting. In Richard Hasen's telling, "voting rights activists" have "resurrected" the Court's conservative doctrine from the racial gerrymandering cases and have, ironically and with the support of Democrats (including the Obama administration), used it "to police Republican overreach" in mostly Southern districts.[196] They claimed in *Alabama Legislative Black Caucus v. Alabama* (2015), *Bethune-Hill v. Virginia State Board of Elections* (2017), and *Cooper v. Harris* (2017) that state legislators went beyond what the Voting Rights Act requires and excessively and unconstitutionally packed African American voters into too few districts in order to limit their power.[197] These arguments found a receptive ear on the Court, especially among its four Democratic justices (Ginsburg, Breyer, Kagan, and Sotomayor), who voted together in the majority in all three cases. Interestingly, Clarence Thomas, a Republican justice and the Court's most conservative member, joined Justice Kagan's majority opinion in *Harris* that invalidated two frequently litigated majority-black districts in North Carolina, the First and Twelfth Congressional Districts, as unconstitutional gerrymanders.[198] In an especially significant move, Justice Kagan offered a footnote weakening *Easley*'s race-versus-party distinction, holding that "the sorting of voters on the grounds of their race remains suspect even if race is meant to function as a proxy for other (including political) characteristics"; strict scrutiny is required even if legislators' "ultimate objective . . . [is] advancing their partisan interests."[199] *Harris* may have thus reinvigorated *Shaw* and invited more lawsuits challenging majority-minority districts.

Several conclusions can be drawn from the Court's rulings in *Shaw* and its progeny. First, the Court has been quite willing to intervene, to challenge states that appear to rely too much on race in their redistricting decisions, and to impose a very tough standard for judging majority-minority districts. This is very different from the Court's approach in the partisan gerrymandering cases. Second, racial gerrymandering has generated what might be called "high-leverage" cases in terms of the challenge discussed in chapter 1 of disentangling partisan and ideological influences in judicial decision-making. For Republican judges in particular, partisan loyalty and ideology lead to different outcomes when it comes to majority-minority redistricting. This framing, however, is somewhat simplistic. After all, although the Republican Court did not support the GOP's strategic endeavor in this area, its approach and decisions are a product of "the color-blind jurisprudential regime of the New Right" in which the Court has "act[ed] in concert with Republican elites to help implement racial conservatives' preferences."[200] Over the "past 40-plus years"—from *Washington v. Davis* (1976) and *Milliken v. Bradley* (1974) to *Parents Involved* (2007) and *Shelby County* (2013)—the Court has "support[ed] the policies of racial conservatives," typically by invoking the principle of color blindness.[201] The power of this color-blind jurisprudential tradition, emerging from "the conservative knowledge structure"[202] and promoted by Reagan regime leaders, helped to insure that the Court's conservatives would overcome their usual reluctance to intervene in the "dirty business"[203] of redistricting and, ironically, resist any potential temptation to favor their party's short-term electoral interests. Although the Court's decisions easily lead to the rejection of any claim of simple or crass partisanship, they support an alternate conclusion: the Republican Court in the racial gerrymandering field has been a loyal partner in the New Right regime's racial conservatism and devotion to color blindness.

The racial gerrymandering and partisan gerrymandering decisions, though quite different in terms of the Court's willingness to intervene, are very similar in other respects. For example, considerable divisions exist among the justices in both areas, with the racial gerrymandering cases also producing frequent 5–4 rulings and multiple plurality opinions. Whether the Court upholds or invalidates a particular majority-minority district is often determined by the vote of the median justice—which, for much of this period, has been either Justice O'Connor or Justice Kennedy. It also appears that, in both areas, the voting patterns are better explained by ideology than partisanship. Several pieces of evidence support this conclusion. First, the justices who initially warned mapmakers that they could not craft majority-minority districts unimpeded by strict judicial scrutiny were exclusively Republican, despite such districts having a pro-Republican impact. Instead, in *Shaw v. Reno* and *Miller v. Johnson*, O'Connor, Kennedy, Scalia, Rehnquist, and Thomas voted their sincere preferences, offering their frequently expressed skepticism toward government-imposed racial preferences. Making an inference of partisan behavior even more of a stretch, three of the four justices dissenting in *Shaw I*—Stevens, Souter, and Blackmun—were Republican. These more moderate (and some would say liberal) Republican justices have typically adopted a more deferential approach to race-conscious policies that seek to help racial and ethnic minorities, and they reasserted that position in the racial gerrymandering cases; this is true as well for the Democratic justices. Thus, justices on both sides of the issue appear to be advancing their sincere philosophical beliefs, unlike Republican Party leaders who abandoned their party's typical opposition to racial preferences for the purpose of advancing the GOP's electoral interests.

Another difficulty in imputing partisan motives to the justices is that both parties have been torn internally and have vacillated in their positions on majority-minority redistricting. Unsurprisingly, given their close alliance with civil rights groups and leaders, Democrats initially supported majority-minority districts as a tool to improve the electoral prospects of minority candidates. This included filing an amicus brief in support of the majority-black districts in North Carolina in *Shaw I*. Democratic support wavered, however, as concern grew over the harmful impact of majority-minority districts on the party's candidates and policies. The Republican Party has also been divided over the years; the (H. W.) Bush Justice Department strongly encouraged majority-minority districting and Republican strategists energetically promoted it behind the scenes, yet the Republican National Committee filed an amicus brief supporting the white plaintiffs in *Shaw I*, a position more consistent with its long-standing ideological commitment to color blindness. These divisions within both parties complicate and confound the task of characterizing the justices' votes as partisan. The more recent second-generation cases, however, present more conventional claims of negative racial gerrymandering and have triggered sharper partisan alignments.

Another sign that the justices have been motivated more by principle than partisanship in the racial gerrymandering cases is the Court's greater willingness to "uphold against *Shaw* challenges districts designed outside the legislative process."[204] Both generally and in the racial gerrymandering field more specifically, the justices have been more skeptical of redistricting plans drawn by partisan legislators than by courts or independent commissions.[205] Rather than supporting the self-interested electoral aims of the party with which they affiliate, justices have been suspicious of the motives and machinations of both parties.

In conclusion, when it comes to racial gerrymandering, the Court has not been reluctant to intervene. Characterizing that intervention as partisan, however, is not so simple. In judging majority-minority districts, conservative Republican justices continued to be highly skeptical of the government's use of racial criteria, and liberal justices, whether Democratic or Republican, continued to be tolerant of them as long as the government's aim was to aid minority representation and influence. No Republican justice acted as a loyal partisan, insincerely siding with their party's strategy of pursuing majority-minority districts in order to hurt the Democratic Party electorally. Instead, the Republican justices, or at least the more conservative ones, faithfully adhered to the color-blind jurisprudential regime that conservative intellectuals and Republican leaders had carefully developed and advanced since the 1970s and 1980s. They rejected race-conscious measures in redistricting, just as they had in school desegregation, government contracting, and affirmative action. A more accurate conclusion, then, is that the New Right Court has been regimist, but not crassly partisan.

A final twist comes from the recent uptick in *Shaw*-related claims that is certainly fueled by partisanship. Democrats and civil rights groups are challenging Republican gerrymanders that in the post-2010 era are alleged to be too aggressive, particularly in packing more minority voters than necessary into existing majority-minority districts. Although it was Republican justices who, in the past, were more skeptical of such districts, opposition is now coming mostly from the Democratic justices, with a more traditional partisan voting pattern emerging. Hasen wonders, however, whether this is only temporary and if the "malleability of Supreme Court constitutional doctrine, especially in the area of election law," will enable "a new, more conservative Supreme Court [to] revert to its original treatment of the gerrymandering claim as a tool to limit minority voting power."[206]

The Future of Redistricting

As in other areas of election law, judges have actively participated in constructing the legal framework of redistricting and shaping its policies and its politics. Compared to the Voting Rights Act and voter identification, however, the New Right Court has not decided as consistently with Republican preferences in the area of redistricting. That is most obviously the case in *Evenwel* and *Department of Commerce*, where the Roberts Court refused to endorse the GOP's strategic efforts to alter, for the party's benefit, the process and methodology for counting US residents both in the census and for purposes of representation. Nor did the New Right Court support the Republican Party's strategic initiative to promote majority-minority districts that would disadvantage the Democratic Party in winning House and state legislative seats. Such resistance, however, was a product of the conservative justices' devotion to the color-blind principle, a central philosophical pillar of the New Right regime. In the partisan gerrymandering cases, the Court's divisions and indecision had the practical effect of permitting politicians great freedom to gerrymander. Yet, it is not clear that this either reflected GOP preferences or worked to the party's advantage—at least not until recently. The new *Rucho* precedent established by the Roberts Court's five Republican justices firmly supports the GOP's emerging preference for judicial noninterference in partisan gerrymandering and potentially continues the party's recent advantage in the redistricting process.

As far as the future of redistricting, an easy prediction is that substantial judicial involvement will continue. Politicians will not stop trying to employ courts for partisan advantage, either to uphold their preferred plans or to invalidate those of the opposing party. Furthermore, while the Roberts Court may have forbidden partisan gerrymandering lawsuits in the federal courts, state courts can still hear those challenges and may choose to invalidate partisan gerrymanders under their state constitutions as, for example, the Pennsylvania Supreme Court did in 2018 with respect to a congressional map.[207] Of course, an important question is whether the Roberts Court will try to restrain the power of state courts to intervene in a process that the Constitution explicitly grants to state legislatures, subject only to congressional regulation. What, too, about the extensive reform efforts aimed at partisan gerrymandering that are being pursued across the nation? Might the Court no longer remain on the sidelines but actively intervene to block the reforms that voters and legislatures wish to adopt? After all, in 2015 the Court upheld—by only a single vote—a constitutional amendment passed by Arizona voters to empower an independent redistricting commission to draw congressional districts.[208] Anthony Kennedy was the only Republican justice to join the majority, with the four other Republicans dissenting, including the new Court median, Chief Justice John Roberts. Should Kennedy's replacement, Brett Kavanaugh, support the dissenters' point of view in a similar case in the future, the Court would set a new precedent that provides even greater judicial tolerance of partisan gerrymandering. Such a ruling would likely prove unpopular and be attacked as undemocratic, as the Court "would have closed off one of the few ways to break the vicious circle of gerrymandering," blocking voters themselves from ending a practice that they find repugnant.[209]

Rucho and *LULAC* may have unleashed forces that will further fuel such voter hostility. Because of *Rucho*, politicians are guaranteed that federal courts will not interfere in even the most extreme partisan gerrymanders. Because of *LULAC*, such restraints are also absent when it comes to mid-decade redistricting. In this era of hyperpartisanship, it is possible that the frequency of gerrymandering could become greater, with each party coming into power in the state legislature seeking to craft new maps that expand and preserve its power. Any marginal partisan advantages from gerrymandering could accumulate from one election to another. This is especially true if more research confirms the recent finding of Gary Jacobson that partisanship is lessening the power of incumbency in congressional elections.[210]

A final potential development is that Democrats will be able to overcome the GOP's electoral advantages that flow from structural features like the Senate and Electoral College that amplify rural power. Should the Democrats, in 2020 and beyond, find significant electoral success across the nation, they could secure control of redistricting processes and freely and aggressively engage in gerrymandering to preserve and expand their power, a development they would likely see as *Rucho's* revenge.

5 | Courts, Parties, and Campaign Finance

Have courts exercised friendly judicial review with respect to campaign finance? Did the Republican Party, as regime politics theory predicts, both cause and benefit from Citizens United *and the Supreme Court's growing hostility to campaign finance regulations?*

In this chapter I ask whether interbranch cooperation and friendly judicial review have occurred in the area of campaign finance. I examine doctrinal developments and discern three noteworthy trends. The first is growing opposition to government regulation in this area, particularly since John Roberts and Samuel Alito joined the Court. The second development is a heightened level of activism in the Roberts Court's approach to campaign finance, seen in its willingness to abandon long-standing precedent and creatively construct a path for major doctrinal change. The third trend is a sharply partisan pattern of decision-making, seen in cases like *Citizens United v. Federal Election Commission* (2010), *McCutcheon v. Federal Election Commission* (2014), and *Janus v. American Federation of State, County, and Municipal Employees, Council 31* (2018).[1] This represents a substantial shift from the last quarter of the twentieth century, when bipartisan coalitions were common.

These revolutionary changes in the area of campaign finance can be traced to broader developments in US politics such as partisan polarization and the "weaponization" of the First Amendment by business interests and conservative legal groups.[2] How exactly campaign finance fits into the GOP's strategy is not straightforward, however, primarily because of the uncertain partisan impact of ending regulatory restrictions in election financing. *Janus*, however, represents an exception as the anti-Democratic intentions and likely impact of ending fair-share fees for public-sector unions are quite clear.

I will first describe landmark campaign finance rulings by the Supreme Court and then highlight three prominent trends revealed in those doctrinal developments: an increasingly antiregulatory approach, heightened activism, and sharp partisan division. Next, I connect these changes to broader shifts in American politics and the Republican Party. Finally, I examine the impact of "the end of limits" in the campaign finance field, being especially attentive to any distinctive partisan advantage caused by the doctrinal changes made by the Roberts Court.[3]

Constitutional Doctrine in the Campaign Finance Field

In *Buckley v. Valeo* (1976) the Court established a framework for evaluating campaign finance laws that persists to this day.[4] At issue in this case were the 1974 amendments to the Federal Election Campaign Act (FECA) adopted by Congress in the wake of the Watergate scandal. In addition to creating the Federal Election Commission to enforce the act, these reforms created a comprehensive set of rules for the financing of federal elections that provided restrictions on both contributions and expenditures, public disclosure requirements, and partial public financing of presidential elections. The complicated 138-page per curiam opinion in *Buckley* upheld much of this scheme, with the notable exception of limits on expenditures. In so doing, the Court established several major principles that have endured in how it treats campaign finance regulations under the Constitution.

"Money is speech" is the first important principle anchoring the Supreme Court's jurisprudence in this area. If money was regarded as property instead of speech or if campaign donations and expenditures were seen more as conduct than speech, the government would have a freer hand in regulating it. In the view of justices across the ideological spectrum, however, government restrictions in the campaign finance area—for example, requiring public disclosure or limiting how much an individual or group can spend on behalf of a candidate or ballot measure—directly implicate the First Amendment. They threaten to limit the political speech at the amendment's core and the freedom of individuals to organize, pool their resources, and advance their shared interests by participating in election campaigns. As the Court noted in *Buckley*, "virtually every means of communicating ideas in today's mass society require the expenditure of money."[5] Because campaign finance regulations directly threaten freedom of speech and association, the

Court evaluates them using a heightened scrutiny standard—intermediate or strict scrutiny, depending on the type of regulation—and requires a strong justification from the government.

One justification that the Court readily accepts is the prevention of corruption or the appearance of corruption. The government has a legitimate concern, the justices have all agreed, with preventing quid pro quo corruption, in which a politician offers a favor in exchange for a campaign donation. In contrast, a governmental interest that is not uniformly accepted by the justices, particularly by conservative justices, is the promotion of equality. This "antidistortion" rationale would justify government intervention that prevents wealthy individuals or businesses from playing an outsized role in financing elections and thereby acquiring disproportionate influence. According to this view, the government can seek to level the playing field and prevent the distortion of democratic politics. The Court typically rejects this justification, however, explaining in *Buckley* that "the concept that government may restrict the speech of some elements of our society in order to enhance the relative voice of others is wholly foreign to the First Amendment."[6]

Flowing from this acceptance of the anticorruption, but not the antidistortion, rationale is another enduring pillar in the *Buckley* framework: contribution limits are considered less troublesome constitutionally and are, thus, treated more leniently than spending limits. Contributions to a candidate, most justices have reasoned,[7] pose a direct risk of quid pro quo corruption, unlike independent expenditures, which are not coordinated with a candidate and, thus, could not be repaid with a political favor. Additionally, the Court views spending limits as a more direct and substantial restriction on speech compared to a donation to a candidate, as the latter communicates a "symbolic expression of support" rather than a specific message.[8] For both of these reasons, limits on expenditures are judged under the strict scrutiny test whereas limits on contributions are judged using a more lenient intermediate scrutiny standard.

How have these general principles been applied to the various efforts of the federal and state governments to regulate the campaign finance marketplace? With regard to public disclosure requirements, the Court has, in *Buckley* and consistently since, applied what amounts to an intermediate scrutiny standard. Under this test, it has upheld nearly all of the state and federal provisions that it has reviewed. This includes, in both *McConnell v. Federal Election Commission* (2003) and *Citizens United*, the more expansive disclosure requirements adopted by Congress in 2002 in the Bipartisan Campaign Reform Act (BCRA), also known as McCain-Feingold.[9] In so doing, the Court has accepted that the government may legitimately require disclosure in order to deter corruption, inform voters about the source of candidate funds, and gather information necessary to detect and enforce contribution limits. While public disclosure rules are regarded as less intrusive than other regulations, the Court has nonetheless recognized their potential to chill political speech. A donation to an unpopular candidate or cause could, for example, trigger unwanted publicity or even reprisals that might discourage would-be donors. Compliance with onerous disclosure requirements could additionally impose burdens on candidates, as well as organizations that participate extensively in campaign activities.[10]

In *Buckley* the Supreme Court also upheld FECA's system for public financing of presidential elections, which provided matching funds during the nomination phase and full funding for major party candidates in the general election.[11] Even though Congress imposed spending limits on candidates accepting those funds, which the Court typically regards as constitutionally dubious, it upheld this public financing scheme because participation was voluntary. Candidates who wished to spend beyond the statutory ceiling could simply refuse to accept the public funds. In fact, serious presidential candidates—all of them since 2008—routinely decline to participate for precisely this reason.[12] The Court in 2011 invalidated a provision in Arizona's public financing scheme that gave additional funding to publicly financed candidates who faced privately financed candidates who spent more than the initial allocation of public funds.[13] The Court divided 5–4 along partisan lines, with the Republican majority ruling that the "rescue funds" provision, like the BCRA's "millionaire's amendment" that it had struck down in 2008,[14] unfairly penalized candidates who privately funded their campaigns, burdening their First Amendment rights and thereby triggering strict scrutiny. The state did so, furthermore, under the disfavored argument that the government has a compelling interest in equalizing candidate resources. The four Democratic dissenters, led by Justice Kagan, disagreed that the law imposed a penalty that infringed on the free speech rights of certain candidates and their supporters; instead, the additional funding was no more than a subsidy. Furthermore, they argued, the state had indeed advanced a compelling interest in reducing candidates' dependence on private donations and, thus, the potential for corruption. Kagan's dissent was most notable for accusing the Court of abandoning the fundamental principles contained in "broad swaths of our First Amendment doctrine" and disrespecting the anticorruption aims of Arizona voters who "deserve better."[15]

When it comes to contributions, the Court has not interfered with long-standing congressional bans on corporations and unions donating directly to federal candidates.[16] Even as late as 2003, in *Federal Election Commission v. Beaumont*, a seven-justice majority upheld FECA's ban on direct corporate donations to federal election campaigns, largely since the individual members of those corporations remained free to donate.[17] In terms of its doctrinal rules, as previously noted, the Court applies a lower standard of review—something akin to intermediate scrutiny—to restrictions on contributions compared to restrictions on expenditures. Contribution limits must be "closely drawn" to a "sufficiently important interest," and the particular monetary amounts need not be "fine tun[ed]."[18] *Buckley*, for example, upheld FECA's $1,000 limit on individual contributions to candidates, its $5,000 limit on donations to political committees (i.e., PACs), and its $25,000 aggregate limit on an individual's contribution to all candidates and committees in a single year. The Court reasoned that direct contributions to candidates do indeed pose a risk of quid pro quo corruption, with its prevention serving as an important government interest.

This logic was used in *Citizens Against Rent Control v. City of Berkeley* to strike down a limit on the amount of money that could be donated to ballot measure campaigns; after all, such donations posed no danger of candidate corruption.[19] Following *Buckley*'s approach, the Court in *Nixon v. Shrink Missouri Government PAC* upheld restrictions on individual contributions to candidates, accepting the state of Missouri's asserted "interest in countering . . . the perception of corruption."[20] Kennedy, Scalia, and Thomas dissented and urged *Buckley*'s reversal, with the latter two justices explicitly advancing strict scrutiny as a more appropriate test for evaluating contribution limits. Joining the six-member majority were O'Connor and Rehnquist, who would soon be replaced (respectively) by Samuel Alito and John Roberts, with profound effects on the Court's campaign finance decisions. For example, in *Randall v. Sorrell* (2006), employing a less deferential approach, six justices—including Alito and Roberts—voted to invalidate Vermont's contribution limits, reasoning that they were set too low and thereby harmed challengers and inhibited electoral competition.[21] This was, notably, the first time in the three decades spanning *Buckley* and *Randall* that the Court had invalidated candidate contribution limits. More evidence of the Court's "deregulatory turn in campaign finance" came in 2014 in *McCutcheon v. FEC*, with Alito and Roberts again playing a critical role.[22] In a strictly partisan 5–4 split, the Court struck down the federal aggregate contribution limit that *Buckley* had previously upheld because it was not closely drawn to the government's concededly important interest in preventing corruption or its appearance.[23]

A prominent dispute among the justices in recent years has focused on the definition of corruption. The liberal justices support a broader conception, expressed in Justice Breyer's *McCutcheon* dissent, "stress[ing] the constitutional importance of Congress' concern that a few large donations not drown out the voices of the many" and its legitimate "interest in maintaining the integrity of our public governmental institutions."[24] In contrast, the Republican justices on the Roberts Court have favored a narrower definition, arguing that the government may only target quid pro quo corruption in which money is exchanged for political favors. As both Michael Kang and Richard Hasen note, this now dominant view on the Court, apparent in *Citizens United*, has had a major doctrinal impact, narrowing the governmental interests that the Court will recognize as sufficiently compelling and the types of regulations it consequently will uphold.[25] A final note with regard to contributions, in *McConnell v. FEC* (2003), a five-member majority that included Justice O'Connor applied intermediate scrutiny and upheld the "soft money" ban enacted by the 2002 BCRA. A significant loophole in the 1974 FECA amendments was that whereas contributions to candidates were restricted, contributions to political parties were not. As a result, unregulated soft money donations grew exponentially in the 1980s and 1990s, a loophole that the BCRA sought to close. In upholding the soft money ban, the Court accepted as sufficiently important the government's concern that "officeholders will decide issues not on the merits or the desires of their constituencies, but according to the wishes of those who have made large, financial contributions valued by the officeholder."[26]

The type of campaign finance regulation toward which the Court has been the most skeptical is expenditure restrictions. Under the exacting standard imposed by the Court in *Buckley* (later confirmed to be strict scrutiny), the limits established by FECA for both campaign spending by candidates and independent expenditures by individuals and groups relative to a specific candidate did not survive. The Court reasoned that the "Act's expenditure ceilings impose direct and substantial restraints on the quantity of political speech . . . [and] political expression 'at the core of our electoral process and of the First Amendment freedoms.'"[27] The Court found "inadequate" the government's asserted interest in preventing corruption and its appearance, given that independent expenditures are not coordinated with a candidate and, therefore, cannot have a corrupting effect.[28] Furthermore, it rejected the argument that spending limits could be justified by the government's interest in equalizing either candidate resources or the ability of individuals and groups to influence elections.

Subsequent cases have provided the opportunity for the Court to clarify the government's regulatory power with regard to more specific types of campaign expenditures, such as those involving ballot measures or spending by unions, corporations, and political parties. With regard to the latter, for example, in *Colorado Republican Federal Campaign Committee v. Federal Election Commission* (1996) and *Federal Election Commission v. Colorado Republican Federal Campaign Committee* (2001), the Court ruled that the government cannot restrict expenditures by political parties that are independent of—that is, not coordinated with—particular congressional candidates.[29] When it comes to spending by corporations and unions, the Court has sometimes clarified the doctrinal rules but has at other times muddied the waters, as seen in the Court's tortured path from *First National Bank of Boston v. Bellotti* (1978) to *Citizens United* (2010).[30]

In *Bellotti* (1978) the Court struck down limits on what corporations and banks could contribute or spend in state elections involving ballot measures. Justice Powell's majority opinion offered a broad view of the free speech rights of corporations and rejected the government's equalizing aim as a permissible justification. In a surprising footnote, however, the Court suggested that corporate spending restrictions might be constitutional in candidate elections given their closer connection to the government's compelling interest in preventing corruption. In *Federal Election Commission v. Massachusetts Citizens for Life, Inc.* (*MCFL*) (1986) the Court ruled that FECA's expenditure limits on express advocacy could not, under the First Amendment, be applied to nonprofit corporations formed for ideological purposes, such as the anti-abortion group at issue in the case that had urged readers of its newsletter to vote for pro-life congressional candidates.[31] In *Austin v. Michigan Chamber of*

Commerce (1990) the Court upheld a Michigan law that limited spending on ballot measures by for-profit corporations because of the government's compelling interest in battling the corrosive and distorting effect of wealth in the political process, offering unexpected support for an antidistortion rationale.[32] The Court reasoned that the *MCFL* exemption did not apply to the Michigan Chamber of Commerce, since it was more of a business association than a political association, with business corporations constituting over three-quarters of its membership. Additionally, the Court noted, corporations could still engage in express advocacy using separate, segregated funds for that purpose. In *McConnell v. FEC* (2003) the Court extended *Austin*'s holding to labor unions and, most significantly, upheld the BCRA ban on corporations and unions using their treasury funds for "electioneering communication," defined as "any broadcast, cable, or satellite communication . . . refer[ring] to a clearly identified candidate for Federal office" within thirty days of a primary election and sixty days of a general election.

With Roberts replacing Rehnquist in 2005 and, especially significant, Alito replacing O'Connor in 2006, the Court shifted direction and became more skeptical of campaign finance regulations generally and limits on corporate campaign spending more specifically. For example, in *Federal Election Commission v. Wisconsin Right to Life, Inc.* (*WRTL*; 2007) the Court narrowed the BCRA's restrictions on corporate-funded electioneering communications by ruling that they could not be applied to a political advertisement unless it was "susceptible of no reasonable interpretation other than as an appeal to vote for or against a specific candidate."[33] In this case, WRTL's ads urged viewers to contact two US senators, one of whom was running for reelection, and encourage them to oppose filibusters of judicial nominees. The Court disagreed with the FEC that the ads were unequivocally express advocacy that could be restricted, as opposed to issue ads that could not. Justices Scalia, Kennedy, and Thomas would have gone further and invalidated the ban entirely as applied to corporate-funded ads.

That major step would be taken by the Court in 2010 in *Citizens United v. Federal Election Commission*. It ruled that the BCRA's restrictions on corporate-funded electioneering communications violated the First Amendment, thereby overruling *Austin* and part of *McConnell*. At issue in this case was a ninety-minute documentary, *Hillary: The Movie*, that was highly critical of Hillary Clinton and that its creator, a nonprofit organization named Citizens United, wished to air via video-on-demand

and advertise for in 2008 while Clinton was competing for the Demo-cratic presidential nomination. The five-member Republican majority, after concluding that Citizens United was not an exempt organization under *MCFL,* applied strict scrutiny to and invalidated the BCRA's ban on corporate-funded electioneering. The Court was no longer persuaded that the First Amendment was sufficiently protected by the ability of corporations to form a political action committee (PAC) and participate in this alternate form. Instead, Justice Kennedy's majority opinion reasoned that banning speech based on the corporate identity of the speaker could not be justified by the government's asserted anti-corruption and antidistortion rationales. The four Democratic dissent-ers rejected the argument that the government could not distinguish between individual and corporate speakers and accepted as valid Con-gress's concern over the undue influence of wealthy corporations that might distort the democratic process. As Justice Stevens's opinion wryly observed, "few outside the majority of this Court would have thought its flaws included a dearth of corporate money in politics."[34] Two years later, in another 5–4 partisan split in *American Tradition Partnership, Inc. v. Bullock* (2012), the Court would reverse a Montana Supreme Court decision upholding state-imposed limits on independent corporate ex-penditures.[35]

Notable Trends in Supreme Court Decision-Making in Campaign Finance Cases

Several noteworthy trends can be discerned in the four decades of Supreme Court decision-making in this doctrinal area. The first is the Court's growing skepticism and hostility toward campaign finance reg-ulation. As Timothy Kuhner notes, and as Table 5.1 clearly indicates, prior to 2005, "campaign finance reformers won in the Supreme Court about as much as they lost"; with Roberts and Alito joining the Court and the three most consistently conservative voices on campaign finance (Scalia, Kennedy, and Thomas), a new Republican majority emerged in 2005 and "political finance" was effectively "deregulat[ed]."[36] Replacing O'Connor with Alito was especially momentous;[37] in fact, as Table 5.1 shows, "the Court has invalidated or severely limited nearly every cam-paign finance restriction it has considered since Alito's arrival."[38] This new Republican coalition has intensified the Court's scrutiny of cam-

Table 5.1. The Supreme Court's Deregulatory Shift in Campaign Finance

1976–2004	2005–2015
Buckley v. Valeo (1976)	*Randall* (2006)
Bellotti (1986)	*WRTL* (2007)
Citizens Against Rent Control (1981)	*Davis* (2008)
MCFL (1986)	*Citizens United* (2010)
Austin (1990)	*Bennett* (2011)
Nixon v. Shrink (2000)	*Bullock* (2012)
McConnell (2003)	*McCutcheon* (2014)
Beaumont (2003)	

*Antiregulation rulings

paign finance laws, employing a "super-strict scrutiny" standard[39] that has proven fatal to multiple regulations: Vermont's contribution limits in 2006 (*Randall*), the BCRA's millionaire's amendment in 2008 (*Davis*), federal restrictions on corporate-funded campaign advertising in 2010 (*Citizens United*), a key component of Arizona's public financing system in 2011 (*Bennett*), and aggregate contribution limits in federal races in 2014 (*McCutcheon*).

As many scholars have observed, these changes in campaign finance decision-making are part of a broader "corporatist" and "Lochnerian" shift in the Court's First Amendment jurisprudence.[40] According to this view, just as the Court in the *Lochner* era[41] offered a robust reading of the due process clause that protected business from progressive regulation, the Court in recent years has offered a robust reading of the First Amendment that similarly protects business from progressive regulation.[42] Employing "a highly formal conception" of the First Amendment[43] that some characterize as "the new *Lochner*'s absolutist 'speech is speech' argument,"[44] the Roberts Court has pursued the protection of speech with "monomaniacal rigor"[45]—whether it involves animal cruelty videos (*U.S. v. Stevens*, 2010), corporate campaign advertising (*Citizens United*, 2010), lies about military awards (*U.S. v. Alvarez*, 2012), hateful protests at military funerals (*Snyder v. Phelps*, 2011), false statements on naturalization documents (*Maslenjuk v. U.S.*, 2017), or violent video games (*Brown v. Entertainment Merchants Association*, 2011).[46] This speech-is-speech approach has, furthermore, insured "virtually categorical protections for campaign speech" that have expanded into new "domains" where regulation was previously permissible.[47] The Court's expansive view of the First Amendment and its solicitude for the rights of corporations has extended to religious liberty as well. It has supported (though, thus far, more on statutory grounds) the freedom of businesses to refuse, for religious reasons, contraceptive coverage to employees (*Burwell v. Hobby Lobby Stores*, 2014) and services to same-sex couples (*Masterpiece Cake Shop v. Colorado Civil Rights Commission*, 2017).[48] As several commentators have aptly put it, "we are in 'the age of the imperial First Amendment.'"[49]

The Court has not only grown more hostile to campaign finance regulation but has also become exceptionally activist in its approach. It has shown no reticence to challenge the judgments of Congress, a co-equal branch of government, in this unusually complex and consequential area of the law.[50] It has also been willing to reverse its own long-standing precedents. *McCutcheon*, for example, overturned part of the thirty-nine-year-old *Buckley* ruling. Also noteworthy is *Janus v. American Federation of State, County, and Municipal Employees, Council 31* (2018). Although this important case does not fit squarely in the campaign finance field, it is likely to have substantial consequences for it given that public-sector unions—disproportionately supporters of the Democratic Party—are expected to lose both membership and revenues as a result. In *Janus* the Court overturned a forty-one-year-old precedent, *Abood v. Detroit Board of Education* (1977), that had permitted states to mandate so-called agency or "fair share" fees for nonunion employees to help cover the union's collective bargaining costs, though not the costs associated with its political activities.[51] The five-member majority in *Janus* held that state-mandated fair-share fees have the potential effect of compelling speech with which nonmembers might disagree, violating the First Amendment and ignoring Jefferson's admonition that "to compel a man to furnish contributions of money for the propagation of opinions which he disbelieves and abhors is sinful and tyrannical."[52] Many scholars see *Janus* as "stunning judicial activism" and "results-oriented hackery."[53] The Court did not take a small step but a sizable one, reversing in toto a long-standing precedent, disrupting thousands of union contracts affecting millions of employees, and unexpectedly requiring that new public employees must actively opt-in to join the union rather than passively consent by not opting out. The majority, furthermore, "usurp[ed] the democratic process," taking from the states their power to resolve an important policy debate regarding the value and costs of agency fees and public-sector unions and substituting their own views in place of the laws of twenty-two states.[54] As Justice Kagan noted in her dissent (and as echoed by Amanda Shanor):[55]

> The majority has chosen the winners [in this debate] by turning the First Amendment into a sword, and using it against workaday economic and regulatory policy. Today is not the first time the Court has wielded the First Amendment in such an aggressive way . . . and it threatens not to be the last. Speech is everywhere—a part of every human activity (employment, health care, securities trading, you name it). For that reason, almost all economic and regulatory policy affects or touches speech. So the majority's road runs long. And at every stop are black-robed rulers overriding citizens' choices. The First Amendment was meant for better things. It was meant not to undermine but to protect democratic governance—including over the role of public-sector unions.[56]

Kagan's dissent also highlighted the majority's "6-year crusade to ban agency fees,"[57] led by Justice Alito, who in cases like *Knox v. Service Employees International Union, Local 1000* (2012) and *Harris v. Quinn* (2014) supplied numerous and unnecessary criticisms of *Abood* that went well beyond those cases' narrow holdings.[58] In so doing, he put *Abood* "on death watch,"[59] "plant[ing] land mines . . . [and] begging for someone to petition the Court with a case that would allow the justices to address the First Amendment issues involved in fair-share agreements."[60] In his majority opinion in *Janus*, Alito cited his own language from *Knox* and *Harris* "more than 30 times as a way to create the illusion of how broken the system was—and how long the Supreme Court had held reservations about labor's use of fair-share fees. But in reality he was mostly citing his own words from the previous few terms."[61]

Citizens United also deserves special notice as an example of the Court's extraordinary activism. First, the ruling "had a profound effect" on existing state laws "governing corporate political activity;" many of the twenty-four states that, at the time of *Citizens United*, banned or limited campaign spending by corporations or unions subsequently revised or repealed their laws.[62] With respect to the majority's "aggressive overreaching,"[63] the attorneys for Citizens United had asked the Court only for a narrow ruling that nonprofit organizations and documentaries were exempt from the BCRA's restrictions on electioneering communications; they did not argue that those restrictions were themselves unconstitutional. On the last day of the term, however, Chief Justice Roberts, "in a highly unusual move,"[64] ordered a new round of arguments for the following term, instructing the parties to discuss whether *Austin* and *McConnell* should be revisited. This was correctly interpreted as an invitation to argue more broadly and aggressively against existing precedent, helping Roberts to "orchestrate . . . the *Citizens United* decision."[65] As Justice Stevens complained in his dissent, the Court's five conservatives "were unhappy with the limited nature of the case before us, so they changed the case to give themselves an opportunity to change the law."[66] Also unusual, oral argument in the case was rescheduled for September, before the Court's typical start on the first Monday in October. Finally, the strategic delay in the Court's decision prevented the publication of what would have been Justice Souter's final opinion prior to his retirement, a dissent described as "an extraordinary, bridge-burning farewell" that "aired some of the Court's dirty laundry."[67] Souter had, reportedly, harshly criticized Kennedy's majority opinion for overreaching and for a results-driven deviation from the traditional practice of deciding only legal questions that have been briefed by the parties.

The final noteworthy trend in the campaign finance field is the sharpening of partisan divisions within the Court. Over the last quarter of the twentieth century, the justices divided in campaign finance cases in ways that could not be predicted solely by ideology or partisanship. For example, the majorities in *Buckley* (1976), *Bellotti* (1978), *Citizens Against Rent Control* (1981), *MCFL* (1986), *Austin* (1990), *Nixon* (2000), and *Beaumont* (2003) consisted of both Democratic and Republican justices. In *Austin*, three Democrats and three Republicans upheld corporate spending limits in ballot measure campaigns, including both the most liberal justice at the time (Marshall) and the most conservative (Rehnquist). In *MCFL*, a bipartisan majority of three Democrats (including liberals Marshall and Brennan) and two Republicans (including the conservative Scalia) agreed that spending limits could not be applied to ideological nonprofit organizations. The *Nixon* majority upholding state limits on contributions to candidates consisted of two Democrats and four Republicans, and the *Beaumont* majority upholding the application of FECA's ban on corporate donations to nonprofit advocacy corporations contained two Democrats and five Republicans; the majority in both cases included the liberal Ginsburg and the conservative Rehnquist. Bipartisan majorities in campaign finance cases since 2005, however, have been quite rare. The majority was exclusively Republican in *WRTL* (2007), *Citizens United* (2010), *Bennett* (2011), *Bullock* (2012), *McCutcheon* (2014), and *Janus* (2018). Additionally, the last four cases on this list were decided in a strictly partisan way, with five Republicans in the majority and four Democrats dissenting. This represents an extraordinary change.

An important question, of course, is whether this change is driven by ideological preference rather than partisan favoritism. After all, the justices' votes were "ideologically ordered" in *Colorado Republican II, McConnell, Randall, WRTL, Davis, Citizens United, Bennett, Bullock,* and *McCutcheon.* A voting alignment is ideologically ordered when the dividing line between the majority and the dissenters does not disrupt the ideological array of the justices from most conservative to most liberal.[68] *McCutcheon* provides one such example where the voting alignment is not only partisan but is also ideologically ordered, since the majority consisted of the most conservative justices (in "descending" order, Thomas, Alito, Scalia, Roberts, and Kennedy) and the dissenters were the most liberal justices (descending further in a liberal direction, Breyer, Kagan, Sotomayor, and Ginsburg). In addition to this predictable ideological array, there is a growing "ideological gulf" between the conservative and liberal justices when it comes to campaign finance issues.[69] Ideology does not, however, always account for a justice's votes in campaign finance cases. After all, the bipartisan coalitions in cases like *Austin, MCFL,* and *Beaumont* included justices from opposite ends of the ideological spectrum. Additionally, Justice Alito's decisions in the campaign finance field are more easily explained in partisan than ideological terms, given that he is not typically a free-speech libertarian, as seen by his dissents in cases like *Snyder v. Phelps* and *U.S. v. Stevens.*[70] Finally, partisanship often explains Justice Scalia's decisions more effectively than would any consistent theory of democracy pertaining to self-dealing by incumbents or deference to legislatures; for example, Scalia expressed concern over self-dealing when it came to campaign finance but not partisan gerrymandering, and he deferred to Congress on the Defense of Marriage Act but not the Voting Rights Act.[71]

It is possible, of course, that both ideology and partisanship could be at work in sharpening voting divisions on the Court in campaign finance cases. Kyle Kopko's 2010 study, for example, found that judicial policy preferences and partisan affiliation both independently influenced votes in campaign finance cases decided by federal district courts and courts of appeals over the 1962 to 2007 period.[72] In fact, of the three election law topics he examined—campaign finance, right to association, and redistricting—campaign finance was the only one in which judicial partisanship had an independent, statistically significant effect on case votes. Kopko's subsequent study of campaign finance cases over the 1971 to 2007 period found that US district court judges were significantly less likely to rule in favor of opposite-party plaintiffs, even when controlling for judicial ideology, although there was no such systematic partisan effect when it came to same-party plaintiffs.[73] While it is difficult to disentangle partisan and ideological influences in this area, it is not impossible.

The GOP's Mission to End Campaign Finance Limits

The Supreme Court's Republican majority has acted aggressively to alter First Amendment doctrine and deregulate the campaign finance marketplace. It remains to discuss why it has done so and with what impact. As with other recent election law changes, regime politics theory offers helpful insights, pointing to the importance of external developments such as the rise of the Reagan regime, the sharp rightward shift of Republican elites, and coalition weaknesses that triggered an intense concern with judicial appointments and election reform. With regard to the latter, campaign finance has received an extraordinary amount of attention from the GOP. It has recently included multiple planks in its national platforms opposing a variety of campaign finance regulations, it has been busy at the state level advancing its preferred legislative proposals, and it has lent support to a vigorous First Amendment litigation campaign launched by business interests and conservative legal groups.

As previously noted and as evident in their national platforms, the Republican Party has shifted sharply to the right on a variety of policy topics, including immigration, civil rights, taxes, climate change, abortion, health care, and same-sex marriage. This is also true for campaign finance. Table 5.2 provides a summary of each party's key statements relating to campaign finance in their national platforms from 1968 to 2016. The most obvious pattern, like with the parties more generally, is growing and asymmetrical polarization, with the two parties taking increasingly divergent positions on campaign finance and the GOP disproportionately responsible for that growing gap. The Democratic Party, for example, has consistently expressed concern over the distorting effect of "big money" and favored public disclosure, contribution limits, expenditure limits, and public financing of federal campaigns; it

Table 5.2. National Party Platform Statements Regarding Campaign Finance, 1968–2016

Year	Republican Party	Democratic Party
1968	"We favor a new Election Reform Act that will apply clear, reasonable restraints to political spending and fund-raising, whether by business, labor, or individuals, ensure timely publication of the financial facts in campaigns, and provide a tax deduction for small contributions."	"We are alarmed at the growing costs of political participation in our country and the consequent reliance of political parties and candidates on large contributors, and we want to assure full public information on campaign expenditures. To encourage citizen participation we urge that limited campaign contributions be made deductible as a credit from the federal income tax."
1972		"A total overhaul of the present system of financing elections is a national necessity. Candidates should not be dependent on large contributors who seek preferential treatment. We call for Congressional action to provide for public financing of more election costs by 1974. We recommend a statutory ceiling on political gifts at a reasonable limit. Publicly owned communications facilities such as television, radio and the postal service should be made available, but on a limited basis, to candidates for federal Office."
1976 1980	"Republicans support public policies that encourage political activity by individual citizens. We support the repeal of those restrictive campaign spending limitations that tend to create obstacles to local grassroots participation in federal elections. We also oppose the	"Recent reforms in the election process have aided immeasurably in opening the process to more people and have begun to reduce the influence of special interests. The limitations on campaign contributions and the public financing of Presidential elections are two

reforms which have worked very well. Business political action committees continue to spend excessively, however. Further reform in this area is essential. In the 1980s we need to enact reforms which will: Provide for public financing of Congressional campaigns; Lower contribution limits for political action committees; Close the loophole that allows private spending in Presidential elections contrary to the intent of the election law reforms."

"We must work to end political action committee funding of federal political campaigns. To achieve that, we must enact a system of public financing of federal campaigns."

"We believe that this country's democratic processes must be revitalized: by . . . minimizing the domination and distortion of our elections by moneyed interests."

"It's time to reform the campaign finance system, to get

(*continued on the next page*)

proposed financing of Congressional campaigns with taxpayers' dollars as an effort by the Democratic Party to protect its incumbent Members of Congress with a tax subsidy."

1984   "The expression of individual political views is guaranteed by the First Amendment; government should protect, not impinge upon First Amendment rights. Free individuals must have unrestricted access to the process of self-government. We deplore the growing labyrinth of bewildering regulations and obstacles which have increased the power of political professionals and discouraged the participation of average Americans. Even well-intentioned restrictions on campaign activity stifle free speech and have a chilling effect on spontaneous political involvement by our citizens."

1988   "Republicans want to broaden involvement in the political process. We oppose government controls that make it harder for average citizens to be politically active. We especially condemn the congressional Democrats' scheme to force taxpayer funding of campaigns."

1992   "We crusade for clean elections. . . . Most of all, we

Table 5.2. *Continued*

Year	Republican Party	Democratic Party
	condemn the Democrats' shameless plots to make taxpayers foot the bills for their campaigns. Their campaign finance bill would have given $1 billion, over six years, in subsidies to candidates. President Bush vetoed that bill. Campaign financing does need reform. It does not need a hand in the public's pocketbook. We will require congressional candidates to raise most of their funds from individuals within their home constituencies. This will limit outside special-interest money and result in less expensive campaigns, with less padding for incumbents. . . . We will eliminate political action committees supported by corporations, unions, or trade associations, and restrict the practice of bundling. . . . To restore competition in elections by attacking the unfair advantages of incumbency, we will stop incumbents from warding off challengers merely by amassing huge war chests. Congressional candidates will be forbidden from carrying campaign funds from one election to the next. We will oppose arbitrary spending limits—cynical devices which hobble challengers to keep politicians in office. . . . We will fully implement the Supreme Court's decision in the *Beck* case, ensuring that workers have the right to stop the use of their union dues for political or other non-collective bargaining purposes."	big money out of our politics and let the people back in. We must limit overall campaign spending and limit the disproportionate and excessive role of PACs."

1996	"Special interests have too much power in the halls of government. They often operate in secret and have special privileges ordinary Americans do not even know exist. Elections have become so expensive that big money can sometimes drown out the voices of ordinary voters—who should always speak the loudest. . . . The President and the Democratic Party support the bipartisan McCain-Feingold campaign finance reform bill. It will limit campaign spending, curb the influence of PACs and lobbyists, and end the soft money system. Perhaps most important of all, this bill provides free TV time for candidates, so they can talk directly to citizens about real issues and real ideas. Unfortunately, Republicans in Congress will not even let this bill come up for a vote. We call on them to stop stonewalling. It is time to take the reins of democracy away from big money and put them back in the hands of the American people, where they belong."	"We will eliminate made-in-Washington schemes to rig the election process under the guise of campaign reform. True reform is indeed needed: ending taxpayer subsidies for campaigns, strengthening party structures to guard against rogue operations, requiring full and immediate disclosure of all contributions, and cracking down on the indirect support, or 'soft money,' by which special interest groups underwrite their favored candidates."
2000	"We must restore Americans' faith in their own democracy by providing real and comprehensive campaign finance reform, creating fairer and more open elections, and breaking the link between special interests and political influence. The Republicans will have none of this. Instead of limiting the influence of the powerful on our politics, they want to raise contribution limits so even more special interest money can flow into campaigns. The big-time lobbyists and special interests were so eager	"The Republican party affirms that any regulation of the political process must not infringe upon the rights of the people to full participation in the political process. . . . Governor Bush's agenda for more honest and more open politics . . . will: Stop the abuses of corporate and labor 'soft' money contributions to political parties. Enact 'Paycheck Protection,' ensuring that no union member is forced to contribute to anybody's campaign—and stopping an annual rip-off of $300 million from

(continued on the next page)

Table 5.2. *Continued*

Year	Republican Party	Democratic Party
	union families by Washington-based politicos. Preserve the right of every individual and all groups—whether for us or against us—to express their opinions and advocate their issues. We will not allow any arm of government to restrict this constitutionally guaranteed right. Level the playing field by forbidding incumbents to roll over their leftover campaign funds into a campaign for a different office. Require full and timely disclosure on the Internet of all campaign contributions—so the media and the public can immediately know who is giving how much to whom. Encourage all citizens to donate their time and resources to the campaigns of their choice by updating for inflation the quarter-century-old limits on individual contributions."	to invest in George W. Bush and deliver campaign cash to him hand-over-fist that he became the first major party nominee to pull out of the primary election financing structure and refuse to abide by campaign spending limits. In this year's presidential primaries it became clear that the Republican establishment is violently opposed to John McCain's call for reforming our democracy. Al Gore supports John McCain's campaign for political reform. In fact, the McCain-Feingold bill is the very first piece of legislation that a President Al Gore will submit to Congress—and he will fight for it until it becomes the law of the land. . . . Most boldly of all, Al Gore has proposed a public-private, non-partisan Democracy Endowment which will raise money from Americans and finance Congressional elections—with no other contributions allowed to candidates who accept the funding. This will let our politics be free from the influence of special interests and let Americans believe in their own democracy again."
2004		
2008	"The rights of citizenship do not stop at the ballot box. They include the free-speech right to devote one's resources to whatever cause or candidate one supports.	"We support campaign finance reform to reduce the influence of moneyed special interests, including public financing of campaigns combined with free television

We oppose any restrictions or conditions upon those activities that would discourage Americans from exercising their constitutional right to enter the political fray or limit their commitment to their ideals."

2012 "The rights of citizenship do not stop at the ballot box. They include the free speech right to devote one's resources to whatever cause or candidate one supports. We oppose any restrictions or conditions that would discourage Americans from exercising their constitutional right to enter the political fray or limit their commitment to their ideals. As a result, we support repeal of the remaining sections of McCain-Feingold, support either raising or repealing contribution limits, and oppose passage of the DISCLOSE Act or any similar legislation designed to vitiate the Supreme Court's recent decisions protecting political speech in *Wisconsin Right to Life v. Federal Election Commission* and *Citizens United v. Federal Election Commission*. . . . To safeguard the free choice of public employees, no government at any level should act as the dues collector for unions. A Republican President will protect the rights of conscience of public employees by proposing legislation to bar mandatory dues for political purposes."

2016 "Freedom of speech includes the right to devote resources to whatever cause or candidate one supports. We oppose any restrictions or conditions that would discourage citizens from participating in the public square or limit

and radio time. We will have the wisdom to put the public interest above special interests. As a national party, we will not take any contributions from Political Action Committees during this election."

"Our political system is under assault by those who believe that special interests should be able to buy whatever they want in our society, including our government. Our opponents have applauded the Supreme Court's decision in *Citizens United* and welcomed the new flow of special interest money with open arms. In stark contrast, we believe we must take immediate action to curb the influence of lobbyists and special interests on our political institutions. . . . We support campaign finance reform, by constitutional amendment if necessary. We support legislation to close loopholes and require greater disclosure of campaign spending. . . . We support requiring groups trying to influence elections to reveal their donors so the public will know who's funding the political ads it sees. President Obama and the Democrats are fighting to reduce the influence of money in politics, and holding Congress to higher conflict-of-interest standards."

"We will fight to reform our broken campaign finance system, which gives outsized influence to billionaires and big corporations. It's time we give back control of our elections to those to whom it belongs—the American

(continued on the next page)

Table 5.2. *Continued*

Year	Republican Party	Democratic Party
	their ability to promote their ideas, such as requiring private organizations to publicly disclose their donors to the government. Limits on political speech serve only to protect the powerful and insulate incumbent officeholders. We support repeal of federal restrictions on political parties in McCain-Feingold, raising or repealing contribution limits, protecting the political speech of advocacy groups, corporations, and labor unions, and protecting political speech on the internet. We likewise call for an end to the so-called Fairness Doctrine, and support free-market approaches to free speech unregulated by government. We believe the forced funding of political candidates through union dues and other mandatory contributions violates the First Amendment. Just as Americans have a First Amendment right to devote resources to favored candidates or views, they have a First Amendment right not to be forced to individually support individuals or ideologies that they oppose. We agree with Thomas Jefferson that 'To compel a man to furnish contributions of money for the propagation of opinions which he disbelieves and abhors is sinful and tyrannical.'"	people. . . . We will fight for real campaign finance reform now. Big money is drowning out the voices of everyday Americans, and we must have the necessary tools to fight back and safeguard our electoral and political integrity. Democrats support a constitutional amendment to overturn the Supreme Court's decisions in *Citizens United* and *Buckley v. Valeo*. We need to end secret, unaccountable money in politics by requiring, through executive order or legislation, significantly more disclosure and transparency. We need to amplify the voices of the American people through a small donor matching public financing system. We need to overhaul and strengthen the Federal Election Commission so that there is real enforcement of campaign finance laws. And we need to fight to eliminate super PACs and outside spending abuses. . . . We will appoint judges who defend the constitutional principles of liberty and equality for all, and will . . . curb billionaires' influence over elections because they understand that *Citizens United* has fundamentally damaged our democracy, and believe the Constitution protects not only the powerful, but also the disadvantaged and powerless."

has also periodically proposed making free air time available for federal candidates. In contrast, platform statements by the Republican Party do not convey a stable message but an evolving one. In 1968, for example, the GOP favored public disclosure and "clear, reasonable restraints to political spending and fund-raising, whether by business, labor or individuals." In 1972 and 1976 the party offered no planks relating to campaign finance, likely due to the prominence of the Watergate scandal that stained a Republican White House and led to Nixon's resignation. In addition to favoring various campaign finance regulations in its 1968 platform, the GOP has periodically supported other reforms like public disclosure (in 1968, 1996, and 2000), the "eliminat[ion]" of corporate and union PACs (in 1992), and a "crack down" on soft money donations (in 1996 and 2000). Republican hostility to campaign finance regulations sometimes appeared in the 1980s and 1990s, such as opposition to spending limits and mandatory agency fees for unions in 1992 and Democratic public financing proposals on four different occasions. The party's broadest and most strident antiregulatory views, however, appear in its 2008, 2012, and 2016 platforms, with the GOP expressing unequivocal opposition to "any restrictions or conditions [on] . . . the free speech right to devote one's resources to whatever cause or candidate one supports." Additionally, the 2012 and 2016 platforms opposed mandatory union fees, urged the repeal of contribution limits and other surviving provisions of the Bipartisan Campaign Reform Act, and opposed the DISCLOSE Act that would strengthen disclosure requirements and ban contributions from US corporations with 20 percent or more foreign ownership.

The GOP has sought to achieve these increasingly antiregulatory platform planks in multiple ways. There have been extensive legislative efforts involving campaign finance across the states in recent years. The National Conference of State Legislatures (NCSL), for example, reports that 782 bills pertaining to campaign finance were introduced in forty-eight states in 2018, and at least 600 have been introduced in each year from 2015 through 2018; a narrower search in the NCSL's database for bills involving contribution limits, disclosure, independent expenditures, and public financing revealed that, on average, 341 bills were introduced in the states in each year from 2015 through 2018.[74] There is, of course, considerable variation in the campaign finance reforms that states have considered and adopted. In 2017, for example, twenty-three states revised their campaign finance laws, with many enhancing criminal and civil penalties; some states (California and Oregon) strengthened and others (Kentucky, North Dakota, and Utah) weakened public disclosure rules; Maryland and Michigan banned campaign contributions and expenditures by foreign nationals in candidate and ballot-initiative campaigns; Iowa repealed key provisions of its public financing system; and South Dakota legislators overturned a sweeping campaign finance and ethics law adopted by voters the previous year. When it comes to Congress, Republicans have mostly played defense and successfully prevented campaign proposals like the DISCLOSE Act from receiving floor consideration. Senate Majority Leader Mitch McConnell has long served as a reliable foe when it comes to campaign finance regulation, helping to block a variety of proposals, including multiple bills sponsored by his copartisan colleague, the late senator John McCain. McConnell's recent efforts include trying to ensure that the first bill passed by the Democratic House in 2019, the For the People Act that includes campaign finance reforms, never received floor time or a vote.

Republicans have also pursued judicial strategies to accomplish their campaign finance policy agenda, both by placing conservatives on the bench and by joining forces with a "business-led social movement [that] has mobilized to embed libertarian-leaning understandings of the First Amendment in constitutional jurisprudence."[75] This represents a considerable change from the absolutist First Amendment arguments that were, in the past, successfully offered by progressive groups representing union workers, journalists, and racial minorities.[76] As Jack Balkin explains, "business interests and other conservative groups [have found] . . . that arguments for property rights and the social status quo can more and more easily be rephrased in the language of the first amendment by using the very same absolutist forms of argument offered by the left in previous generations"; what he characterizes as "ideological drift" means that "what was sauce for the liberal goose increasingly has become sauce for the more conservative gander."[77] Reliance on the First Amendment—a specific and enumerated provision in the Constitution—has, some believe, further enhanced the potency of the movement's legal arguments, particularly "in marshaling the support of . . . conservative judges and justices for [its] deregulatory project."[78]

This litigation campaign has "weaponized the First Amendment" and enabled the Court to alter campaign finance law in critical cases like *WRTL*, *Citizens United*, and *McCutcheon*.[79] Ann Southworth's research reveals that, perhaps unsurprisingly, the lawyers, amici participants, and foundation patrons in these cases "fall into well-defined opposing and partisan camps."[80] For instance, in *Citizens United* the Republican National Committee and Republican-aligned organizations like the US Chamber of Commerce, the National Rifle Association, and Tea Party groups filed briefs on behalf of Citizens United, whereas Democratic members of Congress, the Democratic National Committee, Common Cause, the Brennan Center for Justice, and US PIRG provided briefs siding with the FEC. The Federalist Society has actively organized and participated in campaign finance cases for nearly two decades; it has offered both "a set of litigators finding and bringing well-framed cases and a set of academics working to nurture and develop the intellectual capital that might be used to justify such a radical departure from existing constitutional frames."[81] *Citizens United*, for example, was sponsored by James Bopp, general counsel for the National Right to Life Committee and the James Madison Center for Free Speech, which had also represented Wisconsin Right to Life; Bopp soon thereafter served as co-chair of the RNC's "We the People: A Restoration of Constitutional Government" committee that wrote the party's 2012 platform planks with respect to campaign finance. Ted Olsen, solicitor general under George W. Bush, also served as lead attorney in *Citizens United*. As Amanda Hollis-Brusky further documents, thirteen Federalist Society members signed briefs supporting Citizens United, and eleven Supreme Court clerks at the time were affiliated with the Federalist Society, as were one district court judge and four Supreme Court justices. Those justices' opinions, furthermore, heavily cited Federalist Society scholarship, including that of Bradley Smith, a former FEC chair and an "intellectual powerhouse" in the conservative movement against campaign finance regulation.[82] As Southworth explains, the GOP and various party-affiliated groups "served up promising test cases, funded their progress through the courts, attracted skilled appellate advocates to present their positions, coordinated party and amicus support, and projected consensus among varied amici, which gave the Court a basis for finding that a broad range of affected constituencies supported the rulings;" some of the lawyers interviewed by Southworth "also claimed partial responsibility for encouraging the Court in *Citizens United* to 'go big.'"[83]

The Republican Party has also long engaged in a broad-based attack on labor unions and worker rights. It has done so in party platforms, legislative proposals, and litigation. The group that has been most active in the litigation campaign is the National Right to Work Legal Defense Foundation (NRWLDF); in fact, it has since 1985 participated in as many cases, either as direct party or amicus, as the NAACP.[84] The NRWLDF has brought multiple lawsuits before the Supreme Court in its campaign against public-sector unions, including *Abood*, *Knox*, *Harris*, and *Janus*. It was able to keep the latter lawsuit alive by agreeing to represent state employee Mark Janus, even though the case was triggered by the actions of Illinois Republican governor Bruce Rauner, a wealthy anti-union businessman. In his first month in office, the governor had ordered the state's payroll agency to stop paying to the union the fair-share fees of state workers.[85] Joining the NRWLDF before the Supreme Court was the Trump administration, whose brief urged a reversal of *Abood*, a position also advanced in multiple amicus briefs submitted by business groups, Republican states, and conservative legal groups.[86]

The Reagan regime has also invested considerable effort in making conservative appointments to the federal bench, increasing the chances that the courts would be receptive to the innovative, and some would say extreme, First Amendment arguments of groups like the Federalist Society and the NRWLDF. The evidence does indeed show a sharp increase in the willingness of the Court to entertain free speech claims by conservative groups. Lee Epstein, Andrew Martin, and Kevin Quinn report that only 8 percent of First Amendment cases in the Warren Court involved conservative speech, compared to 22 percent in the Burger Court, 42 percent in the Rehnquist Court, and 65 percent in the Roberts Court.[87] In a similar vein, Lawrence Baum reports a sharp decline in the percentage of free expression cases involving claimants on the left, who comprised 65 percent of free expression cases in the Warren Court but only 16 percent in the early Rehnquist Court and 8 percent in the late Rehnquist Court.[88] This "suggests a fundamental transformation of the Court's free expression agenda likely spearheaded by a combination of attorneys, organizations, and the case-selection process."[89] Not only is the Roberts Court much more likely to accept for review cases in which the government is alleged to have suppressed conservative expression, it also is more likely to rule in favor of conservative speakers over liberal ones. Whereas the Warren Court ruled in favor of speech claims around 80 percent of the time, regardless of their ideological character, the Roberts Court has favored conservative speech claims at a much higher rate (69 percent) than liberal speech claims (21 percent). Additionally, the Roberts Court is distinctive from earlier courts in that partisan differences among the justices in their free-speech support scores are statistically significant; Republican appointees on the Roberts Court have ruled in favor of conservative speech 68 percent of the time and liberal speech 24 percent of the time while the Democratic appointees supported conservative speech 42 percent of the time and liberal speech 47 percent of the time.[90]

The Court's transformation of campaign finance doctrine and its activist and partisan approach are the product of several developments external to the Court—the rise of the Reagan regime; its electoral vulnerability that magnifies the importance of election rules, such as those involving voting and campaign finance; a sharp rightward shift by the party on multiple issues, including campaign finance; a vigorous First Amendment litigation campaign advancing deregulation and defending corporate interests and attacking unions; and a new and intense dedication by the GOP to appointing conservative, originalist justices largely drawn from the Federalist Society. Decisions like *Citizens United* and *Janus* show that the GOP's efforts have been extraordinarily successful.

The Impact of the Court's Deregulatory Shift in Campaign Finance Law

What, however, has been the impact of the Court's deregulatory turn in the campaign finance field? Although there is no doubt that doctrine has shifted sharply to the right and in favor of GOP preferences, has this change been a boon to the party's fundraising efforts and electoral prospects? There is, in fact, little research devoted to this question. It would be surprising, however, given our general knowledge about campaign finance, to find a direct, sizable, and distinctively partisan impact.

This is not what we would expect given the intensity of the GOP's deregulatory crusade and the virulence of Democratic attacks on *Citizens United*. In his 2010 State of the Union address, President Obama condemned *Citizens United*, decided just the week before, for "revers[ing] a century of law that . . . will open the floodgates for special interests—including foreign corporations—to spend without limit in our elections. I don't think American elections should be bankrolled by America's most powerful interests or, worse, by foreign entities."[91] In a 2015 press release, the president added that the "dark money" enabled by *Citizens United* "pulls our politics into the gutter."[92] Hillary Clinton, in her 2016

presidential campaign, pledged to introduce a constitutional amendment reversing *Citizens United* within thirty days of taking office in order
"to protect against the undue influence of billionaires and special interests."[93] Employing particularly harsh language, US senator Sheldon
Whitehouse (D-RI) criticized *Citizens United* as an "appalling" decision
that "unleashed" torrents of outside corporate spending—a "tsunami
of slime" contributing to the "pollution of our democracy."[94] This "near
ubiquitous tale," as Heather Gerken characterizes it, claims that *Citizens United* "ushered in a new era of corporate spending, with wealthy
corporations spending wildly, saturating the airwaves, and taking over
American politics."[95]

Careful analysis of spending in the election cycles following *Citizens United* has failed to confirm these horror stories, offering instead
a more complicated set of findings. First, "direct corporate spending in
elections over the past decade" has not exploded, with "few for-profit
corporations spend[ing] money in their own names boosting or diss-
ing candidates."[96] Quite simply, the direct "influx of corporate cash in
elections" expected from *Citizens United* "has yet to be observed."[97] This
is likely due to risk-averse businesses following "prudentially pusillani-
mous policies" in order to avoid negative publicity and a potentially
hostile public reaction, such as a product boycott.[98]

It is, nonetheless, true that nonparty independent spending has sky-
rocketed in recent years, reaching more than $500 million in 2014, com-
pared to $44 million in 2008, with "Supreme Court decisions spurr[ing]
this trend" and *Citizens United* "assuring the continued growth of outside
spending in future elections."[99] Some claim that the increase in outside
spending began prior to *Citizens United*[100] and that the Court merely "le-
galized an outside spending regime for non-party entities that had been
taking shape since the 1990s."[101] In other words, the Court in *Citizens
United* "sanctioned . . . [preexisting] loopholes . . . as core First Amendment activity" and thereby "turned a license into a blessing."[102] This is
a decidedly minority opinion, however. Most observers credit *Citizens
United* with having "fundamentally altered the financial power dynamics
of federal elections," including paving the way for "Super PACs, 501(c)4
social welfare organizations and 501(c)6 professional associations . . .
[to] become the dominant spenders in congressional contests."[103]

These organizational forms require some explanation. Super PACs
emerged after two key cases in 2010: *Citizens United*, which banned restrictions on independent spending by unions and corporations, and

SpeechNOW.org v. Federal Election Commission, an en banc District of Columbia Circuit Court decision ruling that government could not limit contributions to PACs that engage only in independent spending.[104] An FEC advisory opinion subsequently confirmed that individuals, unions, and corporations could make unlimited donations to "independent-expenditure only committees." These committees came to be known as Super PACs, attracting considerable attention in 2012 by spending extraordinary sums in federal races—over $600 million according to US PIRG and Demos.[105] Their analysis of FEC data from the 2012 election cycle nonetheless revealed that 70 percent of donations to Super PACs came from individuals, compared to only 11 percent from businesses and 5.5 percent from unions; furthermore, 60 percent of Super PAC donations came from 132 individuals giving at least $1 million.[106] Much has been made, perhaps too much, of the substantially greater role in Super PAC funding of "wealthy mega-donors" compared to corporations.[107] This overlooks, however, other significant avenues for corporate spending in election campaigns, including tax-exempt 501(c)4 "social welfare" organizations that engage in issue advocacy and 501(c)6 business league and trade association organizations that promote the common business interests of their members. Because these groups are not required to reveal their contributors, their spending has been referred to as "dark money," with observers concerned about their growing role in federal elections.[108] Democratic critics additionally point to the dominance of conservative organizations in spending by 501(c) groups. According to the Center for Responsive Politics, seven of the top ten spenders in the 501(c)4 and 501(c)6 categories in the 2016 election cycle represented conservative or business interests, including the US Chamber of Commerce (second), the pro-Trump "45 Committee" (third), and the Koch-funded Americans for Prosperity (fourth).[109]

An additional question relating to *Citizens United*'s impact asks whether such outside spending affects election outcomes. A 2017 study by Meilan Chaturvedi and Coleen Holloway found that independent expenditures in the 2010, 2012, and 2014 Senate races in the wake of *Citizens United* had a very small effect on candidate vote share and "paled in significance compared to challenger spending."[110] Victoria Farrar-Myers and Richard Skinner report similar findings for the small impact of independent expenditures on election results in the House.[111] Anne Baker's study focused more narrowly on whether early spending by outside groups served either to "undermine or augment" candidate spending; she found no such impact for super PACs, but a significant and negative effect for spending by 501(c) dark-money organizations.[112] Studies of the impact of independent spending on candidate success and electoral competition are, however, quite few in number. What we generally know is that money is one of many factors, such as candidate quality and voter mobilization, that can affect election outcomes, with its influence stronger under certain conditions: in close contests, in low-expenditure rather than high-expenditure races, and for challengers as compared to incumbents.[113] Nonetheless, it is important to acknowledge that independent groups have tended to concentrate their spending on competitive races, where they hope to have a greater impact. For example, independent spending accounted for nearly 60 percent of the $667 million that was spent in 2014 in nine "toss-up" Senate races, including over 70 percent of the $83 million spent in the contest in Iowa between Democrat Bruce Braley and Republican Joni Ernst.[114]

The problem with outside expenditures representing a growing share of election spending is that such money is less visible and less accountable compared to candidate and party spending.[115] Campaign advertising that is independently financed also tends to be more negative and more deceptive.[116] There are also concerns over whether these expenditures are indeed truly independent as required by law, rather than being coordinated with a candidate's campaign; experience has shown that the dividing line between the two is often blurry.[117] Finally, donors who give to candidates and independent expenditure-only groups like Super PACs are highly unrepresentative; they are disproportionately white, older, male, wealthy, and ideologically extreme, with the latter feature possibly contributing to America's growing polarization and the misalignment between voter preferences on the one hand and legislator preferences and policy outcomes on the other.[118] Balkin has argued, in a similar vein, that *Citizens United* may ironically have hurt the Republican Party as candidates must engage in "radical positioning on the right" to please these ideologically extreme "financial 'warlords' [who] increasingly call the tune in candidate selection and in primary challenges."[119]

Finally, Raymond La Raja and Brian Schaffner's 2014 study deserves special mention.[120] Unlike most studies that focus on candidate spending, their research looked at outside spending and took advantage of the fact that when states had the freedom to choose—that is, prior to *Citizens United* in 2010—they varied in whether they banned or permitted corporate and union election spending. For example, twenty-one states banned corporate spending for at least part of the 1967 to 2008 period that La Raja and Schaffner studied. Their empirical analysis of the impact of state variation with respect to outside spending rules demonstrated that "corporate spending bans have little effect on who wins elections," whether incumbents compared to challengers or Republicans compared to Democrats.[121] There was, however, a very small partisan effect in a few states—Kentucky, Oklahoma, and Wisconsin—and, contrary to expectations, that effect favored Republican candidates. Additional research by La Raja confirmed that the Republican Party did not fare better in states that permit unlimited corporate spending, although GOP seat-share in the legislature suffered a small drop in states that banned corporate *contributions*; this effect, however, was found only in states with small government budgets.[122] Although more research on this question is obviously needed, these two studies suggest that we should "treat with skepticism any claims that *Citizens United* will catapult pro-business Republicans into office."[123] There is little doubt, however, that Republican leaders *believe* that an unregulated campaign finance marketplace helps their party, whether or not it is supported by political science research, and they have worked hard to bend the law in that deregulatory direction.

The impact of *Janus* on campaign finance is a separate but equally important question. The Mackinac Center predicted that public-sector unions would lose as many as three million members and hundreds of millions of dollars in revenues.[124] Its likely partisan impact—a "Big Loss for the coffers of the Democrats!"—was noted in a tweet by President Trump on the day that *Janus* was decided. It is difficult not to see significant losses in union membership, revenues, and power as the primary intention, and the clearly partisan intention, of the campaign to end agency fees for public-sector unions. Even Justice Alito has had difficulty hiding his hostility to public-sector unions; his majority opinion in *Janus* blamed them for runaway state and local spending and labeled the billions of dollars they have received since *Abood* an "unconstitutional exaction" and illegitimate "windfall."[125]

Reports with respect to the impact of *Janus* have been mixed, however, and caution is needed for assessments that are made only a year or two out from the ruling. According to Daniel DiSalvo, public-sector unions have lost substantial revenues, for example, $3.4 million in Connecticut and an estimated $100 million in New York.[126] The National Education Association planned for a 15 percent drop in revenue, and the

Service Employees International Union cut its budget by 30 percent in response to *Janus*.[127] Reduced revenues for public-sector unions would also be expected to reduce union donations to a variety of liberal groups and causes. America Votes, for example, received more than 20 percent of its $10 million budget from public-sector unions in 2016, and the Economic Policy Institute depends on public-sector unions for up to 15 percent of its $6 million annual revenue.[128] Lost revenues for public-sector unions also mean reduced donations to Democratic candidates; in 2016, the four largest public-sector unions contributed 15 percent of the $17 million raised by the Democratic Legislative Campaign Committee, which funds state legislative races.[129] These reductions in donations and spending by public-sector unions could have electoral impacts; one study, for example, found that passage of right-to-work laws that eliminate agency fees for both private and public unions reduced Democratic vote shares in presidential elections by 3.5 percent.[130] Another expected impact of *Janus*, given that worker pay is historically lower in states without agency fee requirements, is reduced wages, estimated to be on average $1,800 per year for public-sector workers; these wage losses would be disproportionately experienced by African Americans, who are overrepresented among state and local government employees.[131]

It is important to acknowledge contrary assessments, such as Rebecca Rainey and Ian Kullgren's claim that "1 year after *Janus*, unions are flush."[132] They assert that public-employee unions have lost some members but are maintaining and, in some cases, increasing their revenues. More time is obviously needed to confirm *Janus*'s impact, particularly since many states have enacted new laws seeking to minimize the damage inflicted by the Court's ruling.[133] New York, New Jersey, and Washington, for example, made union recruiting easier by insuring that unions have access to new employees' personal contact information and allowing union representatives to meet with them for recruiting purposes during work hours. Such laws have also restricted access to new employees' contact information to outside, and possibly anti-union, groups, a strategy that had been employed by Governor Bruce Rauner as he sought to implement *Janus* in Illinois.[134] New York has enacted a state tax deduction for union dues, and some states are considering the more radical step of partial government reimbursement of public-sector unions' collective bargaining costs.[135] Unions, often with state support as in New Jersey and California, have also limited the window during which union members can renounce their membership, reducing it to a ten-

or fifteen-day period. Some blue states have also allowed unions to withhold benefits like life insurance and legal representation in grievance proceedings to nonunion employees. How much public-sector unions will suffer depends on the actions of state legislatures in extending or withholding assistance in a post-*Janus* world. It will also depend critically on courts, both federal and state, that are currently deciding legal challenges to these new state laws. An important research question asks what role judges might play in these intense partisan battles over public-sector unions and whether partisanship will affect their decisions. Of greatest concern to union leaders are class-action lawsuits challenging unions' statutory right to exclusive representation and demanding the retroactive refund of agency fees collected prior to *Janus*, a claim to which Justice Alito appears sympathetic. Multiple cases are percolating in the lower courts, and the Court may accept some for review, although it declined in April 2019 to hear *Uradnik v. Inter Faculty Organization*, an Eighth Circuit case challenging exclusive public-employee union representation.[136]

Conclusion

The electorally vulnerable Reagan regime has unsurprisingly focused on election law in order to enhance its competitiveness and sustain its power. Campaign finance has received considerable attention from Republican politicians and party leaders as part of that effort. They have taken their fight to the legislatures and to the courts. With regard to the latter, they have supported a well-funded and well-organized litigation campaign launched by business interests and conservative legal groups that employ the First Amendment as the vehicle for ending campaign finance restrictions and weakening public-sector unions. They have also worked closely with groups like the Federalist Society to place conservatives and libertarians on the bench who are more receptive to those arguments.

These partisan efforts have been extremely successful in the campaign finance field. Under the Court's new "First Amendment Lochnerism,"[137] the doctrinal rules with respect to campaign finance have been altered in favor of GOP preferences. The Court has, for example, removed aggregate limits on campaign contributions, restrictions on corporate spending, and government-mandated agency fees for public-sector unions—positions that are all found in recent national platforms of the Republican Party. The Court has also divided on these issues in a more sharply partisan way and executed these doctrinal changes in an unusually muscular fashion. This is in no small part enabled by a litigation support structure that has effectively laid the intellectual groundwork for the Court to take sizable doctrinal steps.[138] Even so, the impact of these doctrinal changes has not been as substantial or as partisan as critics have warned, though more research on more election cycles is needed. *Janus* could, as the Republican Party and its business allies intended, substantially reduce public-sector union membership and revenues, as well as donations to Democratic candidates and causes. It is still too early to tell, however, particularly given the efforts of Democratic legislatures to enact policies that mitigate *Janus*'s impact. Courts will, of course, be invited to review these new policies, and public-sector unions should not count on support from the Republican-majority Supreme Court.

The expectation of most election law experts is that the Roberts Court is not finished, and that "the project of the . . . *Citizens United* justices to blow up campaign finance limits continues apace."[139] Disclosure rules are providing an area of "newfound partisan polarization," with considerable pressure "being brought to bear on the existing legal framework for judging disclosure regulation."[140] With Justice Gorsuch less supportive of disclosure rules than his predecessor, Antonin Scalia, "campaign finance disclosure . . . is under threat."[141] Justice Kavanaugh is expected to be at least as hostile to campaign finance regulation as his predecessor, Justice Kennedy, and to support further extensions of the Court's deregulatory agenda. He has, for example, expressed constitutional concerns about contribution limits, which will likely come before the Court in the near future.[142] It is difficult to dispute John Nichols's characterization of recent Republican justices as "conservative judicial activists" and "conservative judicial strategists" who have constructed a First Amendment jurisprudence that is "pro-corporate" and "anti-union" and strongly supportive in the campaign finance field of the antiregulatory aims of their "partisan allies."[143] It is also difficult to imagine a better example of election law being forged between friends.

Conclusion

I now reflect on what has been learned about the relationship between courts and parties after examining four contemporary election law controversies. Additionally, I explore the important normative issues that are raised by the presence of partisan supremacy and friendly judicial review in the election law field. Finally, I speculate on the future of election law and American politics, particularly in light of Donald Trump's late-regime, and likely disjunctive, presidency.

Reviewing the Evidence

Significant cracks in the New Deal–Great Society regime appeared with Richard Nixon's election in 1968, and its collapse was complete by Ronald Reagan's landslide victory in 1980. While the resulting New Right Republican regime has been strong, its electoral performance and control over political institutions has not been as dominant and extensive as that of the previous Democratic regime. In fact, the GOP's electoral vulnerability is growing, largely as a result of a shrinking voter base that is disproportionately white, male, older, and religiously affiliated. In contrast, population groups that are growing—racial and ethnic minorities and the young—strongly lean toward the Democratic Party. It is, uncoincidentally, precisely those groups who are expected to suffer disproportionately under the Republican Party's election reform agenda.

The aging Reagan regime has pursued election reform to protect its interests and stay in power, and it has employed judicial strategies to advance that agenda, mostly succeeding in doing so. On the four election law issues I have examined, evidence shows that courts have most clearly exercised friendly judicial review with regard to two of them—voter identification and campaign finance. The GOP has also achieved a substantial, though long-awaited, judicial victory when it comes to the Voting Rights Act. Evidence of interbranch collaboration is more mixed, however, with respect to redistricting.

The GOP has secured considerable judicial support on the issue of voter identification. This is a high-priority agenda item for the Republican Party and one on which there is extraordinary partisan division, as seen in public opinion polls, party platform statements, and legislative votes. Voter identification policies additionally are adopted nearly exclusively in Republican-controlled states. Evidence from chapter 3 shows that partisan divisions on this issue also exist in the courts. In voter ID cases from 2005 to 2015, the proportion of votes supporting the voter identification law under review was much higher for Republican judges compared to Democratic judges. This gap shrunk, however, after *Crawford*, the 2008 Supreme Court decision upholding Indiana's photo ID law.[1] This change might be characterized as neutral or legalistic, with Democratic judges curbing their partisan behavior and following the legal dictates of the highest court in the land. That ignores, however, that *Crawford* is itself a partisan decision. Six Republican justices endorsed a prominent GOP initiative under an increasingly lax standard of review that was constructed by Republican appointees consistently with the Reagan regime's preference for greater state control over elections and voting.

The Roberts Court has also strongly supported the GOP's deregulatory mission in the campaign finance field. It invalidated federal restrictions on corporate spending in *Citizens United* (2010) and aggregate contributions in *McCutcheon* (2014).[2] It also ended mandatory agency fees for public-sector unions in *Janus* (2018).[3] In all three cases, the majority consisted of five Republican justices who voted consistently with their party's national platform statements and opposed the four Democratic justices in dissent. It is also notable that the Republican justices advanced their party's policy preferences with unusual zeal and activism. In *Citizens United*, for example, the Court did not decide on the narrow grounds originally advanced by the plaintiffs, instead inviting the parties to address the broader question of whether the existing rules from *Austin* and *McConnell* should be reconsidered.[4] This unusual move enabled the Court to leap further ahead in its deregulatory venture, invalidating corporate spending limits immediately and fully. Its robust support of the GOP's policy goals in this area, accelerated by the addition of Roberts and especially Alito, has altered the dynamics of campaign financing in federal elections, mostly by fueling a dramatic increase in independent spending. It is less clear, however, that the Court's rulings and the rise of outside spending have had a disproportionately favorable impact on Republican candidates, although more research on this question is needed. *Janus*, in contrast, is likely to have a distinctively partisan impact by reducing the membership and revenues of public sector unions and, thus, their capacity to support Democratic candidates and causes. That impact may, however, be ameliorated by countermeasures adopted by Democratic politicians.

The GOP has also secured favorable Court rulings on the Voting Rights Act, though party leaders would likely describe that success as partial and belated. Its biggest victory came in *Shelby County* (2013), a decision that effectively ended the VRA's preclearance regime and reduced the federal role in Southern elections that President Nixon and other Republican leaders had long opposed.[5] As in the campaign finance area, this major doctrinal shift was executed by five Republican justices and opposed by four Democratic justices. The Republican majority additionally relied on doctrinal and factual grounds that would generously be described as shaky. *Shelby County* has, furthermore, had a predictable partisan impact, with Republican politicians in covered jurisdictions using their newfound freedom to erect barriers to the ballot like strict photo ID rules, reductions in early voting, and aggressive voter purges. Such actions are likely to harm minority voters disproportionately and would certainly have been challenged under preclearance. This strong case for viewing *Shelby County* as an example of partisan collaboration is further supported by a partisan-regime backstory that reveals repeated efforts by Republican presidents and the Court's Republican appointees to restrict the reach and impact of the Voting Rights Act, the latter with rulings like *Beer, Bolden, Ashcroft,* and *Bossier II.*[6] *Bolden*, for example, imposed an intent requirement for Section 2 lawsuits, a move supported by the Reagan administration and John Roberts, then working in the Justice Department. Congress, however, overturned this decision by amending the VRA to require proof only of discriminatory effects. In this recurring pattern, Republicans in the executive and judicial branches would take steps to restrict the Voting Rights Act, which Congress would then reverse, usually in its periodic reauthorizations. Because these votes were highly visible, Republican presidents and members of Congress hid their opposition and supported more expansive renewal provisions than they truly preferred. Seen in this light, *Shelby County* provided to the GOP a historic victory and a generous gift: eliminating federal preclearance and providing political cover in any future congressional efforts to update the coverage formula and restore preclearance. GOP success in ending preclearance, nonetheless, took a very long time, and the Section 2 effects test survives and remains a potent tool, though some regard it as the next target of the Court's Republican majority.

The record of the Reagan regime in securing judicial aid in the redistricting field does not match its success in the other three election law areas. Nor does it come close to that of its Democratic predecessor, which constructed and benefited from the Warren Court's reapportionment revolution. Republican Party leaders were stymied in the racial gerrymandering cases, with the Court constraining the GOP's strategy of crafting majority-minority districts that reduce the number of Democratic-leaning districts in the House and state legislatures. Most of the Republican justices have opposed the use of race in redistricting decisions, adhering to the principle of color blindness that ironically was part of the intellectual foundation laid by legal conservatives participating in the Reagan revolution.[7] The Republican Party has also failed to gain judicial support for adding a citizenship question to the census and requiring states to count voters rather than residents in the redistricting process.[8] In the partisan gerrymandering cases, the record is mixed. The Court, for example, failed for decades to agree on the proper standard for judging partisan gerrymanders, with a muddled partisan pattern in the justices' votes and no clear advantage accruing to either party. This marginal impact is regarded as unsurprising to political scientists, who find that mapmakers face significant constraints in trying to create sizable and long-lasting partisan bias. Nonetheless, some studies have found a pro-Republican advantage in redistricting in recent years, likely explaining the party's growing commitment to judicial noninterference and matching the contemporary perception of considerable GOP success in securing electoral advantages through aggressive gerrymandering. Seen in this light, the 2019 *Rucho* precedent prohibiting federal judicial consideration of partisan gerrymandering claims, endorsed only by Republican justices, emerges as a more traditional case of partisan cooperation.

Accounting for the GOP's Substantial, but Uneven, Success

The Republican Party's record in securing judicial assistance with its election law preferences is impressive, though somewhat uneven. How do we explain both its success and variation in that success? Judicial appointments present an obvious factor that has enhanced the party's effectiveness. Beginning with Richard Nixon, the GOP's presidential election victories, aided by timely and often strategic departures from the Court, have translated into abundant opportunities to fill the high bench with like-minded copartisans. In fact, the Republican Party has filled fifteen of the nineteen Supreme Court vacancies in the half century from 1968 to 2018, including eleven in a row from 1968 to 1992. While a few of those appointees—most notably Blackmun, Stevens, and Souter—have disappointed the GOP faithful by deviating from conservative positions, they are exceptions; most justices have mostly fulfilled the expectations of the president who appointed them. This is especially the case in recent years, as the Republicans' dedication to conservative judicial appointments has intensified and its reliance on conservative legal groups like the Federalist Society to vet its nominees has grown. The party's commitment to a *judicial* strategy to help accomplish its policy and electoral aims has been considerable, and these efforts have paid substantial dividends. Supreme Court appointments of Republican presidents from Nixon to Trump have clearly produced more conservative decisions in the voting rights and campaign finance field. Presidential election victories have, furthermore, insured control over the Justice Department, enabling lax enforcement of the Voting Rights Act (except when it came to majority-minority districts) and a permissive attitude toward voter ID policies. The Electoral College thus looms large in explaining GOP success in advancing its election reform agenda. It has enabled what some call a minority party to secure political power, to extend it through Supreme Court appointments, and to preserve it even further by rigging the election rules in its favor.

Making multiple appointments that shifted the Court's ideological median to the right cannot, of course, account for variation in the GOP's effectiveness across different areas of election law. It does not, for example, explain why the Republican Party was more successful in winning judicial support on campaign finance compared to redistricting. Several factors appear important and worthy of exploration: the clarity of the party's policy position, the existence of an organized and energetic support structure, and the presence of strong and relevant jurisprudential traditions.

The first factor focuses on the nature of the party's policy commitment. Policy preferences can vary in the degree to which they are clear and precise, supported strongly by a unified party, and communicated prominently and effectively. The GOP's position on voter identification, for example, has been clear and consistent. Its national platforms in 2008, 2012, and 2016 definitively state the party's preference for a photo ID requirement at polling places and for states to have the authority to adopt such a requirement free of federal and judicial interference. The leadership has also been unified in pursuing these policies, and support among the Republican rank and file is extremely high. This has no doubt contributed to the party's great success in its campaign for voter identification. Similarly, the GOP's strong deregulatory stance on campaign finance has been clearly communicated in its national platforms, legal briefs, and legislative proposals. Interestingly, however, Republican leaders have not been fully united, with the late senator John McCain a leading dissenter and rank-and-file members actually favoring government restrictions like spending limits.[9] When it comes to the Voting Rights Act and redistricting, the GOP's policy preferences have been hidden and conflicted. Republican politicians publicly praise the Voting Rights Act, congressional Republicans overwhelmingly vote in favor of expanding and reauthorizing the act, and Republican presidents sign such legislation upon its passage. This comes, however, after they have worked behind the scenes in the early stages of the legislative process to weaken the VRA. Republican presidents have, furthermore, undermined the act in its implementation, with Reagan's Justice Department additionally urging the Court to reverse course by limiting congressional power to protect minority voting rights under the Reconstruction amendments, laying the groundwork for *Shelby County*. On the redistricting issue, Republican politicians and party officials have engaged in partisan gerrymandering, challenged Democratic gerrymanders in court, and aggressively pursued majority-minority districts. These self-interested and electorally strategic actions are not, however, defended publicly and in a principled manner in its national platforms, amicus briefs, or legislative initiatives. In fact, prominent Republican organizations have only recently advanced a strong position urging judicial caution in partisan gerrymandering cases, although it did not do so in the *Benisek* litigation challenging a pro-Democratic gerrymander in Maryland. There is also a disjunction in the redistricting area between public and elite opinion. While party officials and politicians are dedicated practitioners of gerrymandering, rank-and-file Republicans, like most Americans, are disgusted by it and eager for reform.[10] There is thus considerable variation across the four election law issues with regard to how clear, committed, and united the Republican Party is. It scores rather highly on these factors when it comes to voter identification and campaign finance, but lower with respect to the Voting Rights Act and redistricting. Of course, this corresponds closely to the party's success in securing judicial support on each issue.

Related to this, the GOP's commitment to pursuing a *judicial* strategy for achieving its preferred policies has also varied. The party, for example, was strongly committed to building judicial support for ending campaign finance limits through an aggressive deployment of the First Amendment. The Reagan Justice Department also advanced new federalism doctrines and an originalist approach that could generate favorable outcomes in a variety of policy areas, including voting rights. In contrast, Republican leaders did not develop a campaign to convince copartisan judges to support majority-minority districts; the party was not open about this self-interested electoral strategy and did not advance a spirited defense of "affirmative action redistricting" in its legal briefs, perhaps because of the challenge of explaining away its traditional preference for color-blind government policies. Viewed in this light, it seems odd to characterize the Court's racial gerrymandering decisions as "a GOP failure" when the party was not honest about its preferences and did not aggressively employ a judicial strategy to vindicate them. The party's disinclination suggests, perhaps, that not all election issues are equally susceptible of principled legal advocacy and judicial support. Though looking at a different area of constitutional law, Thomas Keck and Kevin McMahon similarly focused on the GOP's judicial strategies in attempting to solve the puzzle of why *Roe v. Wade* has not been overturned despite a plethora of Republican appointments to the Court.[11] The authors concluded that Republican leaders have not always applied "a full-court press" in trying to secure *Roe*'s reversal, sometimes sacrificing it to other priorities like tax cuts or to political realities like a Democratic Senate unwilling to confirm an anti-*Roe* nominee.[12] Without strong and consistent leadership on *Roe*'s reversal, they argue, the Court was unlikely to take such a huge doctrinal step. Similarly, in the racial gerrymandering cases, the Court would be unlikely to abandon its traditional commitment to a color-blind constitutional standard and uphold majority-minority districts without strong leadership and persuasive legal arguments for doing so.

Another factor that likely explains variation in GOP success in securing judicial support on contemporary election law issues is the "support structure" that enables constitutional change.[13] Courts are, relative to Congress and the president, passive institutions that cannot initiate policy change. Although this can be overstated, it is true that the justices must wait for mobilization agents like interest groups and lawyers to fund and design litigation campaigns and craft legal arguments for them to consider. With regard to the Second Amendment, for example, the National Rifle Association and the Federalist Society had to develop new legal scholarship advancing an individual right view that opposed the long dominant collective right view. These legal arguments and the cases they sponsored enabled the Court to take a sizable doctrinal step in *District of Columbia v. Heller* (2008) and create an individual right to gun ownership that exists apart from service in a militia.[14] Conservative legal groups have also contributed mightily to the revolutionary changes adopted by the Court in the campaign finance area. They developed a significant body of innovative scholarship advancing, first, a robust reading of the First Amendment that rendered campaign finance restrictions constitutionally dubious and, second, an interpretive approach that urged judges to reverse precedent when originalist findings require it. Federalist Society members like Jim Bopp played a key role in a well-organized and well-financed legal crusade against campaign finance restrictions that enabled the Court to jump ahead quickly in its doctrinal journey, as seen in *Citizens United* and *McCutcheon*.[15]

A final factor helping to account for variation in the GOP's success on election law issues is legal in nature and relates to the existence of supportive jurisprudential traditions. Keith Whittington has noted that "judicial review is often intertemporal and not just contemporaneous" and that "a newly elected legislature does not immediately bend the entire corpus of law to its will."[16] The latter observation applies with equal force to newly appointed justices, who must act within the constraints of precedents, judicial tests, and legal norms that may be long-standing. Observing partisan influences on the Supreme Court does not change the fact that it is "still a court" whose members are "attentive to norms of collegiality and law-oriented decision making."[17] The justices take seriously legal norms like stare decisis and judicial independence, and they care about the professional judgement of their peers. While they may favor certain policy outcomes or particular groups with which their party is allied, the justices may find it difficult to act in a blatantly partisan way that does not fit with the legal traditions that they have inherited. In

Crawford, for example, the Republican justices could uphold voter identification policies, even if driven by party favoritism or personal political bias, with little difficulty in justifying that outcome legally. The *Anderson-Burdick* precedent was readily available, and it provided a lower standard of review that more easily permitted election regulations affecting the vote to be upheld. In contrast, Republican justices deciding challenges to majority-minority districts favored by their copartisans faced a contrary tradition of judicial skepticism toward race-conscious policies. In the campaign finance area, conservative justices had the First Amendment available as a strong textual hook for invalidating government restrictions like spending limits, but they did not have precedent on their side. They did, however, have a growing body of scholarship and effective litigation strategies designed by conservative legal groups that helped them to move quickly and dramatically in altering constitutional doctrine. As this suggests, there are some limits to the claim that the Court is significantly constrained and slowed by the need to respect precedent and stick closely to the issues briefed by the parties. Rulings like *Citizens United* and *Janus* show the Court's independent capacity to create a path for constitutional change. Finally, *Bush v. Gore* proves that courts can sometimes act in a blatantly partisan way and get away with it, even when persuasive legal reasoning and doctrinal traditions are absent.

Several conclusions are in order. First, evidence gathered from four contemporary election law issues indicates that the Republican Court has greatly aided the Republican Party with its election reform agenda. It has, thus, fulfilled our fears of partisan bias more than it has satisfied our expectations of neutrality. Even so, judicial partisanship has not had a uniform influence across all four issues, a finding offered by Kyle Kopko as well.[18] While an abundance of appointment opportunities has been essential for the GOP to secure judicial aid on issues like campaign finance and voter identification, it is no guarantee of success across the board, as indicated by some of the Court's redistricting decisions. Effectiveness varies depending on the party's clarity and unity with respect to its policy positions, its deployment of an explicitly *judicial* strategy, the presence of supportive doctrinal traditions, and the existence of mobilization agents designing effective litigation strategies, which is especially important when the Court needs to take a large rather than a small doctrinal step.

A final qualification must be added. Although the Court's decisions have often supported the GOP's election reform agenda, social science research does not always confirm that a disproportionate electoral advantage accrued to Republican candidates as a result. Few studies, for example, document a significant reduction in turnout resulting from voter ID requirements, and researchers disagree on whether they disproportionately inhibit youth and minority turnout and harm Democratic candidates. Judicial noninterference in partisan gerrymandering did not significantly advantage either party in the 1980s and 1990s, though it appears to be working in the GOP's favor in recent years. In campaign finance, there is a dearth of empirical research on the partisan impact of recent policy changes, though many experts doubt a sizable pro-Republican electoral impact. *Shelby County*, however, has had a clear partisan impact, with Republican states using their new freedom from federal oversight to adopt a variety of voter suppression laws and practices, including voter purges, which the Court permitted in *Husted* and which are particularly worrisome.[19] It is furthermore possible that the marginal impact of each of several election rule changes could accumulate and produce a significant advantage for the Republican Party, which is clearly what GOP leaders are seeking and intending. They *believe* that these various reforms will help them win elections and survive politically by overcoming the demographic limitations of the coalition that they have constructed. Regardless then of the actual impact—and the verdict is still out—Republican leaders have clearly pursued self-interested election reforms and have been quite successful in enlisting courts in their cause.

Is Friendly Judicial Review in Election Law a Problem?

A number of important questions remain. The first is normative, inquiring about the potential harm to court legitimacy and democracy itself when election law is an interbranch undertaking between friends. One concern is that when courts ignore the law or act outside of it to fulfill their copartisans' electoral needs, they risk their legitimacy. Federal judges are not elected, unlike most state judges, and they cannot draw on electoral validation to legitimate their decisions. As "the least dangerous branch,"[20] the federal judiciary additionally cannot fund or enforce its decisions and may face noncompliance or a political backlash, particularly when it rules against majority preferences. Its legitimacy and power, thus, depend on public confidence that its judgments are independent and rooted in law, or so the argument goes. If the Supreme Court acts in a persistently partisan manner, it could be perceived by the public as a political and not a legal institution, particularly when reinforced by negative comments by the press and politicians, such as President Trump's critical references to "Obama judges" when federal courts have ruled against him.

The claim that a partisan or overly political Court jeopardizes its legitimacy is not well-supported by empirical evidence, however. Research shows that: the Supreme Court enjoys strong, stable, and bipartisan support; public awareness of Supreme Court decisions is limited; Americans hold *both* idealized and realist notions about the Court; and the mix of liberal and conservative decisions issuing from the Court in the modern era has helped to preserve its bipartisan support.[21] James Gibson and Gregory Caldeira find some evidence for a reduction in public support when the Court is politicized, for example, during Senate confirmation hearings, and they acknowledge that the Court's "reservoir of goodwill . . . is far from bottomless"; nonetheless, they find no evidence that "the highly polarized political context in the contemporary United States has metastasized to attitudes toward the Court."[22] Another notable finding is that the Court suffered no overall loss in public support after *Bush v. Gore*, one of the most partisan decisions in its history.[23]

Another concern about interbranch partisan collaboration in election law is the damage it causes to liberal-democratic values and the rule of law. The question of whether courts can stand as independent bulwarks against partisan threats to constitutional values has obvious relevance today, both in the United States and throughout the world. Liberal values are under attack by populist movements and authoritarian leaders around the globe, and many intellectual leaders place considerable faith in the ability and willingness of courts to protect those values. Partisan courts that support the dominant regime obviously cannot be counted on to play this critical role.

It is incontrovertible that Republicans have, in recent years, acted in self-interested fashion to suppress the votes of their Democratic opponents; this has meant targeting young people and racial and ethnic minorities. This strategy is a rational response, but not the only possible response, to its electoral challenges. The party might have followed the advice of the Republican National Committee's post-2012 autopsy report and enacted comprehensive immigration reform and reached out to America's minority voters.[24] The GOP has chosen instead "to give up on trying to reach pluralities or majorities of voters, and to be willing to grab any narrow victory by any means necessary, and in particular by aggressively trying to discount the votes of African-Americans, Hispanics, and Native Americans relative to those of whites."[25] This is more than unfortunate; it is deplorable, particularly in light of America's appalling history of denying the right to vote to people of color, especially African Americans. That sin, many argue, is compounded when presumably independent courts validate those efforts instead of fighting against them. "Democracy has been undermined *pursuant to law*"[26] when courts act in ways that make them "complicit in the disenfranchisement war."[27] I have argued elsewhere that a partisan coalition that succeeds electorally wins the right to populate the bench and shape constitutional policy.[28] That argument is pushed to its limits, however, when that coalition also uses the courts to rig the rules of electoral competition in its favor. Particularly with many election outcomes so close in recent years in the United States, it is a legitimate concern that elections not be "decided by voter suppression and conservative court majorities."[29]

A broader historical perspective helps to clarify that judicial support for the efforts of copartisans to advance their electoral interests is neither new nor confined to a single political party. As we know, Southern Democrats enacted into law a variety of devices to deny African Americans the right to vote, which friendly courts supported. Partisan cooperation across the branches on election rules need not, however, always and inherently weaken democracy. After all, Democrats in all three branches worked together in the 1960s to end the malapportionment that, yes, disadvantaged them electorally but also, more broadly, undermined effective representation. There does exist, nonetheless, the potential for harm when partisan regimes enlist courts in their selfish electoral strategies, an inevitable product of permitting politicians to select judges. Thus, while both *Baker* and *Shelby County* count as examples of the inevitability of friendly judicial review in election law, we easily, properly, and for nonpartisan reasons praise the former and condemn the latter.

Empowering elected officials to shape the courts by selecting their members promotes judicial accountability and enables constitutional law to be a shared democratic enterprise.[30] It also poses risks, however, as like-minded, copartisan elites across the branches cooperate to protect their electoral and policy interests, sometimes through illegitimate means like voter suppression. The best way to address this challenge, ironically, is with more politics. For example, when the Supreme Court, with executive branch support, imposed an intent requirement for Section 2 lawsuits under the Voting Rights Act, civil rights groups mobilized and Democrats and moderate Republicans in Congress worked together to replace it with a results standard, teaching that "the cure for (judicial) politics is more (legislative) politics."[31] Similarly, when the Court displayed an unacceptable form of tribal partisanship in *Bush v. Gore*, the people and their representatives had the right to mobilize against it, perhaps by refusing to confirm George W. Bush's Supreme Court nominees.[32] "More politics" in the form of Congress adding more seats to the Court if a Democratic president wins the White House in 2020 might similarly be an appropriate response to Mitch McConnell's refusal to consider Obama's nominee, Merrick Garland, to fill Justice Scalia's vacant seat. Of course, the danger is that a Republican Court will thwart these efforts, as well as others that seek to address the decline of democratic norms and practices brought about by the New Right regime.

Looking to the Future

If "the remedy for the sort of politics we do not like is more politics," what might those politics look like, and how do we get there?[33] Much depends on the 2020 election and whether Donald Trump's late-regime presidency ends or continues. As conceptualized by Stephen Skowronek and explained in the introduction, a president's authority and success depend on two factors: his relationship to the dominant party regime and the health of that regime. Reconstructive presidents like Franklin Roosevelt and Ronald Reagan transform American politics, reimagining the nation's ideological and policy commitments, restructuring its politics, and realigning its political interests in a dramatic and enduring way. Affiliated presidents who follow, such as Harry Truman and George H. W. Bush, build on and extend those commitments. A regime is then typically interrupted by a preemptive president like Dwight Eisenhower, Bill Clinton, or Barack Obama who belongs to the opposite party and struggles to accommodate their contrary views to those of the still resilient regime. Disjunctive presidents like Herbert Hoover and Jimmy Carter tend to be regarded as failures, an unsurprising result given that they lead and struggle to preserve an old and dying regime. According to this "life cycle of a political regime . . . [a] party that was once subordinate gradually grows in strength. It forms a rising coalition. It dominates politics. It promotes its distinctive agendas of ideology and interest. Its influence peaks. It becomes the victim of its own success. Its factions struggle with each other. It weakens, it withers, and it is eventually pushed aside by a new regime headed by another political party."[34]

In attempting to locate Donald Trump in political time, Skowronek acknowledges the president's reconstructive "ambitions," seen in his claims about a "rigged" and "broken" system, repeated efforts to override "deep state" support in the bureaucracy, and attacks on the courts that he has aggressively packed with young, ideological allies.[35] These ambitions, however, "don't quite square with his circumstances" with "structure and opportunity" not operating in the president's favor; after all, unlike FDR and Reagan, Trump is a member of the long dominant regime, not the opposition party that seeks to dislodge it.[36] Looking at Table C.1, we can see the "sequence of presidents" across political time, with both the New Deal regime and Reagan regime "align[ing] remarkably well."[37] As Skowronek observes, "Donald Trump is readily identifiable in these lines of succession. Political time tags him a late-regime affiliate . . . [and] the conservative regime's fourth administration."[38]

Trump closely resembles other late-regime affiliates like Hoover and Carter, who took over the reins of an aging regime and acted as "conspicuous loners promoting idiosyncratic credentials and independent appeals."[39] They sought to "save the old party from *itself*" and move "a regime long accustomed to rule to reconstruct itself."[40] Trump's tariffs and extreme immigration policies might, in this way, be understood as a populist shift designed "to renovate and repair the regime . . . adapting it to a changing Republican base of white, working class voters, especially those without college degrees."[41] The "common challenge" facing late-regime affiliates like Trump, however, is "to make good on the promise of a new dispensation, while leading a party committed to the old dispensation . . . a working definition of the impossible leadership situation. . . . We have seen this movie before, and it has always ended the same way."[42] Skowronek predicts that "if the clock at work in presidential leadership is still keeping political time . . . we would expect to see the Republican coalition implode under the pressures of Trump's leadership, and for the president to go down with it."[43]

As would be expected for any predictive enterprise, there exists disagreement on this point. Skowronek himself wonders if the dynamics of

Table C.1. The Sequence of Presidents across Political Time in the Modern Era

	Reconstructive →	Affiliated →	Preemptive →	Affiliated →	Preemptive →	Disjunctive
New Deal Regime	FDR	Truman	Eisenhower	JFK/LBJ	Nixon	Carter
Reagan Regime	Reagan	H. W. Bush	Clinton	W. Bush	Obama	Trump?

political time are being constrained by secular developments, such as the growing independence of the presidency and Trump's remarkable power to build a personal brand with his base that his copartisans are too fearful to challenge. Perhaps we are "witnessing the long-awaited arrival of the president as a party unto himself," independent of "received formulas and nominal allies," suggesting that Trump's reelection is possible despite his status as a late-regime affiliate.[44] Enhancing that potential is the president avoiding Senate conviction on the House's impeachment charges in early 2020; public approval ratings that have been modest, but steady; and an economy that, at least prior to the COVID-19 pandemic, was performing quite strongly.[45]

Jack Balkin offers a more optimistic account.[46] He acknowledges that "the transition to [a] new political order" will be "awkward, uncomfortable, and occasionally frightening" but predicts that America will successfully move on from "the recent unpleasantness," with Democrats most likely emerging as the next dominant party.[47] Others, however, see recent phenomena like hyperpolarization and Trump's authoritarian populism as complicating and possibly preventing a successful transition.[48] Theda Skocpol, for example, worries about "the radicalization of the GOP and the apparent willingness of virtually all of its officeholders, candidates, and big donors to go along with authoritarian and antidemocratic measures of many kinds, not just presidential power grabs but legislative and judicial steps to curtail voting and organization rights of opponents, in essence rigging future electoral contests in a very minority rule direction."[49] Republican success with regard to these efforts could leave American politics stuck in a "long disjunction" marked by "strong, ideologically-driven partisan contestation" instead of a realignment and the emergence of a new dominant party.[50] The partisan warfare, gridlock, and dysfunction marking the Obama-Trump years would then continue, replete with government shutdowns and impeachment threats. The judiciary could become a political target as partisan conflict further escalates to include Court-packing efforts.

My sincere hope (it is not yet a firm belief) is that there are limits to the ability of the GOP—or any party—to rig the rules without suffering political consequences. There has been considerable countermobilization in the Trump years, including the massive Women's March in 2017; a potent student movement against gun violence in the aftermath of the Parkland, Florida, school shooting; and nationwide Black Lives Matter protests in 2020. Reactions against the persistent and self-interested efforts by Republicans to restrict voting rights, particularly in the midst of a pandemic, could backfire and lead to massive resistance. America's minorities could rebel against the GOP's relentless attacks on their right to participate and make the party pay with extraordinary turnout and Democratic support in future elections.[51] Growing discontent and the collapse of the Reagan regime are no guarantee, however, that Democrats will take advantage and astutely engineer their comeback to dominant status in American politics. There remain many opportunities for political miscalculations and missteps, with some regarding the Democrats' failed impeachment effort as one such example.[52] Current rules for nominating and electing a president are, furthermore, not effectively geared toward finding either a consensus candidate or a skilled and experienced leader, as Donald Trump's ascendance to the White House proves.

Even if the Democrats emerge as the next dominant party in American politics, it is possible that the Roberts Court could act to limit that transition and obstruct policies that seek to reverse the democratic erosion suffered over the past decade. It is not difficult to imagine the Republican justices striking down new campaign finance regulations, gerrymandering reforms, and a revised preclearance formula.[53] Such judicial activism would represent a very deep entrenchment of the GOP's campaign to alter election rules in order to stay in power. The Court could very well become a target of popular anger and the centerpiece of Democratic election campaigns, much as the Warren Court was for Richard Nixon. Court-packing and Court-curbing legislation could result. A collision between the Court and an electorally dominant Democratic Party might also trigger a constitutional crisis like that of the 1930s. This need not be regarded as a disaster, however. Political mobilization around constitutional law is a positive development, as the nation moves forward in building a consensus around new national commitments, which hopefully will include a desire to promote voter participation and a healthier democracy.

Prediction has for good reason been called a fool's errand. Several things are certain, however. In the short term, voting rights will continue to be vulnerable, as long as the Republican Party and the Court's "Fed Soc Five"[54] remain in power. With the former likely to lose power before the latter, major interbranch conflict could result. Another certainty is that election law will continue to serve as a tool of regime maintenance and an object of partisan rivalry, with courts playing a critical role. Politicians will make sure of this. They will also do their best to ensure that history repeats and that courts will be friendly to the dominant party in its self-serving electoral endeavors. This will sometimes benefit and sometimes harm democracy. The proper response to this challenge, always, is more politics rather than less.

Notes

Introduction

1. No. 19A1016.

2. According to the Court, state law required that ballots be mailed and post-marked by election day, April 7, while the district court permitted them to be mailed and postmarked *after* election day, as long as they were received by April 13. Permitting voters to cast their ballot after election day was the fundamental alteration of the election to which the majority referred. The Court additionally objected to a judicially imposed rule change so close to the election, citing *Purcell v. Gonzalez*, 549 U.S. 1 (2006).

3. Wisconsin Legislature v. Evers, No. 2020AP608-OA.

4. Wisconsin's elections for its supreme court are formally nonpartisan. However, ideological cues and partisan endorsements and campaign donations suggest that, at the time of this ruling, the court was composed of five Republican justices and two Democratic justices. The latter dissented and voted in favor of the Democratic governor, while the former supported the Republican legislature. The majority in this case consisted of only four justices, however, as Justice Daniel Kelly, appointed by Republican governor Scott Walker and endorsed by President Trump, recused himself from the case since he was on the ballot.

5. In a surprise outcome, Justice Kelly lost the election and his seat on the supreme court to Jill Karofsky, who had been endorsed by numerous Democrats, including presidential candidates Joe Biden and Bernie Sanders. In another intriguing development, Kelly has since changed his mind about participating in the voter purge case and could cast a deciding vote, given that the court had previously split 3-3 in deciding whether to accept it. "Wisconsin Democrat Jill Karofsky in Supreme Court Election Upset," BBC News, April 14, 2020, https://www.bbc.com/news/world-us-canada-52279608.

6. Simon Lewis and Julia Harte, "Chaotic Wisconsin Election Signals Virus-Related Voting Battles Ahead," Reuters, April 8, 2020, https://www.reuters.com/article/us-usa-election-voting-rights-insight/chaotic-wisconsin-election-signals-virus-related-voting-battles-ahead-idUSKCN21R01L.

7. Quint Forgey, "Trump: GOP Should Fight Mail-In Voting because It 'Doesn't Work Out Well for Republicans,'" *Politico*, April 8, 2020; Carl Hulse, "As Pandemic Imperils Elections, Democrats Clash with Trump on Voting Changes," *New York Times*, April 8, 2020. Research actually reveals that vote-by-mail "is remarkably neutral," with no disproportionate advantage accruing to either party. Emily Bazelon, "Will Americans Lose Their Right to Vote in the

Pandemic," *New York Times Magazine,* May 5, 2020; Alan S. Gerber, Gregory A. Huber, and Seth J. Hill, "Identifying the Effect of All-Mail Elections on Turnout: Staggered Reform in the Evergreen State," *Political Science Research and Methods* 1 (2013): 91–116; Daniel M. Thompson, Jennifer Wu, Jesse Yoder, and Andrew B. Hall, "The Neutral Partisan Effects of Vote-by-Mail: Evidence from County-Level Roll-Outs," unpublished manuscript, Democracy and Polarization Lab, Stanford University, April 25, 2020, http://www.andrewbenjaminhall.com/Thompson_et_al_VBM.pdf.

8. Cleve R. Wootson Jr., "Donald Trump: 'I Won the Popular Vote If You Deduct the Millions of People Who Voted Illegally,'" *Washington Post,* November 27, 2016. From the start, the Presidential Advisory Commission on Election Integrity was plagued with difficulties—confusion, criticism, and litigation—and lasted only eight months before being disbanded by the president.

9. Garrett Epps, "The Supreme Court's Key Role in Polarizing American Politics," *Atlantic,* September 27, 2013; Ellen D. Katz, "Election Law's Lochnerian Turn," *Boston University Law Review* 94 (2014): 697–709; Stephen Gottlieb, "Democracy Essential to the Legitimacy of Constitutional Interpretation," Albany Law School Research Paper Number 7, 2017, https://papers.ssrn.com/so13/papers.cfm?abstract_id=2931153; Stephen Gottlieb, *Unfit for Democracy: The Roberts Court and the Breakdown of American Politics* (New York: New York University Press), 195–204.

10. Bush v. Gore, 531 U.S. 98 (2000); Shelby County v. Holder, 570 U.S. 529 (2013); Crawford v. Marion County Election Board, 553 U.S. 181 (2008); Vieth v. Jubelirer, 541 U.S. 267 (2004); Rucho v. Common Cause, 139 S. Ct. 2484 (2019); Citizens United v. Federal Election Commission, 558 U.S. 310 (2010); Janus v. American Federation of State, County, and Municipal Employees, Council 31, 138 S. Ct. 2448 (2018); Husted v. A. Philip Randolph Institute, 138 S. Ct. 1833 (2018).

11. Quoted in Senator George W. Plunkitt, "Tammany's Plans Outlined," *Good Government* 21, no. 1 (1904): 15.

12. Ericka Andersen, "Gorsuch: 'There's No Such Thing as a Republican Judge or a Democratic Judge, We Just Have Judges' (VIDEO)," *National Review,* March 21, 2017. Chief Justice Roberts responded similarly to President Trump's complaint about "Obama judges," stating that "We do not have Obama judges or Trump judges, Bush judges or Clinton judges. What we have is an extraordinary group of dedicated judges doing their level best to do equal right to those appearing before them. That independent judiciary is something we should all be thankful for." Eli Watkins and Joan Biskupic, "Trump Slams Chiefs Justice after Roberts Chides the President," CNN, November 21, 2018, https://www.cnn.com/2018/11/21/politics/supreme-court-john-roberts-trump/index.html.

13. Michael S. Kang and Joanna M. Shepherd, "The Long Shadow of *Bush v. Gore:* Judicial Partisanship in Election Cases," *Stanford Law Review* 68 (2016): 1411–1452; Thomas M. Keck, *Judicial Politics in Polarized Times* (Chicago: University of Chicago Press, 2014); Kyle C. Kopko, "Partisanship Suppressed: Judicial Decision-Making in Ralph Nader's 2004 Ballot Access Litigation," *Election Law Journal* 7, no. 4 (2008): 301–324; Mark Jonathan, "The Influence of Partisan-

ship, Ideology, and the Law on Redistricting Decisions in the Federal Courts," *Political Research Quarterly* 65, no. 4 (2012): 799–813; Terri Peretti, "Judicial Partisanship in Voter Identification Litigation," *Election Law Journal* 15 (2016): 214–231; Cass R. Sunstein, David Schkade, Lisa M. Ellman, and Andres Sawicki, *Are Judges Political? An Empirical Analysis of the Federal Judiciary* (Washington, DC: Brookings Institution Press, 2006).

14. Kopko, "Partisanship Suppressed," 301.

15. Kang and Shepherd, "The Long Shadow of *Bush v. Gore,*" 1430–1431.

16. Richard L. Hasen, *The Supreme Court and Election Law: Judging Equality from* Baker v. Carr *to* Bush v. Gore (New York: New York University Press, 2006), 1. Two factors that helped to generate this increase in the Supreme Court's election law caseload were the Voting Rights Act of 1965, which triggered an avalanche of litigation, and the Court's 1962 *Baker v. Carr* ruling that malapportionment claims were justiciable and could be entertained by federal courts. Recent contributing factors to the increase in election law litigation include the close competitive balance between the two parties and *Bush v. Gore,* which intensified attention to the multitude of administrative details governing elections.

17. Charles Anthony Smith and Christopher Shortell, "The Suits that Counted: The Judicialization of Presidential Elections," *Election Law Journal* 6, no. 3 (2007): 260, 262.

18. Alexander Hutzler, "2020 Was Already Expected to Be a Record Year for Election-Related Lawsuits—then Coronavirus Happened," *Newsweek,* April 23, 2020.

19. Smith and Shortell, "The Suits that Counted," 252.

20. Steven F. Huefner, "Remedying Election Wrongs," *Harvard Journal on Legislation* 44 (2007): 306.

21. Smith and Shortell, "The Suits that Counted," 264; Kopko, "Partisanship Suppressed"; Richard L. Hasen, "Keynote Address: Judging the Political and Political Judging: Justice Scalia as Case Study," *Chicago-Kent Law Review* 93, no. 2 (2018): 325–341.

22. Samuel Issacharoff and Richard Pildes, "Politics as Markets: Partisan Lockups of the Democratic Process," *Stanford Law Review* 50 (1998): 643–717.

23. Chad Flanders, "Election Law behind a Veil of Ignorance," *Florida Law Review* 64 (2012): 1369–1403.

24. Christopher S. Elmendorf, "Undue Burdens on Voter Participation: New Pressures for a Structural Theory of the Right to Vote?," *Hastings Constitutional Law Quarterly* 35 (2008): 646; Richard L. Hasen, "The Untimely Death of *Bush v. Gore,*" *Stanford Law Review* 60, no. 1 (2007): 18–28; Daniel P. Tokaji, "Early Returns on Election Reform: Discretion, Disenfranchisement, and the Help America Vote Act," *George Washington Law Review* 73 (2005): 1207; Daniel P. Tokaji, "The New Vote Denial: Where Election Reform Meets the Voting Rights Act," *South Carolina Law Review* 57 (2006): 689–695.

25. Hasen, "The Untimely Death of *Bush v. Gore,*" 26–28; Heather K. Gerken, *The Democracy Index: Why Our Election System Is Failing and How to Fix It* (Princeton, NJ: Princeton University Press).

26. In the 2018 Georgia governor's race, Republican Brian Kemp narrowly

defeated Democrat Stacey Abrams after refusing to step down as secretary of state during the election in order to avoid a conflict of interest. He was also accused of various voter suppression efforts alleged to have boosted his electoral prospects, including purging over a million Georgians who were disproportionately African American from the voting rolls and closing over two hundred polling places, primarily in black precincts. Similar allegations dogged Kris Kobach's unsuccessful gubernatorial run in 2018, conducted while he served as Kansas secretary of state. Ari Berman, "How Gerrymandering and Voter Suppression Paved the Way for Abortion Bans," *Mother Jones*, May 17, 2019; Jelani Cobb, "Voter-Suppression Tactics in the Age of Trump," *New Yorker*, October 21, 2018.

27. Scott Lemieux, "'Wholly Without Merit': The 10th Anniversary of *Bush v. Gore*," *Lawyers, Guns & Money* (blog), December 13, 2010, http://www.lawyers gunsmoneyblog.com/2010/12/wholly-without-merit-the-10th-anniversary-of -bush-v-gore.

28. John G. Geer, "Parties and Partisanship: A Brief Introduction." *Political Behavior* 24, no. 2 (2002): 85.

29. Keith E. Whittington, "'Interpose Your Friendly Hand': Political Supports for the Exercise of Judicial Review by the United States Supreme Court," *American Political Science Review* 99 (2005): 583–596; Mark A. Graber, "The Nonmajoritarian Difficulty: Legislative Deference to the Judiciary," *Studies in American Political Development* 7 (1993): 48–54; Cornell W. Clayton and David May, "A Political Regimes Approach to the Analysis of Legal Decisions," *Polity* 32 (1999): 233–252.

30. Robert H. Salisbury and Michael MacKuen, "On the Study of Party Realignment," *Journal of Politics* 43, no. 2 (1981): 523; V. O. Key Jr., "A Theory of Critical Elections," *Journal of Politics* 17 (1955): 1–18; James L. Sundquist, *Dynamics of the Party System* (Washington, DC: Brookings Institution, 1973); Walter Dean Burnham, "The Changing Shape of the American Political Universe," *American Political Science Review* 59 (1965): 7–28; Walter Dean Burnham, *Critical Elections and the Mainsprings of American Politics* (New York: W. W. Norton, 1970).

31. Eric Schickler, *Racial Realignment: The Transformation of American Liberalism, 1932–1965* (Princeton, NJ: Princeton University Press, 2016); Keneshia N. Grant, *The Great Migration and the Democratic Party: Black Voters and the Realignment of American Politics in the 20th Century* (Philadelphia: Temple University Press, 2020); Kevin M. Kruse, *White Flight: Atlanta and the Making of Modern Conservatism* (Princeton, NJ: Princeton University Press, 2007).

32. Cornell W. Clayton and J. Mitchell Pickerill, "The Politics of Criminal Justice: How the New Right Regime Shaped the Rehnquist Court's Criminal Justice Jurisprudence," *Georgetown Law Journal* 94 (2006): 1387; Cornell W. Clayton and J. Mitchell Pickerill, "Guess What Happened on the Way to the Revolution? Precursors to the Supreme Court's Federalism Revolution," *Publius: The Journal of Federalism* 34, no. 3 (2004): 85–114.

33. Mr. Dooley was a fictional character created by American journalist Finley Peter Dunne. The Irish immigrant bartender dispensed both liquor and humorous insights on the issues of the day.

34. Whittington, "'Interpose Your Friendly Hand'"; McCulloch v. Maryland, 17 U.S. 316 (1819); Martin v. Hunter's Lessee, 14 U.S. 304 (1816).

35. Howard Gillman, "How Political Parties Can Use the Courts to Advance Their Agendas: Federal Courts in the United States, 1875–1891," *American Political Science Review* 96, no. 3 (2002): 511–524.

36. Kevin J. McMahon, *Reconsidering Roosevelt on Race: How the Presidency Paved the Road to* Brown (Chicago: University of Chicago Press, 2004), 20; Martin M. Shapiro, "The Constitution and Economic Rights," in *Essays on the Constitution of the United States*, ed. M. Judd Harmon (Port Washington, NY: Kennikat, 1978), 74–98.

37. Lucas A. Powe Jr., *The Warren Court and American Politics* (Cambridge, MA: Harvard University Press, 2000); Ken I. Kersch, *Constructing Civil Liberties: Discontinuities in the Development of American Constitutional Law* (New York: Cambridge University Press, 2004).

38. Terri Peretti, "Constructing the State Action Doctrine, 1940–1990," *Law and Social Inquiry* 35 (2010): 273–310; Shelley v. Kraemer, 334 U.S. 1 (1948).

39. Stephen Skowronek, *Presidential Leadership in Political Time: Reprise and Reappraisal*, 2nd ed. (Lawrence: University Press of Kansas, 2011), 85.

40. Skowronek, *Presidential Leadership in Political Time*, 2nd ed.

41. Skowronek, 84.

42. Stephen Skowronek, *Presidential Leadership in Political Time*, 3rd ed. (Lawrence: University Press of Kansas, 2020); Jack M. Balkin, "The Recent Unpleasantness: Understanding the Cycles of Constitutional Time," *Indiana Law Journal* 94 (2019): 253–296; Sanford Levinson and Jack M. Balkin, *Democracy and Dysfunction* (Chicago: University of Chicago Press, 2019).

43. McMahon, *Reconsidering Roosevelt on Race*, 16–17.

44. Stephen Ansolabehere and James M. Snyder Jr., *The End of Inequality: One Person, One Vote, and the Transformation of American Politics* (New York: W. W. Norton, 2008), 89.

45. 369 U.S. 186 (1962).

46. Gordon E. Baker, *The Reapportionment Revolution: Representation, Political Power, and the Supreme Court* (New York: Random House, 1966).

47. Barry Friedman, "The Birth of an Academic Obsession: The History of the Countermajoritarian Difficulty, Part Five," *Yale Law Journal* 112 (2002): 153–259.

48. Clayton and Pickerill, "The Politics of Criminal Justice," 2006.

49. Jack M. Balkin, "All Hail Ed Meese!" (Review of Neal Devins and Lawrence Baum, *The Company They Keep*), *Balkinization Blogspot*, April 3, 2019, https://balkin.blogspot.co/2019/04/all-hail-ed-meese.html.

50. Kevin J. McMahon, *Nixon's Court: His Challenge to Judicial Liberalism and Its Political Consequences* (Chicago: University of Chicago Press, 2011); Clayton and Pickerill, "The Politics of Criminal Justice," 2006.

51. Nixon, with the help of attorney general John Mitchell and assistant attorney general William Rehnquist, has been credited with orchestrating the resignation of Justice Abe Fortas by pursuing, and possibly leaking, multiple investigations involving Fortas, his wife, and a former law partner. A less suc-

cessful campaign to create another Supreme Court vacancy involved then congressman Gerald Ford's efforts, supported by Nixon, to impeach Justice William Douglas.

52. Balkin, "All Hail Ed Meese!," 2019; Neal Devins and Lawrence Baum, *The Company They Keep: How Partisan Divisions Came to the Supreme Court* (New York: Oxford University Press, 2019), 124–125; Steven M. Teles, *Rise of the Conservative Movement: The Battle for Control of the Law* (Princeton, NJ: Princeton University Press, 2008).

53. Clayton and Pickerill, "Guess What Happened on the Way to the Revolution?"; Jack M. Balkin and Sanford Levinson, "Understanding the Constitutional Revolution," *Virginia Law Review* 87 (2001): 1045–1109.

54. Whittington, "'Interpose Your Friendly Hand,'" 585, 589.

55. Jeffrey M. Jones, "Democrats Hold Edge in U.S. Party Affiliation in 3rd Quarter," *Gallup News*, October 7, 2019, https://news.gallup.com/poll/267239/democrats-hold-edge-party-affiliation-3rd-quarter.aspx.

56. Alec Tyson and Shiva Maniam, "Behind Trump's Victory: Divisions by Race, Gender, Education," Pew Research Center, November 9, 2016, https://www.pewresearch.org/fact-tank/2016/11/09/behind-trumps-victory-divisions-by-race-gender-education/.

57. Danielle Kurtzleben, "Rural Voters Played a Big Part in Helping Trump Defeat Clinton," National Public Radio, November 14, 2016, https://www.npr.org/2016/11/14/501737150/rural-voters-played-a-big-part-in-helping-trump-defeat-clinton; Roper Center, "How Groups Voted 2016," 2016, https://ropercenter.cornell.edu/polls/us-elections/how-groups-voted/groups-voted-2016/; Jessica Martinez and Gregory A. Smith, "How the Faithful Voted: A Preliminary 2016 Analysis," Pew Research Center, November 9, 2016, https://www.pewresearch.org/fact-tank/2016/11/09/how-the-faithful-voted-a-preliminary-2016-analysis/.

58. Roper Center, "How Groups Voted 2016"; Martinez and Smith, "How the Faithful Voted."

59. Pew Research Center, "U.S. Public Becoming Less Religious," November 3, 2015, http://www.pewforum.org/2015/11/03/u-s-public-becoming-less-religious/; Pew Research Center, "In U.S., Decline of Christianity Continues at Rapid Pace," October 17, 2019, https://www.pewforum.org/2019/10/17/in-u-s-decline-of-christianity-continues-at-rapid-pace/.

60. Reid Wilson, "Metro Area Populations Surge as Rural America Shrinks," *The Hill*, March 22, 2018; John Cromartie, "Rural Areas Show Overall Population Decline and Shifting Regional Patterns of Population Change," *Amber Waves*, US Department of Agriculture Economic Research Service, September 5, 2017; Justin Fox, "Rural America Is Aging and Shrinking," *Bloomberg*, June 20, 2017, https://www.bloomberg.com/view/articles/2017–06–20/rural-america-is-aging-and-shrinking.

61. Kim Parker, Juliana Menasce Horowitz, Anna Brown, Richard Fry, D'Vera Cohn, and Ruth Igielnik, "What Unites and Divides Urban, Suburban, and Rural Communities," Pew Research Center, May 22, 2018, https://www.pew

socialtrends.org/2018/05/22/what-unites-and-divides-urban-suburban-and
-rural-communities/.

62. Roper Center, "How Groups Voted 2016"; Anthony Cilluffo and Richard Fry, "An Early Look at the 2020 Electorate," Pew Research Center, January 30, 2019, https://www.pewsocialtrends.org/essay/an-early-look-at-the-2020-elec torate/.

63. William H. Frey, "Minorities Are the Demographic Engine of Millennial Urban Growth," *Brookings Blog*, February 21, 2018.

64. Frey, "Minorities Are the Demographic Engine."

65. Frey; Cilluffo and Fry, "An Early Look at the 2020 Electorate."

66. While party elites are much more polarized since the mid-1970s, it is less clear whether party identifiers in the electorate have also polarized. Morris P. Fiorina, *Culture War? The Myth of a Polarized America* (New York: Pearson, 2005); Alan I. Abramowitz and Kyle L. Saunders, "Is Polarization a Myth?," *Journal of Politics* 70, no. 2 (2008): 542–555.

67. https://legacy.voteview.com/political_polarization_2015.htm.

68. Geoffrey C. Layman and Thomas M. Carsey, "Party Polarization and 'Conflict Extension' in the American Electorate," *American Journal of Political Science* 46, no. 4 (2002): 786–802.

69. https://legacy.voteview.com/political_polarization_2014.htm; Gary C. Jacobson, "Partisanship, Money, and Competition: Elections and the Transformation of Congress since the 1970s," in *Congress Reconsidered*, ed. Lawrence C. Dodd and Bruce I. Oppenheimer (Washington, DC: Congressional Quarterly Press, 2017), 89–117.

70. Matt Grossman and David A. Hopkins, *Asymmetric Politics: Ideological Republicans and Group Interest Democrats* (New York: Oxford University Press, 2016), 11; https://legacy.voteview.com/political_polarization_2015.htm.

71. Grace Sparks, "The Majority of Americans Tend to Agree with Democrats on Top Issues, Polling Shows," CNN, April 7, 2019, https://www.cnn.com/2019/04/07/politics/democratic-positions-majority/index.html.

72. Grossman and Hopkins, *Asymmetric Politics*, 3–4.

73. Grossman and Hopkins, 4, 12.

74. Thomas E. Mann and Norman J. Ornstein, "Let's Just Say It: The Republicans Are the Problem," *Washington Post,* April 27, 2012.

75. Quoted in Ian Chipman, "Political Polarization's Geographic Roots Run Deep," *Insight* (Stanford Graduate School of Business), May 2, 2017, https://www.gsb.stanford.edu/insights/political-polarizations-geographic-roots-run -deep; Jonathan Rodden, *Why Cities Lose: Political Geography and the Representation of the Left* (New York: Basic, 2019).

76. Nicholas R. Seabrook, *Drawing the Lines: Constraints on Partisan Gerrymandering in U.S. Politics* (Ithaca, NY: Cornell University Press, 2017); Rodden, *Why Cities Lose*; Steven Mulroy, *Rethinking U.S. Election Law: Unskewing the System* (Northampton, MA: Edward Elgar, 2018); Gary C. Jacobson, "Partisanship, Money, and Competition: Elections and the Transformation of Congress since the 1970s," in *Congress Reconsidered*, 11th ed., ed. Lawrence C. Dodd and Bruce

I. Oppenheimer (Washington, DC: Congressional Quarterly Press, 2017), 89–118.

77. "The Minority Majority: America's Electoral System Gives the Republicans Advantages over Democrats," *Economist,* July 12, 2018.

78. Jacob T. Levy, "Democracy for Republicans: Simple Voting Rules for a Complex World," Niskanen Center, February 20, 2019, https://www.niskanen center.org/democracy-for-republicans/.

79. Francis E. Lee and Bruce I. Oppenheimer, *Sizing Up the Senate: The Unequal Consequences of Equal Representation* (Chicago: University of Chicago Press, 1999); Mulroy, *Rethinking U.S. Election Law.*

80. Benjamin Highton, "How the Senate Is Biased toward Republicans," *Washington Post,* January 31, 2014.

81. Paul Waldman, "We're Living in an Age of Minority Rule," *Washington Post,* July 13, 2018.

82. Sabrina Siddiqui, "Democrats Got Millions More Votes—So How Did Republicans win the Senate?" *Guardian,* November 8, 2018.

83. Philip Bump, "In about 20 Years, Half the Population Will Live in Eight states," *Washington Post,* July 12, 2018 (quoting Norman Ornstein).

84. Lee and Oppenheimer, *Sizing Up the Senate,* 115–121.

85. Kevin J. McMahon, "Will the Supreme Court Still 'Seldom Stray Very Far'?: Regime Politics in a Polarized America," *Chicago-Kent Law Review* 93 (2018): 343–371.

86. Stephen Jessee and Neil Malhotra, "The Chart That Shows the Supreme Court Will Be Out of Step with the Country," *New York Times,* July 12, 2018.

87. Waldman, "We're Living in an Age of Minority Rule;" Dana Milbank, "An Explosion Is Coming," *Washington Post,* June 29, 2018; Scott Lemieux, "Justice Kennedy's Retirement Cements His Legacy as an Enabler of Trump's Pro-Business, Racist, Anti-Woman Agenda," NBC News, June 27, 2018, https://www.nbcnews.com/think/opinion/justice-kennedy-s-retirement-cements-his-legacy-enabler-trump-s-ncna887106.

88. Frey, "Minorities Are the Democratic Engine."

89. Sean McElwee, "The GOP's Stunning Election Advantage," *Salon,* December 5, 2015.

90. Some party planks relating to elections or voting were excluded from Table I.1 due to space limitations, such as repeated statements in recent RNC platforms regarding the importance of protecting "the voting rights of our citizen soldiers."

91. Keith G. Bentele and Erin O'Brien, "Jim Crow 2.0?: Why States Consider and Adopt Restrictive Voter Access Policies," *Perspectives on Politics* 11, no. 4 (2013): 1089–1090.

92. Keith G. Bentele and Erin O'Brien, "Resolved, States Should Enact Voter ID Laws and Reduce Early Voting, CON," in *Debating Reform: Conflicting Perspectives on How to Fix the American Political System,* 3rd ed., ed. Richard J. Ellis and Michael C. Nelson (Washington, DC: Congressional Quarterly Press, 2016), 106–117.

93. Ann Bandolik, "Life after the Voting Rights Act: Identifying Partisan and

Racialised Trends in the Proposal and Passage of Restrictive Voter-Access Policy in the United States of America," M.S. thesis, London School of Economics and Political Science, 2017. In contrast to Bentele and O'Brien's study, Bandolik did not so consistently find that Republican government control helped to explain a state's propensity to propose or adopt restrictive voting policies; nonetheless, she found that the percentage of Republican state legislators significantly increased the likelihood of a state adopting the controversial Voter Registration Crosscheck Program, which the 2016 GOP platform explicitly endorsed. Bentele and O'Brien, "Jim Crow 2.0?"

94. Cobb, "Voter-Suppression Tactics in the Age of Trump."

95. Dar Kam, "Former Florida GOP Leaders Say Voter Suppression Was Reason They Pushed New Election Law," *Palm Beach Post*, November 25, 2012.

96. Elise Viebeck, Amy Gardner, and Michael Scherer, "Trump, GOP Challenge Efforts to Make Voting Easier Amid Coronavirus Pandemic," *Washington Post*, April 4, 2020.

97. Viebeck, Gardner, and Scherer, "Trump, GOP Challenge Efforts."

98. Mark Graber, email to lawcourt list-serv, January 4, 2020.

99. Jennifer Rubin, "GOP Autopsy Report Goes Bold," *Washington Post*, March 18, 2013.

100. Ari Berman, "How the 2000 Election in Florida Led to a New Wave of Voter Disenfranchisement," *Nation*, July 28, 2015; Richard L. Hasen, *The Voting Wars: From Florida 2000 to the Next Election Meltdown* (New Haven, CT: Yale University Press, 2012), 28–30; Robert E. Pierre, "Botched Name Purge Denied Some the Right to Vote," *Washington Post*, May 31, 2001.

101. Berman, "How the 2000 Election in Florida."

102. Hasen, *The Voting Wars*, 5.

103. Berman, "How the 2000 Election in Florida."

104. Bob Egelko, "Trump Outsources Supreme Court Picks to Federalist Society," *San Francisco Chronicle*, July 8, 2018.

105. For example, in 2016, the Republicans pledged to "reaffirm the Constitution's fundamental principles: limited government, separation of powers, individual liberty, and the rule of law"; identified "an activist judiciary" as a "critical threat to our country's constitutional order"; encouraged Congress to use its impeachment power against "judges who unconstitutionally usurp Article I powers"; and promised that "a new Republican president will restore to the Court a strong conservative majority that will follow the text and original meaning of the Constitution."

106. The 2016 RNC platform mentioned *Constitution* or *constitutional* eighty times and *amendment* forty-seven times.

107. Scott Lemieux, "Trump's Plan to Make Voters Older, Wealthier, and Whiter," *Reuters*, July 12, 2017, https://www.reuters.com/article/us-lemieux-voting-commentary/commentary-trumps-plan-to-make-voters-older-wealthier-and-whiter-idUSKBN19X28H.

108. Department of Commerce v. New York, 139 S. Ct. 2551 (2019); Evenwel v. Abbott, 136 S. Ct. 1120 (2016).

Chapter 1: Understanding Judicial Partisanship

1. Charles Gardner Geyh, *Courting Peril: The Political Transformation of the American Judiciary* (New York: Oxford University Press, 2016), 54, 55; Richard L. Pacelle Jr., Brett W. Curry, and Bryan W. Marshall, *Decision Making by the Supreme Court* (New York: Cambridge University Press, 2011); Michael A. Bailey and Forrest Maltzman, *The Constrained Court: Law, Politics, and the Decisions Justices Make* (Princeton, NJ: Princeton University Press, 2011).

2. Morton J. Horwitz, "The Rise of Legal Formalism," *American Journal of Legal History* 19 (1975): 251–264; Lawrence M. Friedman, *A History of American Law*, 2nd ed. (New York: Simon & Schuster, 1985); Thomas Grey, "Langdell's Orthodoxy," *University of Pittsburgh Law Review* 45 (1983): 1–53.

3. Oliver Wendell Holmes, "The Path of the Law," *Harvard Law Review* 10 (1897): 457–478; Benjamin Cardozo, *The Nature of the Judicial Process* (New Haven, CT: Yale University Press, 1921).

4. Roscoe Pound, "Liberty of Contract," *Yale Law Journal* 18 (1909): 454–487; Jerome Frank, *Law and the Modern Mind* (New York: Brentano's, 1930); Jerome Frank, *Courts on Trial* (Princeton, NJ: Princeton University Press, 1949); Felix S. Cohen, "Transcendental Nonsense and the Functional Approach," *Columbia Law Review* 35 (1935): 809–849.

5. Holmes, "The Path of the Law," 466.

6. Thomas G. Walker, Lee Epstein, and William J. Dixon, "On the Mysterious Demise of Consensual Norms in the United States Supreme Court," *Journal of Politics* 50 (1988): 361–389.

7. Pamela C. Corley, Amy Steigerwalt, and Artemus Ward, *The Puzzle of Unanimity: Consensus on the United States Supreme Court* (Palo Alto, CA: Stanford University Press, 2013), 17–19.

8. Walker et al., "On the Mysterious Demise of Consensual Norms in the United States Supreme Court," 363.

9. C. Herman Pritchett, *The Roosevelt Court: A Study in Judicial Politics and Values, 1937–47* (New York: Macmillan, 1948).

10. David W. Rohde and Harold J. Spaeth, *Supreme Court Decision Making* (San Francisco: W. H. Freeman, 1976); Glendon Schubert, "The 1960 Term of the Supreme Court," *American Journal of Political Science* 56, no. 1 (1962): 90–107; Glendon Schubert, *The Judicial Mind* (Chicago: Northwestern University Press, 1965); Glendon Schubert, *The Judicial Mind Revisited: Psychometric Analysis of Supreme Court Ideology* (San Francisco: W. H. Freeman, 1974); Harold J. Spaeth, "An Approach to the Study of Attitudinal Differences as an Aspect of Judicial Behavior," *Midwest Journal of Political Science* 5 (1961): 165–180; Harold J. Spaeth, "An Analysis of Judicial Attitudes in the Labor Relations Decisions of the Warren Court," *Journal of Politics* 25 (1963): 290–311; Harold J. Spaeth, *Supreme Court Policy Making: Explanation and Prediction* (San Francisco: W. H. Freeman, 1979); S. Sydney Ulmer, "Supreme Court Behavior and Civil Rights," *Western Political Quarterly* 13, no. 2 (1960): 288–311.

11. Jeffrey A. Segal and Harold J. Spaeth, *The Supreme Court and the Attitudinal Model* (New York: Cambridge University Press, 1993); Jeffrey A. Segal and

Harold J. Spaeth, *The Supreme Court and the Attitudinal Model Revisited* (New York: Cambridge University Press, 2002).

12. Segal and Spaeth, *The Supreme Court and the Attitudinal Model Revisited*, 48.

13. Segal and Spaeth, *The Supreme Court and the Attitudinal Model Revisited*, 86. Judicial behavior scholars tend to use terms like "ideology," "attitudes," "values," and "preferences" interchangeably. As Braman correctly notes, however, they are distinct concepts. Ideology, she explains, is "a coherent set of beliefs that individual judges hold about the proper role of government in society," whereas attitudes and preferences are more specific: attitudes are the "positive or negative feelings judges have toward . . . a particular issue or class of litigant," and preferences are the particular outcomes judges favor in legal or policy disputes. Eileen Braman, *Law, Politics and Perception: How Policy Preferences Influence Legal Reasoning* (Charlottesville: University of Virginia Press, 2009). While distinctive, these concepts are obviously interrelated. This book tends to use "ideology" and "policy preferences" most often and typically interchangeably, though ideology might best be understood as summated preferences.

14. Jeffrey A. Segal and Albert Cover, "Ideological Values and the Votes of U.S. Supreme Court Justices," *American Political Science Review* 83, no. 2 (1989): 557–565; Andrew Martin and Kevin Quinn, "Dynamic Ideal Point Estimation via Markov Chain Monte Carlo for the U.S. Supreme Court, 1953–1999," *Political Analysis* 10, no. 2 (2002): 134–153; Lee Epstein, Andrew D. Martin, Jeffrey A. Segal, and Chad Westerland, "The Judicial Common Space," *Journal of Law, Economics, and Organization* 23 (2007): 303–325; Michael W. Giles, Virginia. Hettinger, and Todd Peppers, "Picking Federal Judges: A Note on Policy and Partisan Selection Agendas," *Political Research Quarterly* 54 (2001): 623–641; Bailey and Maltzman, *The Constrained Court*; Benjamin E. Lauderdale and Tom S. Clark, "The Supreme Court's Many Median Justices," *American Political Science Review* 106, no. 4 (2012): 847–866; Adam Bonica and Michael J. Woodruff, "A Common-Space Measure of State Supreme Court Ideology," *Journal of Law, Economics, and Organization* 31, no. 3 (2014): 472–498; Jason H. Windett, Jeffrey J. Harden, and Matthew E. K. Hall, "Estimating Dynamic Ideal Points for State Supreme Courts," *Political Analysis* 23, no. 3 (2015): 461–469.

15. Segal and Spaeth, *The Supreme Court and the Attitudinal Model Revisited*, 112.

16. Bailey and Maltzman, *The Constrained Court*; Tim Hagle and Harold Spaeth, "Ideological Patterns in the Justices' Voting in the Burger Court Business Cases," *Journal of Politics* 55, no. 2 (1993): 492–505; Rohde and Spaeth, *Supreme Court Decision Making*; Segal and Cover, "Ideological Values and the Votes of U.S. Supreme Court Justices"; Segal and Spaeth, *The Supreme Court and the Attitudinal Model Revisited*; Spaeth, *Supreme Court Policy Making*; Frank B. Cross and Emerson H. Tiller, "Judicial Partisanship and Obedience to Legal Doctrine: Whistleblowing on the Federal Courts of Appeals," *Yale Law Journal* 107 (1998): 2155–2176.

17. Virginia Armstrong and Charles A. Johnson, "Certiorari Decisionmaking by the Warren and Burger Courts: Is Cue Theory Time Bound?" *Polity* 15 (1982): 141–150; Robert Boucher and Jeffrey Segal, "Supreme Court Justices as Strategic Decision Makers: Aggressive Grants and Defensive Denials on the

Vinson Court," *Journal of Politics* 57 (1995): 824–837; Gregory A. Caldeira, John R. Wright, and Christopher J. W. Zorn, "Sophisticated Voting and Gate-Keeping in the Supreme Court." *Journal of Law, Economics, and Organization* 15, no. 3 (1999): 549–572; Vanessa A. Baird, *Answering the Call of the Court: How Justices and Litigants Set the Supreme Court Agenda* (Charlottesville: University of Virginia Press, 2007).

18. Timothy R. Johnson, Paul J. Wahlbeck, and James F. Spriggs II, "The Influence of Oral Arguments on the U.S. Supreme Court," *American Political Science Review* 100, no. 1 (2006): 99–113.

19. Chris W. Bonneau, Thomas H. Hammond, Forrest Maltzman, and Paul J. Wahlbeck, "Agenda Control, the Median Justice, and the Majority Opinion on the U.S. Supreme Court," *American Journal of Political Science* 51, no. 4 (2007): 890–905; Forrest Maltzman, James F. Spriggs II, and Paul J. Wahlbeck, *Crafting Law on the Supreme Court: The Collegial Game* (New York: Cambridge University Press, 2000); Ryan J. Owens and Justin P. Wedeking, "Justices and Legal Clarity: Analyzing the Complexity of U.S. Supreme Court Opinions," *Law and Society Review* 45 (2011): 1027–1061.

20. Lawrence Baum, "Membership Change and Collective Voting Change in the United States Supreme Court," *Journal of Politics* 54 (1992): 3–24; Helmut Norpoth and Jeffrey A. Segal, "Popular Influence on Supreme Court Decisions: Comment," *American Political Science Review* (1994): 711–716; Richard L. Pacelle Jr., *The Transformation of the Supreme Court's Agenda: From the New Deal to the Reagan Administration* (Boulder, CO: Westview, 1991).

21. Paul Brace, Laura Langer, and Melinda Gann Hall, "Measuring the Preferences of State Supreme Court Judges," *Journal of Politics* 62, no. 2 (2000): 387–413; Frank B. Cross, "Decisionmaking in the U.S. Circuit Courts of Appeals," *California Law Review* 91 (2003): 1457–1515; Craig F. Emmert and Carol Ann Traut, "The California Supreme Court and the Death Penalty," *American Politics Research* 22, no. 1 (1994): 41–61; Lee Epstein, William M. Landes, and Richard A. Posner, *The Behavior of Federal Judges: A Theoretical and Empirical Study of Rational Choice* (Cambridge, MA: Harvard University Press, 2013); Virginia A. Hettinger, Stefanie A. Lindquist, and Wendy L. Martinek, *Judging on a Collegial Court: Influences on Federal Appellate Decision Making* (Charlottesville: University of Virginia Press, 2006); Kyle Casimir Kopko, "The Effect of Partisanship in Election Law Judicial Decision-Making" (PhD diss., Ohio State University, 2010); Thomas J. Miles and Cass R. Sunstein, "The Real World of Arbitrariness Review." *University of Chicago Law Review* 75 (2008): 761–814; Daniel R. Pinello, "Linking Party to Judicial Ideology in American Courts: A Meta-Analysis," *Justice System Journal* 20, no. 3 (1999): 219–254; Richard L. Revesz, "Environmental Regulation, Ideology, and the D.C. Circuit," *Virginia Law Review* 83 (1997): 1717–1772; Max M. Schanzenbach and Emerson H. Tiller, "Reviewing the Sentencing Guidelines: Judicial Politics, Empirical Evidence, and Reform," *University of Chicago Law Review* 75 (2008): 715–760; Gregory C. Sisk, Michael Heise, and Andrew P. Morris, "Searching for the Soul of Judicial Decision Making: An Empirical Study of Religious Freedom Decisions," *Ohio State Law Journal* 65 (2004): 491–614; Cass R. Sunstein, David Schkade, Lisa M. Ellman, and Andres

Sawicki, *Are Judges Political? An Empirical Analysis of the Federal Judiciary* (Washington, DC: Brookings Institution, 2006).

22. Walter Murphy, *Elements of Judicial Strategy* (Chicago: University of Chicago Press, 1964); Lee Epstein and Jack Knight, *The Choices Justices Make* (Washington, DC: Congressional Quarterly Press, 1998).

23. Forrest Maltzman, James F. Spriggs II, and Paul J. Wahlbeck, *Crafting Law on the Supreme Court: The Collegial Game* (New York: Cambridge University Press, 2000).

24. Gerald N. Rosenberg, *The Hollow Hope: Can Courts Bring About Social Change?*, 2nd ed. (Chicago: University of Chicago Press, 2008); Tom S. Clark, *The Limits of Judicial Independence* (New York: Cambridge University Press, 2011); Anna Harvey and Barry Friedman, "Pulling Punches: Congressional Constraints on the Supreme Court's Constitutional Rulings, 1987–2000," *Legislative Studies Quarterly* 31, no. 4 (2006): 533–562; Bailey and Maltzman, *The Constrained Court.*

25. Melinda Gann Hall, "Constituent Influence in State Supreme Courts: Conceptual Notes and a Case Study," *Journal of Politics* 49, no. 4 (1987): 1117–1124; Melinda Gann Hall, "Voluntary Retirements from State Supreme Courts: Assessing Democratic Pressures to Relinquish the Bench," *Journal of Politics* 63, no. 4 (2001): 1112–1140; Gregory A. Huber and Sanford C. Gordon, "Accountability and Coercion: Is Justice Blind when It Runs for Office?" *American Journal of Political Science* 48 (2004): 247–263.

26. Barry Friedman, "Taking Law Seriously," *Perspectives on Politics* 4, no. 2 (2006): 261–276; Frank B. Cross, "Political Science and the New Legal Realism: A Case of Unfortunate Interdisciplinary Ignorance," *Northwestern University Law Review* 92 (1997): 251–326.

27. Harry T. Edwards, "Collegiality and Decision Making on the D.C. Circuit," *Virginia Law Review* 84, no. 7 (1998): 1335–1370; Alex Kozinski, "What I Ate for Breakfast, and Other Mysteries of Judicial Decision Making," in *Judges on Judging: Views from the Bench*, 2nd ed., ed. David M. O'Brien (Washington, DC: Congressional Quarterly Press, 2004), 76–81; Patricia M. Wald, "A Response to Tiller and Cross," *Columbia Law Review* 99, no. 1 (1999): 235–261.

28. Corley et al., *The Puzzle of Unanimity*, 4–5; Paul H. Edelman, David E. Klein, and Stefanie A. Lindquist, "Consensus, Disorder, and Ideology on the Supreme Court," *Journal of Empirical Legal Studies* 9, no. 1 (2012): 129–148.

29. Bailey and Maltzman, *The Constrained Court*, 16.

30. Friedman, "Taking Law Seriously"; Howard Gillman, "What's Law Got to Do with It? Judicial Behavioralists Test the 'Legal Model' of Judicial Decision Making," *Law and Social Inquiry* 26 (2001): 465–504; David E. Klein, "Law in Judicial Decision-Making," in *The Oxford Handbook of U.S. Judicial Behavior*, ed. Lee Epstein and Stefanie A. Lindquist (New York: Oxford University Press, 2017), 236–252.

31. Cross, "Decisionmaking in the U.S. Circuit Courts of Appeals"; Thomas G. Hansford and James F. Spriggs II, *The Politics of Precedent on the U.S. Supreme Court* (Princeton, NJ: Princeton University Press, 2006); Michael J. Gerhardt, *The Power of Precedent* (New York: Oxford University Press, 2008); Bailey and

Maltzman, *The Constrained Court*; Eric A. Posner, "What Do Judges and Justices Maximize? (The Same Thing Everybody Else Does)," *Supreme Court Economic Review* 3 (1993): 1–41.

32. Joshua B. Fischman and Tonja Jacobi, "The Second Dimension of the Supreme Court," *William and Mary Law Review* 57 (2015): 1671–1715; Alexander Volokh, "Choosing Interpretive Methods: A Positive Theory of Judges and Everyone Else," *New York University Law Review* 83 (2008): 769–846.

33. Mark J. Richards and Herbert M. Kritzer, "Jurisprudential Regimes in Supreme Court Decision Making," *American Political Science Review* 96, no. 2 (2002): 305–320; Brandon L. Bartels, "The Constraining Capacity of Legal Doctrine on the U.S. Supreme Court," *American Political Science Review* 103, no. 3 (2009): 474–495; Tonja Jacobi and Emerson H. Tiller, "Legal Doctrine and Political Control," *Journal of Law, Economics, and Organization* 23 (2007): 326–345; Frank B. Cross, *Decision-Making in the U.S. Court of Appeals* (Palo Alto, CA: Stanford University Press, 2007).

34. Corley et al., *The Puzzle of Unanimity*; Owens and Wedeking, "Justices and Legal Clarity"; Nancy C. Staudt, "Modeling Standing," *New York University Law Review* 79 (2004): 612–684.

35. Timothy R. Johnson, Paul J. Wahlbeck, and James F. Spriggs II, "The Influence of Oral Arguments on the U.S. Supreme Court," *American Political Science Review* 100, no. 1 (2006): 99–113.

36. Bailey and Maltzman, *The Constrained Court*.

37. Cross, *Decision-Making in the U.S. Court of Appeals*; Epstein et al., *The Behavior of Federal Judges*.

38. David E. Klein, *Making Law in the United States Courts of Appeals* (New York: Cambridge University Press, 2002), 6.

39. Klein, *Making Law in the United States Courts of Appeals*; Lawrence Baum, *The Puzzle of Judicial Behavior* (Ann Arbor: University of Michigan Press, 1997); Lawrence Baum, *Judges and Their Audiences: A Perspective on Judicial Behavior* (Princeton, NJ: Princeton University Press, 2006); Ronald Kahn, "Institutionalized Norms and Supreme Court Decision Making: The Rehnquist Court on Privacy and Religion," in *Supreme Court Decision-Making: New Institutionalist Approaches*, ed. Cornell W. Clayton and Howard Gillman (Chicago: University of Chicago Press, 1999), 177–198; Howard Gillman and Cornell Clayton, "Beyond Judicial Attitudes: Institutional Approaches to Supreme Court Decision-Making," in *Supreme Court Decision-Making: New Institutionalist Approaches*, ed. Cornell W. Clayton and Howard Gillman (Chicago: University of Chicago Press, 1999), 1–14.

40. Geyh, *Courting Peril*, 55.

41. Bailey and Maltzman, *The Constrained Court*, 16, 47; Richard L. Pacelle Jr., Brett W. Curry, and Bryan W. Marshall, *Decision Making by the Supreme Court* (New York: Cambridge University Press, 2011).

42. Bailey and Maltzman, *The Constrained Court*; Bartels, "The Constraining Capacity of Legal Doctrine on the U.S. Supreme Court"; Epstein et al., *The Behavior of Federal Judges*; Stephen M. Feldman, "Supreme Court Alchemy: Turning Law and Politics Into Mayonnaise," *Georgetown Journal of Law and Public Policy* 12 (2014): 57–97; Joshua B. Fischman and Tonja Jacobi, "The Second Dimension

of the Supreme Court," *William and Mary Law Review* 57 (2015): 1671–1715; Benjamin E. Lauderdale and Tom S. Clark, "The Supreme Court's Many Median Justices," *American Political Science Review* 106, no. 4 (2012): 847–866; Jeffrey R. Lax, "The New Judicial Politics of Legal Doctrine," *Annual Review of Political Science* 14 (2011): 131–157; Pacelle et al., *Decision Making by the Supreme Court*; Lawrence Solum, "The Positive Foundations of Formalism: False Necessity and American Legal Realism," *Harvard Law Review* 120 (2014): 2464–2497.

43. Eileen Braman and Thomas E. Nelson, "Mechanism of Motivated Reasoning? Analogical Perception in Discrimination Disputes," *American Journal of Political Science* 51, no. 4 (2007): 940.

44. Pritchett, *The Roosevelt Court*; Glendon Schubert, ed., *Judicial Decision-Making* (New York: Free Press, 1963); Schubert, *The Judicial Mind*; Spaeth, *Supreme Court Policy Making*.

45. Braman, *Law, Politics and Perception*, 28.

46. Lawrence Baum, "Motivation and Judicial Behavior: Expanding the Scope of Inquiry," in *The Psychology of Judicial Decision Making*, ed. David Klein and Gregory Mitchell (New York: Oxford University Press, 2010), 24; Baum, *Judges and Their Audiences*; Neal Devins and Lawrence Baum, *The Company They Keep: How Partisan Divisions Came to the Supreme Court* (New York: Oxford University Press, 2019), 18–19.

47. Cross, "Decisionmaking in the U.S. Circuit Courts of Appeals"; Klein, *Making Law in the United States Courts of Appeals*; Gillman, "What's Law Got to Do with It?"

48. Baum, "Motivation and Judicial Behavior," 21.

49. Posner, "What Do Judges and Justices Maximize?"

50. Lawrence Baum, "What Judges Want: Judges' Goals and Judicial Behavior," *Political Research Quarterly* 47 (1994): 749–768; Baum, *Judges and Their Audiences*; Christopher R. Drahozal, "Judicial Incentives and the Appeals Process," *Southern Methodist University Law Review* 51 (1998): 469–503; Nuno Garoupa and Tom Ginsberg, *Judicial Reputation: A Comparative Theory* (Chicago: University of Chicago Press, 2015); Thomas J. Miceli and Metin M. Cosgel, "Reputation and Judicial Decision-Making," *Journal of Law, Economics, and Organization* 23 (1994): 31–51.

51. Matthew E. K. Hall, *What Justices Want: Goals and Personality on the U.S. Supreme Court* (New York: Cambridge University Press, 2018); Ryan C. Black, Ryan J. Owens, Justin Wedeking, and Patrick C. Wohlfarth, *The Conscientious Justice: How Supreme Court Justices' Personalities Influence the Law, the High Court, and the Constitution* (Cambridge: Cambridge University Press, 2020).

52. C. K. Rowland and Robert A. Carp, *Politics and Judgment in Federal District Courts* (Lawrence: University Press of Kansas, 1996), 136.

53. Ziva Kunda, "The Case for Motivated Reasoning," *Psychological Bulletin* 108, no. 3 (1990): 480–498.

54. Braman, *Law, Politics and Perception*, 7.

55. Braman and Nelson, "Mechanism of Motivated Reasoning?"

56. Dan Kahan, "'Ideology in' or 'Cultural Cognition of' Judging: What Difference Does It Make?" *Marquette Law Review* 92, no. 3 (2009): 413; Feldman, "Supreme Court Alchemy."

57. Segal and Spaeth, *The Supreme Court and the Attitudinal Model Revisited.*
58. David W. Adamany, "The Party Variable in Judges' Voting: Conceptual Notes and a Case Study," *American Political Science Review* 63, no. 1 (1969): 57–73; Paul Brace and Melinda Gann Hall, "The Interplay of Preferences, Case Facts, Context, and Rules in the Politics of Judicial Choice," *Journal of Politics* 59, no. 4 (1997): 1206–1231; Robert A. Carp and C. K. Rowland, *Policymaking and Politics in the Federal District Courts* (Knoxville: University of Tennessee Press, 1983); Sheldon Goldman, "Voting Behavior on the United States Courts of Appeals, 1961–1964," *American Political Science Review* 60 (1966): 374–383; Sheldon Goldman, "Voting Behavior on the United States Courts of Appeals Revisited," *American Political Science Review* 69 (1975): 491–506; Melinda Gann Hall and Paul Brace, "Toward an Integrated Model of Judicial Voting Behavior," *American Politics Quarterly* 20 (1992): 147–168; Melinda Gann Hall and Paul Brace, "The Vicissitudes of Death by Decree: Forces Influencing Capital Punishment Decision Making in State Supreme Courts," *Social Science Quarterly* 75, no. 1 (1994): 136–151; Stuart Nagel, "Political Party Affiliation and Judges' Decisions," *Political Science Review* 55 (1961): 843–850; Stuart Nagel, "Multiple Correlation of Judicial Backgrounds and Decisions," *Florida State University Law Review* 2 (1974): 258–280; Glendon Schubert, *Quantitative Analysis of Judicial Behavior* (Glencoe, IL: Free Press, 1959); Donald R. Songer, "Consensual and Nonconsensual Decisions in Unanimous Opinions of the United States Courts of Appeals," *American Journal of Political Science* 26 (1982): 225–239; Donald R. Songer and Sue Davis, "The Impact of Party and Region on Voting Decisions in the United States Courts of Appeals, 1955–1986," *Western Political Quarterly* 43 (1990): 317–334; C. Neal Tate, "Personal Attribute Models of the Voting Behavior of U.S. Supreme Court Justices' Liberalism in Civil Liberties and Economics Decisions, 1946–1978," *American Political Science Review* 75, no. 2 (1981): 355–367; C. Neal Tate and Roger Handberg, "Time Binding and Theory Building in Personal Attribute Models of Supreme Court Voting Behavior, 1916–88," *American Journal of Political Science* 35 (1991): 460–480; S. Sidney Ulmer, "The Political Party Variable in the Michigan Supreme Court," *Journal of Public Law* 11 (1962): 352–362.
59. Nagel, "Political Party Affiliation and Judges' Decisions," 846.
60. Schubert, *Quantitative Analysis of Judicial Behavior,* 129–142; Ulmer, "The Political Party Variable in the Michigan Supreme Court."
61. Tate, "Personal Attribute Models of the Voting Behavior of U.S. Supreme Court Justices' Liberalism in Civil Liberties and Economics Decisions, 1946–1978."
62. Hall and Brace, "The Vicissitudes of Death by Decree: Forces Influencing Capital Punishment Decision Making in State Supreme Courts."
63. Pinello, "Linking Party to Judicial Ideology in American Courts."
64. Brian Z. Tamanaha, *Realistic Socio-Legal Theory: Pragmatism and a Social Theory of Law* (New York: Oxford University Press, 1999); Cross, "Political Science and the New Legal Realism"; Thomas J. Miles and Cass R. Sunstein, "The New Legal Realism," *University of Chicago Law Review* 75 (2008): 831.
65. Sunstein et. al., *Are Judges Political?*

66. Cross and Tiller, "Judicial Partisanship and Obedience to Legal Doctrine."

67. Thomas M. Keck, *Judicial Politics in Polarized Times* (Chicago: University of Chicago Press, 2014).

68. Cross and Tiller, "Judicial Partisanship and Obedience to Legal Doctrine"; Joshua B. Fischman, "Estimating Preferences of Circuit Judges: A Model of Consensus Voting," *Journal of Law and Economics* 54 (2011): 781–809; Hettinger et al., *Judging on a Collegial Court*; Thomas J. Miles and Cass R. Sunstein, "The Real World of Arbitrariness Review," *University of Chicago Law Review* 75 (2008): 761–814; Jaya Ramji-Nogales, Andres I. Schoenholtz, and Phillip G. Schrag, "Refugee Roulette: Disparities in Asylum Adjudication," *Stanford Law Review* 60 (2007): 295–411; Revesz, "Environmental Regulation, Ideology, and the D.C. Circuit"; Cass R. Sunstein and Thomas J. Miles, "Depoliticizing Administrative Law," *Duke Law Journal* 58 (2009): 2193–2230.

69. Miles and Sunstein, "The New Legal Realism," 838.

70. Randall D. Lloyd, "Separating Partisanship from Party in Judicial Research: Reapportionment in the U.S. District Courts," *American Political Science Review* 89, no. 2 (1995): 413, 418.

71. Nagel, "Political Party Affiliation and Judges' Decisions," 847.

72. Justine D'Elia-Kueper and Jeffrey A. Segal, "Ideology and Partisanship," in *The Oxford Handbook of U.S. Judicial Behavior*, ed. Lee Epstein and Stefanie A. Lindquist (New York: Oxford University Press, 2017), 303.

73. Neal Devins and Lawrence Baum, "Split Definitive: How Party Polarization Turned the Supreme Court into a Partisan Court," *Supreme Court Review* (2016): 301–365; Devins and Baum, *The Company They Keep*.

74. Devins and Baum, *The Company They Keep*, 2.

75. Lee Epstein and Gary King, "The Rules of Inference," *University of Chicago Law Review* 69 (2002): 87–96.

76. Nagel, "Political Party Affiliation and Judges' Decisions," 847.

77. Epstein and King, "The Rules of Inference," 88–89.

78. Epstein and King, 89, 95.

79. Cox and Miles, "Judging the Voting Rights Act."

80. Cox and Miles, 19.

81. Cox and Miles, 20; Epstein and King, "The Rules of Inference."

82. Cox and Miles, "Judging the Voting Rights Act," 20.

83. Cox and Miles, 21.

84. D'Elia-Kueper and Segal, "Ideology and Partisanship," 303.

85. Kevin J. McMahon, "The Justices Decide: Analyzing Attitudes, Politics and the Law (reviewing Bailey and Maltzman, *The Constrained Court*, Stephen Engel, *American Politicians Confront the Court*, and Pacelle, Curry and Marshall's *Decision Making by the Supreme Court*)," *Tulsa Law Review* 48 (2012): 269; Cornell W. Clayton and David May, "A Political Regimes Approach to the Analysis of Legal Decisions," *Polity* 32 (1999): 233–252.

86. Robert A. Dahl, "Decision-Making in a Democracy: The Supreme Court as a National Policy-Maker," *Journal of Public Law* 6 (1957): 285.

87. Dahl, "Decision-Making in a Democracy," 293.

88. Keith E. Whittington, "'Interpose Your Friendly Hand': Political Supports

for the Exercise of Judicial Review by the United States Supreme Court," *American Political Science Review* 99 (2005): 583–596.

89. Mark Tushnet, *A Court Divided: The Rehnquist Court and the Future of Constitutional Law* (New York: W. W. Norton, 2006).

90. Cornell W. Clayton and Howard Gillman, eds., *Supreme Court Decision-Making: New Institutionalist Approaches* (Chicago: University of Chicago Press, 1999); Cornell W. Clayton and J. Mitchell Pickerill, "Guess What Happened on the Way to the Revolution? Precursors to the Supreme Court's Federalism Revolution," *Publius: The Journal of Federalism* 34, no. 3 (2004): 85–114; Howard Gillman, "How Political Parties Can Use the Courts to Advance Their Agendas: Federal Courts in the United States, 1875–1891," *American Political Science Review* 96, no. 3 (2002): 511–524; Gillman and Clayton, "Beyond Judicial Attitudes"; Mark A. Graber, "The Nonmajoritarian Difficulty: Legislative Deference to the Judiciary," *Studies in American Political Development* 7 (1993): 48–54; Mark A. Graber, "Constructing Judicial Review," *Annual Review of Political Science* 8, no. 1 (2005): 425–451; George I. Lovell, *Legislative Deferrals: Statutory Ambiguity, Judicial Power, and American Democracy* (New York: Cambridge University Press, 2003); Kevin J. McMahon, *Reconsidering Roosevelt on Race: How the Presidency Paved the Road to Brown* (Chicago: University of Chicago Press, 2004); Kevin J. McMahon, *Nixon's Court: His Challenge to Judicial Liberalism and Its Political Consequences* (Chicago: University of Chicago Press, 2011); Terri Peretti, *In Defense of a Political Court* (Princeton, NJ: Princeton University Press, 1999); Martin M. Shapiro, "The Constitution and Economic Rights," in *Essays on the Constitution of the United States*, ed. M. Judd Harmon (Port Washington, NY: Kennikat, 1978), 74–98; Tushnet, *A Court Divided*; Whittington, "'Interpose Your Friendly Hand'"; Keith E. Whittington, *The Political Foundations of Judicial Supremacy* (Princeton, NJ: Princeton University Press, 2007).

91. Howard Gillman, "Regime Politics, Jurisprudential Regimes, and Unenumerated Rights," *Journal of Constitutional Law* 9 (2006): 108; Sarah A. Binder and Forrest Maltzman, *Advise and Dissent: The Struggle to Shape the Federal Judiciary* (Washington, DC: Brookings Institution, 2009); Lee Epstein and Jeffrey A. Segal, *Advice and Consent: The Politics of Judicial Appointments* (New York: Oxford University Press, 2005); Christine L. Nemacheck, *Strategic Selection: Presidential Nomination of Supreme Court Justices from Herbert Hoover through George W. Bush* (Charlottesville: University of Virginia Press, 2007); Nancy Maveety, *Picking Judges* (New Brunswick, NJ: Transaction, 2016); Byron J. Moraski and Charles R. Shipan, "The Politics of Supreme Court Nominations: A Theory of Institutional Constraints and Choices," *American Journal of Political Science* 43 (1999): 1069–1095; Jeffrey A. Segal, Charles M. Cameron, and Albert D. Cover, "A Spatial Model of Roll Call Voting: Senators, Constituents, Presidents, and Interest Groups in Supreme Court Confirmations," *American Journal of Political Science* 36, no. 1 (1992): 96–121.

92. McMahon, *Reconsidering Roosevelt on Race*.

93. Teles, *Rise of the Conservative Movement*; Amanda Hollis-Brusky, *Ideas with Consequences: The Federalist Society and the Conservative Counterrevolution* (New York: Oxford University Press, 2015).

94. McMahon, *Nixon's Court.*

95. Deborah J. Barrow, Gary Zuk, and Gregory Gryski, *The Federal Judiciary and Institutional Change* (Ann Arbor: University of Michigan Press, 1996).

96. Clayton and May, "A Political Regimes Approach to the Analysis of Legal Decisions."

97. Calvin TerBeek, "The Constitution as Political Program: The Republican Party and Originalism, 1977–1988," paper presented at the annual meeting of the Midwest Political Science Association, Chicago, April 2019.

98. Mathew E. K. Hall, "Rethinking Regime Politics," *Law and Social Inquiry* 37, no. 4 (2012): 878–907.

99. Thomas Keck and Kevin McMahon, "Why *Roe* Still Stands: Abortion Law, the Supreme Court and the Republican Regime," *Studies in Law, Politics and Society* 70 (2015): 3383.

100. Keith E. Whittington, *Repugnant Laws: Judicial Review of Acts of Congress from the Founding to the Present* (Lawrence: University Press of Kansas), 288.

101. Eric A. Posner, "Does Political Bias in the Judiciary Matter: Implications of Judicial Bias Studies for Legal and Constitutional Reform," *University of Chicago Law Review* 85 (2008): 853–883; Thomas J. Miles and Cass R. Sunstein, "The Real World of Arbitrariness Review," *University of Chicago Law Review* 75 (2008): 761–814.

102. Bush v. Gore, 531 U.S. 98 (2000).

103. Gillman, "What's Law Got to Do with It?," 189.

104. Lawrence Solum, "I'm Gonna Get High, High, High, or Deconstructing the Up-Down Distinction Revisited," *Legal Theory Blog*, May 4, 2003, http://lsolum.typepad.com/legaltheory/2003/05/im_gonna_get_hi.html.

105. Michael S. Kang and Joanna M. Shepherd, "The Long Shadow of *Bush v. Gore*: Judicial Partisanship in Election Cases," *Stanford Law Review* 68 (2016): 1419.

106. Michael J. Klarman, "*Bush v. Gore* through the Lens of Constitutional History," *California Law Review* 89 (2001): 1721–1765.

107. Balkin and Levinson, "Understanding the Constitutional Revolution," 1062.

108. Harold J. Spaeth, David M. Meltz, Gregory J. Rathjen, and Michael V. Haselswerdt, "Is Justice Blind: An Empirical Investigation of a Normative Ideal," *Law and Society Review* 7, no. 1 (1972): 119–138; Harold J. Spaeth and Douglas R. Parker, "Effects of Attitude toward Situation upon Attitude toward Object," *Journal of Psychology* 73, no. 2 (1969): 173–182; Segal and Spaeth, *The Supreme Court and the Attitudinal Model Revisited*, 313.

109. Segal and Spaeth, 313.

110. Geyh, *Courting Peril.*

111. Justin Levitt, "The Partisanship Spectrum," *William and Mary Law Review* 55 (2014): 1787–1868.

112. Peretti, *In Defense of a Political Court.*

113. Levitt, "The Partisanship Spectrum."

114. Kyle Casimir Kopko, "Partisanship Suppressed: Judicial Decision-Making in Ralph Nader's 2004 Ballot Access Litigation," *Election Law Journal* 7, no. 4 (2008): 306.

115. Richard A. Posner, *Overcoming Law* (Cambridge, MA: Harvard University Press, 1995), 13.

116. Steven Greene, "Social Identity Theory and Party Identification," *Social Science Quarterly* 85, no. 1 (2004): 136–153; Donald P. Green, Bradley Palmquist, and Eric Schickler, *Partisan Hearts and Minds* (New Haven, CT: Yale University Press, 2004).

117. Angus Campbell, Philip E. Converse, Warren E. Miller, and Donald E. Stokes, *The American Voter* (New York: John Wiley & Sons, 1960); Larry M. Bartels, "Beyond the Running Tally: Partisan Bias in Political Perceptions," *Political Behavior* 24, no. 2 (2002): 117–150.

118. Baum, *Ideology in the Supreme Court*, 17.

119. Lloyd, "Separating Partisanship from Party in Judicial Research."

120. Kopko, "Litigant Partisan Identity and Challenges to Campaign Finance Policies," 228.

121. Baum, *Judges and Their Audiences*; Baum, "Motivation and Judicial Behavior."

122. Devins and Baum, *The Company They Keep*, 14.

123. Hollis-Brusky, *Ideas with Consequences*, 155–158.

124. Devins and Baum, *The Company They Keep*, 13.

125. Baum, *Ideology in the Supreme Court*, xiii, xiv.

126. Lee Epstein, Andrew D. Martin, and Kevin Quinn, "6+ Decades of Freedom of Expression in the U.S. Supreme Court," 2018, http://epstein.wustl.edu /research/FreedomOfExpression.pdf.

127. Terri Peretti, "Constructing the State Action Doctrine, 1940–1990," *Law and Social Inquiry* 35 (2010): 273–310.

128. Baum, *Ideology in the Supreme Court*.

129. Shapiro, "The Constitution and Economic Rights"; Martin M. Shapiro, "The Supreme Court: From Warren to Burger," in *The New American Political System*, ed. Anthony King (Washington, DC: American Enterprise Institute, 1978), 179–211.

130. Baum, *Ideology in the Supreme Court*, 189.

131. Brandice Canes-Wrone and Tom S. Clark, "Judicial Independence and Nonpartisan Elections," *Wisconsin Law Review* (2009): 21–65; Kyle Cheek and Anthony Champagne, *Judicial Politics in Texas: Partisanship, Money, and Politics in State Courts* (New York: Peter Lang, 2005).

132. John R. Schmidhauser, "The Justices of the Supreme Court: A Collective Portrait," *Midwest Journal of Political Science* 3 (1959): 56–57.

133. Terri Peretti, "Where Have All the Politicians Gone? Recruiting for the Modern Supreme Court," *Judicature* 91, no. 3 (2007): 112–122; Lee Epstein, Jack Knight, and Andrew Martin, "The Norm of Prior Judicial Experience and Its Consequences for Career Diversity on the U.S. Supreme Court," *California Law Review* 91 (2003): 903–966.

134. Baum, "Motivation and Judicial Behavior," 24.

135. Terri Peretti, "Judicial Partisanship in Voter Identification Litigation," *Election Law Journal* 15 (2016): 225.

136. Kopko, "The Effect of Partisanship in Election Law Judicial Decision-

Making"; Kopko, "Litigant Partisan Identity and Challenges to Campaign Finance Policies"; Devins and Baum, *The Company They Keep.*

137. For example, with respect to the influence of unconscious racial bias, see Jeffrey J. Rachlinski, Sheri Lynn Johnson, Andrew J. Wistrich, and Chris Guthrie, "Does Unconscious Racial Bias Affect Trial Judges?" *Notre Dame Law Review* 84 (2009): 1195–1246.

138. Kopko, "The Effect of Partisanship in Election Law Judicial Decision-Making," 9, 30–34; Mark Jonathon McKenzie, "The Influence of Partisanship, Ideology, and the Law on Redistricting Decisions in the Federal Courts," *Political Research Quarterly* 65, no. 4 (2012): 799–813.

139. Jordan Carr Peterson, "The Mask of Neutrality: Judicial Partisan Calculation and Legislative Redistricting," *Law and Policy* 41, no. 3 (2019): 336–359.

140. Jackson Williams, "Irreconcilable Principles: Law, Politics, and the Illinois Supreme Court," *Northern Illinois University Law Review* 18 (1998): 285–287.

141. 417 U.S. 642 (1974); Corley et al., *The Puzzle of Unanimity,* 102.

142. Kyle C. Kopko, Sarah McKinnon Bryner, Jeffrey Budziak, Christopher J. Devine, and Steven P. Nawara, "In the Eye of the Beholder? Motivated Reasoning in Disputed Elections," *Political Behavior* 33, no. 2 (2011): 271–290.

143. McKenzie, "The Influence of Partisanship, Ideology, and the Law on Redistricting Decisions in the Federal Courts."

144. Roe v. Wade, 410 U.S. 113 (1973).

145. Kang and Shepherd, "The Long Shadow of *Bush v. Gore*," 1415–1416.

146. Kang and Shepherd, 1429, 1415.

147. Kopko, "Partisanship Suppressed: Judicial Decision-Making in Ralph Nader's 2004 Ballot Access Litigation."

148. Keck, *Judicial Politics in Polarized Times*; Sunstein et al., *Are Judges Political?*

149. Kopko, "The Effect of Partisanship in Election Law Judicial Decision-Making."

150. Baum, *Judges and Their Audiences,* 126–128; Kopko, "Litigant Partisan Identity and Challenges to Campaign Finance Policies," 218.

151. Shaw v. Reno, 509 U.S. 630 (1993).

152. Kang and Shepherd, "The Long Shadow of *Bush v. Gore*," 1423.

153. Kang and Shepherd, 1451.

154. Kopko, "Partisanship Suppressed: Judicial Decision-Making in Ralph Nader's 2004 Ballot Access Litigation."

155. Scott Graves, "Competing Interests in State Supreme Courts: Justices' Votes and Voting Rights," *American Review of Politics* 24 (2003): 267–283.

156. Williams, "Irreconcilable Principles: Law, Politics, and the Illinois Supreme Court."

157. Lloyd, "Separating Partisanship from Party in Judicial Research"; McKenzie, "The Influence of Partisanship, Ideology, and the Law on Redistricting Decisions in the Federal Courts." Both studies, however, characterized this partisan favoritism as conditional. Lloyd, for example, found that judges were more likely to strike down opposite-party plans compared to same-party plans, but he also found that they were more likely to strike down plans crafted by same-party legislatures compared to divided or neutral legislatures. The judges in McKen-

zie's study were indeed more likely to strike down opposite-party plans, but this pattern of partisan favoritism occurred where legal precedents were ambiguous (e.g., in racial gerrymandering and Voting Rights Act cases), not where they were clear (e.g., with equal population claims).

158. Gary W. Cox and Jonathan N. Katz, *Elbridge Gerry's Salamander: The Electoral Consequences of the Reapportionment Revolution* (New York: Cambridge University Press, 2002).

159. Kopko, "Litigant Partisan Identity and Challenges to Campaign Finance Policies."

160. Kopko, "The Effect of Partisanship in Election Law Judicial Decision-Making."

161. Cox and Miles, "Judging the Voting Rights Act."

162. Kopko, "The Effect of Partisanship in Election Law Judicial Decision-Making"; McKenzie, "The Influence of Partisanship, Ideology, and the Law on Redistricting Decisions in the Federal Courts."

163. Peretti, "Judicial Partisanship in Voter Identification Litigation."

164. Corey Rayburn Yung, "Beyond Ideology: An Empirical Study of Partisanship and Independence in the Federal Courts," *George Washington Law Review* 80 (2012): 505–567.

165. Keck, *Judicial Politics in Polarized Times.*

166. Keck, 148.

167. Keck, 257.

168. Levitt, "The Partisanship Spectrum," 1787, 1791, 1796–1800.

169. Kopko, "The Effect of Partisanship in Election Law Judicial Decision-Making," 33.

170. Solum, "I'm Gonna Get High, High, High, or Deconstructing the Up-Down Distinction Revisited."

171. Yung, "Beyond Ideology"; Kang and Shepherd, "The Long Shadow of *Bush v. Gore.*"

Chapter 2: Courts, Parties, and the Voting Rights Act

1. 570 U.S. 529 (2013).

2. Heather K. Gerken, "An Academic Elegy: Comment on *The Voting Rights Act in Winter: The Death of a Superstatute.*" *Iowa Law Review* 100 (2015): 109–116.

3. Rick Valelly, "*Shelby* and the Sisyphean Struggle for Black Disenfranchisement," 2014, http://digitalcommons.law.umaryland.edu/cgi/viewcontent.cgi?article=1175&context=schmooze_papers.

4. Scott Lemieux, "Republicans' Coup de Grace on Voting Rights?" *The Week,* December 15, 2015, http://theweek.com/articles/593609/republicans-coup-de-grace-voting-rights.

5. Ari Berman, *Give Us the Ballot: The Modern Struggle for Voting Rights in America* (New York: Farrar, Straus & Giroux, 2015).

6. Stephen Gottlieb, *Unfit for Democracy: The Roberts Court and the Breakdown of American Politics* (New York: New York University Press, 2016); Berman, *Give*

Us the Ballot, Scott Lemieux, "John Roberts Has Been Trying to Gut the Voting Rights Act for Decades," *The Week*, August 3, 2015, https://theweek.com/articles/568963/john-roberts-been-trying-gut-voting-rights-act-decades.

7. Jesse H. Rhodes, *Ballot Blocked: The Political Erosion of the Voting Rights Act* (Palo Alto, CA: Stanford University Press, 2017), 3–4, 17, 21–22, 67–69, 77, 101–106, 131, 146–153.

8. Rhodes, *Ballot Blocked*, 3, 131, 160–162, 176.

9. 92 U.S. 542 (1876). *U.S. v. Cruikshank* arose from the 1873 Colfax Massacre, in which an armed white militia killed over a hundred African Americans, following hotly contested Louisiana elections in which federal intervention was needed to seat the victorious Republican governor and a Republican-majority legislature. Three white men were convicted of violating the 1870 Enforcement Act, aimed at Ku Klux Klan violence, which forbade conspiracies to deny the constitutional rights of any citizen. The Supreme Court reversed those convictions in *Cruikshank*, reasoning in part that the rights to due process and equal protection under the Fourteenth Amendment applied only to actions by the state and not by private individuals. This ruling inhibited federal efforts to protect the civil rights of African Americans and left them to suffer at the hands of hostile state governments and the KKK.

10. 92 U.S. 214 (1876). The Enforcement Act of 1870 provided that if an official refused to permit a citizen to perform an act required for voting, that citizen could present an affidavit that would qualify him to vote; additionally, the official could be penalized for violating the citizen's voting rights under the Fifteenth Amendment. In *U.S. v. Reese* (1876), the Supreme Court dismissed the indictments of the two Kentucky election officials who had refused to accept the affidavit of an African American man who had been prevented from paying a mandatory $1.50 poll tax. The Court ruled these provisions of the Enforcement Act as overly broad and exceeding congressional power to enforce the Fifteenth Amendment.

11. 109 U.S. 3 (1883). In the *Civil Rights Cases*, the Supreme Court struck down the Civil Rights Act of 1875 that prohibited race discrimination in public accommodations. The Court held that congressional power to enforce the Thirteenth and Fourteenth Amendments extended only to state actors and not private actors.

12. The Court in *Williams v. Mississippi* (1898) upheld several voter disenfranchisement tools in Mississippi's new constitution, including poll taxes and literacy tests, since they were not racially discriminatory in "their language or effects" and were applicable to all potential voters. 170 U.S. 213 (1898).

13. Guinn v. U.S., 238 U.S. 347 (1915); Smith v. Allwright, 321 U.S. 649 (1944).

14. Drew Kurlowski, *Rules Matter: Election Law Revealed* (St. Paul, MN: West Academic Publishing, 2019), 13.

15. Other important advancements for voting rights included the Twenty-Fourth Amendment, ratified in 1964, which prohibited poll taxes in federal elections, and the Court's 1966 decision in *Harper v. Virginia Board of Elections*, which that forbade them in state elections. 383 U.S. 663 (1966).

16. A 1975 amendment added language minorities to the Section 2 ban on voting discrimination.

17. Congress later made this ban permanent and nationwide.

18. Most preclearance requests have been administrative (i.e., directed to the Justice Department) rather than judicial since the former is quicker and less costly and objections can be judicially appealed.

19. Poll taxes were not included in the original definition of a "test or device," which excluded Texas and Arkansas from the list of covered jurisdictions, serving to reduce opposition to the VRA from these two states' congressional delegations. The 1975 reauthorization expanded the definition of "test or device" to include jurisdictions providing English-only ballots despite the presence of a language minority group constituting more than 5 percent of the voting-age population.

20. Berman, *Give Us the Ballot*, 6.

21. Guy-Uriel E. Charles and Luis Fuentes-Rohwer, "The Voting Rights Act in Winter: The Death of a Superstatute," *Iowa Law Review* 100 (2015): 1394–1396.

22. Charles S. Bullock III, Ronald Keith Gaddie, and Justin J. Wert, *The Rise and Fall of the Voting Rights Act* (Norman: University of Oklahoma Press, 2016), 59–77; Jeffrey Rosen, "Give Us the Ballot, by Ari Berman," *New York Times Sunday Book Review*, August 25, 2015; Daniel Tokaji, "The New Vote Denial: Where Election Reform Meets the Voting Rights Act," *South Carolina Law Review* 57 (2006): 689–732.

23. Berman, *Give Us the Ballot*, 46.

24. By 2005, black registration had reached 73 percent. Berman, *Give Us the Ballot*, 240.

25. Berman, 240; Rhodes, *Ballot Blocked*, 47.

26. Bullock et al., *The Rise and Fall of the Voting Rights Act*, 61–62.

27. Bernard Grofman and Lisa Handley, "The Impact of the Voting Rights Act on Black Representation in Southern State Legislatures," *Legislative Studies Quarterly* 16, no. 1 (1991): 112; Berman, *Give Us the Ballot*, 240.

28. Charles and Fuentes-Rohwer, "The Voting Rights Act in Winter," 1394.

29. 383 U.S. 301 (1966).

30. *South Carolina v. Katzenbach*, 383 U.S. at 309.

31. Section 4(e) provided that "no person who has completed the sixth grade in a public school, or an accredited private school, in Puerto Rico in which the language of instruction was other than English shall be disenfranchised for inability to read or write English." Katzenbach v. Morgan, 384 U.S. 641 (1966).

32. Samuel Issacharoff, Pamela S. Karlan, Richard H. Pildes, and Nathaniel Persily, *The Law of Democracy*, 5th ed. (St. Paul, MN: Foundation, 2016), 726.

33. Expanding the time period to fifty-three years instead of fifty would include Neil Gorsuch and Brett Kavanaugh and increase the number of Republican appointees to fifteen. The six Democratic appointees include Justices Marshall, Ginsburg, Breyer, Kagan, and Sotomayor, and Abe Fortas, who was confirmed in the Senate five days after President Johnson signed the Voting Rights Act.

34. Kurlowski, *Rules Matter*, 15.

35. 446 U.S. 55 (1980).

36. Whitcomb v. Chavis, 403 U.S. 124 (1971); White v. Regester, 412 U.S. 755 (1973).

37. *White*, 412 U.S. at 769, 766.

38. Berman, *Give Us the Ballot*, 135.

39. 478 U.S. 30 (1986).

40. Morgan Kousser, "Do the Facts of Voting Rights Support Chief Justice Roberts's Opinion in *Shelby County*?" *Transatlantica* 1 (2015): 10.

41. *Gingles*, 478 U.S. at 47.

42. Johnson v. De Grandy, 512 U.S. 997 (1994).

43. Miller v. Johnson, 515 U.S. 900, 916 (1995); Shaw v. Reno, 509 U.S. 630 (1993).

44. Daniel Tokaji, "Restricting Race-Conscious Redistricting," *Regulatory Review*, July 31, 2017.

45. Allen v. State Board of Elections, 393 U.S. 544 (1969).

46. *Allen*, 393 U.S. at 565.

47. *Allen*, 393 U.S. at 566.

48. Issacharoff et al., *The Law of Democracy*, 733.

49. Berman, *Give Us the Ballot*, 92.

50. Issacharoff et al., *The Law of Democracy*, 733.

51. Georgia v. United States, 411 U.S. 526 (1973); Dougherty County Board of Education v. White, 439 U.S. 32 (1978); Perkins v. Matthews, 400 U.S. 379 (1971).

52. 446 U.S. 156 (1980).

53. 521 U.S. 507, 529 (1997).

54. Nevada Department of Human Resources v. Hibbs, 538 U.S. 721 (2003); Tennessee v. Lane, 541 U.S. 509 (2004).

55. 425 U.S. 130 (1976).

56. Rhodes, *Ballot Blocked*, 90.

57. Kousser, "Do the Facts of Voting Rights Support Chief Justice Roberts's Opinion in *Shelby County*?" 11; John C. Jeffries and Daryl J. Levinson, "The Non-Retrogression Principle in Constitutional Law," *California Law Review* 86 (1998): 1211–1249.

58. 539 U.S. 461 (2003).

59. 422 U.S. 358 (1975).

60. 528 U.S. 320 (2000).

61. Rhodes, *Ballot Blocked*, 126.

62. 557 U.S. 193 (2009).

63. Kiefer Cox, "The Voting Rights Act under Review: *Shelby County v. Holder* and the Consequences of Change," *Wayne Law Review* 60 (2014): 500.

64. Howard Gillman, Mark A. Graber, and Keith E. Whittington, *American Constitutionalism*, vol. 2 (New York: Oxford University Press, 2013), 978.

65. *Northwest Austin*, 557 U.S. at 203, 204.

66. Damien Cave, "Ruling Prompts a Mixed Response," *New York Times*, June 22, 2009.

67. *Shelby County*, 570 U.S. at 551, 554.

68. *Shelby County,* 570 U.S. at 547.
69. *Shelby County,* 570 U.S. at 552.
70. *Shelby County,* 570 U.S. at 545.
71. *Shelby County,* 570 U.S. at 544.
72. *Shelby County,* 570 U.S. at 593.
73. *Shelby County,* 570 U.S. at 565.
74. *Shelby County,* 570 U.S. at 565.
75. *Shelby County,* 570 U.S. at 587, 566.
76. Lawrence Baum, "Judges and Their Audiences," in *The Oxford Handbook of U.S. Judicial Behavior,* ed. Lee Epstein and Stefanie A. Lindquist (New York: Oxford University Press, 2017), 353.
77. Adam B. Cox and Thomas J. Miles, "Judging the Voting Rights Act," *Columbia Law Review* 108 (2008): 1–54.
78. Richard Hasen, "*Shelby County* and the Illusion of Minimalism," *William and Mary Bill of Rights Journal* 22 (2014): 727; Richard Posner, "The Voting Rights Act Ruling Is about the Conservative Imagination," *Slate,* June 26, 2013; Lemieux, "Republicans' Coup de Grace on Voting Rights?." *Shelby County* has a few, though only a few, defenders. Thomas Colby, for example, claims that there is "a deep principle of equal sovereignty that runs through the Constitution," even if the majority failed to articulate it effectively. Mark Rush defends the Court as acting appropriately in the face of "congressional malfeasance" in not making "timely adjustments" to the "antiquated" coverage formula; it correctly refused to "uphold . . . a bad law in order to achieve good ends." Richard Hasen, in a forceful and multipronged attack on *Shelby County,* does not spare the dissenters who failed to acknowledge Congress's refusal to address serious problems with the coverage formula and "minimized the difficult constitutional questions before Congress and before the Court." Thomas B. Colby, "In Defense of the Equal Sovereignty Principle," *Duke Law Journal* 65, no. 6 (2016): 1087–1088; Mark Rush, "*Shelby County v. Holder.* A Case of Judicial *Hubris* or a Clash of Ancient Principles?" *Election Law Journal* 12, no. 3 (2013): 323; Hasen, "*Shelby County* and the Illusion of Minimalism," 715.
79. *Shelby County,* 570 U.S. at 544.
80. *Shelby County,* 570 U.S. at 545.
81. 383 U.S. at 308, 309, 334 (1966).
82. *Shelby County,* 570 U.S. at 547, 554.
83. *Coyle v. Smith,* 221 U.S. 559 (1911).
84. Nina Totenberg "Whose Term Was It? A Look Back at the Supreme Court," *National Public Radio,* July 5, 2013, https://www.npr.org/2013/07/05/198708325/whose-term-was-it-a-look-back-at-the-supreme-court.
85. Posner, "The Voting Rights Act Ruling Is about the Conservative Imagination."
86. Leah Litman, "Inventing Equal Sovereignty," *Michigan Law Review* 114 (2016): 1207–1273.
87. James Blacksher and Lani Guinier, "Free at Last: Rejecting Equal Sovereignty and Restoring the Constitutional Right to Vote *Shelby County v. Holder,*"

Harvard Law and Policy Review 8 (2014): 39–69; Lemieux, "Republicans' Coup de Grace on Voting Rights?"; William Yeomans, "Judicial Hubris," *Justice Watch,* June 25, 2013, http://afjjusticewatch.blogspot.com/2013/06/judicial-hubris .html.

88. Blacksher and Guinier, "Free at Last," 39.

89. Bullock et al., *The Rise and Fall of the Voting Rights Act,* 151.

90. Hasen, "*Shelby County* and the Illusion of Minimalism."

91. *Shelby County,* 570 U.S. at 588.

92. Berman, *Give Us the Ballot,* 284.

93. Cox, "The Voting Rights Act under Review," 501.

94. Hasen, "*Shelby County* and the Illusion of Minimalism," 723–724; Cox, "The Voting Rights Act under Review," 493–514.

95. Hasen, "*Shelby County* and the Illusion of Minimalism," 714.

96. Berman, *Give Us the Ballot,* 280.

97. Yeomans, "Judicial Hubris"; Ellen D. Katz, "What Was Wrong with the Record?" *Election Law Journal* 12, (2013): 329–331; Hasen, "*Shelby County* and the Illusion of Minimalism," 713–745.

98. *Shelby County,* 570 U.S. at 554.

99. *Shelby County,* 570 U.S. at 553.

100. *Shelby County,* 570 U.S. at 546.

101. Guy-Uriel E. Charles and Luis Fuentes-Rohwer, "States' Rights, Last Rites, and Voting Rights," *Connecticut Law Review* 47 (2014): 497.

102. David Kimball, "Judges Are Not Social Scientists (Yet)," *Election Law Journal* 12 (2013): 325.

103. Kousser, "Do the Facts of Voting Rights Support Chief Justice Roberts's Opinion?," 1.

104. Kimball, "Judges Are Not Social Scientists (Yet)," 325.

105. Kousser, "Do the Facts of Voting Rights Support Chief Justice Roberts's Opinion?," 25–26; David Gartner, "The Voting Rights Act and the Enduring Challenge of Participation," *Election Law Journal:* 14, no. 3 (2015): 278–281.

106. Kousser, 26.

107. Kousser, 26.

108. Pamela Karlan, "Section 5 Squared: Congressional Power to Extend and Amend the Voting Rights Act," *Houston Law Review* 44 (2007): 1–31; Kousser, 26.

109. Ian Vanderwalker and Keith Gunnar Bentele, "Vulnerability in Numbers: Racial Composition of the Electorate, Voter Suppression, and the Voting Rights Act," *Harvard Latino Law Review* 18 (2015): 99.

110. Kimball, "Judges Are Not Social Scientists (Yet)," 325.

111. Kimball, 324–326.

112. Kousser, "Do the Facts of Voting Rights Support Chief Justice Roberts's Opinion?," 1, 3, 10. Kousser explains that "events include any successful or unsuccessful case, published or not, decided or settled; Section 5 objections and 'more information requests' by the Department of Justice; and election law changes that manifestly took place as a result of the threat or reality of legal challenges."

113. *Shelby County,* 570 U.S. at 557.

114. Desmond S. King and Rogers M. Smith, "The Last Stand? *Shelby County v. Holder,* White Political Power, and America's Racial Policy Alliances," *Du Bois Review* 13 (2016): 26.

115. Bullock et al., *The Rise and Fall of the Voting Rights Act,* 171–188; Bruce Cain, "Moving Past Section 5: More Fingers or a New Dike?" *Election Law Journal* 12, no. 3 (2013): 338–340; David Epstein, Richard H. Pildes, Rodolfo O. de la Garza, and Sharyn O'Halloran, eds., *The Future of the Voting Rights Act* (New York: Russell Sage Foundation, 2006); Bernard Grofman, "Devising a Sensible Trigger for Section 5 of the Voting Rights Act," *Election Law Journal* 12, no. 3 (2013): 332–337; Samuel Issacharoff, "Beyond the Discrimination Model on Voting," *Harvard Law Review* 127 (2013): 95–126; Daniel Tokaji, "Responding to *Shelby County*: A Grand Election Bargain," *Harvard Law and Policy Review* 8 (2014): 71–108; Franita Tolson, "Congressional Authority to Protect Voting Rights after *Shelby County* and *Arizona Inter Tribal,*" *Election Law Journal* 13 (2014): 322–335; Vandewalker and Bentele, "Vulnerability in Numbers," 99–150.

116. Rhodes, *Ballot Blocked,* 175–176.

117. Ari Berman, "Congressional Democrats Introduce Ambitious New Bill to Restore the Voting Rights Act," *Nation,* June 24, 2015.

118. Benjamin Barber, "The States Facing Federal Preclearance under Proposed Voting Rights Act Fix," *Facing South,* March 13, 2019, https://www.facingsouth.org/2019/03/states-facing-federal-preclearance-under-proposed-voting-rights-act-fix.

119. Sarah Binder, "Reading Congressional Tea Leaves from the 2006 Renewal of the Voting Rights Act," *Washington Post/The Monkey Cage,* June 27, 2013.

120. Kimball, "Judges Are Not Social Scientists (Yet)," 324–326; Gerken, "An Academic Elegy," 109–116; Hasen, "*Shelby County* and the Illusion of Minimalism," 713–745.

121. *Shelby County,* 570 U.S. at 545, 557.

122. Gerken, "An Academic Elegy," 111.

123. Jeffrey Toobin, "Holder v. Roberts," *New Yorker,* February 17, 2014 (quoting Richard Hasen).

124. North Carolina State Conference of the NAACP v. McCrory, 831 F.3d 204, 214 (4th Cir. 2016).

125. National Association for the Advancement of Colored People Legal Defense and Educational Fund, "Democracy Diminished: State and Local Threats to Voting Post-*Shelby County, Alabama v. Holder*" (Washington, DC: Thurgood Marshall Institute at LDF, 2016), https://www.naacpldf.org/wp-content/uploads/Democracy-Diminished-State-and-Local-Threats-to-Voting-Post-Shelby-County-Alabama-v.-Holder.pdf.

126. Thomas Lopez, "*Shelby County*: One Year Later," Brennan Center for Justice, June 24, 2014, http://www.brennacenter.org/analysis/shelby-county-one-year-later.

127. "Election 2016: Restrictive Voting Laws by the Numbers," Brennan Center for Justice, September 28, 2016, https://www.brennancenter.org/our-work/research-reports/election-2016-restrictive-voting-laws-numbers. The

number of states would have been higher—at seventeen—if not for successful legal challenges in three states.

128. Wendy R. Weiser and Max Feldman, "The State of Voting 2018," Brennan Center for Justice, June 5, 2018, https://www.brennancenter.org/publication/state-voting-2018.

129. Jonathan Brater, Kevin Morris, Myrna Perez, and Christopher Deluzio, "Purges: A Growing Threat to the Right to Vote," Brennan Center for Justice, July 20, 2018, https://www.brennancenter.org/sites/default/files/publications/Purges_Growing_Threat_2018.1.pdf.

130. The Leadership Conference Education Fund, "Warning Signs: The Potential Impact of *Shelby County v. Holder* on the 2016 General Election," June 2016, http://civilrightsdocs.info/pdf/reports/2016-Voting-Rights-Report-FOR-WEB.pdf.

131. Brater et al., "Purges: A Growing Threat to the Right to Vote"; Theodore R. Johnson and Max Feldman, "The New Voter Suppression," Brennan Center for Justice, January 16, 2020, https://www.brennancenter.org/our-work/research-reports/new-voter-suppression.

132. Keith G. Bentele and Erin O'Brien, "Jim Crow 2.0?: Why States Consider and Adopt Restrictive Voter Access Policies," *Perspectives on Politics* 11, no. 4 (2013): 1088–1116; Vandewalker and Bentele, "Vulnerability in Numbers," 99–150.

133. Five Republican House members and two Republican senators did not vote.

134. https://www.supremecourt.gov/oral_arguments/argument_transcripts/2012/12-96_7648.pdf.

135. Richard H. Pildes, "Political Avoidance, Constitutional Theory, and the VRA," *Yale Law Journal Pocket Part* 117 (2007): 148, http://yalelawjournal.org/forum/political-avoidance-constitutional-theory-and-the-vra.

136. Richard H. Pildes, "What Does the Court's Decision Mean?" *Election Law Journal* 12 (2013): 317.

137. King and Smith, "The Last Stand?," 27.

138. Berman, "Give Us the Ballot"; Jim Rutenberg, "A Dream Undone: Inside the 50-Year Campaign to Roll Back the Voting Rights Act," *New York Times Magazine,* July 29, 2015; Jim Rutenberg, "Nine Years Ago, Republicans Favored Voting Rights. What Happened?," *New York Times Magazine,* August 12, 2015.

139. Alexander Keyssar, *The Right to Vote: The Contested History of Democracy in the United States,* rev. ed. (New York: Basic, 2009); Gary May, *Bending toward Justice: The Voting Rights Act and the Transformation of American Democracy* (New York: Basic, 2013).

140. Richard Hasen, "The 2012 Voting Wars, Judicial Back-Stops, and the Resurrection of *Bush v. Gore,*" *George Washington Law Review* 81 (2013): 1865–1901.

141. Rhodes, *Ballot Blocked*; Bullock et al., *The Rise and Fall of the Voting Rights Act.*

142. King and Smith, "The Last Stand?," 29; Rhodes, *Ballot Blocked,* 3–4, 17, 21–22, 67–69, 77, 101–106, 131, 146–153.

143. Rhodes, *Ballot Blocked,* 95.

144. Rutenberg, "A Dream Undone."

145. Berman, *Give Us the Ballot*, 10.

146. Rutenberg, "A Dream Undone"; Berman, *Give Us the Ballot*, 128–131, 149, 217–219, 232–233, 236–239, 273.

147. Berman, *Give Us the Ballot*, 73.

148. Rhodes, *Ballot Blocked*, 68.

149. Rhodes, 74–75.

150. Berman, *Give Us the Ballot*, 124.

151. Berman, 145; Rhodes, *Ballot Blocked*, 102.

152. Berman, 152.

153. Rhodes, *Ballot Blocked*, 102–105.

154. Rhodes, 103.

155. Rhodes, 142.

156. Bullock et al., *The Rise and Fall of the Voting Rights Act*, 111–122.

157. Binder, "Reading Congressional Tea Leaves from the 2006 Renewal of the Voting Rights Act."

158. Bullock et al., *The Rise and Fall of the Voting Rights Act*, 122.

159. Rhodes, *Ballot Blocked*, 3–7, 16–20, 59, 79–93, 95–98, 107–118, 122–128, 130–141, 153–162, 183–186; Berman, *Give Us the Ballot*, 143–151, 165–168, 180–181, 203, 213–214, 216–219, 224–230.

160. Rhodes, 78.

161. Rhodes, 79.

162. Berman, *Give Us the Ballot*, 89.

163. Rhodes, *Ballot Blocked*, 109.

164. Rhodes, *Ballot Blocked*, 109–110.

165. Rhodes, 108–110; Berman, *Give Us the Ballot*, 167–168.

166. Rhodes, 109; Berman, 166.

167. Berman, 229.

168. Rhodes, *Ballot Blocked*, 137, 229.

169. Rhodes, 136.

170. 548 U.S. 399 (2006).

171. Rutenberg, "A Dream Undone."

172. Berman, *Give Us the Ballot*, 229.

173. Berman, 225.

174. Rhodes, *Ballot Blocked*, 134.

175. "How Bush Watered Down Civil-Rights Enforcement," *Newsweek*, December 9, 2009, https://www.newsweek.com/how-bush-watered-down-civil-rights-enforcement-75741.

176. http://sblog.s3.amazonaws.com/wp-content/uploads/2012/08/12-96-Amicus-Brief-former-DOJ-Officials-filed-8-23-12.pdf.

177. The US Supreme Court Database, http://scdb.wustl.edu/.

178. 512 U.S. 874 (1994).

179. Roberts and Alito each voted the conservative position in three additional Voting Rights Act cases in the 2018 term. Neither Justice Gorsuch nor Justice Kavanaugh voted the liberal position in the (admittedly few) voting rights cases they decided in the 2018 term.

180. Jack M. Balkin and Sanford Levinson, "Understanding the Constitutional Revolution," *Virginia Law Review* 87 (2001): 1045–1109; Mitchell J. Pickerill and Clayton W. Clayton, "The Rehnquist Court and the Political Dynamics of Federalism," *Perspectives on Politics* 2 (2004): 233–248; Steven M. Teles, *Rise of the Conservative Movement: The Battle for Control of the Law* (Princeton, NJ: Princeton University Press, 2008).

181. New York v. U.S., 505 U.S. 144 (1992); Printz v. U.S., 521 U.S. 898 (1997); U.S. v. Lopez, 514 U.S. 549 (1995); and U.S. v. Morrison, 529 U.S. 598 (2000).

182. Victor Andres Rodriguez, "Section 5 of the Voting Rights Act of 1965 after *Boerne*: The Beginning of the End of Preclearance?," *California Law Review* 91, no. 3 (2003): 769–826; Sylvia A. Law, "In the Name of Federalism: The Supreme Court's Assault on Democracy and Civil Rights," *University of Cincinnati Law Review* 70 (2002): 367–432.

183. King and Smith, "The Last Stand?," 29; Rhodes, *Ballot Blocked*, 3–4, 17, 21–22, 67–69, 77, 101–106, 131, 146–153.

184. Rhodes, 3–7, 16–20, 59, 79–93, 95–98, 107–118, 122–128, 130–141, 153–162, 183–186.

185. King and Smith, "The Last Stand?," 29.

186. Nathan Pippenger, "John Roberts and the Shifting Politics of Race," *Democracy: The Alcove*, October 27, 2016.

187. Rhodes, *Ballot Blocked*, 176–177.

188. Cain, "Moving Past Section 5," 339–340; Valelly, "*Shelby* and the Sisyphean Struggle"; Issacharoff et al., *The Law of Democracy*, 764–765.

189. Christopher S. Elmendorf and Douglas M. Spencer, "Administering Section 2 of the Voting Rights Act after *Shelby County*," *Columbia Law Review* 115 (2015): 2158.

190. 138 S. Ct. 2305 (2018).

191. Richard L. Hasen, "How Justice Kennedy's Successor Will Wreak Havoc on Voting Rights and American Democracy," *Slate*, July 2, 2018.

192. Ari Berman, "Does Brett Kavanaugh Spell the End of Voting Rights?," *New York Times*, July 13, 2018.

193. Michael Waldman, "An Alarming Day for Democracy," *Politico*, July 9, 2018.

194. South Carolina v. U.S., 898 F. Supp.2d 30 (2012).

195. Hasen, "How Justice Kennedy's Successor Will Wreak Havoc"; Luis Fuentes-Rohwer, "The Future of Section 2 of the Voting Rights Act in the Hands of a Conservative Court," *Duke Journal of Constitutional Law and Public Policy* 5 (2010): 144.

Chapter 3: Courts, Parties, and Voter Identification

1. 553 U.S. 181 (2008).
2. National Conference of State Legislatures, "Voter Identification Requirements/Voter ID Laws," January 17, 2019, http://www.ncsl.org/research/elections-and-campaigns/voter-id.aspx.

3. National Conference of State Legislatures, "Voter Identification Requirements/Voter ID Laws."

4. National Conference of State Legislatures, "Voter Identification Requirements/Voter ID Laws."

5. These states are Alabama, Alaska, Arizona, Arkansas, Colorado, Connecticut, Delaware, Florida, Georgia, Hawaii, Idaho, Indiana, Iowa, Kansas, Kentucky, Louisiana, Michigan, Mississippi, Missouri, Montana, New Hampshire, North Dakota, Ohio, Oklahoma, Rhode Island, South Carolina, South Dakota, Tennessee, Texas, Utah, Virginia, Washington, West Virginia, and Wisconsin. The list excludes Pennsylvania and North Carolina, whose laws were invalidated by courts.

6. 570 U.S. 529 (2013).

7. Brief of the Republican National Committee as Amicus Curiae Supporting Respondents in *Crawford v. Marion County Election Board* and *Indiana Democratic Party v. Rokita*, Nos. 07-21 and 07-25, December 10, 2007, 1, 3–6, https://www.americanbar.org/content/dam/aba/publishing/preview/publiced_preview_briefs_pdfs_07_08_07_21_RespondentAmCuRepNatComm.pdf.

8. The nine states are Florida, Georgia, Indiana, Kansas, Missouri, New Hampshire, Pennsylvania, Texas, and Wisconsin.

9. Richard L. Hasen, *The Voting Wars: From Florida 2000 to the Next Election Meltdown* (New Haven, CT: Yale University Press, 2012), 43; Chandler Davidson, "The Historical Context of Voter Photo-ID Laws," *PS: Political Science and Politics* 42 (2009): 94.

10. William D. Hicks, Seth C. McKee, and Daniel A. Smith, "The Determinants of State Legislator Support for Restrictive Voter ID Laws," *State Politics and Policy Quarterly* 16, no. 4 (2016): 424.

11. Hicks et al., "The Determinants of State Legislator Support," 415. The simple measure of party polarization that Hicks et al. develop subtracts the percentage of Democratic legislators voting "nay" from the percentage of Republican legislators voting "yea" and then subtracts that number from 100.

12. http://www.govtrack.us/congress/bills/109/hr4844.

13. Hasen, *The Voting Wars,* 52–53.

14. Hasen, *The Voting Wars,* 127; Tova Andrea Wang, "A Rigged Report on U.S. Voting," *Washington Post,* August 30, 2007, www.washingtonpost.com/wp-dyn/content/article/2007/08/29/AR2007082901928_pf.html.

15. Hasen, *The Voting Wars,* 54–58; Gary May, *Bending toward Justice: The Voting Rights Act and the Transformation of American Democracy* (New York: Basic, 2013), 242.

16. Keith G. Bentele and Erin O'Brien, "Jim Crow 2.0?: Why States Consider and Adopt Restrictive Voter Access Policies," *Perspectives on Politics* 11, no. 4 (2013): 1088–1116; Daniel R. Biggers and Michael J. Hanmer, "Understanding the Adoption of Voter Identification Laws in the American States," *American Politics Research* 45 (2017): 560–588; Lorraine C. Minnite, "Voter Identification Laws: The Controversy over Voter Fraud," in *Law and Elections Politics: The Rules of the Game 2013,* 2nd ed., ed. Matthew J. Streb (New York: Routledge, 2013), 88; Rene R. Rocha and Tetsuya Matsubayashi, "The Politics of Race and Voter ID Laws in the States: The Return of Jim Crow?," *Political Research Quarterly* 67,

no. 3 (2014): 666–679. Rhode Island offers a rare exception, with its Democratic legislature enacting a voter ID law in 2011.

17. Minnite, "Voter Identification Laws," 92.

18. Minnite, "Voter Identification Laws," 88; Kathleen Hale and Ramona McNeal, "Election Administration Reform and State Choice: Voter Identification Requirements and HAVA," *Policy Studies Journal* 38, no. 2 (2010): 281–302.

19. Rocha and Matsubayashi, "The Politics of Race and Voter ID Laws in the States," 671.

20. Hicks et al., "The Determinants of State Legislator Support."

21. Seth C. McKee, "Politics Is Local: State Legislator Voting on Restrictive Voter Identification Legislation," *Research and Politics* 2 (2015): 1–7.

22. Biggers and Hanmer, "Understanding the Adoption of Voter Identification Laws in the American States."

23. Hale and McNeal, "Election Administration Reform and State Choice."

24. Rocha and Matsubayashi, "The Politics of Race and Voter ID Laws in the States."

25. William D. Hicks, Seth C. McKee, Mitchell D. Sellers, and Daniel A. Smith, "A Principle or a Strategy? Voter Identification Laws and Partisan Competition in the American States," *Political Research Quarterly* 68, no. 1 (2015): 18–33.

26. Bentele and O'Brien, "Jim Crow 2.0?"; Vandewalker and Bentele, "Vulnerability in Numbers."

27. Hicks et al., "A Principle or a Strategy?" 19–20; Tova Andrea Wang, *The Politics of Voter Suppression: Defending and Expanding Americans' Right to Vote* (Ithaca, NY: Cornell University Press, 2012).

28. Associated Press/NORC Center for Public Affairs Research, "Views on the American Election Process and Perceptions of Voter Fraud," 2016, http://www.apnorc.org/projects/Pages/HTML%20Reports/views-on-the-american-election-process-and-perceptions-of-voter-fraud-issue-brief.aspx; Justin McCarthy, "Four in Five Americans Support Voter ID Laws, Early Voting," *Gallup News*, August 22, 2016, https://news.gallup.com/poll/194741/four-five-americans-support-voter-laws-early-voting.aspx; Paul Gronke, William D. Hicks, Seth C. McKee, Charles Stewart III, and James Dunham, "Voter ID Laws: A View from the Public," MIT Political Science Department Research Paper No. 13, 2015, http://papers.ssrn.com/so13/papers.cfm?abstract_id=2594290.

29. Justin McCarthy, "Four in Five Americans Support Voter ID Laws, Early Voting," *Gallup News*, August 22, 2016, https://news.gallup.com/poll/194741/four-five-americans-support-voter-laws-early-voting.aspx; David C. Wilson and Paul R. Brewer, "The Foundations of Public Opinion on Voter ID Laws: Political Predispositions, Racial Resentment, and Information Effects," *Public Opinion Quarterly* 77, no. 4 (2013): 962–984; John V. Kane, "Why Can't We Agree on ID? Partisanship, Perceptions of Fraud, and Public Support for Voter Identification Laws," *Public Opinion Quarterly* 81, no. 4 (2017): 943–955.

30. Rasmussen Reports, "Voters Want IDs at the Polls, Don't See Them as Discriminatory," *Rasmussen Reports*, October 3, 2018.

31. Charles Stewart III, Stephen Ansolabehere, and Nathaniel Persily, "Re-

visiting Public Opinion on Voter Identification and Voter Fraud in an Era of Increasing Partisan Polarization," *Stanford Law Review* 68 (2016): 1455–1489.

32. Stewart et al., "Revisiting Public Opinion on Voter Identification and Voter Fraud in an Era of Increasing Partisan Polarization," 1461–1462.

33. Wilson and Brewer, "The Foundations of Public Opinion on Voter ID Laws."

34. McCarthy, "Four in Five Americans Support Voter ID Laws, Early Voting"; Stewart et al., "Revisiting Public Opinion on Voter Identification and Voter Fraud in an Era of Increasing Partisan Polarization," 1470–1473; Wilson and Brewer, "The Foundations of Public Opinion on Voter ID Laws;" Pamela Johnston Conover and Patrick R. Miller, "How Republicans Won on Voter Identification Laws: The Roles of Strategic Reasoning and Moral Conviction," *Social Science Quarterly* 99, no. 2 (2018): 490–511; Stewart et al., "Revisiting Public Opinion on Voter Identification and Voter Fraud," 1482; Herman Schwartz, "The Public Doesn't Support Restrictive Voter ID Laws, but Many New Ones Will Be in Force in 2016," *Reuters*, December 8, 2015, https://blogs.reuters.com/great-debate/2015/12/08/the-public-does-not-support-voter-id-laws-but-many-new-ones-will-be-in-force-in-2016/; David C. Wilson, "Public Opinion on Voter ID Laws: Strong Support, Shaky Foundation," *Huffington Post*, September 7, 2012, www.huffingtonpost.com/david-c-wilson/public-opinion-on-voter-i_b_1683873.html; Wilson and Brewer, "The Foundations of Public Opinion on Voter ID Laws."

35. This is not to say that voter fraud never happens, but it is more common with other types of voting, such as absentee balloting. A prominent example occurred in a 2018 congressional race in Bladen County, North Carolina, which the Republican candidate, Mark Harris, won narrowly. Evidence came to light that a Harris political operative had hired workers who collected absentee ballots, disproportionately in African American neighborhoods, filling out some ballots for Harris with forged signatures and discarding others. The state's Board of Elections invalidated the results and ordered a new election.

36. US Elections Assistance Commission, Election Crimes: An Initial Review and Recommendations for Future Study, 2006, 2–3, www.eac.gov/clearinghouse/docs/reportsandsurveys2006electioncrimes.pdf/; Lorraine C. Minnite, *The Myth of Voter Fraud* (Ithaca, NY: Cornell University Press, 2010); David A. Schultz, "Less Than Fundamental: The Myth of Voter Fraud and the Coming of the Second Great Disenfranchisement," *William Mitchell Law Review* 34 (2008): 498.

37. Juan Williams, "GOP's Voter ID Campaign Aimed at Suppressing Constitutional Rights," *The Hill*, October 15, 2012, http://thehill.com/opinion/columnists/juan-williams/261945-opinion-gops-voter-id-campaign-aimed-at-supressing-constitutional-rights; V. M. Hood III and William Gillespie, "They Just Do Not Vote Like They Used To: A Methodology to Empirically Assess Election Fraud," *Social Science Quarterly* 93 (2012): 76–94.

38. Justin Levitt, "A Comprehensive Investigation of Voter Impersonation Finds 31 Credible Incidents out of One Billion Ballots Cast," *Washington Post*, August 6, 2014.

39. Justin Levitt, "The Truth about Voter Fraud," Brennan Center for Justice, 2007, https://www.brennancenter.org/sites/defalt/files/legacy/The%20Truth%20About%20Voter%20Fraud.pdf.

40. Stephen Ansolabehere, Samantha Luks, and Brian F. Schaffner, "The Perils of Cherry Picking Low Frequency Events in Large Sample Surveys," *Electoral Studies* 40 (2015): 409–410; Jesse T. Richman, Gulshan A. Chattha, and David C. Earnest. "Do Non-citizens Vote in U.S. Elections?," *Electoral Studies* 36 (2014): 149–157.

41. David Cottrell, Michael C. Herron, and Sean J. Westwood, "An Exploration of Donald Trump's Allegations of Massive Voter Fraud in the 2016 General Election," *Electoral Studies* 51 (2018): 123–142.

42. Quoted in Peter Katel, "Voter Rights: Should Photo IDs Be Required at the Ballot Box?," *Congressional Quarterly Researcher* 22, no. 19 (2012): 452.

43. Hasen, *The Voting Wars*, 52–53.

44. May, *Bending toward Justice*, 242.

45. Davidson, "The Historical Context of Voter Photo-ID Laws."

46. Christopher Ingraham, "7 Papers, 4 Government Inquiries, 2 News Investigations and 1 Court Ruling Proving Voter Fraud Is Mostly a Myth," *Washington Post,* July 9, 2014.

47. Minnite, "Voter Identification Laws," 99–100.

48. Jane C. Timm and Adam Edelman, "Illegal Voting? Not Much in Kobach's Home State," *NBC News,* July 19, 2017.

49. *Crawford,* 553 U.S. at 195.

50. Hasen, *The Voting Wars,* 61.

51. Minnite, "Voter Identification Laws," 114.

52. Jack Citrin, Donald P. Green, and Morris Levy, "The Effects of Voter ID Notification on Voter Turnout: Results from a Large-Scale Field Experiment," *Election Law Journal* 13, no. 2 (2014): 228–242; Hopkins et al., "Voting But for the Law;" Jacob R. Neiheisel and Rich Horner, "Voter Identification Requirements and Aggregate Turnout in the U.S.: How Campaigns Offset the Costs of Turning Out When Voting Is Made More Difficult," *Election Law Journal* 18, no. 3 (2019): 227–242; Nicholas A. Valentino and Fabian G. Neuner, "Why the Sky Didn't Fall: Mobilizing Anger in Reaction to Voter ID Laws," *Political Psychology* 38, no. 2 (2017): 331–350.

53. John H. Aldrich, "Rational Choice and Turnout," *American Journal of Political Science* 37, no. 1 (1993): 246–278; Anthony Downs, *An Economic Theory of Democracy* (New York: Harper & Brothers, 1957); Quan Li, Michael J. Pomante II, and Scot Schraufnagel, "Cost of Voting in the American States," *Election Law Journal* 17, no. 3 (2018): 234–247; Raymond E. Wolfinger and Steven J. Rosenstone, *Who Votes?* (New Haven, CT: Yale University Press 1980).

54. Richard Sobel, "The High Cost of 'Free' Photo Voter Identification Cards," Charles Hamilton Houston Institute for Race and Justice, Harvard Law School, 2014, https://today.law.harvard.edu/wp-content/uploads/2014/06/FullReportVoterIDJune20141.pdf.

55. Benjamin Highton, "Voter Identification Laws and Turnout in the United States," *Annual Review of Political Science* 20 (2017): 150.

56. Stephen Ansolabehere, "Effects of Identification Requirements on Voting: Evidence from the Experiences of Voters on Election Day," *PS: Political Science and Politics* 42 (2009): 127–130; Enrico Cantoni and Vincent Pons, "Strict ID Laws Don't Stop Voters: Evidence from a U.S. Nationwide Panel, 2008–2016," National Bureau of Economic Research, 2019, http://www.nber.org/papers/w25522; Robert S. Erikson and Lorraine C. Minnite, "Modeling Problems in the Voter Identification–Voter Turnout Debate," *Election Law Journal* 8 (2009): 85–101; Phoebe Henninger, Marc Meredith, and Michael Morse, "Who Votes without Identification? Using Affidavits from Michigan to Learn about the Potential Impact of Strict Photo Voter Identification Laws," paper prepared for the 2018 Election Sciences, Reform, and Administration Conference, 2017, https://esra.wisc.edu/papers/HMM.pdf; M. V. Hood III and Charles S. Bullock, "Much Ado About Nothing? An Empirical Assessment of the Georgia Voter Identification Statute," *State Politics and Policy Quarterly* 12, no. 4 (2012): 394–414; Hopkins et al., "Voting But for the Law"; Jason D. Mycoff, Michael W. Wagner, and David C. Wilson, "The Empirical Effects of Voter-ID Laws: Present or Absent?," *PS: Political Science and Politics* 42 (2009): 121–126; Robert A. Pastor, Robert Santos, Alison Prevost, and Vassia Stoilov, "Voting and ID Requirements: A Survey of Registered Voters in Three States," *American Review of Public Administration* 40 (2010): 461–481; Rocha and Matsubayashi, "The Politics of Race and Voter ID Laws in the States"; Charles Stewart III, "Voter ID: Who Has Them? Who Shows Them?" *Oklahoma Law Review* 66 (2013): 21–52; Valentino and Neuner, "Why the Sky Didn't Fall"; Timothy Vercellotti and David Andersen, "Voter-Identification Requirements and the Learning Curve," *PS: Political Science and Politics* 42 (2009): 117–120.

57. Michael R. Alvarez, Delia Bailey, and Jonathan N. Katz, "The Effect of Voter Identification Laws on Turnout," Social Science Working Paper 1267R, California Institute of Technology, 2008; Michael R. Alvarez, Delia Bailey, and Jonathan N. Katz, "An Empirical Bayes Approach to Estimating Ordinal Treatment Effects," *Political Analysis* 19 (2011): 20–31; Shelley De Alth, "ID at the Polls: Assessing the Impact of Recent State Voter ID Laws on Voter Turnout," *Harvard Law and Policy Review* 3 (2009): 185–202; Kyle A. Dropp, "Voter Identification Laws and Voter Turnout," unpublished manuscript, 2013, http://kyledropp.weebly.com/uploads/1/2/0/9/12094568/dropp_voter_id.pdf; US Government Accountability Office, "Elections: Issues Related to State Voter Identification Laws," Report to Congressional Requesters, September 2014, https://www.gao.gov/assets/670/665966.pdf.

58. Stewart, "Voter ID: Who Has Them? Who Shows Them?"; Stephen Ansolabehere and Eitan D. Hersh, "ADGN: An Algorithm for Record Linkage Using Address, Date of Birth, Gender, and Name," *Journal of Statistics and Public Policy* 4, no. 1 (2017): 6.

59. Mark Jones, Renee Cross, Jim Granato, Ching-Hsing Wang, and Kwok-Wai Wan, "The Texas Voter ID Law and the 2016 Election: A Study of Harris County and Congressional District 23," University of Houston Hobby School of Public Affairs, 2017, www.uh.edu/hobby/voterid2016/voterid2016.pdf.

60. Minnite, "Voter Identification Laws," 105.

61. For this phrase, Bronner cites Jorge Luis Borges's comments on the Falklands War. Ethan Bronner, "Partisan Rifts Hinder Efforts to Improve U.S. Voting System," *New York Times,* July 31, 2012.

62. Justin Levitt, "New State Voting Laws: Barriers to the Ballot?," statement before Subcommittee on Constitution, Civil Rights and Human Rights of the Committee on the Judiciary, US Senate, 112th Cong., 1st session, September 8, 2011, 13.

63. Ansolabehere and Hersch, "ADGN"; Matt A. Barreto, Stephen A. Nuno, and Gabriel R. Sanchez, "The Disproportionate Impact of Voter-ID Requirements on the Electorate—New Evidence from Indiana," *PS: Political Science and Politics* 42 (2009): 111–115; Henninger et al., "Who Votes without Identification?"; Jon C. Rogowski and Cathy J. Cohen, "The Racial Impact of Voter Identification Laws in the 2012 Election," Black Youth Project, November 2015, blackyouthproject.com/wp-content/uploads/2015/11/voter_id_after_2008.pdf; Stewart, "Voter ID: Who Has Them? Who Shows Them?"

64. Stephen Ansolabehere, "Effects of Identification Requirements on Voting: Evidence from the Experiences of Voters on Election Day," *PS: Political Science and Politics* 42 (2009): 127–130; Barreto et al., "The Disproportionate Impact of Voter-ID Requirements on the Electorate"; Rachael V. Cobb, D. James Greiner, and Kevin M. Quinn, "Can Voter ID Laws Be Administered in a Race-Neutral Manner? Evidence from the City of Boston in 2008," *Quarterly Journal of Political Science* 7 (2012): 1–33; Zoltan Hajnal, Nazita Lajevardi, and Lindsay Nielson, "Voter Identification Laws and the Suppression of Minority Votes," *Journal of Politics* 79, no. 2 (2017): 363–379; M. V. Hood III and Charles S. Bullock, "Worth a Thousand Words? An Analysis of Georgia's Voter Identification Statute," *American Politics Research* 36 (2008): 555–579; Ariel R. White, Noah L. Nathan, and Julie K. Faller, "What Do I Need to Vote? Bureaucratic Discretion and Discrimination by Local Election Officials," *American Political Science Review* 109 (2015): 129–142.

65. Cantoni and Pons, "Strict ID Laws Don't Stop Voters"; Erikson and Minnite, "Modeling Problems in the Voter Identification–Voter Turnout Debate"; Hood and Bullock, "Much Ado About Nothing?"; Rocha and Matsubayashi, "The Politics of Race and Voter ID Laws in the States."

66. Dropp, "Voter Identification Laws and Voter Turnout"; Bernard L. Fraga and Michael G. Miller, "Who Does Voter ID Keep from Voting?," paper prepared for the 2018 State Politics and Policy Conference, Pennsylvania State University, State College, 2018, https://ucaeb23e1b76b331484a06c8f1d8.previews.dropboxusercontent.com/nativeprint?file=https%3A%2F%2Fwww.dropbox.com%2Fs%2Ff30qui1jhq6nqie%2FFragaMiller_TXID_2018.pdf%3Fdisable_range%3D1%26from_native_print%3D1%26preview%3D1; US Government Accountability Office, "Elections"; Zolton Hajnal, Nazita Lajevardi, and Lindsay Nielson, "Voter Identification Laws and the Suppression of Minority Votes," *Journal of Politics* 79, no. 2 (2017): 363–379; Zolton Hajnal, John Kuk, and Nazita Lajevardi, "We All Agree: Strict Voter ID Laws Disproportionately Burden Minorities," *Journal of Politics* 80, no. 3 (2018): 1052–1059; Henninger et al., "Who Votes without Identification?"; Stewart, "Voter ID: Who Has Them? Who

Shows Them?"; Vercellotti and Andersen, "Voter-Identification Requirements and the Learning Curve."

67. Hajnal et al., "We All Agree," 1059. Some studies have concluded that voter ID laws have discriminatory impacts that are nonracial, including disproportionately negative effects on turnout for the young, the elderly, the poor, and Democrats. Barretto et al., "The Disproportionate Impact of Voter-ID Requirements"; Dropp, "Voter Identification Laws and Voter Turnout"; Hajnal et al., "Voter Identification Laws and the Suppression of Minority Votes"; Hopkins et al., "Voting But for the Law"; Rogowski and Cohen, "The Racial Impact of Voter Identification Laws in the 2012 Election"; Vercellotti and Andersen, "Voter-Identification Requirements and the Learning Curve." Cantoni and Pons, however, dispute that voter ID laws have disparate effects based on race, gender, age, or party affiliation. Cantoni and Pons, "Strict ID Laws Don't Stop Voters."

68. Ansolabehere, "Effects of Identification Requirements on Voting"; Lonna Rae Atkeson, R. Michael Alvarez, Thad E. Hall, and J. Andrew Sinclair, "Balancing Fraud Prevention and Electoral Participation: Attitudes toward Voter Identification," *Social Science Quarterly* 95 (2014): 1381–1398; Shaun Bowler and Todd Donovan, "A Partisan Model of Electoral Reform: Voter Identification Laws and Confidence in State Elections," *State Politics and Policy Quarterly* 16, no. 3 (2016): 340–361; Cantoni and Pons, "Strict ID Laws Don't Stop Voters."

69. Hasen, *The Voting Wars*, 41–43.

70. Hasen, 42.

71. Texas v. Holder, 888 F. Supp. 2d 113 (D.D.C. 2012).

72. Texas v. Holder, 133 S. Ct. 2886 (2013).

73. Veasey v. Perry, 71 F. Supp. 3d 627 (S.D. Tex. 2014).

74. Veasey v. Perry, 769 F.3d 890 (5th Cir. 2014).

75. Veasey v. Perry, 135 S. Ct. 6 (2014).

76. Veasey v. Abbott, 796 F.3d 487 (5th Cir. 2015).

77. Veasey v. Abbott, 830 F.3d 216 (5th Cir. 2016) (en banc).

78. Vann R. Newkirk, "The Department of Justice Stands by Texas's Voter ID Law," *Atlantic,* July 8, 2017.

79. Veasey v. Abbott, No. 17-40884 (5th Cir. 2018).

80. Daniel P. Tokaji. "Voter Registration and Election Reform," *William and Mary Bill of Rights Journal* 17, no. 2 (2008): 494.

81. Lassiter v. Northampton County Board of Elections, 360 U.S. 45 (1959); Louisiana v. U.S., 380 U.S. 145 (1965).

82. Harper v. Virginia Board of Elections, 383 U.S. 663 (1966); Kramer v. Union Free School District No. 15, 395 U.S. 621 (1969); Dunn v. Blumstein, 405 U.S. 330 (1972); Oregon v. Mitchell, 400 U.S. 112 (1970).

83. 400 U.S. 112 (1970).

84. Language suggesting that the right to vote is fundamental is also found in *Reynolds v. Sims,* the reapportionment ruling dictating that state legislatures must adhere to a one person, one vote equality standard. 377 U.S. 533 (1964).

85. Richardson v. Ramirez, 418 U.S. 24 (1974); Holt Civic Club v. City of Tuscaloosa 439 U.S. 60 (1978).

86. Anderson v. Celebrezze, 460 U.S. 780 (1983); Burdick v. Takushi, 504 U.S. 428 (1992).

87. *Anderson*, 460 U.S. at 788.

88. *Anderson*, 460 U.S. at 789.

89. *Burdick*, 504 U.S. at 434.

90. Technically, *Purcell v. Gonzalez* (2006) was the first Supreme Court case involving voter identification. The Court's per curiam opinion did not, however, address the merits of the substantive claim, instead vacating an injunction against Arizona's voter ID law since changing the rules too closely to election day might cause voter confusion and inhibit turnout. 549 U.S. 1 (2006).

91. *Crawford*, 553 U.S. at 197.

92. *Crawford*, 553 U.S. at 200.

93. *Crawford*, 553 U.S. at 205–206.

94. *Crawford*, 553 U.S. at 209.

95. *Crawford*, 553 U.S. at 209.

96. Crawford v. Marion County Election Board, 472 F.3d 949 (7th Cir. 2007).

97. Lawrence Baum, *Ideology* in *the Supreme Court* (Princeton, NJ: Princeton University Press, 2017).

98. Indiana Democratic Party v. Rokita, 458 F. Supp. 2d 775 (2006).

99. Jesse Bravin, "Voter-ID Laws Worry Jurist," *Wall Street Journal*, October 17, 2013.

100. Citizens United v. Federal Election Commission, 558 U.S. 310 (2010).

101. Carol Nackenoff, "What Became of Fundamental Rights? Of Voter IDs and Voting Rights," paper presented at the "Constitutional Schmooze" at the University of Maryland, 2014, https://digitalcomons.law.umaryland.edu/schmooze_papers/195/.

102. *Anderson*, 460 U.S. at 789.

103. Samuel Issacharoff, Pamela S. Karlan, Richard H. Pildes, and Nathaniel Persily, *The Law of Democracy: Legal Structure of the Political Process*, 5th ed. (St. Paul, MN: Foundation, 2016), 350.

104. Thomas Keck and Kevin McMahon, "Why *Roe* Still Stands: Abortion Law, the Supreme Court, and the Republican Regime," *Studies in Law, Politics and Society* 70 (2015): 33–83; Calvin TerBeek, "The Constitution as Political Program: The Republican Party and Originalism, 1977–1988," paper Presented at the annual meeting of the Midwest Political Science Association, Chicago, April 4–7, 2019.

105. Tokaji, "Restricting Race-Conscious Redistricting," 165.

106. Thomas Basile, "Inventing the 'Right to Vote' in *Crawford v. Marion County Election Board*," *Harvard Journal of Law and Public Policy* 32 (2009): 431–447; Edward B. Foley, "Details, Equal Citizenship, and Reasonable Fairness," *University of Pennsylvania Law Review* 156 (2007): 247–257; Joel Heller, "Fearing Fear Itself: Photo Identification Laws, Fear of Fraud, and the Fundamental Right to Vote," *Vanderbilt Law Review* 62, no. 6 (2009): 1871–1912; Bryan P. Jensen, "*Crawford v. Marion County Election Board*: The Missed Opportunity to Remedy the Ambiguity and Unpredictability of *Burdick*," *Denver University Law Review* 86 (2009): 535–563; Mary Jo Lang, "The Importance of Being Narrowly

Tailored: A Call for Strict Scrutiny for a Fundamental Right in *Crawford v. Marion County Election Board,*" *Nebraska Law Review* 88 (2009): 582–611; Matthew J. McGuane, "*Crawford v. Marion County Election Board*: The Disenfranchised Must Wait," *University of Miami Law Review* 64 (2009): 713–734; Nackenoff, "What Became of Fundamental Rights?"; Schultz, "Less Than Fundamental: The Myth of Voter Fraud and the Coming of the Second Great Disenfranchisement"; *William Mitchell Law Review* 34 (2008): 483–532; Robert Ellis Smith and Richard Sobel, "Demands for Voter Identification Require a Constitutional Standard of Reasonable Suspicion of Illegal Activity," *PS: Political Science and Politics* 42, no. 1 (2009): 103–105; Kathleen M. Stoughton, "A New Approach to Voter ID Challenges: Section 2 of the Voting Rights Act," *George Washington Law Review* 81, no. 1 (2013): 292–320.

107. Cox and Miles, "Judging the Voting Rights Act"; Kimi Lynn King, Jennifer Morbitt, and John Ryan, "Voting Rights and Wrongs: Federal District Court Decisions, 1965–1993," paper presented at the annual meeting of the American Political Science Association in San Francisco, 1996; Michael E. Solimine, "The Three-Judge District Court in Voting Rights Litigation," *University of Michigan Journal of Legal Reform* 79 (1996): 123, 140.

108. Hasen, *The Voting Wars,* 8, 42n201.

109. Christopher S. Elmendorf, "Undue Burdens on Voter Participation: New Pressures for a Structural Theory of the Right to Vote?," *Hastings Constitutional Law Quarterly* 35 (2008): 643–712.

110. Joshua A. Douglas, "Is the Right to Vote Really Fundamental?," *Cornell Journal of Law and Public Policy* 18 (2008): 143–201.

111. An excellent resource for finding and accessing these cases is the Election Law at Moritz website, sponsored by Ohio State University's Moritz College of Law and found at http://moritzlaw.osu.edu/election-law/.

112. I thus did not include *Arizona v. Inter Tribal Council,* in which both the Ninth Circuit and the Supreme Court invalidated Arizona's requirement of documentary evidence of citizenship for voter registration applicants. 570 U.S. 1 (2013).

113. Multiple lawsuits challenging a particular voter ID law were sometimes consolidated, which then counted as a single challenge. For example, two federal lawsuits challenging Wisconsin's photo identification law—*Frank v. Walker* and *Jones v. Deininger*—were joined as *Frank v. Walker.* Three federal suits challenging North Carolina's voter ID law—*League of Women Voters of North Carolina v. Howard, North Carolina Conference of NAACP v. McCrory,* and *U.S. v. North Carolina*—were consolidated as *League of Women Voters of North Carolina v. Howard.*

114. The voter identification law in New Mexico is a municipal ordinance in the city of Albuquerque rather than a statewide law enacted by the state legislature.

115. 472 F.3d 929 (7th Cir. 2007).

116. Michael Hiltzik, "A Conservative Judge's Devastating Take on Why Voter ID Laws Are Evil," *Los Angeles Times,* October 13, 2014.

117. In re Request for Advisory Opinion Regarding Constitutionality of 2005 PA 71, 740 N.W.2d 444 (Mich. 2007).

118. City of Memphis v. Hargett, No. M2012–02141-COA-R3-CV (Tenn. Ct. App. Oct. 25, 2012).
119. South Carolina v. U.S., 898 F. Supp.2d 30 (2012).
120. Applewhite, et al. v. Commonwealth of Pennsylvania, et al. (2012).
121. Joseph L. Fleiss, *Statistical Methods for Rates and Proportions*, 2nd ed. (New York: John Wiley, 1981); J. Richard Landis and Gary G. Koch, "The Measurement of Observer Agreement for Categorical Data," *Biometrics* 33 (1977): 159–174. A Kappa value of 0 indicates agreement equivalent to chance, and a value of 1 indicates perfect agreement.
122. http://www.cas.sc.edu/poli/juri/attributes.htm.
123. Mark Jonathan McKenzie, "The Influence of Partisanship, Ideology, and the Law on Redistricting Decisions in the Federal Courts," *Political Research Quarterly* 65, no. 4 (2012): 799–813.
124. American Civil Liberties Union of New Mexico v. Santillanes, 506 F. Supp.2d 598 (D.N.M. 2007).
125. Michael A. Bailey and Forrest Maltzman, *The Constrained Court: Law, Politics, and the Decisions Justices Make* (Princeton, NJ: Princeton University Press, 2011), 47, 53.
126. Joshua A. Douglas, "State Judges and the Right to Vote," *Ohio State Law Journal* 77 (2016): 1–48.
127. Schultz, "Less Than Fundamental: The Myth of Voter Fraud and the Coming of the Second Great Disenfranchisement," 523.
128. National Conference of State Legislatures, "Voter Identification Requirements/Voter ID Laws," January 17, 2019, http://www.ncsl.org/research/elections-and-campaigns/voter-id.aspx.
129. Additional states whose strict photo ID laws were challenged in court include Kansas, Mississippi, North Dakota, and Virginia.
130. Douglas, "State Judges and the Right to Vote," 16.
131. Democratic Party of Georgia v. Perdue, 288 Ga. 720 (2011).
132. Hasen, *The Voting Wars*.
133. Eileen Braman, *Law, Politics and Perception: How Policy Preferences Influence Legal Reasoning* (Charlottesville: University of Virginia Press, 2009); Kyle Casimir Kopko, "Litigant Partisan Identity and Challenges to Campaign Finance Policies: An Examination of U.S. District Court Decisions, 1971–2007," *Justice System Journal* 36, no. 3 (2015): 225, 228–229.
134. The asterisk indicates that the variable is statistically significant at the .05 level; the p-value, however, is actually 0.000.
135. The p-value here is 0.001.
136. This difference is statistically significant according to Pearson's chi-square test (pr = .001).
137. Pearson's chi-square test confirms that these differences are statistically significant for both federal and state court judges.
138. Jon Gottschall, "Reagan's Appointments to the U.S. Courts of Appeals: The Continuation of a Judicial Revolution," *Judicature* 70 (1986): 48–54.
139. Obviously, ideology matters more as we travel up the judicial hierarchy, with judges at the highest level, such as the US Supreme Court, more

likely to face difficult cases lacking clear and simple answers. Lee Epstein, William M. Landes, and Richard A. Posner, *The Behavior of Federal Judges: A Theoretical and Empirical Study of Rational Choice* (Cambridge, MA: Harvard University Press, 2013). Nonetheless, even here, many decisions—around a third from 1953 to 2004—are unanimous, with Democratic and Republican justices across the ideological spectrum agreeing on the correct legal answer. Pamela C. Corley, Amy Steigerwalt, and Artemus Ward, *The Puzzle of Unanimity: Consensus on the United States Supreme Court* (Palo Alto, CA: Stanford University Press, 2013), 3.

140. Douglas, "State Judges and the Right to Vote."

141. Bailey and Maltzman, *The Constrained Court*, 83.

142. Thomas M. Keck, *Judicial Politics in Polarized Times* (Chicago: University of Chicago Press, 2014), 148.

143. Keck, *Judicial Politics in Polarized Times*, 150.

Chapter 4: Courts, Parties, and Redistricting

1. Commerce Department v. New York, 139 S. Ct. 2551 (2019).

2. Evenwel v. Abbott, 136 S. Ct. 1120 (2016).

3. Shaw v. Reno, 509 U.S. 630 (1993).

4. Anthony J. McGann, Charles Anthony Smith, Michael Latner, and Alex Keena, *Gerrymandering in America: The House of Representatives, the Supreme Court, and the Future of Popular Sovereignty* (New York: Cambridge University Press, 2016); Rucho v. Common Cause, 139 S. Ct. 2484 (2019); Vieth v. Jubelirer, 541 U.S. 267 (2004).

5. Gordon E. Baker, *The Reapportionment Revolution: Representation, Political Power, and the Supreme Court* (New York: Random House, 1966).

6. Article I, Section 2 also specified that the population count would include all "free Persons" and "three fifths of all other Persons" (i.e., slaves) but would exclude "Indians not taxed." Section 2 of the Fourteenth Amendment removed the three-fifths provisions. It also authorized a reduction in a state's representation in the House if the right to vote was denied to any male citizen who was at least twenty-one years of age, though this was never enforced despite massive disenfranchisement of African Americans in Southern states.

7. Georgia v. U.S., 411 U.S. 526 (1973).

8. Wesberry v. Sanders, 376 U.S. 1 (1964).

9. Thornburg v. Gingles, 478 U.S. 30 (1986); Shaw v. Reno, 509 U.S. 630 (1993).

10. National Conference of State Legislatures, "Redistricting Commissions," January 9, 2020, https://www.ncsl.org/research/redistricting/2009-redistricting-commissions-table.aspx.

11. Seven states currently have only one House seat: Alaska, Delaware, Montana, North Dakota, South Dakota, Vermont, and Wyoming. Montana might gain a second seat after the 2020 census.

12. Justin Levitt, "Professor Justin Levitt's Guide to Drawing the Lines," All About Redistricting (website), 2017, http://redistricting.lls.edu/.

13. National Conference of State Legislatures, "Redistricting Commissions." The number of states assigning primary responsibility for crafting House districts to a commission will increase to nine if Montana gains a second seat after the next census.

14. Jordan Carr Peterson, "The Mask of Neutrality: Judicial Partisan Calculation and Legislative Redistricting," *Law and Policy* 41, no. 3 (2019): 336–359.

15. Bernard Grofman and German Feierherd, "The U.S. Could Be Free of Gerrymandering. Here's How Other Countries Do Redistricting," *Washington Post*, August 7, 2017.

16. Justin Levitt, "Litigation in the 2010 Cycle," All About Redistricting (website), 2018, http://redistricting.lls.edu/cases.php.

17. Nathaniel Persily, "When Judges Carve Democracies: A Primer on Court-Drawn Redistricting Plans," *George Washington University Law Review* 73 (2005): 1701–1739.

18. 328 U.S. 549 (1946).

19. *Colegrove*, 328 at 569, 570.

20. *Colegrove*, 328 at 553–554, 556.

21. Earl Warren, *The Memoirs of Earl Warren* (New York: Doubleday, 1977), 306; Baker v. Carr, 369 U.S. 186 (1962).

22. 376 U.S. 1, 7–8 (1964).

23. 377 U.S. 533, 577 (1964).

24. Lucas v. Colorado 44th General Assembly, 377 U.S. 713 (1964).

25. Brown v. Thomson, 462 U.S. 835 (1983).

26. 462 U.S. 725 (1983).

27. Stephen Ansolabehere and James M. Snyder Jr., *The End of Inequality: One Person, One Vote and the Transformation of American Politics* (New York: W. W. Norton, 2008), 31.

28. Lucas Powe, *The Warren Court and American Politics* (Cambridge, MA: Harvard University Press, 2002), 200.

29. *Reynolds*, 377 at 566–568.

30. *Reynolds*, 377 at 565.

31. *Reynolds*, 377 at 565, 562.

32. Ansolabehere and Snyder, *The End of Inequality*, 31.

33. Mathew D. McCubbins and Thomas Schwartz, "Congress, the Courts, and Public Policy: Consequences of the One Man, One Vote Rule," *American Journal of Political Science* 32, no. 2 (1988): 388–415.

34. Ansolabehere and Snyder, *The End of Inequality*, 233–238. Some scholars dispute this claim that increased education and social welfare spending resulted from the Warren Court's egalitarian intervention in redistricting. Robert S. Erikson, "Reapportionment and Policy: A Further Look at Some Intervening Variables," in "Democratic Representation and Apportionment: Quantitative Methods, Measures, and Criteria," *Annals of the New York Academy of Sciences* 29 (1973): 280–290; Matthew D. Lassiter, *The Silent Majority: Suburban Politics in*

the Sunbelt South (Princeton, NJ: Princeton University Press, 2006); Gerald N. Rosenberg, *The Hollow Hope: Can Courts Bring About Social Change?*, 2nd ed. (Chicago: University of Chicago Press, 2008); Timothy O'Rourke, *The Impact of Reapportionment* (New Brunswick, NJ: Transaction, 1980).

35. Robert G. McCloskey, "The Supreme Court, 1961 Term—Foreword: The Reapportionment Case," *Harvard Law Review* 76 (1962): 54–222; Alexander M. Bickel, "The Durability of *Colegrove v. Green*," *Yale Law Journal* 72 (1962): 39–45; Allan P. Sindler, "*Baker v. Carr*: How to 'Sear the Conscience' of Legislators," *Yale Law Journal* 72 (1962): 23–38.

36. Daniel H. Lowenstein and Jonathan Steinberg, "The Quest for Legislative Districting in the Public Interest: Elusive or Illusory?" *UCLA Law Review* 33 (1985): 1–75; Samuel Issacharoff and Pamela S. Karlan, "Where to Draw the Lines: Judicial Review of Political Gerrymandering," *University of Pennsylvania Law Review* 153 (2004): 541–578; Michael McConnell, "The Redistricting Cases: Original Mistakes and Current Consequences," *Harvard Journal of Law and Public Policy* 24 (2000): 103–118.

37. John Hart Ely, *Democracy and Distrust: A Theory of Judicial Review* (Cambridge, MA: Harvard University Press, 1980).

38. Jeffrey Rosen, *The Most Democratic Branch: How the Courts Serve America* (New York: Oxford University Press, 2006), 126.

39. Ron Replogle, "The Scope of Representation-Reinforcing Judicial Review," *Columbia Law Review* 92, no. 6 (1992):1592–1624; Cass R. Sunstein, *The Partial Constitution* (Cambridge, MA: Harvard University Press, 1993); David A. Strauss, "Modernization ad Representation Reinforcement: An Essay in Memory of John Hart Ely," *Stanford Law Review* 57 (2004): 761–778; Robert C. Post, "Justice William J. Brennan and the Warren Court," *Constitutional Commentary* 8 (1991): 11–25; Erwin Chemerinsky, *Interpreting the Constitution* (New York: Praeger , 1987).

40. Jack M. Balkin and Sanford Levinson, "The Canons of Constitutional Law," *Harvard Law Review* 111 (1998): 963–1024.

41. I credit Sunstein for this particular phrasing of the timing question which he used in analyzing the Court's *District of Columbia v. Heller* decision, 554 US 570 (2008). Cass R. Sunstein, "Second Amendment Minimalism: *Heller* as *Griswold*," *Harvard Law Review* 122 (2008): 246–274.

42. Harold J. Spaeth, Lee Epstein, Andrew D. Martin, Jeffrey A. Segal, Theodore J. Ruger, and Sara C. Benesh, The U.S. Supreme Court Database, Version 2018, Release 01, http://supremecourtdatabase.org.

43. Andrew Martin and Kevin Quinn, "Dynamic Ideal Point Estimation via Markov Chain Monte Carlo for the U.S. Supreme Court, 1953–1999," *Political Analysis* 10, no. 2 (2002): 134–153.

44. Ansolabehere and Snyder, *The End of Inequality*, 89.

45. John F. Kennedy, "The Shame of the States," *New York Times Magazine*, May 18, 1958, 37.

46. Ansolabehere and Snyder, *The End of Inequality*, 1, 4–5.

47. Keith E. Whittington, "'Interpose Your Friendly Hand': Political Supports

for the Exercise of Judicial Review by the United States Supreme Court," *American Political Science Review* 99 (2005): 588–589.

48. Whittington, "Interpose Your Friendly Hand," 589.

49. Powe, *The Warren Court and American Politics*, 204.

50. Whittington, "Interpose Your Friendly Hand," 589.

51. Rosen, *The Most Democratic Branch*, 127–128.

52. Powe, *The Warren Court and American Politics*, 494.

53. Whittington, "Interpose Your Friendly Hand," 588.

54. Martin M. Shapiro, "Gerrymandering, Unfairness, and the Supreme Court," *UCLA Law Review* 33 (1985): 241.

55. Lucas A. Powe Jr., "The Warren Court and the Political Process," in *The American Congress: The Building of Democracy*, ed., Julian E. Zelizer (New York: Houghton Mifflin, 2004), 548–556.

56. Gary W. Cox and Jonathan N. Katz, *Elbridge Gerry's Salamander: The Electoral Consequences of the Reapportionment Revolution* (New York: Cambridge University Press, 2002), 72–81.

57. Cox and Katz, *Elbridge Gerry's Salamander*, 25–26, 32.

58. Cox and Katz, i.

59. Jamie L. Carson and Michael H. Crespin, "The Effect of State Redistricting Methods on Competition in United States House of Representatives Races," *State Politics and Policy Quarterly* 4 (2004): 455–469; Jamie L. Carson, Michael H. Crespin, and Ryan D. Williamson, "Reevaluating the Effects of Redistricting on Electoral Competition, 1972–2012," *State Politics and Policy Quarterly* 14, no. 2 (2014): 165–177; James B. Cottrill, "The Effects of Non-Legislative Redistricting on Competition in Congressional Elections," *Polity* 44 (2012): 32–50; Eric Lindgren and Priscilla Southwell, "The Effect of Redistricting Commissions on Electoral Competitiveness in U.S. House Elections, 2002–2010," *Journal of Law and Politics* 6, no. 2 (2013): 13–18; Peterson, "The Mask of Neutrality." Most studies also find that commission-drawn plans produce more competitive elections relative to legislative plans. Although not directly focusing on electoral competition, Peress and Zhao, in contrast, found that redistricting commissions do not actually "preserve" rather than reduce "partisan bias in the districting process." Michael Peress and Yangzi Zhao, "How Many Seats in Congress Is Control of Redistricting Worth?," *Legislative Studies Quarterly* 45 (2020).

60. Carson and Crespin, "The Effect of State Redistricting Methods."

61. Carson et al., "Reevaluating the Effects of Redistricting."

62. James B. Cottrill and Terri J. Peretti, "Gerrymandering from the Bench? The Electoral Consequences of Judicial Redistricting," *Election Law Journal* 12 (2013): 261–276.

63. Peterson, "The Mask of Neutrality."

64. Corbett A. Grainger, "Redistricting and Polarization: Who Draws the Lines in California?," *Journal of Law and Economics* 53, no. 3 (2010): 545–567.

65. Kathleen L. Barber, "Partisan Values in the Lower Courts: Reapportionment in Ohio and Michigan," *Case Western Reserve Law Review* 20, no. 2 (1969): 420.

66. Peterson, "The Mask of Neutrality."

67. Randall D. Lloyd, "Separating Partisanship from Party in Judicial Research: Reapportionment in the U.S. District Courts," *American Political Science Review* 89, no. 2 (1995): 413–420.

68. Mark Jonathan McKenzie, "Beyond Partisanship? An Analysis of Judicial Decisions on Redistricting in State Supreme Courts," paper presented at the annual meeting of the Midwest Political Science Association, Chicago, April 2010.

69. Mark Jonathan McKenzie, "The Influence of Partisanship, Ideology, and the Law on Redistricting Decisions in the Federal Courts," *Political Research Quarterly* 65, no. 4 (2012): 799–813.

70. McKenzie, "The Influence of Partisanship, Ideology, and the Law," 802.

71. Kyle Casimir Kopko, "The Effect of Partisanship in Election Law Judicial Decision-Making" (PhD diss., Ohio State University, 2010).

72. Cox and Katz, *Elbridge Gerry's Salamander*, 9.

73. Cottrill and Peretti, "Gerrymandering from the Bench?"

74. Peterson, "The Mask of Neutrality."

75. Peterson, 337.

76. Peterson, 336.

77. Peterson, 336.

78. Charles S. Bullock III, *Redistricting: The Most Political Activity in America* (Lanham, MD: Rowmand & Littlefield, 2012), 230.

79. *New York Times* Editorial Board, "Kris Kobach's Voting Sham Gets Exposed in Court," *New York Times*, March 17, 2018.

80. Robert Draper, "The League of Dangerous Mapmakers," *Atlantic*, October 2012; Carl Hulse, "Seeking to End Gerrymandering's Enduring Legacy," *New York Times*, January 25, 2016; Stuart Leavenworth, "Gerrymandering Hurts Cities Such as Elk Grove," *Sacramento Bee*, February 21, 2010.

81. Jamal Greene, "Judging Partisan Gerrymanders under the Election Clause," *Yale Law Review* 114 (2005): 2012–1061; Samuel Issacharoff, "Gerrymandering and Political Cartels," *Harvard Law Review* 116 (2002): 593–648; Stephen Gottlieb, *Unfit for Democracy: The Roberts Court and the Breakdown of American Politics* (New York: New York University Press, 2016), 120.

82. David Daley, "This Is How We End Gerrymandering," FairVote, January 26, 2018, https://www.fairvote.org/this_is_how_we_end_gerrymandering; Common Cause, "End Gerrymandering Now," commoncause.org/actions/end-gerrymandering-now/# (accessed February 11, 2020); Brennan Center for Justice, "Gerrymandering & Fair Representation," https://www.brennancenter.org/issues/gerrymandering-fair-representation (accessed February 11, 2020).

83. Bernard Grofman and Gary King, "The Future of Partisan Symmetry as a Judicial Test for Partisan Gerrymandering after *LULAC v. Perry*," *Election Law Journal* 6, no. 1 (2007): 2–35; McGann et al., *Gerrymandering in America*.

84. Brennan Center for Justice, "American Leaders Talk about Gerrymandering," June 15, 2017, https://www.brennancenter.org/analysis/american-leaders-talk-about-gerrymandering.

85. Sam Wang, "The Great Gerrymander of 2012," *New York Times*, February

2, 2013; Vann Newkirk II, "How Redistricting Became a Technological Arms Race," *Atlantic*, October 28, 2017.

86. Richard Fleisher and Jon R. Bond, "Partisanship and the President's Quest for Votes on the Floor of Congress," in *Polarized Politics: Congress and the President in a Partisan Era*, ed. Jon R. Bond and Richard Fleisher (Washington, DC: Congressional Quarterly Press, 2000), 154–184. Some scholars challenge these democratic concerns over partisan gerrymandering. Thomas Brunell, for example, criticizes the reflexive approval of competitive elections, noting that they can produce negative consequences. The number of voters who are disappointed or angry when their preferred candidate loses is much greater in a close election than in a lopsided one; these voters are also more likely to be dissatisfied with their representative and with Congress as a whole. Uncompetitive elections, in contrast, can increase the proportion of voters in a district who share the policy views of and are satisfied with their congressional representative. Thomas L. Brunell, *Redistricting and Representation: Why Competitive Elections Are Bad for America* (New York: Routledge, 2008); Thomas Brunell and Justin Buchler, "Ideological Representation and Competitive Elections," *Electoral Studies* 28 (2009): 448–457; Justin Buchler, "Competition, Representation, and Redistricting: The Case against Competitive Congressional Districts," *Journal of Theoretical Politics* 17 (2005): 431–463. Persily echoes this view and observes a variety of benefits produced by safe districts and incumbent reelection—not only higher voter satisfaction but also the presence of experienced and more effective legislators. Nathaniel Persily, "Reply: In Defense of Foxes Guarding Henhouses: The Case for Judicial Acquiescence to Incumbent Protecting Activities," *Harvard Law Review* 116 (2002): 649–683.

87. National Conference of State Legislatures, "2015 Redistricting Legislation," December 30, 2015, http://www.ncsl.org/research/redistricting/2015 -redistricting-legislation.aspx; National Conference of State Legislatures, "Redistricting Legislation Database: 2018 Onward," April 30, 2019, http://www .ncsl.org/research/redistricting/redistricting-legislation-database.aspx.

88. Bush v. Gore, 531 U.S. 98 (2000); Shelby County v. Holder, 570 U.S. 529 (2013).

89. 478 U.S. 109 (1986).

90. *Davis*, 109 at 132.

91. *Davis*, 109 at 147.

92. Thomas H. Crouch, "Political Gerrymandering: Judicial Scrutiny under the Equal Protection Clause," *Hamline Law Review* 10 (1987): 313–344.

93. Oddly, the only redistricting plan to be struck down under *Bandemer* by a lower court prior to *Whitford v. Gill* (2016) involved a 1992 challenge to North Carolina's statewide election of superior court judges, which had produced only one Republican judge since 1900. The federal district court in *Republican Party of North Carolina v. Martin* (1988) reasonably concluded that the Republican Party had been, and would likely continue to be consistently, excluded from the electoral process. In the election immediately following the court's decision, however, Republican candidates won every contested race, leading the court of

appeals to reverse. Whitford v. Gill, 218 F. Supp. 3d 837 (W.D. Wis. 2016); Republican Party of North Carolina v. Martin, 682 F. Supp. 834 (M.D.N.C. 1988).

94. Michael A. Smith, "Minority Representation and Majority-Minority Districts after *Shaw v. Reno*: Legal Challenges, Empirical Evidence and Alternate Approaches," *Politics and Policy* 29 (2001): 245. The best possibility for success in partisan gerrymandering cases has come when a gerrymandering claim is "bootstrapped" to a more promising legal argument—for example, involving the one-person, one-vote standard, which Issacharoff and Karlan refer to as a "second-order political gerrymandering claim." Issacharoff and Karlan, "Where to Draw the Lines," 695; J. Gerald Herbert and Marina K. Jenkins, "The Need for State Redistricting Reform to Rein in Partisan Gerrymandering," *Yale Law and Policy Review* 29 (2001): 551; McKenzie, "The Influence of Partisanship, Ideology, and the Law," 808. For example, in *Larios v. Cox* (2004) a three-judge court accepted a one-person, one-vote challenge to a post-2000 redistricting plan enacted by the Democratic-controlled Georgia legislature because the deviation from population equality was motivated by partisanship and not more legitimate grounds such as those suggested in *Karcher v. Daggett* like promoting compactness, respecting municipal boundaries, or preserving the core of previous districts. Larios v. Cox, 300 F. Supp.2d 1320 (N.D. Ga. 2004).

95. Richard L. Hasen, "Looking for Standards (in All the Wrong Places): Partisan Gerrymandering Claims after *Vieth*," *Election Law Journal* 3, no. 4 (2004): 626–642.

96. Daniel H. Lowenstein, "*Vieth*'s Gap: Has the Supreme Court Gone from Bad to Worse on Partisan Gerrymandering?," *Cornell Journal of Law and Public Policy* 14 (2005): 367.

97. *Vieth*, 541 at 306.

98. Justice Stevens would forbid partisan factors to play a dominant role, Justice Breyer advanced an "unjustified minority entrenchment" standard, and Justices Souter and Ginsburg offered a multifactor test involving whether the legislature had manipulated district lines to pack or crack the plaintiff's party, disregarded traditional criteria such as contiguity and compactness, and overlooked alternate plans that better achieved those criteria.

99. Nicholas O. Stephanopoulos, "Lessons from Litigating for Reform," *Election Law Journal* 16, no. 2 (2017): 231.

100. Thomas L. Brunell, review of *Gerrymandering in America: The House of Representatives, the Supreme Court, and the Future of Popular Sovereignty*, by Anthony J. McGann, Charles Anthony Smith, Michael Latner, and Alex Keena, *Congress and the Presidency* 44 (2017): 176–178.

101. McGann et al., *Gerrymandering in America*.

102. Lowenstein, "*Vieth*'s Gap," 370.

103. 548 US 399 (2006).

104. 138 S. Ct. 1916 (2018).

105. *Gill*, 138 S. Ct. at 1929, 1930. In *Gill*, Justice Kagan, joined by Justices Ginsburg, Breyer, and Sotomayor, offered an interesting concurrence that followed up on Kennedy's suggestion in *Vieth* that the First Amendment might be a more relevant constitutional provision when it comes to partisan gerryman-

dering claims. She noted to future plaintiffs that they might avoid the district-specific requirement by arguing instead that their First Amendment right of association was infringed. If this was an appeal for Justice Kennedy's vote, the strategy failed.

106. 138 S. Ct. 1942 (2018).

107. Mark Joseph Stern, "The Supreme Court Punted on Partisan Gerry-mandering: The Fight to Kill It Is Far from Over," *Slate*, June 18, 2018; Richard Levick, "SCOTUS, for Now, Largely Chooses to Punt on Partisan Gerrymander-ing," *Forbes*, June 19, 2018.

108. Rucho v. Common Cause, 139 S. Ct. at 2506–2507.

109. *Rucho,* 139 at 2491, 2500.

110. *Rucho,* 139 at 2501.

111. *Rucho,* 139 at 2525, 2509.

112. *Rucho,* 139 at 2516, 2519.

113. *Rucho* 139 at 2516, 2521.

114. Richard L. Engstrom, "The Post-2000 Round of Redistricting: An En-tangled Thicket within the Federal System," *Publius* 32, no. 4 (2002): 51–70; Heather K. Gerken, "Lost in the Political Thicket: The Court, Election Law, and the Doctrinal Interregnum," *University of Pennsylvania Law Review* 153 (2004): 503–540; Issacharoff, "Gerrymandering and Political Cartels"; Michael S. Kang, "When Courts Won't Make Law: Partisan Gerrymandering and a Struc-tural Approach to the Law of Democracy," *Ohio State Law Journal* 68 (2007): 1097–1120; J. Gerald Hebert and Marina K. Jenkins, "The Need for State Re-districting Reform to Rein in Partisan Gerrymandering," *Yale Law and Policy Review* 29 (2011): 543–558; Kang, "When Courts Won't Make Law"; Michael S. Kang, "Gerrymandering and the Constitutional Norm against Government Partisanship," *Michigan Law Review* 116 (2017): 351–419; Levitt, "Litigation in the 2010 Cycle"; David A. Schultz, "Regulating the Political Thicket: Congress, the Courts, and State Reapportionment Commissions," *Charleston Law Review* 3 (2008):109–145.

115. Kang, "When Courts Won't Make Law," 1100.

116. Lowenstein, "*Vieth*'s Gap," 368.

117. McGann et al., *Gerrymandering in America.*

118. Some attribute the GOP's success in 2010 to its Redistricting Majority Project, also known as REDMAP, which sought to flip party control of state legislatures with thin Democratic majorities in the 2010 elections in order to expand GOP power in the next round of redistricting. David Daley, *Ratf**ked: The True Story behind the Secret Plan to Steal America's Democracy* (New York: Liver-ight, 2016). Karl Rove described this plan in a 2010 *Wall Street Journal* editorial, noting that fundraising efforts were underway, with campaign strategists "fo-cused on 107 seats in 16 states. Winning these seats would give [the Republican Party] . . . control of drawing district lines for nearly 190 congressional seats." Karl Rove, "The GOP Targets State Legislatures: He Who Controls Redistricting Can Control Congress," *Wall Street Journal*, March 3, 2010. Targets included dis-tricts in Ohio, Florida, North Carolina, Wisconsin, Indiana, and Pennsylvania. If judged solely by the outcome of the 2010 election, this $30 million campaign

was remarkably successful, with Democrats suffering devastating losses and Republicans winning exclusive control over redistricting in twenty states with two hundred congressional seats; Democrats, in contrast, controlled redistricting in two states, Oregon and Rhode Island, with only seven House seats. Geoffrey Skelley and Kyle Kondik, "2018 Governors: The Battle Lines for Drawing the Lines," *Sabato's Crystal Ball,* February 23, 2017, http://crystalball.centerfor politics.org/crystalball/articles/2018-governors-the-battle-lines-for-drawing -the-lines/. This represents a major change from both the 2000 redistricting cycle, where Democrats drew boundaries for 136 House districts compared to ninety-eight for the Republicans, and the 1990s round in which Democrats drew the lines for 172 House districts compared to only five for Republicans. Daley, *Rat**fucked,* xx.

119. Wang, "The Great Gerrymander of 2012."

120. McGann et al., *Gerrymandering in America,* 56–57.

121. McGann et al., 71.

122. McGann et al., 72. In many Southern states, asymmetry scores were so extreme that the GOP could win two-thirds to three-fourths of the state's House seats by winning only half of the votes. Among the thirty-eight states with three or more congressional districts, twenty were unbiased and eighteen were biased, with seventeen of the eighteen states biased in favor of the Republican Party. Additionally, of the eighteen states with significant partisan bias, fourteen were states in which a single party controlled the redistricting process, supporting the study's claim that politics and not demography or geography, such as the urban concentration of Democrats, was the primary cause. McGann et al., 74, 79–80, 157.

123. McGann et al., 177.

124. McGann et al., 18.

125. The Democratic Party offered a statement regarding redistricting in four of its thirteen national platforms from 1968 through 2016. The party recognized "the principle of one man, one vote" in 1968, proclaimed the importance of "count[ing] . . . every American" in the census in 1988 and 2004, and called for an end to partisan and racial gerrymandering in 2016.

126. William H. Frey, "Trump Put the Census Citizenship Question Back in Play," *Brookings Brief,* July 9, 2019, https://www.brookings.edu/blog/the-ave nue/2019/07/09/trump-puts-the-census-citizenship-question-back-in-play/; Ted Mellnik and Kate Rabinowitz, "Where a Citizenship Question Could Cause the Census to Miss Millions of Hispanics—and Why That's a Big Deal," *Washington Post,* June 6, 2019. An unpublished study by Thomas Hofeller, a prominent redistricting strategist for the Republican Party, concluded that requiring a citizenship question would be "advantageous to Republicans and Non-Hispanic Whites" in redrawing districts." Hanso Lo Wang, "Deceased GOP Strategist's Daughter Makes Files Public That Republicans Wanted Sealed," *National Public Radio,* January 5, 2020.

127. 139 S. Ct. 2551 (2019).

128. Ari Berman, "Trump's Stealth Plan to Preserve White Electoral Power," *Mother Jones,* January/February 2020.

129. Rebecca Klar, "DHS to Share Citizenship Data with Census Bureau in Wake of Court Decision," *The Hill,* January 6, 2020.

130. Executive Order on Collecting Information about Citizenship Status in Connection with the Decennial Census, July 11, 2019, https://www.white house.gov/presidential-actions/executive-order-collecting-information-citizen ship-status-connection-decennial-census/.

131. The National Republican Redistricting Trust is described as "the GOP's data and legal hub preparing for redistricting after the next census." It was founded in 2017, reportedly in response to the National Democratic Redistricting Committee that former president Obama founded and former attorney general Eric Holder leads. Both groups seek to position their party favorably for the 2020 round of redistricting. Scott Bland, "Republicans Expand Redistricting Strategy for 2020," *Politico,* September 29, 2017.

132. McGann et al., *Gerrymandering in America,* quotations on 19.

133. Nicholas R. Seabrook, *Drawing the Lines: Constraints on Partisan Gerrymandering in U.S. Politics* (Ithaca, NY: Cornell University Press, 2017), 9.

134. Nicholas O. Stephanopoulos, "The Causes and Consequences of Gerrymandering," *William and Mary Law Review* 59 (2018): 2115–2149; David Cottrell, "Using Computer Simulations to Measure the Effect of Gerrymandering on Electoral Competition in the U.S. Congress," *Legislative Studies Quarterly* 44, no. 3 (2019): 487–514.

135. Seabrook, *Drawing the Lines,* 14–15.

136. Seabrook, 14.

137. Skelley and Kondik, "2018 Governors."

138. McGann et al., *Gerrymandering in America.*

139. John Sides and Eric McGhee, "Redistricting Didn't Win Republicans the House," *Washington Post,* February 17, 2013.

140. Vladimir Kogan and Eric McGhee, "Redistricting and Representation: Searching for 'Fairness' between the Lines," in *Changing How America Votes,* ed. Todd Donovan (New York: Rowman & Littlefield, 2018), 84–99; Andrew Gelman and Gary King, "Enhancing Democracy through Legislative Districting," *American Political Science Review* 88, no. 3 (1994): 541–559; David Butler and Bruce Cain, eds., *Congressional Redistricting: Comparative and Theoretical Perspectives* (New York: Macmillan, 1992).

141. Bruce E. Cain, Karin MacDonald, and Michael McDonald, "From Equality to Fairness: The Path of Political Reform since *Baker v. Carr,*" in *Party Lines: Competition, Partisanship, and Congressional Redistricting,* ed., Thomas E. Mann and Bruce E. Cain (Washington, DC: Brookings Institution, 2005), 6–30; Nicholas Goedert, "The Pseudoparadox of Partisan Mapmaking and Congressional Competition," *State Politics and Policy Quarterly* 17, no. 1 (2017): 47–75; Antoine Yoshinaka and Chad Murphy, "The Paradox of Redistricting: How Partisan Mapmakers Foster Competition but Disrupt Representation," *Political Research Quarterly* 64 (2011): 435–447; Seabrook, *Drawing the Lines.*

142. John A. Ferejohn, "On the Decline of Competitiveness of Congressional Elections," *American Political Science Review* 71 (1977): 166–176; Seth E. Masket, Jonathan Winburn, and Gerald C. Wright, "The Gerrymanderers Are Com-

ing! Legislative Redistricting Won't Affect Competition or Polarization Much, No Matter Who Does It," *Political Science and Politics* 45, no. 1 (2012): 39–43; Seabrook, *Drawing the Lines*.

143. Alan I. Abramowitz, Brad Alexander, and Matthew Gunning, "Incumbency, Redistricting, and the Decline of Competition in US House Elections," *Journal of Politics* 68, no. 1 (2006): 75–88.

144. Cottrell, "Using Computer Simulations," 505.

145. Michael McDonald, "The 2010 Midterm Elections: Signs and Portents for the Decennial Redistricting," *Political Science and Politics* 44, no. 2 (2011): 311–315.

146. Sides and McGhee, "Redistricting Didn't Win Republicans the House"; Nicholas Goedert, "Gerrymandering or Geography? How Democrats Won the Popular Vote but Lost the Congress in 2012," *Research and Politics* 1, no. 1 (2014): 1–8; Gary C. Jacobson, "Partisanship, Money, and Competition: Elections and the Transformation of Congress since the 1970s," in *Congress Reconsidered*, 11th ed., ed. Lawrence C. Dodd and Bruce I. Oppenheimer (Washington, DC: Congressional Quarterly Press, 2017), 110–111; Jonathan Rodden, *Why Cities Lose: Political Geography and the Representation of the Left* (New York: Basic, 2019); David Wasserman, "Introducing the 2017 Cook Political Report Partisan Voter Index," *Cook Political Report*, April 7, 2017.

147. Goedert, "Gerrymandering or Geography?," 1, 7.

148. Stephanopoulos, "The Causes and Consequences of Gerrymandering," 2115.

149. Seabrook, *Drawing the Lines*, 30.

150. Kogan and McGhee, "Redistricting and Representation," 94.

151. Bernard Grofman and Thomas L. Brunell, "The Art of the Dummymander: The Impact of Recent Redistrictings on the Partisan Makeup of Southern House Seats," in *Redistricting in the New Millennium*, ed. Peter F. Galderisi (New York: Rowman & Littlefield, 2005), 183–200.

152. Nicholas Goedert, "The Pseudoparadox of Partisan Mapmaking and Congressional Competition," *State Politics and Policy Quarterly* 17, no. 1 (2017): 47.

153. Eric McGhee, "Measuring Partisan Bias in Single-Member District Electoral Systems," *Legislative Studies Quarterly* 39, no. 1 (2014): 55.

154. Seabrook, *Drawing the Lines*, 72.

155. Wasserman, "Introducing the 2017 Cook Political Report Partisan Voter Index"; Bill Bishop, *The Big Sort: Why the Clustering of Like-Minded America is Tearing Us Apart* (New York: Houghton Mifflin, 2008).

156. Goedert, "The Pseudoparadox of Partisan Mapmaking and Congressional Competition," 51–52; Seabrook, *Drawing the Lines*, 17–19.

157. Nicholas Goedert, "The Case of the Disappearing Bias: A 2014 Update to the 'Gerrymandering or Geography' Debate," *Research and Politics* 2, no. 4 (2015): 3.

158. Elena Schneider, "The Biggest Threat to the GOP Majority No One's Talking About," *Politico*, September 14, 2018; Center for Responsive Politics, "Departures Resulting in Open Seat Races by Cycle," https://www.opensecrets.org/members-of-congress/departures-by-cycle (accessed January 19, 2020).

159. David A. Lieb, "AP: GOP Won More Seats in 2018 Than Suggested by Vote Share," *AP News*, March 21, 2019.

160. Molly E. Reynolds, "Republicans in Congress Got a 'Seats Bonus' This Election (Again)," *Brookings Institution FixGov* (blog), November 22, 2016, https://www.brookings.edu/blog/fixgov/2016/11/22/gop-seats-bonus-in -congress/.

161. Reynolds, "Republicans in Congress Got a 'Seats Bonus.'"

162. Sides and McGhee, "Redistricting Didn't Win Republicans the House."

163. Hasen, "Looking for Standards (in All the Wrong Places)"; Lowenstein, "*Vieth*'s Gap"; Peter Schuck, "The Thickest Thicket: Partisan Gerrymandering and Judicial Regulation of Politics," *Columbia Law Review* 87, no. 7 (1987): 1325–1384.

164. Different methods for measuring partisan bias include a "partisan symmetry" approach (employed by Grofman and King and by McGann et al.), the "efficiency gap" standard that emphasizes wasted votes (used by Stephanopoulos and by McGhee), compactness metrics such as the Polsby-Popper test (used by Polsby and Popper and by Najmabadi), and an "equal vote weight standard" that compares a party's median vote share with its mean vote share (used by McDonald and Best and by Wang). Grofman and King, "The Future of Partisan Symmetry as a Judicial Test for Partisan Gerrymandering after *LULAC v. Perry*"; McGann et al., *Gerrymandering in America*; Daniel D. Polsby and Robert D. Popper, "The Third Criterion: Compactness as a Procedural Safeguard against Partisan Gerrymandering," *Yale Law and Policy Review* 9, no. 2 (1991): 301–353; Shannon Najmabadi, "Meet the Math Professor Who's Fighting Gerrymandering with Geometry," *Chronicle of Higher Education*, February 22, 2017; Michael D. McDonald and Robin E. Best, "Unfair Partisan Gerrymanders in Politics and Law: A Diagnostic Applied to Six Cases," *Election Law Journal* 14, no. 4 (2015): 312–330; Sam Wang, "Three Tests for Practical Evaluation of Partisan Gerrymandering," *Stanford Law Review* 68, no. 6 (2016): 1263–1321.

165. A key factor in Orban gaining a parliamentary supermajority, Scheppele explains, was the redrawing of electoral districts that were "highly unequal in size," with left-leaning districts containing many more voters compared to right-leaning districts. Kim Lane Scheppele, "Legal but not Fair: Viktor Orban's New Supermajority," *Conscience of a Liberal* (blog), April 13, 2014; Kim Lane Scheppele, "Hungary and the End of Politics," *Nation*, May 6, 2014; Cas Mudde, "The 2014 Hungarian Parliamentary Elections, or How to Craft a Constitutional Majority," *Washington Post*, April 14, 2014.

166. Seabrook, *Drawing the Lines*.

167. Michael Peress and Yangzi Zhao, "How Many Seats in Congress Is Control of Redistricting Worth?" *Legislative Studies Quarterly* 45 (2020).

168. Lieb, "AP: GOP Won More Seats"; Wang, "The Great Gerrymander of 2012"; Christopher Ingraham, "Republicans Are so Much Better than Democrats at Gerrymandering," *Washington Post*, June 6, 2017; McGann et al., *Gerrymandering in America*.

169. Newkirk, "How Redistricting Became a Technological Arms Race"; Karl Rove, "The National Battle for Redistricting," *Republican State Leadership Com-*

mittee News, September 5, 2019, https://rslc.gop/news/2019/09/05/the-national-battle-for-redistricting/.

170. Donald E. Stokes, "Minority Representation and the Tradeoffs in Legislative Redistricting," in *Race and Representation*, ed. Georgia A. Persons (New Brunswick, NJ: Transaction, 1997), 27–34.

171. 364 U.S. 339 (1960).

172. Charles S. Bullock III, "The Impact of Changing the Racial Composition of Congressional Districts on Legislators' Roll Call Behavior," *American Politics Research* 23, no. 2 (1995): 141–158; Kevin A. Hill, "Does the Creation of Majority Black Districts Aid Republicans? An Analysis of the 1992 Congressional Elections in Eight Southern States," *Journal of Politics* 57 (1995): 384–401; Seth C. McKee, "Majority Black Districts, Republican Ascendancy, and Party Competition in the South, 1988–2000," *American Review of Politics* 23 (2002): 123–139.

173. Jesse H. Rhodes, *Ballot Blocked: The Political Erosion of the Voting Rights Act* (Palo Alto, CA: Stanford University Press, 2017), 112.

174. Winnett W. Hagens, "Redistricting the Commonwealth: A Narrative and Analysis of the Virginia Outcome, 1991–1995," in *Race and Representation*, ed. Georgia A. Persons (New Brunswick, NJ: Transaction, (1997), 44–62.

175. 509 U.S. 630 (1993).

176. Dale E. Ho, "Something Old, Something New, or Something *Really* Old? Second Generation Racial Gerrymandering Litigation as Intentional Racial Discrimination Cases," *William and Mary Law Review* 59 (2018): 1887–1919; Guy-Uriel E. Charles and Luis Fuentes-Rohwer, "Race and Representation Revisited: The New Racial Gerrymandering Cases and Section 2 of the VRA," *William and Mary Law Review* 59 (2018): 1559–1600.

177. Alabama Legislative Black Caucus v. Alabama, 135 S. Ct. 1257 (2015); Cooper v. Harris, 137 S. Ct. 1455 (2017).

178. 446 U.S. 55 (1980).

179. 478 U.S. 30, 46 (1986).

180. *Thornburg*, 478 at 50–51.

181. David T. Canon, *Race, Redistricting, and Representation: The Unintended Consequences of Black Majority Districts* (Chicago: University of Chicago Press, 1999), 57; Bernard Grofman, "The 1990s Round of Redistricting: A Schematic Outline of Some Key Features," in *Race and Representation*, ed. Georgia A. Persons (New Brunswick, NJ: Transaction, 1997), 21.

182. Daniel P. Tokaji, "The Story of *Shaw v. Reno*: Representation and Race-blindness," in *Race Law Stories*, ed. Rachel F. Moran and Devon Wayne Carbado (St. Paul, MN: Foundation, 2008), 497–538.

183. Steven Hill, "How the Voting Rights Act Hurts Democrats and Minorities," *Atlantic*, June 17, 2013.

184. Bullock, *Redistricting*, 238–239; Howard Gillman, Mark A. Graber, and Keith E. Whittington, *American Constitutionalism, Volume II* (New York: Oxford University Press, 2013), 817.

185. Wayne Arden, Bernard Grofman, and Lisa Handley, "The Impact of Redistricting on African-American Representation in the U.S. Congress and State

Legislatures in the 1990s," in *Race and Representation,* ed. Georgia A. Persons (New Brunswick, NJ: Transaction, 1997), 35–43.

186. Bernard Grofman and Lisa Handley, "1990s Issues in Voting Rights," *Mississippi Law Journal* 65 (1995): 205–270; Tokaji, "The Story of *Shaw v. Reno.*"

187. Kimball Brace, Bernard Grofman, and Lisa Handley, "Does Redistricting Aimed to Help Blacks Necessarily Help Republicans?," *Journal of Politics* 49 (1987): 143–156; Grofman and Handley, "1990s Issues in Voting Rights"; Grant M. Hayden, "Resolving the Dilemma of Minority Representation," *California Law Review* 92 (2004): 1589–1637; Hill, "Does the Creation of Majority Black Districts Aid Republicans?"; David Lublin, *The Paradox of Representation: Racial Gerrymandering and Minority Interests in Congress* (Princeton, NJ: Princeton University Press, 1997); John R. Petrocik and Scott W. Desposato, "The Partisan Consequences of Majority-Minority Redistricting in the South, 1991 and 1994," *Journal of Politics* 60 (1998): 613–633; Kenneth W. Shotts, "The Effect of Majority-Minority Mandates on Partisan Gerrymandering," *American Journal of Political Science* 45, no. 1 (2001): 120–135.

188. Charles Cameron, David Epstein, and Sharyn O'Halloran, "Do Majority-Minority Districts Maximize Substantive Black Representation in Congress?," *American Political Science Review* 90, no. 4 (1996): 794–812; Canon, *Race, Redistricting, and Representation*; Lublin, *The Paradox of Representation*; Kenneth W. Shotts, "Does Racial Redistricting Cause Conservative Policy Outcomes? Policy Preferences of Southern Representatives in the 1980s and 1990s," *Journal of Politics* 65, no. 1 (2003): 216–226; Smith, "Minority Representation and Majority-Minority Districts After *Shaw v. Reno*"; Carol M. Swain, *Black Faces, Black Interests: The Representation of African Americans in Congress* (Cambridge, MA: Harvard University Press, 1993); Katherine Tate, *From Protest to Politics: The New Black Voters in American Elections* (Cambridge, MA: Harvard University Press, 1993); Damian Waymer and Robert L. Heath, "Black Voter Dilution, American Exceptionalism, and Racial Gerrymandering," *Journal of Black Studies* 47, no. 7 (2016): 635–658.

189. *Shaw,* 509 U.S. at 647, 657.

190. 515 U.S. 900, 909 (1995).

191. Shaw v. Hunt, 517 U.S. 899 (1996); Bush v. Vera, 517 U.S. 952 (1996); Meadows v. Moon, 521 U.S. 113 (1997).

192. Lawyer v. Department of Justice, 521 U.S. 567 (1997); King v. Illinois Board of Elections, 522 U.S. 1087 (1998); Easley v. Cromartie, 532 U.S. 234 (2001).

193. Richard H. Pildes, "Is Voting-Rights Law Now at War with Itself? Social Science and Voting Rights in the 2000s," *North Carolina Law Review* 80 (2002): 1517–1573.

194. Richard L. Hasen, "Race or Party? How Courts Should Think about Republican Efforts to Make It Harder to Vote in North Carolina and Elsewhere," *Harvard Law Review Forum* 127 (2014): 58–75; Smith, "Minority Representation and Majority-Minority Districts after *Shaw v. Reno,*" 249–250.

195. Katharine Inglis Butler, "Redistricting in a Post-*Shaw* Era," *University of Richmond Law Review* 36 (2002): 214–219.

196. Richard L. Hasen, "Resurrection: *Cooper v. Harris* and the Transformation of Racial Gerrymandering into a Voting Rights Tool," *ACS Supreme Court Review 2016–2017* (2017): 106.

197. Wendy Smooth, "Gendering Redistricting: Race, Gender, and the New Southern Strategy," annual meeting of the National Conference of Black Political Scientists (NCOBPS), 2016, https://ssrn.co/abstract=2684927; *Alabama Legislative Black Caucus,* 135 S. Ct. 1257; Bethune-Hill v. Virginia State Board of Elections, 137 S. Ct. 788 (2017); *Cooper,* 137 S. Ct. 1455. In 2019 the Court issued another ruling in this litigation, this time dismissing the racial gerrymandering claim on grounds of standing. Virginia House of Delegates v. Bethune-Hill, 139 S. Ct. 1945 (2019).

198. Thomas's concurring opinion, which no other justice joined, took a further step in offering an unusual response to the state's defense that the Voting Rights Act required it to rely heavily on race in crafting its majority-minority districts. Thomas asserted that the VRA does not apply to redistricting and, therefore, cannot be invoked as a justification for racial gerrymandering.

199. *Harris,* 137 S. Ct. at 1473–1474.

200. Calvin TerBeek, "Dog Whistling, the Color-Blind Jurisprudential Regime, and the Constitutional Politics of Race," *Constitutional Commentary* 30 (2014): 169. Richards and Kritzer define a jurisprudential regime as "the way in which judges translate their political ideologies and identities into a preferred legal analysis [that includes] rules, concepts, doctrines, precedents, and tests that collectively establish a standard operating procedure for the treatment of certain kinds of claims." Mark J. Richards and Herbert M. Kritzer, "Jurisprudential Regimes in Supreme Court Decision Making," *American Political Science Review* 96 (2002): 305, 308.

201. TerBeek, "Dog Whistling," 167, 168. Washington v. Davis, 426 U.S. 229 (1976); Milliken v. Bradley, 418 U.S. 717 (1974); Parents Involved in Community Schools v. Seattle School District No. 1, 551 U.S. 701 (2007); Shelby County v. Holder, 570 U.S. 529 (2013).

202. Calvin TerBeek, "Originalist Scholarship and Conservative Politics: Review of *A Republic, If You Can Keep It,* by Neil Gorsuch, and *Originalism's Promise: A Natural Law Account of the American Constitution,* by Lee J. Strang," *New Rambler Review,* October 9, 2019.

203. Guy-Uriel E. Charles and Luis E. Fuentes-Rohwer, "Dirty Thinking about Law and Democracy in *Rucho v. Common Cause,*" *ACS Supreme Court Review 2018–2019* (2019): 293–317.

204. Samuel Issacharoff, Pamela S. Karlan, Richard H. Pildes, and Nathaniel Persily, *The Law of Democracy: Legal Structure of the Political Process,* 5th ed. (St. Paul, MN: Foundation, 2016), 940.

205. Nicholas O. Stephanopoulos, "Our Electoral Exceptionalism," *University of Chicago Law Review* 80 (2013): 769–858; Samuel Issacharoff, "Judging Politics: The Elusive Quest for Judicial Review of Political Fairness," *Texas Law Review* 71 (1993): 1643–1704.

206. Hasen, "Resurrection," 106.

207. League of Women Voters v. Commonwealth of Pennsylvania, Supreme

Court of Pennsylvania, No. 159 MM 2017; Nicholas Goedert, "Partisan Gerry-mandering in the Courts: The Search for a Common Standard," paper presented at the annual meeting of the Midwest Political Science Association Meeting, Chicago, April 4–7, 2019.

208. Arizona State Legislators v. Arizona Independent Redistricting Commission, 135 S. Ct. 2652 (2015).

209. Charles Fried, "A Day of Sorrow for American Democracy," *Atlantic*, July 3, 2019.

210. Gary C. Jacobson, "Partisanship, Money, and Competition: Elections and the Transformation of Congress since the 1970s," in *Congress Reconsidered*, 11th ed., ed. Lawrence C. Dodd and Bruce I. Oppenheimer (Washington DC: Congressional Quarterly Press, 2017), 89–118.

Chapter 5. Courts, Parties, and Campaign Finance

1. Citizens United v. Federal Election Commission, 558 U.S. 310 (2010); Mc-Cutcheon v. Federal Election Commission, 572 US 185 (2014); Janus v. American Federation of State, County, and Municipal Employees, Council 31, 138 S. Ct. 2448 (2018).

2. Adam Liptak, "How Conservatives Weaponized the First Amendment," *New York Times*, June 30, 2018.

3. Lonna Rae Atkeson and Wendy L. Hansen, "Campaign Finance in U.S. Politics," in *Changing How America Votes*, ed. Todd Donovan (Lanham, MD: Rowman & Littlefield, 2018), 187–202.

4. 424 U.S. 1 (1976).

5. *Buckley*, 424 U.S. at 19.

6. *Buckley*, 424 U.S. at 48–49.

7. In *Buckley*, Justice White expressed his doubts about whether a direct donation would have a significantly different impact on a candidate compared to an independent expenditure. In *Nixon v. Shrink Missouri Government PAC* (2000), Justices Thomas and Scalia rejected the idea that there is a meaningful constitutional difference between the two and would, thus, apply strict scrutiny to restrictions on both contributions and expenditures. 528 U.S. 377 (2000).

8. *Buckley*, 424 U.S. at 21.

9. McConnell v. Federal Election Commission, 540 U.S. 93 (2003).

10. In recognition of these costs, the Court has consequently narrowed their application, exempting "issue advocacy" and permitting disclosure requirements only for "express advocacy," defined as the use of certain "magic words" (like "support," "vote for," "defeat," or "vote against") that expressly advocate for the election or defeat of a particular candidate.

11. To be eligible for matching funds from the government during the nomination period, candidates must prove that they are viable by raising a sufficient amount of money in at least twenty states; once proven, the federal government will match each individual donation up to a maximum of $250. Candidates who volunteer to receive matching funds must agree to spending limits, which were

$48 million in 2016. In the general election, major party candidates can opt to receive a flat grant, set at $96 million in 2016, but may not raise or spend any other money.

12. In 2000, George W. Bush became the first major-party candidate to decline public funds and its attendant spending limits in the nomination phase, and in 2008, Barack Obama became the first major-party candidate to opt out of the public financing system in the general election. No major party candidate accepted public funds in 2012 and 2016.

13. Arizona Free Enterprise Club's Freedom Club PAC v. Bennett, 564 U.S. 721 (2011).

14. In *Davis v. Federal Election Commission* (2008) the Court invalidated the BCRA's "millionaire's amendment," which tripled the contribution limits for candidates who faced a self-financed opponent spending more than $350,000 of their own money. The five-member majority found that the provision substantially burdened candidates' First Amendment freedom to finance their own campaign and could not be justified by the government's stated interest in "level[ing] electoral opportunities for candidates of different personal wealth." 554 U.S. 724, 741 (2008).

15. Arizona Free Enterprise Club's Freedom Club PAC, 564 U.S. at 784–785.

16. The 1907 Tillman Act banned corporations and national banks from donating money in any federal election campaign, and the 1947 Taft-Hartley Act included a ban on labor unions using their treasury funds to contribute to federal candidates.

17. 539 U.S. 146 (2003).

18. *Buckley*, 424 U.S. at 25, 30.

19. 454 U.S. 290 (1981).

20. 528 U.S. 377, 390 (2000).

21. 548 U.S. 230 (2006).

22. Timothy Kuhner, "The Market Metaphor, Radicalized: How a Capitalist Theology Trumped Democracy," *Election Law Journal* 16, no. 1 (2017): 96.

23. The aggregate limits imposed by the 1974 FECA amendments were indexed to inflation in the 2002 BCRA. Under the 2013/2014 limits challenged in *McCutcheon*, an individual could not donate more than $48,600 to all federal candidates and $74,600 to all PACs and political parties, for a total of $123,200.

24. *McCutcheon*, 134 S. Ct. at 1467–1468.

25. Michael S. Kang, "After *Citizens United*," *Indiana Law Review* 44 (2010): 243–254; Richard L. Hasen, *Plutocrats United: Campaign Money, the Supreme Court, and the Distortion of American Elections* (New Haven, CT: Yale University Press, 2016).

26. *McConnell*, 540 U.S. at 153.

27. *Buckley*, 424 U.S. at 39.

28. *Buckley*, 424 U.S. at 39.

29. Colorado Republican Federal Campaign Committee v. Federal Election Commission, 518 U.S. 604 (1996); Federal Election Commission v. Colorado Republican Federal Campaign Committee, 533 U.S. 431 (2001).

30. First National Bank of Boston v. Bellotti, 435 U.S. 765 (1978).

31. 479 U.S. 238 (1986).

32. 494 U.S. 652 (1990).

33. 551 U.S. 449, 470 (2007).

34. *Citizens United*, 558 U.S. at 479.

35. 567 U.S. 516 (2012).

36. Kuhner, "The Market Metaphor, Radicalized," 100.

37. Robert E. Mutch, *Buying the Vote: A History of Campaign Finance Reform* (New York: Oxford University Press, 2014), 175; Hasen, *Plutocrats United*, 108.

38. Ann Southworth, "Elements of the Support Structure for Campaign Finance Litigation in the Roberts Court," *Law and Social Inquiry* 43, no. 2 (2018): 320. The few exceptions include BCRA's soft money ban and enhanced disclosure rules. The Court additionally upheld a state ban on judicial candidates personally soliciting campaign funds on the grounds that judges' nonpolitical position justified such restrictions. Williams-Yulee v. The Florida Bar, 135 S. Ct. 1656 (2015).

39. Allie Boldt, "Scrutinizing Independent Expenditure Limits: A Case against Super-Strict Scrutiny," *Election Law Journal* 16, no. 1 (2017): 33–56.

40. Jack M. Balkin, "Some Realism about Pluralism: Legal Realist Approaches to the First Amendment," *Duke Law Journal* 1990, no. 3 (1990): 375–430; Amanda Shanor, "The New *Lochner*," *Wisconsin Law Review* 2016 (2016): 133–206; Jeremy K. Kessler and David E. Pozen, "The Search for an Egalitarian First Amendment," *Columbia Law Review* 118, no. 7 (2018): 1953–2010.

41. This phrase references *Lochner v. New York* (1905), a Supreme Court ruling invalidating a New York law limiting the hours of bakers. This case has taken on enormous significance in normative debates over judicial review. It is used to describe an entire era in which the Court is claimed to have exceeded its proper role, invalidating economic policies the people desired and doing so illegitimately on the basis of personal biases rather than the Constitution. Lochner v. New York, 198 U.S. 45 (1905). Some scholars would like to see the end of "the normative *Lochner.*" Howard Gillman, "De-Lochnerizing *Lochner*," *Boston University Law Review* 85 (2005): 859–865.

42. Genevieve Lakier, "Imagining an Antisubordinating First Amendment," *Columbia Law Review* 118, no. 7 (2018): 2117–2160; Kessler and Pozen, "The Search for an Egalitarian First Amendment."

43. Lakier, "Imagining an Antisubordinating First Amendment," 2117.

44. Shanor, "The New *Lochner*," 2014; Kyle Langvardt, "A Model of First Amendment Decision-Making at a Divided Court," *Tennessee Law Review* 84 (2017): 833–891.

45. Jedediah Purdy, "That We Are Underlings: The Real Problems in Disciplining Political Spending and the First Amendment," *Constitutional Commentary* 30 (2015): 393.

46. U.S. v. Stevens, 559 U.S. 460 (2010); U.S. v. Alvarez, 567 U.S. 709 (2012); Snyder v. Phelps, 562 U.S. 443 (2011); Maslenjuk v. U.S., 137 S. Ct. 1918 (2017); Brown v. Entertainment Merchants Association, 564 U.S. 786 (2011).

47. Bertrall L. Ross II, "Paths of Resistance to Our Imperial First Amendment," review of *Citizens Divided: Campaign Finance Reform and the Constitution,* by Robert C. Post, *Michigan Law Review* 113 (2015): 917.

48. Burwell v. Hobby Lobby Stores, 134 S. Ct. 2751 (2014); Masterpiece Cake Shop v. Colorado Civil Rights Commission, 137 S. Ct. 1918 (2017).

49. Ross, "Paths of Resistance to Our Imperial First Amendment"; Robert C. Post, *Citizens Divided: Campaign Finance Reform and the Constitution* (Cambridge, MA: Harvard University Press, 2014); Paul D. Carrington, "Our Imperial First Amendment," *University of Richmond Law Review* 34 (2001): 1167–1211; Ann Southworth, "The Consequences of *Citizens United*: What Do the Lawyers Say?" *Chicago-Kent Law Review* 93 (2018): 525–560.

50. Geoffrey R. Stone, "*Citizens United* and Conservative Judicial Activism," *University of Illinois Law Review* 2012, no. 2 (2012): 485–500.

51. 431 U.S. 209 (1977).

52. *Janus,* 138 S. Ct. at 2464.

53. Langvardt, "A Model of First Amendment Decision-Making at a Divided Court," 878; Erwin Chemerinsky, "The Supreme Court's *Janus* Ruling Was Pure Judicial Activism: Unions, Look Out," *Sacramento Bee,* July 9, 2018; John Nichols, "'*Janus*' Was Decided by Conservative Judicial Activists Who Are Legislating from the Bench," *Nation,* June 27, 2018; Robert Bruno, "A Supreme Court Ruling for Janus Would Be Judicial Activism at Its Worst," *Herald and Review,* May 25, 2018.

54. Chemerinsky, "The Supreme Court's *Janus* Ruling Was Pure Judicial Activism."

55. Shanor, "The New *Lochner,*" 135.

56. *Janus,* 138 S. Ct. at 2501–2502.

57. *Janus,* 138 S. Ct. at 2500.

58. Knox v. Service Employees International Union, Local 1000, 567 U.S. 298 (2012); Harris v. Quinn, 134 S. Ct. 2618 (2014).

59. Langvardt, "A Model of First Amendment Decision-Making at a Divided Court," 879.

60. Moshe Z. Marvit, "For 60 Years, This Powerful Conservative Group Has Worked to Crush Labor," *Nation,* July 5, 2018. It was widely expected that *Friedrichs v. California Teachers Association* (2016) would invalidate agency fees and overturn *Abood,* but Scalia's death left the Court divided 4–4. Friedrichs v. California Teachers Association, 136 S. Ct. 1083 (2016).

61. Marvit, "For 60 Years, This Powerful Conservative Group Has Worked to Crush Labor"; William A. Herbert and Joseph A. McCartin, "*Janus*'s Progeny? A Supreme Court Threat to Majority Rule Looms," *Prospect,* March 21, 2019.

62. National Conference of State Legislatures, "*Citizens United* and the States," July 21, 2016, http://www.ncsl.org/research/elections-and-campaigns/citizens -united-and-the-states.aspx.

63. Stone, "*Citizens United* and Conservative Judicial Activism," 489.

64. Southworth, "The Consequences of *Citizens United,*" 528.

65. Jeffrey Toobin, "Money Unlimited," *New Yorker,* May 21, 2012; Kang, "After *Citizens United,*" 247.

66. *Citizens United,* 558 U.S. at 398.

67. John Hudson, "How Justice Souter Almost Left the Supreme Court in a Blaze of Glory," *Atlantic,* May 14, 2012.

68. To determine the ideological alignment of the justices, I used Martin-Quinn ideal point estimates for each justice in the particular term in which the case was decided. To access these scores, see the following link: https://mqscores.lsa.umich.edu/measures.php. Andrew D. Martin and Kevin M. Quinn, "Dynamic Ideal Point Estimation via Markov Chain Monte Carlo for the U.S. Supreme Court, 1953–1999," *Political Analysis* 10 (2002): 134–153.

69. Post, *Citizens Divided*; Lillian R. BeVier, "Full of Surprises—and More to Come: *Randall v. Sorrell,* The First Amendment, and Campaign Finance Regulation," *Supreme Court Review* 2006 (2006): 173–200.

70. Neil S. Siegel, "The Distinctive Role of Justice Samuel Alito: From a Politics of Restoration to a Politics of Dissent," *Yale Law Journal Forum* 126 (2016): 172; Stephanie Mencimer, "Conservatives Say They Want Another Antonin Scalia: They Really Want Another Sam Alito," *Mother Jones,* May/June 2016.

71. Richard L. Hasen, "Keynote Address: Judging the Political and Political Judging: Justice Scalia as Case Study," *Chicago-Kent Law Review* 93, no. 2 (2018): 325–341.

72. Kyle Casimir Kopko, "The Effect of Partisanship in Election Law Judicial Decision-Making" (PhD diss., Ohio State University, 2010).

73. Kyle Casimir Kopko, "Litigant Partisan Identity and Challenges to Campaign Finance Policies: An Examination of U.S. District Court Decisions, 1971–2007," *Justice System Journal* 36, no. 3 (2015): 212–232.

74. National Conference of State Legislatures, "Campaign Finance Legislation Database/2015 Onward," May 7, 2019, http://www.ncsl.org/research/elections-and-campaigns/campaign-finance-database-2015-onward.aspx. Of course, some of these bills are carried over from previous years, which is permitted in about half of the states. Unfortunately, the NCSL database is not searchable by the party affiliation of bill sponsor(s).

75. Shanor, "The New *Lochner,*" 133.

76. Lawrence Baum, *Ideology in the Supreme Court* (Princeton, NJ: Princeton University Press, 2017).

77. Balkin, "Some Realism about Pluralism," 383–384.

78. Charlotte Garden, "The Deregulatory First Amendment at Work," *Harvard Civil Rights–Civil Liberties Law Review* 51 (2016): 324.

79. Adam Liptak, "How Conservatives Weaponized the First Amendment," *New York Times,* June 30, 2018; Amanda Hollis-Brusky, *Ideas with Consequences: The Federalist Society and the Conservative Counterrevolution* (New York: Oxford University Press, 2015); Mutch, *Buying the Vote.*

80. Southworth, "Elements of the Support Structure for Campaign Finance Litigation in the Roberts Court," 319.

81. Hollis-Brusky, *Ideas with Consequences,* 62.

82. Eric Lichtblau, "Long Battle by Foes of Campaign Finance Rules Shifts Landscape," *New York Times,* October 15, 2010.

83. Southworth, "Elements of the Support Structure for Campaign Finance Litigation in the Roberts Court," 353.

84. Marvit, "For 60 Years, This Powerful Conservative Group Has Worked to Crush Labor."

85. Marvit.

86. The Obama administration's brief in the *Friedrichs* case had urged the Court to uphold *Abood*.

87. Lee Epstein, Andrew D. Martin, and Kevin Quinn, "6+ Decades of Freedom of Expression in the U.S. Supreme Court," 2018, http://epstein.wustl.edu/research/FreedomOfExpression.pdf.

88. Baum, *Ideology in the Supreme Court*, 71–73.

89. Epstein et al., "6+ Decades." Pettys offered a potent critique of a similar study by Epstein, Parker, and Segal that was presented at a 2013 academic conference and received considerable media attention because of its accusation of "in-group bias" against the Court's conservatives. Pettys pointed out multiple coding errors that had led to inflated claims of in-group bias, particularly for Chief Justice Roberts and Justice Alito. Todd E. Pettys, "Free Expression, In-Group Bias, and the Court's Conservatives: A Critique of the Epstein-Parker-Segal Study," *Buffalo Law Review* 63, no. 1 (2015): 1–83; Lee Epstein, Christopher M. Parker, and Jeffrey A. Segal, "Do Justices Defend the Speech They Hate? In-Group Bias, Opportunism, and the First Amendment," paper presented at the annual meeting of the American Political Science Association, Chicago, August/September 2013.

90. Epstein et al., "6+ Decades," 17.

91. Television cameras caught Justice Alito's response from the audience—frowning and mouthing the words "not true"—which received considerable attention.

92. Barack Obama, "The *Citizens United* Decision Was Wrong," press release, January 21, 2015, https://www.whitehouse.gov/the-press-office/2015/01/21/statement-president.

93. Benjamin Oreskes, "Clinton Pledges Constitutional Amendment to Overturn *Citizens United* Ruling," *Politico*, July 16, 2016.

94. Senator Sheldon Whitehouse, "The Many Sins of *Citizens United*," *Nation*, September 24, 2015.

95. Heather K. Gerken, "The Real Problem with *Citizens United*: Campaign Finance, Dark Money, and Shadow Parties," *Marquette Law Review* 97, no. 4 (2014): 904.

96. Richard L. Hasen, "The Decade of *Citizens United*," *Slate*, December 19, 2019.

97. Michael S. Kowal, "Corporate Politicking, Together: Trade Association Ties, Lobbying, and Campaign Giving," *Business and Politics* 20, no. 1 (2018): 125; Daniel I. Weiner, "*Citizens United* Five Years Later," Brennan Center for Justice, January 15, 2015, https://www.brennancenter.org/our-work/research-reports/citizens-united-five-years-later; Wendy L. Hansen, Michael S. Rocca, and Brittany Leigh Ortiz, "The Effects of *Citizens United* on Corporate Spending in the 2012 Presidential Election," *Journal of Politics* 77, no. 2 (2015): 535.

98. Richard A. Epstein, "*Citizens United v. FEC:* The Constitutional Right That

Big Corporations Should Have But Do Not Want," *Harvard Journal of Law and Public Policy* 34, no. 2 (2011): 653; Hansen et al., "The Effects of *Citizens United* on Corporate Spending in the 2012 Presidential Election."

99. Gary C. Jacobson, "Partisanship, Money, and Competition: Elections and the Transformation of Congress since the 1970s," in *Congress Reconsidered*, 11th ed., ed. Lawrence C. Dodd and Bruce I. Oppenheimer (Washington, DC: Congressional Quarterly Press, 2017), 103–104; Lonna Rae Atkeson and Wendy L. Hansen, "Campaign Finance in U.S. Politics," in *Changing How America Votes*, ed. Todd Donovan (Lanham, MD: Rowman & Littlefield, 2018), 187–202; Hansen et al., "The Effects of *Citizens United* on Corporate Spending in the 2012 Presidential Election"; Weiner, "*Citizens United* Five Years Later."

100. Matt Bai, "How Much Has *Citizens United* Changed the Political Game?," *New York Times Magazine*, July 17, 2012; Hasen, *Plutocrats United*, 45; Weiner, "*Citizens United* Five Years Later"; Bob Biersack, "8 Years Later: How *Citizens United* Changed Campaign Finance," *OpenSecrets News*, February 7, 2015, https://www.opensecrets.org/news/2018/02/how-citizens-united-changed-campaign-finance/.

101. Nathaniel Persily, "The Court's Campaign Finance Jurisprudence and Its Impact on the Electoral Process," SCOTUSblog, November 8, 2011, https://www.scotusblog.com/community/the-court's-campaign-finance-jurisprudence-and-its-impact-on-the-electoral-process/; Eric S. Heberling and Bruce A. Larson, "U.S. House Incumbent Fundraising and Spending in a Post-*Citizens United* and Post-*McCutcheon* World," *Political Science Quarterly* 129, no. 4 (2014): 613–642; Richard H. Pildes, "The Court's Campaign Finance Jurisprudence and Its Impact on the Electoral Process," SCOTUSblog, November 8, 2011, https://www.scotusblog.com/community/the-court's-campaign-finance-jurisprudence-and-its-impact-on-the-electoral-process/; Richard L. Hasen, "What the Court Did—and Why?" *American Interest*, July 2, 2010.

102. Nathaniel Persily, "The Court's Campaign Finance Jurisprudence and Its Impact on the Electoral Process," SCOTUSblog, November 8, 2011, https://www.scotusblog.com/community/the-court's-campaign-finance-jurisprudence-and-its-impact-on-the-electoral-process/; Raymond J. La Raja, "The Court's Campaign Finance Jurisprudence and Its Impact on the Electoral Process," SCOTUSblog, November 8, 2011, https://www.scotusblog.com/community/the-court's-campaign-finance-jurisprudence-and-its-impact-on-the-electoral-process/; Richard H. Pildes, "The Court's Campaign Finance Jurisprudence and Its Impact on the Electoral Process," SCOTUSblog, November 8, 2011, https://www.scotusblog.com/community/the-court's-campaign-finance-jurisprudence-and-its-impact-on-the-electoral-process/; Richard L. Hasen, "What the Court Did—and Why?," *American Interest*, July 2, 2010.

103. Anne E. Baker, "Help or Hindrance? Outside Group Advertising Expenditures in House Races," *Forum* 16, no. 2 (2018): 313; Melissa Smith and Larry Powell, *Dark Money, Super PACs, and the 2012 Election* (New York: Lexington, 2013).

104. 599 F.3d 686 (D.C. Cir. 2010).

105. Blair Bowie and Adam Lioz, "Billion-Dollar Democracy: The Unprecedented Role of Money in the 2012 Elections," *Demos,* January 17, 2013, https://www.demos.org/sites/default/files/publications/billion.pdf.

106. Bowie and Lioz, "Billion-Dollar Democracy."

107. Weiner, "*Citizens United* Five Years Later," 1; Bowie and Lioz, "Billion-Dollar Democracy; Victoria Farrar-Myers and Richard Skinner, "Super PACs and the 2012 Elections," *Forum* 10 (2012): 105–118; Wendy L. Hansen, Michael S. Rocca, and Brittany Leigh Ortiz, "The Effects of *Citizens United* on Corporate Spending in the 2012 Presidential Election," *Journal of Politics* 77, no. 2 (2015): 535–545; Michael S. Kowal, "Corporate Politicking, Together: Trade Association Ties, Lobbying, and Campaign Giving," *Business and Politics* 20, no. 1 (2018): 98–131; Richard L. Hasen, "The Decade of *Citizens United*," *Slate,* December 29, 2019.

108. "Political Nonprofits (Dark Money)," OpenSecrets.org, Center for Responsive Politics, https://www.opensecrets.org/outsidespending/nonprof_summ.php (accessed February 11, 2020).

109. "Top Election Spenders," OpenSecrets.org, Center for Responsive Politics, https://www.opensecrets.org/dark-money/top-election-spenders (accessed February 11, 2020).

110. Meilan S. Chaturvedi and Coleen Holloway, "Postdiluvian? The Effects of Outside Group Spending on Senate Elections after *Citizens United* and *Speechnow.org v. FEC*," *Forum* 15, no. 2 (2017): 251.

111. Farrar-Myers and Skinner, "Super PACs and the 2012 elections."

112. Baker, "Help or Hindrance?," 313.

113. Alan Abramowitz, "Explaining Senate Election Outcomes," *American Political Science Review* 82 (1988): 385–403; Chaturvedi and Holloway, "Postdiluvian?"; Richard Engstrom and Christopher Kenny, "The Effects of Independent Expenditures in Senate Elections," *Political Research Quarterly* 55, no. 4 (2002): 885–905; Hasen, *Plutocrats United,* 4–45; Gary C. Jacobson, *Money in Congressional Elections* (New Haven, CT: Yale University Press, 1980); Gary C. Jacobson, "The Effects of Campaign Spending in House Elections: New Evidence for Old Arguments," *American Journal of Political Science* 34 (1990): 334–362; Gary C. Jacobson, "How the Economy and Partisanship Shaped the 2012 Presidential and Congressional Elections," *Political Science Quarterly* 128, no. 1 (2013): 1–38. There is mixed evidence on this latter point, however, with some studies concluding that incumbent spending does not matter while challenger spending does (Abramowitz, "Explaining Senate Election Outcomes"; Chaturvedi and Holloway, "Postdiluvian?"; Jacobson, "The Effects of Campaign Spending in House Elections") and other studies concluding that incumbent and challenger spending both affect election outcomes: Donald Green and Jonathan Krasno, "Salvation for the Spendthrift Incumbent: Reestimating the Effects of Campaign Spending in House Elections," *American Journal of Political Science* 32 (1988): 884–907; Robert, S. Erikson and Thomas R. Palfrey, "Campaign Spending and Incumbency: An Alternative Simultaneous Equations Approach," *Journal of Politics* 60, no. 2 (1998): 355–373.

114. Jacobson, "Partisanship, Money, and Competition," 105.

115. Michael M. Franz, "Campaign Finance Law: The Changing Role of Parties and Interest Groups," in *Rethinking American Electoral Democracy*, 2nd ed., ed. Matthew Streb (New York: Routledge, 2012), 6–28; Gerken, "The Real Problem with *Citizens United*," Raymond J. La Raja and Brian Schaffner, *Campaign Finance and Political Polarization: When Purists Prevail* (Ann Arbor: University of Michigan Press, 2015); Richard H. Pildes, "Romanticizing Democracy, Political Fragmentation, and the Decline of American Government," *Yale Law Journal* 124 (2014): 804–852.

116. Jacobson, "Partisanship, Money, and Competition," 105.

117. Richard Briffault, "Coordination Reconsidered," *Columbia Law Review Sidebar* 113 (2013): 88–101; Abby K. Wood, "Campaign Finance Disclosure," *Annual Review of Law and Social Science* 14 (2018): 15–16.

118. Nicholas O. Stephanopoulos, "Aligning Campaign Finance Law," *Virginia Law Review* 101 (2015): 1425–1500; McCarty, Nolan McCarty, Keith T. Poole, and Howard Rosenthal, *Polarized America: The Dance of Ideology and Unequal Riches* (Cambridge, MA: MIT Press, 2006); Jacobson, "Partisanship, Money, and Competition," 100, 104–105.

119. Jack M. Balkin, "All Hail Ed Meese!" (review of Neal Devins and Lawrence Baum, *The Company They Keep*), *Balkinization Blogspot*, April 3, 2019, https://balkin.blogspot.co/2019/04/all-hail-ed-meese.html.

120. Raymond J. La Raja and Brian Schaffner, "The Effects of Campaign Finance Spending Bans on Electoral Outcomes: Evidence from the States about the Potential Impact of *Citizens United v. FEC*," *Electoral Studies* 33 (2014): 102–114.

121. La Raja and Schaffner, "The Effects of Campaign Finance Spending Bans," 110.

122. La Raja, "The Court's Campaign Finance Jurisprudence and Its Impact."

123. La Raja.

124. Matthew Forys, "Symposium: Free Speech for Public Employees Restored—Justice Alito Plays the Long Game," SCOTUSblog, June 28, 2018, https://www.scotusblog.com/2018/06/syposium-free-speech-for-public-employees-restored-justice-alito-plays-the-long-game/.

125. *Janus*, 138 S. Ct. at 2486.

126. Daniel DiSalvo, "Public-Sector Unions after *Janus*: An Update," Manhattan Institute Issue Brief, February 14, 2019, https://www.manhattan-institute.org/public-sector-unions-after-janus.

127. Noam Scheiber, "Supreme Court Labor Decision Wasn't Just a Loss for Unions," *New York Times*, July 1, 2018.

128. Scheiber, "Supreme Court Labor Decision Wasn't Just a Loss for Unions."

129. Scheiber.

130. James Feigenbaum, Alexander Hertel-Fernandez, and Vanessa Williamson, "From the Bargaining Table to the Ballot Box: Political Effects of Right to Work Laws," National Bureau of Economic Research Working Paper No. 24259, January 2018.

131. Bruno, "A Supreme Court Ruling for Janus Would Be Judicial Activism at Its Worst"; Alana Semuels, "Is This the End of Public-Sector Unions in America?" *Atlantic*, June 27, 2018.

132. Rebecca Rainey and Ian Kullgren, "1 Year after *Janus*, Unions Are Flush," *Politico*, May 17, 2020.

133. DiSalvo, "Public-Sector Unions after *Janus*"; Forys, "Symposium."

134. Ted Cox, "*Janus* Unleashes Coordinated Attack on Unions," *One Illinois*, June 28, 2018, https://www.oneillinois.com/stories/2018/6/28/from-fair-share-to-opt-out.

135. Aaron Tang, "Life after *Janus*," *Columbia Law Review* 119, no. 3 (2019): 677–762.

136. *Uradnik v. Inter Faculty Organization*, 18–719 (2019).

137. Kessler and Pozen, "The Search for an Egalitarian First Amendment," 1953.

138. Hollis-Brusky, *Ideas with Consequences.*

139. Hasen, *Plutocrats United*, 35.

140. Issacharoff et al., *The Law of Democracy*, 543.

141. Wood, "Campaign Finance Disclosure," 11.

142. Richard L. Hasen, "Brett Kavanaugh May Soon Unshackle All Rich Political Donors," *Slate*, September 3, 2018.

143. Nichols, "'*Janus*' Was Decided by Conservative Judicial Activists."

Conclusion

1. Crawford v. Marion County Election Board, 553 U.S. 181 (2008).

2. Citizens United v. Federal Election Commission, 558 U.S. 310 (2010); McCutcheon v. Federal Election Commission, 572 U.S. 185 (2014).

3. Janus v. American Federation of State, County, and Municipal Employees, Council 31, 138 S. Ct. 2448 (2018).

4. Austin v. Michigan Chamber of Commerce, 494 U.S. 652 (1990); McConnell v. Federal Election Commission, 540 U.S. 93 (2003).

5. Shelby County v. Holder, 570 U.S. 529 (2013).

6. Beer v. United States, 425 U.S. 130 (1976); City of Mobile v. Bolden, 446 U.S. 55 (1980); Georgia v. Ashcroft, 539 U.S. 461 (2003); Reno v. Bossier Parish School Board, 528 U.S. 320 (2000).

7. Calvin TerBeek, "The Constitution as Political Program: The Republican Party and Originalism, 1977–1988," paper presented at Midwest Political Science Association, Chicago, April 4–7, 2019.

8. Department of Commerce v. New York, 139 S. Ct. 2551 (2019); Evenwel v. Abbott, 136 S. Ct. 1120 (2016).

9. Bradley Jones, "Most Americans Want to Limit Campaign Spending, Say Big Donors Have Greater Political Influence," Pew Research Center, May 8, 2018, https://www.pewresearch.org/fact-tank/2018/05/08/most-americans-want-to-limit-campaign-spending-say-big-donors-have-greater-political-influence/.

10. Campaign Legal Center, "New Bipartisan Poll Shows Support for Su-

preme Court to Establish Clear Rules for Gerrymandering," Campaign Legal Center, January 28, 2019, https://campaignlegal.org/update/new-bipartisan-poll-shows-support-supreme-court-establish-clear-rules-gerrymandering; David Daley, "One Thing Voters Agree On—They Hate Gerrymandering," *Boston Globe*, November 12, 2018; Kylee Groft, "The Results Are In: Most Americans Want Limits on Gerrymandering," Campaign Legal Center, September 11, 2017, https://campaignlegal.org/update/results-are-most-americans-want-limits-gerrymandering.

11. Thomas Keck and Kevin McMahon, "Why *Roe* Still Stands: Abortion Law, the Supreme Court, and the Republican Regime," *Studies in Law, Politics and Society* 70 (2015): 33–83; Roe v. Wade, 410 U.S. 113 (1973).

12. Keck and McMahon, "Why *Roe* Still Stands," 40.

13. Charles R. Epp, *The Rights Revolution: Lawyers, Activists, and Supreme Courts in Comparative Perspective* (Chicago: University of Chicago Press, 1998); Charles R. Epp, "External Pressures and the Supreme Court's Agenda," in *Supreme Court Decision-Making: New Institutionalist Approaches*, ed. Cornell W. Clayton and Howard Gillman (Chicago: University of Chicago Press, 1999), 255–278; Michael W. McCann, *Rights at Work: Pay Equity Reform and the Politics of Legal Mobilization* (Chicago: University of Chicago Press, 1994); Amanda Hollis-Brusky, *Ideas with Consequences: The Federalist Society and the Conservative Counterrevolution* (New York: Oxford University Press, 2015); TerBeek, "The Constitution as Political Program."

14. Carl T. Bogus, "The History and Politics of Second Amendment Scholarship," *Chicago-Kent Law Review* 76 (2000): 3–25; Hollis-Brusky, *Ideas with Consequences*, 31–60; District of Columbia v. Heller, 554 U.S. 570 (2008).

15. Hollis-Brusky, *Ideas with Consequences*, 61–89; Ann Southworth, "Elements of the Support Structure for Campaign Finance Litigation in the Roberts Court," *Law and Social Inquiry* 43, no. 2 (2018): 319–359.

16. Keith E. Whittington, *Repugnant Laws: Judicial Review of Acts of Congress from the Founding to the Present* (Lawrence: University Press of Kansas), 19.

17. Neal Devins and Lawrence Baum, *The Company They Keep: How Partisan Divisions Came to the Supreme Court* (New York: Oxford University Press, 2019), 140.

18. Kyle Casimir Kopko, "The Effect of Partisanship in Election Law Judicial Decision-Making" (PhD diss., Ohio State University, 2010).

19. Husted v. A. Philip Randolph Institute, 138 S. Ct. 1833 (2018).

20. Alexander M. Bickel, *The Least Dangerous Branch: The Supreme Court at the Bar of Politics* (New Haven, CT: Yale University Press, 1962).

21. James L. Gibson and Gregory A. Caldeira, *Citizens, Courts, and Confirmations: Positivity Theory and the Judgments of the American People* (Princeton, NJ: Princeton University Press, 2009), 205; James L. Gibson, Gregory A. Calderia, and Vanessa Baird, "On the Legitimacy of National High Courts," *American Political Science Review* 92 (1998): 343–358; James L. Gibson and Michael J. Nelson, "The Legitimacy of the U.S. Supreme Court: Conventional Wisdoms and Recent Challenges Thereto," *Annual Review of Law and Social Science* 10 (2014): 201–219; Michael F. Salamone, *Perceptions of a Polarized Court: How Division among Justices Shapes the Supreme Court's Public Image* (Philadelphia: Temple University

Press, 2018); Benjamin Woodson, James L. Gibson, and Milton Lodge, "Judicial Symbols and the Link between Institutional Legitimacy and Acquiescence," paper presented at the annual meeting of the American Political Science Association, 2011; Michael Zilis, *The Limits of Legitimacy: Dissenting Opinions, Media Coverage, and Public Responses to Supreme Court Decisions* (Ann Arbor: University of Michigan Press, 2015).

22. Gibson and Caldeira, *Citizens, Courts, and Confirmations*, 204–205.

23. James L. Gibson, Gregory A. Caldeira, and Lester Kenyatta Spence, "The Supreme Court and the U.S. Presidential Election of 2000: Wounds, Self-Inflicted or Otherwise?," *British Journal of Political Science* 33 (2003): 535–556. Kritzer found that support for the Court dropped among Democrats after *Bush v. Gore*, but this was offset by an increase in support among Republicans. Herbert M. Kritzer, "The Impact of *Bush v. Gore* on Public Perceptions and Knowledge of the Supreme Court," *Judicature* 85, no. 1 (2001): 32–38.

24. Jennifer Rubin, "GOP Autopsy Report Goes Bold," *Washington Post*, March 18, 2013.

25. Jacob T. Levy, "Democracy for Republicans: Simple Voting Rules for a Complex World," Niskanen Center, February 20, 2019.

26. Timothy Kuhner, "The Market Metaphor, Radicalized: How a Capitalist Theology Trumped Democracy," *Election Law Journal* 16, no. 1 (2017): 97.

27. Gilda R. Daniels, "*Husted v. A. Philip Randolph Institute*—To Vote, or Not to Vote: That is the Question," *ACS Supreme Court Review 2017–2018* (2018): 74.

28. Terri Jennings Peretti, *In Defense of a Political Court* (Princeton, NJ: Princeton University Press, 1999).

29. Dan McCready, "Voter Fraud Is Part of the G.O.P. Playbook," *New York Times*, April 24, 2020.

30. Peretti, *In Defense of a Political Court.*

31. Pamela S. Karlan, "The Rights to Vote: Some Pessimism about Formalism," *Texas Law Review* 71 (1993): 1738; Stephen M. Griffin, "Judicial Supremacy and Equal Protection in a Democracy of Rights," *Journal of Constitutional Law* 4 (2002): 281–313.

32. Jack M. Balkin, "*Bush v. Gore* and the Boundary between Law and Politics," *Yale Law Journal* 110 (2001): 1459.

33. Balkin, "*Bush v. Gore* and the Boundary Between Law and Politics," 1458.

34. Jack M. Balkin, "All Hail Ed Meese!," review of *The Company They Keep*, by Neal Devins and Lawrence Baum, *Balkinization Blogspot*, April 3, 2019, 260.

35. Stephen Skowronek, *Presidential Leadership in Political Time*, 3rd ed. (Lawrence: University Press of Kansas, 2020).

36. Skowronek, *Presidential Leadership in Political Time.*

37. Skowronek.

38. Skowronek.

39. Skowronek.

40. Skowronek.

41. Balkin, "All Hail Ed Meese!," 269.

42. Skowronek, *Presidential Leadership in Political Time.*

43. Skowronek.

44. Skowronek.

45. Jeffrey M. Jones, "Trump Job Approval at Personal Best 49%," *Gallup News*, February 4, 2020, https://news.gallup.com/poll/284156/trump-job-approval-personal-best.aspx.

46. Balkin, "All Hail Ed Meese!"

47. Balkin, 257, 253.

48. Steven Levitsky and Daniel Ziblatt, *How Democracies Die* (New York: Crown, 2018).

49. Quoted in Thomas B. Edsall, "The Fight Over How Trump Fits in with the Other 44 Presidents," *New York Times*, May 15, 2019.

50. Julia Azari and Scott Lemieux, "The Long Disjunction: Donald Trump in Political Time," paper presented at the 2019 meeting of the Western Political Science Association, Los Angeles, 2019.

51. Jim Rutenberg, "Nine Years Ago, Republicans Favored Voting Rights. What Happened?," *New York Times Magazine*, August 12, 2015.

52. Michael Collins and Rebecca Morin, "The trial Is Over. Trump Won. Now Get Ready for the Political Fallout," *USA Today*, February 5, 2020; Peter Beinart, "Impeachment Hurt Somebody. It Wasn't Trump," *Atlantic*, February 6, 2020.

53. Thomas M. Keck, "These Are the Roadblocks to the Democrats' Big Voting Rights Bill," *Washington Post*, March 7, 2019.

54. "Fed Soc" is the phrase that Federalist Society members themselves employ to refer to their group. The Fed Soc five refers to the Court's Republican justices—Thomas, Roberts, Alito, Gorsuch, and Kavanaugh—who belong to and closely align with this organization.

Bibliography

Abramowitz, Alan. "Explaining Senate Election Outcomes." *American Political Science Review* 82 (1988): 385–403.

Abramowitz, Alan I., Brad Alexander, and Matthew Gunning. "Incumbency, Redistricting, and the Decline of Competition in US House Elections." *Journal of Politics* 68, no. 1 (2006): 75–88.

Abramowitz, Alan I., and Kyle L. Saunders. "Is Polarization a Myth? *Journal of Politics* 70, no. 2 (2008): 542–555.

Adamany, David W. "The Party Variable in Judges' Voting: Conceptual Notes and a Case Study." *American Political Science Review* 63, no. 1 (1969): 57–73.

Aldrich, John H. "Rational Choice and Turnout." *American Journal of Political Science* 37, no. 1 (1993): 246–278.

Aliotta, Jilda M. "Social Backgrounds, Social Motives and Participation on the U.S. Supreme Court." *Political Behavior* 10, no. 3 (1988): 267–284.

Alvarez, Michael R., Delia Bailey, and Jonathan N. Katz. "The Effect of Voter Identification Laws on Turnout." Social Science Working Paper 1267R, California Institute of Technology, 2008.

———."An Empirical Bayes Approach to Estimating Ordinal Treatment Effects." *Political Analysis* 19 (2011): 20–31.

Andersen, Ericka. "Gorsuch: 'There's No Such Thing as a Republican Judge or a Democratic Judge, We Just Have Judges' (VIDEO)." *National Review*, March 21, 2017.

Ansolabehere, Stephen. "Effects of Identification Requirements on Voting: Evidence from the Experiences of Voters on Election Day." *PS: Political Science and Politics* 42 (2009): 127–130.

Ansolabehere, Stephen, and Eitan D. Hersh. "ADGN: An Algorithm for Record Linkage Using Address, Date of Birth, Gender, and Name." *Journal of Statistics and Public Policy* 4, no. 1 (2017): 1–10.

Ansolabehere, Stephen, Samantha Luks, and Brian F. Schaffner. "The Perils of Cherry Picking Low Frequency Events in Large Sample Surveys." *Electoral Studies* 40 (2015): 409–410.

Ansolabehere, Stephen, and James M. Snyder Jr. *The End of Inequality: One Person, One Vote and the Transformation of American Politics.* New York: W. W. Norton, 2008.

Arden, Wayne, Bernard Grofman, and Lisa Handley. "The Impact of Redistricting on African-American Representation in the U.S. Congress and State Legislatures in the 1990s." In *Race and Representation,* ed. Georgia A. Persons, 35–43. New Brunswick, NJ: Transaction, 1997.

Armstrong, Virginia, and Charles A. Johnson. "Certiorari Decisionmaking by the Warren and Burger Courts: Is Cue Theory Time Bound?" *Polity* 15 (1982): 141–150.

Associated Press/National Opinion Research Center. "Views on the American Election Process and Perceptions of Voter Fraud." 2016. http://www.ap norc.org/projects/Pages/HTML%20Reports/views-on-the-american-elec tion-process-and-perceptions-of-voter-fraud-issue-brief.aspx.

Atkeson, Lonna Rae, R. Michael Alvarez, Thad E. Hall, and J. Andrew Sinclair. "Balancing Fraud Prevention and Electoral Participation: Attitudes toward Voter Identification." *Social Science Quarterly* 95 (2014): 1381–1398.

Atkeson, Lonna Rae, and Wendy L. Hansen. "Campaign Finance in U.S. Politics." In *Changing How America Votes*, ed. Todd Donovan, 187–202. Lanham, MD: Rowman & Littlefield, 2018.

Azari, Julia, and Scott Lemieux. "The Long Disjunction: Donald Trump in Political Time." Paper presented at the annual meeting of the Western Political Science Association, San Diego, CA, April 2019.

Bai, Matt. "How Much Has *Citizens United* Changed the Political Game?" *New York Times Magazine,* July 17, 2012.

Bailey, Michael A., and Forrest Maltzman. *The Constrained Court: Law, Politics, and the Decisions Justices Make.* Princeton, NJ: Princeton University Press, 2011.

Baird, Vanessa A. *Answering the Call of the Court: How Justices and Litigants Set the Supreme Court Agenda.* Charlottesville: University of Virginia Press, 2007.

Baker, Anne E. "Help or Hindrance? Outside Group Advertising Expenditures in House Races." *Forum* 16, no. 2 (2018): 313–330.

Baker, Gordon E. *The Reapportionment Revolution: Representation, Political Power, and the Supreme Court.* New York: Random House, 1966.

Baker, Kelly J. "Note: Senior Judges: Valuable Resources, Partisan Strategists or Self-Interested Maximizers?" *Journal of Law and Politics* 16 (2000): 139–161.

Balkin, Jack M. "All Hail Ed Meese!" Review of *The Company They Keep,* by Neal Devins and Lawrence Baum. *Balkinization Blogspot,* April 3, 2019.

———. "*Bush v. Gore* and the Boundary Between Law and Politics." *Yale Law Journal* 110 (2001): 1407–1458.

———. "The Recent Unpleasantness: Understanding the Cycles of Constitutional Time." *Indiana Law Journal* 94 (2019): 253–296.

———. "Some Realism about Pluralism: Legal Realist Approaches to the First Amendment." *Duke Law Journal* 1990, no. 3 (1990): 375–430.

Balkin, Jack M., and Sanford Levinson. "The Canons of Constitutional Law." *Harvard Law Review* 111 (1998): 963–1024.

———. "Understanding the Constitutional Revolution." *Virginia Law Review* 87 (2001): 1045–1109.

Bandolik, Ann. "Life after the Voting Rights Act: Identifying Partisan and Racialised Trends in the Proposal and Passage of Restrictive Voter-Access Policy in the United States of America." MS thesis, London School of Economics and Political Science, 2017.

Barber, Benjamin. "The States Facing Federal Preclearance under Proposed Voting Rights Act Fix." *Facing South,* March 13, 2019.

Barber, Kathleen L. "Partisan Values in the Lower Courts: Reapportionment in Ohio and Michigan." *Case Western Reserve Law Review* 20, no. 2 (1969): 401–421.

Barreto, Matt A., Stephen A. Nuno, and Gabriel R. Sanchez. "The Disproportionate Impact of Voter-ID Requirements on the Electorate—New Evidence from Indiana." *PS: Political Science and Politics* 42 (2009): 111–115.

Barrow, Deborah J., Gary Zuk, and Gregory Gryski. *The Federal Judiciary and Institutional Change.* Ann Arbor: University of Michigan Press, 1996.

Bartels, Brandon L. "The Constraining Capacity of Legal Doctrine on the U.S. Supreme Court." *American Political Science Review* 103, no. 3 (2009): 474–495.

Bartels, Larry M. 2002. "Beyond the Running Tally: Partisan Bias in Political Perceptions." *Political Behavior* 24, no. 2 (2002): 117–150.

Bartlett, John. *Bartlett's Familiar Quotations,* 16th ed. New York: Little, Brown, 1992.

Basile, Thomas. "Inventing the 'Right to Vote' in *Crawford v. Marion County Election Board.*" *Harvard Journal of Law and Public Policy* 32 (2009): 431–447.

Baum, Lawrence. *Ideology in the Supreme Court.* Princeton, NJ: Princeton University Press, 2017.

———. *Judges and Their Audiences: A Perspective on Judicial Behavior.* Princeton, NJ: Princeton University Press, 2006.

———. "Judges and Their Audiences." In *The Oxford Handbook of U.S. Judicial Behavior,* eds. Lee Epstein and Stefanie A. Lindquist, 343–360. New York: Oxford University Press, 2017.

———. "Membership Change and Collective Voting Change in the United States Supreme Court." *Journal of Politics* 54 (1992): 3–24.

———. "Motivation and Judicial Behavior: Expanding the Scope of Inquiry." In *The Psychology of Judicial Decision Making,* ed. David Klein and Gregory Mitchell, 3–25. New York: Oxford University Press, 2010.

———. *The Puzzle of Judicial Behavior.* Ann Arbor: University of Michigan Press, 1997.

———. "What Judges Want: Judges' Goals and Judicial Behavior." *Political Research Quarterly* 47 (1994): 749–768.

Bazelon, Emily. "Will Americans Lose Their Right to Vote in the Pandemic." *New York Times Magazine,* May 5, 2020.

Beinart, Peter. "Impeachment Hurt Somebody. It Wasn't Trump," *Atlantic,* February 6, 2020.

Bentele, Keith G., and Erin O'Brien. "Jim Crow 2.0?: Why States Consider and Adopt Restrictive Voter Access Policies." *Perspectives on Politics* 11, no. 4 (2013): 1088–1116.

———. "Resolved, States Should Enact Voter ID Laws and Reduce Early Voting, CON." In *Debating Reform: Conflicting Perspectives on How to Fix the American Political System,* 3rd ed., ed. Richard J. Ellis and Michael C. Nelson, 106–117. Washington, DC: Congressional Quarterly Press, 2016.

Berman, Ari. "Congressional Democrats Introduce Ambitious New Bill to Restore the Voting Rights Act." *Nation,* June 24, 2015.

————. "Does Brett Kavanaugh Spell the End of Voting Rights?" *New York Times*, July 13, 2018.

————. *Give Us the Ballot: The Modern Struggle for Voting Rights in America*. New York: Farrar, Straus & Giroux, 2015.

————. "How Gerrymandering and Voter Suppression Paved the Way for Abortion Bans." *Mother Jones*, May 17, 2019.

————. "How the 2000 Election in Florida Led to a New Wave of Voter Disenfranchisement." *Nation*, July 28, 2015.

————. "Trump's Stealth Plan to Preserve White Electoral Power." *Mother Jones*, January/February 2020.

BeVier, Lillian R. "Full of Surprises—and More to Come: *Randall v. Sorrell*, The First Amendment, and Campaign Finance Regulation." *Supreme Court Review* (2006): 173–200.

Bickel, Alexander M. "The Durability of *Colegrove v. Green*." *Yale Law Journal* 72 (1962): 39–45.

————. *The Least Dangerous Branch: The Supreme Court at the Bar of Politics*. New Haven, CT: Yale University Press, 1962.

Biersack, Bob. "8 Years Later: How *Citizens United* Changed Campaign Finance." *Open Secrets News*, February 7, 2018.

Biggers, Daniel R., and Michael J. Hanmer. "Understanding the Adoption of Voter Identification Laws in the American States. *American Politics Research* 45 (2017): 560–588.

Binder, Sarah A. "Reading Congressional Tea Leaves from the 2006 Renewal of the Voting Rights Act." *Monkey Cage*, June 27, 2013.

Binder, Sarah A., and Forrest Maltzman. *Advise and Dissent: The Struggle to Shape the Federal Judiciary*. Washington, DC: Brookings Institution Press, 2009.

Bishop, Bill. *The Big Sort: Why the Clustering of Like-Minded America Is Tearing Us Apart*. New York: Houghton Mifflin, 2008.

Black, Ryan C., Ryan J. Owens, Justin Wedeking, and Patrick C. Wohlfarth. *The Conscientious Justice: How Supreme Court Justices' Personalities Influence the Law, the High Court, and the Constitution*. Cambridge: Cambridge University Press, 2020.

Blacksher, James, and Lani Guinier. "Free at Last: Rejecting Equal Sovereignty and Restoring the Constitutional Right to Vote: *Shelby County v. Holder*." *Harvard Law and Policy Review* 8 (2014): 39–69.

Bland, Scott. "Republicans Expand Redistricting Strategy for 2020." *Politico*, September 29, 2017.

Bogus, Carl T. "The History and Politics of Second Amendment Scholarship." *Chicago-Kent Law Review* 76 (2000): 3–25.

Boldt, Allie. "Scrutinizing Independent Expenditure Limits: A Case against Super-Strict Scrutiny." *Election Law Journal* 16, no. 1 (2017): 33–56.

Bonica, Adam, and Michael J. Woodruff. "A Common-Space Measure of State Supreme Court Ideology." *Journal of Law, Economics, and Organization* 31, no. 3 (2014): 472–498.

Bonneau, Chris W., Thomas H. Hammond, Forrest Maltzman, and Paul J. Wahlbeck. "Agenda Control, the Median Justice, and the Majority Opinion on the U.S. Supreme Court." *American Journal of Political Science* 51, no. 4 (2007): 890–905.

Boucher, Robert, and Jeffrey Segal. "Supreme Court Justices as Strategic Decision Makers: Aggressive Grants and Defensive Denials on the Vinson Court." *Journal of Politics* 57 (1995): 824–837.

Bowie, Blair, and Adam Lioz. "Billion-Dollar Democracy: The Unprecedented Role of Money in the 2012 Elections." *Demos,* January 17, 2013, https://www.demos.org/sites/default/files/publications/billion.pdf.

Bowler, Shaun, and Todd Donovan. "A Partisan Model of Electoral Reform: Voter Identification Laws and Confidence in State Elections." *State Politics and Policy Quarterly* 16, no. 3 (2016): 340–361.

Brace, Kimball, Bernard Grofman, and Lisa Handley. "Does Redistricting Aimed to Help Blacks Necessarily Help Republicans?" *Journal of Politics* 49 (1987): 143–156.

Brace, Paul, and Melinda Gann Hall. "The Interplay of Preferences, Case Facts, Context, and Rules in the Politics of Judicial Choice." *Journal of Politics* 59, no. 4 (1997): 1206–1231.

Brace, Paul, Laura Langer, and Melinda Gann Hall. "Measuring the Preferences of State Supreme Court Judges." *Journal of Politics* 62, no. 2 (2000): 387–413.

Braman, Eileen. *Law, Politics and Perception: How Policy Preferences Influence Legal Reasoning.* Charlottesville: University of Virginia Press, 2009.

Braman, Eileen, and Thomas E. Nelson. "Mechanism of Motivated Reasoning? Analogical Perception in Discrimination Disputes." *American Journal of Political Science* 51, no. 4 (2007): 940–956.

Brater, Jonathan, Kevin Morris, Myrna Perez, and Christopher Deluzio. "Purges: A Growing Threat to the Right to Vote." Brennan Center for Justice, July 20, 2018. https://www.brennancenter.org/sites/default/files/publications/Purges_Growing_Threat_2018.1.pdf.

Bravin, Jesse. "Voter-ID Laws Worry Jurist." *Wall Street Journal,* October 17, 2013.

Brennan Center for Justice. "American Leaders Talk about Gerrymandering." June 15, 2017.

———. "Election 2016: Restrictive Voting Laws by the Numbers." September 28, 2016. https://www.brennancenter.org/our-work/research-reports/election-2016-restrictive-voting-laws-numbers.

———. "Gerrymandering & Fair Representation." https://www.brennancenter.org/issues/gerrymandering-fair-representation (accessed February 11, 2020).

———. "New Voting Restrictions in Place for 2016 Presidential Elections." August 20, 2016.

Briffault, Richard. "Coordination Reconsidered." *Columbia Law Review Sidebar* 113 (2013): 88–101.

Bronner, Ethan. "Partisan Rifts Hinder Efforts to Improve U.S. Voting System." *New York Times,* July 31, 2012.

Brunell, Thomas L. *Redistricting and Representation: Why Competitive Elections Are Bad for America.* New York: Routledge, 2008.

————. Review of *Gerrymandering in America: The House of Representatives, the Supreme Court, and the Future of Popular Sovereignty*, by Anthony J. McGann, Charles Anthony Smith, Michael Latner, and Alex Keena. *Congress and the Presidency* 44 (2017): 176–178.

Brunell, Thomas, and Justin Buchler. "Ideological Representation and Competitive Elections." *Electoral Studies* 28 (2009): 448–457.

Bruno, Robert. "A Supreme Court Ruling for Janus would Be Judicial Activism at Its Worst." *Herald and Review*, May 25, 2018.

Buchler, Justin. "Competition, Representation, and Redistricting: The Case against Competitive Congressional Districts." *Journal of Theoretical Politics* 17 (2005): 431–463.

Bullock, Charles S., III. "The Impact of Changing the Racial Composition of Congressional Districts on Legislators' Roll Call Behavior." *American Politics Research* 23, no. 2 (1995): 141–158.

————. *Redistricting: The Most Political Activity in America*. Lanham, MD: Rowman & Littlefield, 2012.

Bullock, Charles S., III, Ronald Keith Gaddie, and Justin J. Wert. *The Rise and Fall of the Voting Rights Act*. Norman: University of Oklahoma Press, 2016.

Bump, Philip. "In about 20 Years, Half the Population Will Live in Eight States." *Washington Post*, July 12, 2018.

Burnham, Walter Dean. "The Changing Shape of the American Political Universe." *American Political Science Review* 59 (1965): 7–28.

————. *Critical Elections and the Mainsprings of American Politics*. New York: W. W. Norton, 1970.

Butler, David, and Bruce Cain, eds. *Congressional Redistricting: Comparative and Theoretical Perspectives*. New York: Macmillan, 1992.

Butler, Katharine Inglis. "Redistricting in a Post-*Shaw* Era." *University of Richmond Law Review* 36 (2002): 137–270.

Cain, Bruce E. "Moving Past Section 5: More Fingers or a New Dike?" *Election Law Journal* 12, no. 3 (2013): 338–340.

Cain, Bruce E., Karin MacDonald, and Michael McDonald. "From Equality to Fairness: The Path of Political Reform since *Baker v. Carr*." In *Party Lines: Competition, Partisanship, and Congressional Redistricting*, ed. Thomas E. Mann and Bruce E. Cain, 6–30. Washington, DC: Brookings Institution Press, 2005.

Caldeira, Gregory A., John R. Wright, and Christopher J. W. Zorn. "Sophisticated Voting and Gate-Keeping in the Supreme Court." *Journal of Law, Economics and Organization* 15, no. 3 (1999): 549–572.

Cameron, Charles, David Epstein, and Sharyn O'Halloran. "Do Majority-Minority Districts Maximize Substantive Black Representation in Congress?" *American Political Science Review* 90, no. 4 (1996): 794–812.

Campaign Legal Center. "New Bipartisan Poll Shows Support for Supreme Court to Establish Clear Rules for Gerrymandering." Campaign Legal Center, January 28, 2019. https://campaignlegal.org/update/new-bipartisan-poll-shows-support-supreme-court-establish-clear-rules-gerrymandering.

Campbell, Angus, Philip E. Converse, Warren E. Miller, and Donald E. Stokes. *The American Voter*. New York: John Wiley, 1960.

Canes-Wrone, Brandice, and Tom S. Clark. "Judicial Independence and Non-partisan Elections." *Wisconsin Law Review* (2009): 21–65.

Canon, David T. *Race, Redistricting, and Representation: The Unintended Consequences of Black Majority Districts.* Chicago: University of Chicago Press, 1999.

Cantoni, Enrico, and Vincent Pons. "Strict ID Laws Don't Stop Voters: Evidence from a U.S. Nationwide Panel, 2008–2016." National Bureau of Economic Research, 2019. http://www.nber.org/papers/w25522.

Cardozo, Benjamin. *The Nature of the Judicial Process.* New Haven, CT: Yale University Press, 1921.

Carp, Robert A., and C. K. Rowland. *Policymaking and Politics in the Federal District Courts.* Knoxville: University of Tennessee Press, 1983.

Carrington, Paul D. "Our Imperial First Amendment." *University of Richmond Law Review* 34 (2001): 1167–1211.

Carson, Jamie L., and Michael H. Crespin. "The Effect of State Redistricting Methods on Competition in United States House of Representatives Races." *State Politics and Policy Quarterly* 4 (2004): 455–469.

Carson, Jamie L., Michael H. Crespin, and Ryan D. Williamson. "Reevaluating the Effects of Redistricting on Electoral Competition, 1972–2012." *State Politics and Policy Quarterly* 14, no. 2 (2014): 165–177.

Cave, Damien. "Ruling Prompts a Mixed Response." *New York Times,* June 22, 2009.

Center for Responsive Politics. "Departures Resulting in Open Seat Races by Cycle." https://www.opensecrets.org/members-of-congress/departures-by-cycle (accessed January 19, 2020).

Charles, Guy-Uriel E., and Luis E. Fuentes-Rohwer. "Dirty Thinking about Law and Democracy in *Rucho v. Common Cause.*" *ACS Supreme Court Review 2018–2019* (2019): 293–317.

———. "Race and Representation Revisited: The New Racial Gerrymandering Cases and Section 2 of the VRA." *William and Mary Law Review* 59 (2018): 1559–1600.

———. "States' Rights, Last Rites, and Voting Rights." *Connecticut Law Review* 47 (2014): 481–527.

———. "The Voting Rights Act in Winter: The Death of a Superstatute." *Iowa Law Review* 100 (2015): 1389–1439.

Chaturvedi, Neilan S., and Coleen Holloway. "Postdiluvian? The Effects of Outside Group Spending on Senate Elections after *Citizens United* and *Speechnow.org v. FEC.*" *Forum* 15, no. 2 (2017): 251–267.

Cheek, Kyle, and Anthony Champagne. *Judicial Politics in Texas: Partisanship, Money, and Politics in State Courts.* New York: Peter Lang, 2005.

Chemerinsky, Erwin. *Interpreting the Constitution.* New York: Praeger, 1987.

———. "The Supreme Court's *Janus* Ruling Was Pure Judicial Activism. Unions, Look Out." *Sacramento Bee,* July 9, 2018.

Chipman, Ian. "Political Polarization's Geographic Roots Run Deep." *Insight.* Stanford Graduate School of Business, May 2, 2017.

Cilluffo, Anthony, and Richard Fry. "An Early Look at the 2020 Electorate."

Pew Research Center, January 30, 2019. https://www.pewsocialtrends.org
/essay/an-early-look-at-the-2020-electorate/.

Citrin, Jack, Donald P. Green, and Morris Levy. "The Effects of Voter ID Notification on Voter Turnout: Results from a Large-Scale Field Experiment."
Election Law Journal 13, no. 2 (2014): 228–242.

Clark, Tom S. *The Limits of Judicial Independence.* New York: Cambridge University Press, 2011.

Clayton, Cornell W., and Howard Gillman, eds. *Supreme Court Decision-Making:
New Institutionalist Approaches.* Chicago: University of Chicago Press, 1999.

Clayton, Cornell W., and David May. "A Political Regimes Approach to the
Analysis of Legal Decisions." *Polity* 32 (1999): 233–252.

Clayton, Cornell W., and J. Mitchell Pickerill. "Guess What Happened on the
Way to the Revolution? Precursors to the Supreme Court's Federalism Revolution" *Publius: The Journal of Federalism* 34, no. 3 (2004): 85–114.

———. "The Politics of Criminal Justice: How the New Right Regime Shaped
the Rehnquist Court's Criminal Justice Jurisprudence." *Georgetown Law Journal* 94 (2006): 1385–1425.

Cobb, Jelani. "Voter-Suppression Tactics in the Age of Trump." *New Yorker*, October 21, 2018.

Cobb, Rachael V., D. James Greiner, and Kevin M. Quinn. "Can Voter ID Laws
Be Administered in a Race-Neutral Manner? Evidence from the City of Boston in 2008." *Quarterly Journal of Political Science* 7 (2012): 1–33.

Cohen, Felix S. "Transcendental Nonsense and the Functional Approach." *Columbia Law Review* 35 (1935): 809–849.

Colby, Thomas B. "In Defense of the Equal Sovereignty Principle." *Duke Law
Journal* 65, no. 6 (2016): 1087–1171.

Collins, Michael, and Rebecca Morin. "The trial Is Over. Trump Won. Now Get
Ready for the Political Fallout." *USA Today*, February 5, 2020.

Common Cause. "End Gerrymandering Now." commoncause.org/actions
/end-gerrymandering-now/# (accessed February 11, 2020).

Conover, Pamela Johnston, and Patrick R. Miller. "How Republicans Won on
Voter Identification Laws: The Roles of Strategic Reasoning and Moral Conviction." *Social Science Quarterly* 99, no. 2 (2018): 490–511.

Corley, Pamela C., Amy Steigerwalt, and Artemus Ward. *The Puzzle of Unanimity:
Consensus on the United States Supreme Court.* Palo Alto, CA: Stanford University Press, 2013.

Cottrell, David. "Using Computer Simulations to Measure the Effect of Gerrymandering on Electoral Competition in the U.S. Congress." *Legislative Studies Quarterly* 44, no. 3 (2019): 487–514.

Cottrell, David, Michael C. Herron, and Sean J. Westwood. "An Exploration of
Donald Trump's Allegations of Massive Voter Fraud in the 2016 General
Election." *Electoral Studies* 51 (2018): 123–142.

Cottrill, James B. "The Effects of Non-Legislative Redistricting on Competition
in Congressional Elections." *Polity* 44 (2012): 32–50.

Cottrill, James B., and Terri J. Peretti. "Gerrymandering from the Bench? The

Electoral Consequences of Judicial Redistricting." *Election Law Journal* 12 (2013): 261–276.

Cox, Adam B., and Thomas J. Miles. "Judging the Voting Rights Act." *Columbia Law Review* 108 (2008): 1–54.

Cox, Gary W., and Jonathan N. Katz. *Elbridge Gerry's Salamander: The Electoral Consequences of the Reapportionment Revolution.* New York: Cambridge University Press, 2002.

Cox, Kiefer. "The Voting Rights Act under Review: *Shelby County v. Holder* and the Consequences of Change." *Wayne Law Review* 60 (2014): 493–514.

Cox, Ted. "*Janus* Unleashes Coordinated Attack on Unions." *One Illinois,* June 28, 2018. https://www.oneillinois.com/stories/2018/6/28/from-fair-share -to-opt-out.

Cromartie, John. "Rural Areas Show Overall Population Decline and Shifting Regional Patterns of Population Change." *Amber Waves,* US Department of Agriculture Economic Research Service, September 5, 2017.

Cross, Frank B. "Decisionmaking in the U.S. Circuit Courts of Appeals." *California Law Review* 91 (2003): 1457–1515.

———. *Decision-Making in the U.S. Court of Appeals.* Palo Alto, CA: Stanford University Press, 2007.

———. "Political Science and the New Legal Realism: A Case of Unfortunate Interdisciplinary Ignorance." *Northwestern University Law Review* 92 (1997): 251–326.

Cross, Frank B., and Emerson H. Tiller. "Judicial Partisanship and Obedience to Legal Doctrine: Whistleblowing on the Federal Courts of Appeals." *Yale Law Journal* 107 (1998): 2155–2176.

———. "The Three Faces of Federalism: An Empirical Assessment of Supreme Court Federalism Jurisprudence." *Southern California Law Review* 73 (2000): 741–771.

Crouch, Thomas H. "Political Gerrymandering: Judicial Scrutiny under the Equal Protection Clause." *Hamline Law Review* 10 (1987): 313–344.

Dahl, Robert A. "Decision-Making in a Democracy: The Supreme Court as a National Policy-Maker." *Journal of Public Law* 6 (1957): 279–295.

Daley, David. "One Thing Voters Agree on—They Hate Gerrymandering." *Boston Globe,* November 12, 2018.

———. *Ratf**ked: The True Story behind the Secret Plan to Steal America's Democracy.* New York: Liveright, 2016.

———. "This Is How We End Gerrymandering." FairVote, January 26, 2018. https://www.fairvote.org/this_is_how_we_end_gerrymandering.

Daniels, Gilda R. "*Husted v. A. Philip Randolph Institute*—To Vote, or Not to Vote: That Is the Question." *ACS Supreme Court Review* 2017–2018 (2018): 49–75.

Davidson, Chandler. "The Historical Context of Voter Photo-ID Laws." *PS: Political Science and Politics* 42 (2009): 93–96.

De Alth, Shelley. "ID at the Polls: Assessing the Impact of Recent State Voter ID Laws on Voter Turnout." *Harvard Law and Policy Review* 3 (2009): 185–202.

D'Elia-Kueper, Justine, and Jeffrey A. Segal. "Ideology and Partisanship." In *The Oxford Handbook of U.S. Judicial Behavior*, ed. Lee Epstein and Stefanie A. Lindquist, 303–319. New York: Oxford University Press, 2017.

Devins, Neal, and Lawrence Baum. *The Company They Keep: How Partisan Divisions Came to the Supreme Court.* New York: Oxford University Press, 2019.

———. "Split Definitive: How Party Polarization Turned the Supreme Court into a Partisan Court." *Supreme Court Review* (2016): 301–365.

DiSalvo, Daniel. "Public-Sector Unions after *Janus*: An Update." Manhattan Institute Issue Brief, February 14, 2019. https://www.manhattan-institute .org/public-sector-unions-after-janus.

Douglas, Joshua A. "Is the Right to Vote Really Fundamental?" *Cornell Journal of Law and Public Policy* 18 (2008): 143–201.

———. "State Judges and the Right to Vote." *Ohio State Law Journal* 77 (2016): 1–48.

Downs, Anthony. *An Economic Theory of Democracy.* New York: Harper, 1957.

Drahozal, Christopher R. "Judicial Incentives and the Appeals Process." *Southern Methodist University Law Review* 51 (1998): 469–503.

Draper, Robert. "The League of Dangerous Mapmakers." *Atlantic*, October 2012.

Dropp, Kyle A. "Voter Identification Laws and Voter Turnout." Unpublished manuscript, 2013. http://kyledropp.weebly.com/uploads/1/2/0/9/1209 4568/dropp_voter_id.pdf.

Edelman, Paul H., David E. Klein, and Stefanie A. Lindquist. "Consensus, Disorder, and Ideology on the Supreme Court." *Journal of Empirical Legal Studies* 9, no. 1 (2012): 129–148.

Edsall, Thomas B. "The Fight over How Trump Fits in with the Other 44 Presidents." *New York Times*, May 15, 2019.

Edwards, Harry T. "Collegiality and Decision Making on the D.C. Circuit." *Virginia Law Review* 84, no. 7 (1998): 1335–1370.

Egelko, Bob. "Trump Outsources Supreme Court Picks to Federalist Society." *San Francisco Chronicle*, July 8, 2018.

Elmendorf, Christopher S. "Undue Burdens on Voter Participation: New Pressures for a Structural Theory of the Right to Vote?" *Hastings Constitutional Law Quarterly* 35 (2008): 643–712.

Elmendorf, Christopher S., and Douglas M. Spencer. "Administering Section 2 of the Voting Rights Act after *Shelby County*." *Columbia Law Review* 115 (2015): 2143–2217.

Ely, John Hart. *Democracy and Distrust: A Theory of Judicial Review.* Cambridge, MA: Harvard University Press, 1980.

Emmert, Craig F., and Traut, Carol Ann. "The California Supreme Court and the Death Penalty." *American Politics Research* 22, no. 1 (1994): 41–61.

Engstrom, Richard L. "The Post-2000 Round of Redistricting: An Entangled Thicket within the Federal System." *Publius* 32, no. 4 (2002): 51–70.

Engstrom, Richard, and Christopher Kenny. "The Effects of Independent Expenditures in Senate Elections." *Political Research Quarterly* 55, no. 4 (2002): 885–905.

Epp, Charles R. "External Pressures and the Supreme Court's Agenda." In *Supreme Court Decision-Making: New Institutionalist Approaches*, ed. Cornell W. Clayton and Howard Gillman, 255–278. Chicago: University of Chicago Press, 1999.

———. *The Rights Revolution: Lawyers, Activists, and Supreme Courts in Comparative Perspective*. Chicago: University of Chicago Press, 1998.

Epps, Garrett. "The Supreme Court's Key Role in Polarizing American Politics." *Atlantic*, September 27, 2013.

Epstein, David, Richard H. Pildes, Rodolfo O. de la Garza, and Sharyn O'Halloran, eds. *The Future of the Voting Rights Act*. New York: Russell Sage Foundation, 2006.

Epstein, Lee, and Gary King. "The Rules of Inference." *University of Chicago Law Review* 69 (2002): 1–209.

Epstein, Lee, and Jack Knight. *The Choices Justices Make*. Washington, DC: Congressional Quarterly Press, 1998.

Epstein, Lee, Jack Knight, and Andrew Martin. "The Norm of Prior Judicial Experience and Its Consequences for Career Diversity on the U.S. Supreme Court." *California Law Review* 91 (2003): 903–966.

Epstein, Lee, William M. Landes, and Richard A. Posner. *The Behavior of Federal Judges: A Theoretical and Empirical Study of Rational Choice*. Cambridge, MA: Harvard University Press, 2013.

Epstein, Lee, Andrew D. Martin, and Kevin Quinn. "6+ Decades of Freedom of Expression in the U.S. Supreme Court." 2018. http://epstein.wustl.edu/research/FreedomOfExpression.pdf.

Epstein, Lee, Andrew D. Martin, Jeffrey A. Segal, and Chad Westerland. "The Judicial Common Space." *Journal of Law, Economics, and Organization* 23 (2007): 303–325.

Epstein, Lee, Christopher M. Parker, and Jeffrey A. Segal. "Do Justices Defend the Speech They Hate? In-Group Bias, Opportunism, and the First Amendment." Paper presented at the annual meeting of the American Political Science Association, Chicago, August/September 2013.

Epstein, Lee, and Jeffrey A. Segal. *Advice and Consent: The Politics of Judicial Appointments*. New York: Oxford University Press, 2005.

Epstein, Richard A. "*Citizens United v. FEC*: The Constitutional Right That Big Corporations Should Have but Do Not Want." *Harvard Journal of Law and Public Policy* 34, no. 2 (2011): 639–661.

Erikson, Robert S. "Reapportionment and Policy: A Further Look at Some Intervening Variables." In "Democratic Representation and Apportionment: Quantitative Methods, Measures, and Criteria." *Annals of the New York Academy of Sciences* 29 (1973): 280–290.

Erikson, Robert S., and Lorraine C. Minnite. "Modeling Problems in the Voter Identification-Voter Turnout Debate." *Election Law Journal* 8 (2009): 85–101.

Erikson, Robert, S., and Thomas R. Palfrey. "Campaign Spending and Incumbency: An Alternative Simultaneous Equations Approach." *Journal of Politics* 60, no. 2 (1998): 355–373.

Executive Order on Collecting Information about Citizenship Status in Connection with the Decennial Census. July 11, 2019. https://www.whitehouse .gov/presidential-actions/executive-order-collecting-information-citizen ship-status-connection-decennial-census/.

Farrar-Myers, Victoria, and Richard Skinner. "Super PACs and the 2012 elections." *Forum* 10 (2012): 105–118.

Feigenbaum, James, Alexander Hertel-Fernandez, and Vanessa Williamson. "From the Bargaining Table to the Ballot Box: Political Effects of Right to Work Laws." National Bureau of Economic Research Working Paper No. 24259, January 2018.

Feldman, Stephen M. "Supreme Court Alchemy: Turning Law and Politics into Mayonnaise." *Georgetown Journal of Law and Public Policy* 12 (2014): 57–97.

Ferejohn, John A. "On the Decline of Competitiveness of Congressional Elections." *American Political Science Review* 71 (1977): 166–176.

Fiorina, Morris P. *Culture War? The Myth of a Polarized America.* New York: Pearson, 2005.

Fischman, Joshua B. "Estimating Preferences of Circuit Judges: A Model of Consensus Voting." *Journal of Law and Economics* 54 (2011): 781–809.

Fischman, Joshua B., and Tonja Jacobi. "The Second Dimension of the Supreme Court." *William and Mary Law Review* 57 (2015): 1671–1715.

Flanders, Chad. "Election Law behind a Veil of Ignorance." *Florida Law Review* 64 (2012): 1369–1403.

Fleisher, Richard, and Jon R. Bond. "Partisanship and the President's Quest for Votes on the Floor of Congress." In *Polarized Politics: Congress and the President in a Partisan Era,* ed. Jon R. Bond and Richard Fleisher, 154–184. Washington, DC: Congressional Quarterly Press, 2000.

Fleiss, Joseph L. *Statistical Methods for Rates and Proportions,* 2nd ed. New York: John Wiley, 1981.

Foley, Edward B. "Details, Equal Citizenship, and Reasonable Fairness." *University of Pennsylvania Law Review* 156 (2007): 247–257.

Forgey, Quint. "Trump: GOP Should Fight Mail-In Voting because It 'Doesn't Work Out Well for Republicans.'" *Politico,* April 8, 2020.

Forys, Matthew. "Symposium: Free Speech for Public Employees Restored—Justice Alito Plays the Long Game." SCOTUSblog, June 28, 2018. https:// www.scotusblog.com/2018/06/syposium-free-speech-for-public-employ ees-restored-justice-alito-plays-the-long-game/.

Fox, Justin. "Rural America Is Aging and Shrinking." *Bloomberg,* June 20, 2017. https://www.bloomberg.com/view/articles/2017-06-20/rural-america-is -aging-and-shrinking.

Fraga, Bernard L., and Michael G. Miller. "Who Does Voter ID Keep from Voting?" Paper prepared for the 2018 State Politics and Policy Conference, Pennsylvania State University, State College, PA, 2018. https://ucaeb23e 1b76b331484a06c8f1d8.previews.dropboxusercontent.com/nativeprint ?file=https%3A%2F%2Fwww.dropbox.com%2Fs%2Ff30qui1jhq6nqie% 2FFragaMiller_TXID_2018.pdf%3Fdisable_range%3D1%26from_native _print%3D1%26preview%3D1.

Frank, Jerome. *Courts on Trial*. Princeton, NJ: Princeton University Press, 1949.
———. *Law and the Modern Mind*. New York: Brentano's, 1930.
Franz, Michael M. "Campaign Finance Law: The Changing Role of Parties and Interest Groups." In *Rethinking American Electoral Democracy*, 2nd ed., ed. Matthew Streb, 6–28. New York: Routledge, 2012.
Frey, William H. "Minorities Are the Demographic Engine of Millennial Urban Growth." *Brookings Blog*, February 21, 2018. https://www.brookings.edu/blog/the-avenue/2018/02/20/minorities-are-the-demographic-engine-of-millennial-urban-growth/.
———. "Trump Put the Census Citizenship Question Back in Play." *Brookings Brief*, July 9, 2019. https://www.brookings.edu/blog/the-avenue/2019/07/09/trump-puts-the-census-citizenship-question-back-in-play/.
Fried, Charles. "A Day of Sorrow for American Democracy." *Atlantic*, July 3, 2019.
Friedman, Barry. "The Birth of an Academic Obsession: The History of the Countermajoritarian Difficulty, Part Five." *Yale Law Journal* 112 (2002): 153–259.
———. "Taking Law Seriously." *Perspectives on Politics* 4, no. 2 (2006): 261–276.
Friedman, Lawrence M. *A History of American Law*, 2nd ed. New York: Simon & Schuster, 1985.
Fuentes-Rohwer, Luis. "The Future of Section 2 of the Voting Rights Act in the Hands of a Conservative Court." *Duke Journal of Constitutional Law and Public Policy* 5 (2010): 125–158.
Garden, Charlotte. "The Deregulatory First Amendment at Work." *Harvard Civil Rights–Civil Liberties Law Review* 51 (2016): 323–362.
Garoupa, N., and T. Ginsberg. *Judicial Reputation: A Comparative Theory*. Chicago: University of Chicago Press, 2015.
Gartner, David. "The Voting Rights Act and the Enduring Challenge of Participation." *Election Law Journal* 14, no. 3 (2015): 278–281.
Geer, John G. "Parties and Partisanship: A Brief Introduction." *Political Behavior* 24, no. 2 (2002): 85–91.
Gelman, Andrew, and Gary King. "Enhancing Democracy through Legislative Districting." *American Political Science Review* 88, no. 3 (1994): 541–559.
Gerber, Alan S., Gregory A. Huber, and Seth J. Hill. "Identifying the Effect of All-Mail Elections on Turnout: Staggered Reform in the Evergreen State." *Political Science Research and Methods* 1 (2013): 91–116.
Gerhardt, Michael J. *The Power of Precedent*. New York: Oxford University Press, 2008.
Gerken, Heather K. "An Academic Elegy: Comment on *The Voting Rights Act in Winter: The Death of a Superstatute*." *Iowa Law Review* 100 (2015): 109–116.
———. *The Democracy Index: Why Our Election System Is Failing and How to Fix It*. Princeton, NJ: Princeton University Press, 2009.
———. "Lost in the Political Thicket: The Court, Election Law, and the Doctrinal Interregnum." *University of Pennsylvania Law Review* 153 (2004): 503–540.
———. "The Real Problem with *Citizens United:* Campaign Finance, Dark Money, and Shadow Parties." *Marquette Law Review* 97, no. 4 (2014): 903–923.

Geyh, Charles Gardner. *Courting Peril: The Political Transformation of the American Judiciary.* New York: Oxford University Press, 2016.

Gibson, James L., and Gregory A. Caldeira. *Citizens, Courts, and Confirmations: Positivity Theory and the Judgments of the American People.* Princeton, NJ: Princeton University Press, 2009.

Gibson, James L., Gregory A. Calderia, and Vanessa Baird. "On the Legitimacy of National High Courts." *American Political Science Review* 92 (1998): 343–358.

Gibson, James L., Gregory A. Caldeira, and Lester Kenyatta Spence. "The Supreme Court and the U.S. Presidential Election of 2000: Wounds, Self-Inflicted or Otherwise?" *British Journal of Political Science* 33 (2003): 535–556.

Gibson, James L., and Michael J. Nelson. "The Legitimacy of the U.S. Supreme Court: Conventional Wisdoms and Recent Challenges Thereto." *Annual Review of Law and Social Science* 10 (2014): 201–219.

Giles, Michael W., Virginia Hettinger, and Todd Peppers. "Picking Federal Judges: A Note on Policy and Partisan Selection Agendas." *Political Research Quarterly* 54 (2001): 623–641.

Gillman, Howard. "De-Lochnerizing *Lochner.*" *Boston University Law Review* 85 (2005): 859–865.

———. "How Political Parties Can Use the Courts to Advance Their Agendas: Federal Courts in the United States, 1875–1891." *American Political Science Review* 96, no. 3 (2002): 511–524.

———. "Regime Politics, Jurisprudential Regimes, and Unenumerated Rights." *Journal of Constitutional Law* 9 (2006): 107–119.

———. *The Votes That Counted: How the Court Decided the 2000 Presidential Election.* Chicago: University of Chicago Press, 2003.

———. "What's Law Got to Do with It? Judicial Behavioralists Test the 'Legal Model' of Judicial Decision Making." *Law and Social Inquiry* 26 (2001): 465–504.

Gillman, Howard, and Cornell Clayton. "Beyond Judicial Attitudes: Institutional Approaches to Supreme Court Decision-Making. In *Supreme Court Decision-Making: New Institutionalist Approaches,* ed. Cornell W. Clayton and Howard Gillman, 1–14. Chicago: University of Chicago Press, 1999.

Gillman, Howard, Mark A. Graber, and Keith E. Whittington. *American Constitutionalism, Volume II.* New York: Oxford University Press, 2013.

Goedert, Nicholas. "The Case of the Disappearing Bias: A 2014 Update to the 'Gerrymandering or Geography' Debate." *Research and Politics* 2, no. 4 (2015): 1–6.

———. "Gerrymandering or Geography? How Democrats Won the Popular Vote but Lost the Congress in 2012." *Research and Politics* 1, no. 1 (2014): 1–8.

———. "Partisan Gerrymandering in the Courts: The Search for a Common Standard." Paper presented at the annual meeting of the Midwest Political Science Association, Chicago, April 2019.

———. "The Pseudoparadox of Partisan Mapmaking and Congressional Competition." *State Politics and Policy Quarterly* 17, no. 1 (2017): 47–75.

Goldman, Sheldon. "Voting Behavior on the United States Courts of Appeals, 1961–1964." *American Political Science Review* 60 (1966): 374–383.
———. "Voting Behavior on the United States Courts of Appeals Revisited." *American Political Science Review* 69 (1975): 491–506.
Gottlieb, Stephen. "Democracy Essential to the Legitimacy of Constitutional Interpretation." Albany Law School Research Paper Number 7, 2017. https://papers.ssrn.com/so13/papers.cfm?abstract_id=2931153.
———. *Unfit for Democracy: The Roberts Court and the Breakdown of American Politics.* New York: New York University Press, 2016.
Gottschall, Jon. "Reagan's Appointments to the U.S. Courts of Appeals: The Continuation of a Judicial Revolution." *Judicature* 70 (1986): 48–54.
Graber, Mark A. "Constructing Judicial Review." *Annual Review of Political Science* 8, no. 1 (2005): 425–451.
———. "The Nonmajoritarian Difficulty: Legislative Deference to the Judiciary." *Studies in American Political Development* 7 (1993): 48–54.
Grainger, Corbett A. "Redistricting and Polarization: Who Draws the Lines in California?" *Journal of Law and Economics* 53, no. 3 (2010): 545–567.
Grant, Keneshia N. *The Great Migration and the Democratic Party: Black Voters and the Realignment of American Politics in the 20th Century.* Philadelphia: Temple University Press, 2020.
Graves, Scott. "Competing Interests in State Supreme Courts: Justices' Votes and Voting Rights." *American Review of Politics* 24 (2003): 267–283.
Green, Donald, and Jonathan Krasno. "Salvation for the Spendthrift Incumbent: Reestimating the Effects of Campaign Spending in House Elections." *American Journal of Political Science* 32 (1988): 884–907.
Green, Donald P., Bradley Palmquist, and Eric Schickler. *Partisan Hearts and Minds.* New Haven, CT: Yale University Press, 2004.
Greene, Jamal. "Judging Partisan Gerrymanders under the Election Clause." *Yale Law Review* 114 (2005): 1021–1061.
Greene, Steven. "Social Identity Theory and Party Identification." *Social Science Quarterly* 85, no. 1 (2004): 136–153.
Grey, Thomas. "Langdell's Orthodoxy." *University of Pittsburgh Law Review* 45 (1983): 1–53.
Griffin, Stephen M. "Judicial Supremacy and Equal Protection in a Democracy of Rights." *Journal of Constitutional Law* 4 (2002): 281–313.
Grofman, Bernard. "Devising a Sensible Trigger for Section 5 of the Voting Rights Act." *Election Law Journal* 12, no. 3 (2013): 332–337.
———. "The 1990s Round of Redistricting: A Schematic Outline of Some Key Features." In *Race and Representation,* ed. Georgia A. Persons, 17–26. New Brunswick, NJ: Transaction, 1997.
Grofman, Bernard, and Thomas L. Brunell. "The Art of the Dummymander: The Impact of Recent Redistrictings on the Partisan Makeup of Southern House Seats." In *Redistricting in the New Millennium,* ed. Peter F. Galderisi, 183–200. New York: Rowman & Littlefield, 2005.
Grofman, Bernard, and German Feierherd. "The U.S. Could Be Free of Gerry-

mandering. Here's How Other Countries Do Redistricting." *Washington Post,* August 7, 2017.

Grofman, Bernard, and Lisa Handley. "The Impact of the Voting Rights Act on Black Representation in Southern State Legislatures." *Legislative Studies Quarterly* 16, no. 1 (1991): 111–128.

———. "1990s Issues in Voting Rights." *Mississippi Law Journal* 65 (1995): 205–270.

Grofman, Bernard, and Gary King. "The Future of Partisan Symmetry as a Judicial Test for Partisan Gerrymandering after *LULAC v. Perry.*" *Election Law Journal* 6, no. 1 (2007): 2–35.

Groft, Kylee. "The Results Are In: Most Americans Want Limits on Gerrymandering." Campaign Legal Center, September 11, 2017. https://campaign legal.org/update/results-are-most-americans-want-limits-gerrymandering.

Gronke, Paul, William D. Hicks, Seth C. McKee, Charles Stewart III, and James Dunham. "Voter ID Laws: A View from the Public." MIT Political Science Department Research Paper No. 2015–13, 2015. http://papers.ssrn.com /so13/papers.cfm?abstract_id=2594290.

Grossman, Matt, and David A. Hopkins. *Asymmetric Politics: Ideological Republicans and Group Interest Democrats.* New York: Oxford University Press, 2016.

Guthrie, Chris, Jeffrey J. Rachlinski, and Andrew J. Wistrich. "Blinking on the Bench: How Judges Decide Cases." *Cornell Law Review* 93 (2007): 1–43.

———. "Inside the Judicial Mind." *Cornell Law Review* 86 (2001): 777–830.

Hagens, Winnett W. "Redistricting the Commonwealth: A Narrative and Analysis of the Virginia Outcome, 1991–1995." In *Race and Representation,* ed. Georgia A. Persons, 44–62. New Brunswick, NJ: Transaction, 1997.

Hagle, Timothy M. "Strategic Retirements: A Political Model of Turnover on the United States Supreme Court." *Political Behavior* 15 (1993): 25–48.

Hagle, Tim, and Harold Spaeth. "Ideological Patterns in the Justices' Voting in the Burger Court Business Cases." *Journal of Politics* 55, no. 2 (1993): 492–505.

Hajnal, Zoltan, John Kuk, and Nazita Lajevardi. "We All Agree: Strict Voter ID Laws Disproportionately Burden Minorities." *Journal of Politics* 80, no. 3 (2018): 1052–1059.

Hajnal, Zoltan, Nazita Lajevardi, and Lindsay Nielson. "Voter Identification Laws and the Suppression of Minority Votes." *Journal of Politics* 79, no. 2 (2017): 363–379.

Hale, Kathleen, and Ramona McNeal. "Election Administration Reform and State Choice: Voter Identification Requirements and HAVA." *Policy Studies Journal* 38, no. 2 (2010): 281–302.

Hall, Matthew E. K. *What Justices Want: Goals and Personality on the U.S. Supreme Court.* New York: Cambridge University Press, 2018.

Hall, Melinda Gann. "Constituent Influence in State Supreme Courts: Conceptual Notes and a Case Study." *Journal of Politics* 49, no. 4 (1987): 1117–1124.

———. "Electoral Politics and Strategic Voting in State Supreme Courts." *Journal of Politics* 54 (1992): 427–446.

———. "Voluntary Retirements from State Supreme Courts: Assessing Democratic Pressures to Relinquish the Bench." *Journal of Politics* 63, no. 4 (2001): 1112–1140.

Hall, Melinda Gann, and Paul Brace. "Toward an Integrated Model of Judicial Voting Behavior." *American Politics Quarterly* 20 (1992): 147–168.

———. "The Vicissitudes of Death by Decree: Forces Influencing Capital Punishment Decision Making in State Supreme Courts." *Social Science Quarterly* 75, no. 1 (1994): 136–151.

Hansen, Wendy L., Michael S. Rocca, and Brittany Leigh Ortiz. "The Effects of *Citizens United* on Corporate Spending in the 2012 Presidential Election." *Journal of Politics* 77, no. 2 (2015): 535–545.

Hansford, Thomas G., and James F. Spriggs II. *The Politics of Precedent on the U.S. Supreme Court.* Princeton, NJ: Princeton University Press, 2006.

Harvey, Anna, and Barry Friedman. "Pulling Punches: Congressional Constraints on the Supreme Court's Constitutional Rulings, 1987–2000." *Legislative Studies Quarterly* 31, no. 4 (2006): 533–562.

Hasen, Richard L. "Brett Kavanaugh May Soon Unshackle All Rich Political Donors." *Slate*, September 3, 2018.

———. "The Decade of *Citizens United*." *Slate*, December 19, 2019.

———. "How Justice Kennedy's Successor Will Wreak Havoc on Voting Rights and American Democracy." *Slate*, July 2, 2018.

———. "Keynote Address: Judging the Political and Political Judging: Justice Scalia as Case Study." *Chicago-Kent Law Review* 93, no. 2 (2018): 325–341.

———. "Looking for Standards (in All the Wrong Places): Partisan Gerrymandering Claims after *Vieth*." *Election Law Journal* 3, no. 4 (2004): 626–642.

———. *Plutocrats United: Campaign Money, the Supreme Court, and the Distortion of American Elections.* New Haven, CT: Yale University Press, 2016.

———. "Race or Party? How Courts Should Think about Republican Efforts to Make It Harder to Vote in North Carolina and Elsewhere." *Harvard Law Review Forum* 127 (2014): 58–75.

———. "Resurrection: *Cooper v. Harris* and the Transformation of Racial Gerrymandering into a Voting Rights Tool." *ACS Supreme Court Review* 2016–2017 (2017): 105–129.

———. "*Shelby County* and the Illusion of Minimalism." *William and Mary Bill of Rights Journal* 22 (2014): 713–745.

———. *The Supreme Court and Election Law: Judging Equality from* Baker v. Carr *to* Bush v. Gore. New York: New York University Press, 2006.

———. "The 2012 Voting Wars, Judicial Back-stops, and the Resurrection of *Bush v. Gore*." *George Washington Law Review* 81 (2013): 1865–1901.

———. "The Untimely Death of *Bush v. Gore*." *Stanford Law Review* 60, no. 1 (2007): 1–44.

———. *The Voting Wars: From Florida 2000 to the Next Election Meltdown.* New Haven, CT: Yale University Press, 2012.

———. "What the Court Did—and Why?" *American Interest*, July 2, 2010.

Hayden, Grant M. "Resolving the Dilemma of Minority Representation." *California Law Review* 92 (2004): 1589–1637.

Heberling, Eric S., and Bruce A. Larson. "U.S. House Incumbent Fundraising and Spending in a Post-*Citizens United* and Post-*McCutcheon* World." *Political Science Quarterly* 129, no. 4 (2014): 613–642.

Hebert, J. Gerald, and Marina K. Jenkins. "The Need for State Redistricting Reform to Rein in Partisan Gerrymandering." *Yale Law and Policy Review* 29 (2011): 543–558.

Heller, Joel. "Fearing Fear Itself: Photo Identification Laws, Fear of Fraud, and the Fundamental Right to Vote." *Vanderbilt Law Review* 62, no. 6 (2009): 1871–1912.

Henninger, Phoebe, Marc Meredith, and Michael Morse. "Who Votes without Identification? Using Affidavits from Michigan to Learn about the Potential Impact of Strict Photo Voter Identification Laws." Paper prepared for the 2018 Election Sciences, Reform, and Administration Conference. https://esra.wisc.edu/papers/HMM.pdf.

Herbert, William A., and Joseph A. McCartin. "*Janus*'s Progeny? A Supreme Court Threat to Majority Rule Looms." *Prospect,* March 21, 2019.

Hershey, Marjorie Randon. "What We Know about Voter-ID Laws, Registration, and Turnout." *PS: Political Science and Politics* 42 (2009): 87–91.

Hettinger, Virginia A., Stefanie A. Lindquist, and Wendy L. Martinek. *Judging on a Collegial Court: Influences on Federal Appellate Decision Making.* Charlottesville: University of Virginia Press, 2006.

Hicks, William D., Seth C. McKee, Mitchell D. Sellers, and Daniel A. Smith. "A Principle or a Strategy? Voter Identification Laws and Partisan Competition in the American States." *Political Research Quarterly* 68, no. 1 (2015): 18–33.

Hicks, William D., Seth C. McKee, and Daniel A. Smith. "The Determinants of State Legislator Support for Restrictive Voter ID Laws." *State Politics and Policy Quarterly* 16, no. 4 (2016): 411–431.

Highton, Benjamin. "How the Senate Is Biased toward Republicans," *Washington Post,* January 31, 2014.

———. "Voter Identification Laws and Turnout in the United States." *Annual Review of Political Science* 20 (2017): 149–167.

Hill, Kevin A. "Does the Creation of Majority Black Districts Aid Republicans? An Analysis of the 1992 Congressional Elections in Eight Southern States." *Journal of Politics* 57 (1995): 384–401.

Hill, Steven. "How the Voting Rights Act Hurts Democrats and Minorities." *Atlantic,* June 17, 2013.

Hiltzik, Michael. "A Conservative Judge's Devastating Take on Why Voter ID Laws Are Evil." *Los Angeles Times,* October 13, 2014.

Ho, Dale E. "Something Old, Something New, or Something *Really* Old? Second Generation Racial Gerrymandering Litigation as Intentional Racial Discrimination Cases." *William and Mary Law Review* 59 (2018): 1887–1919.

Hollis-Brusky, Amanda. *Ideas with Consequences: The Federalist Society and the Conservative Counterrevolution.* New York: Oxford University Press, 2015.

Holmes, Oliver Wendell. "The Path of the Law." *Harvard Law Review* 10 (1897): 457–478.

Hood, M. V., III, and Charles S. Bullock. "Much Ado About Nothing? An Empirical Assessment of the Georgia Voter Identification Statute." *State Politics and Policy Quarterly* 12, no. 4 (2012): 394–414.
———. "Worth a Thousand Words? An Analysis of Georgia's Voter Identification Statute." *American Politics Research* 36 (2008): 555–579.
Hood, M. V, III, and William Gillespie. "They Just Do Not Vote Like They Used To: A Methodology to Empirically Assess Election Fraud." *Social Science Quarterly* 93 (2012): 76–94.
Hopkins, Daniel J., Marc Meredith, Michael Morse, Sarah Smith, and Jesse Yoder. "Voting but for the Law: Evidence from Virginia on Photo Identification Requirements." *Journal of Empirical Legal Studies* 14, no. 1 (2017): 79–128.
Horwitz, Morton J. "The Rise of Legal Formalism." *American Journal of Legal History* 19 (1975): 251–264.
"How Bush Watered Down Civil-Rights Enforcement." *Newsweek*, December 9, 2009. https://www.newsweek.com/how-bush-watered-down-civil-rights-en forcement-75741.
Huber, Gregory A., and Sanford C. Gordon. "Accountability and Coercion: Is Justice Blind When It Runs for Office?" *American Journal of Political Science* 48 (2004): 247–263.
Hudson, John. "How Justice Souter Almost Left the Supreme Court in a Blaze of Glory." *Atlantic*, May 14, 2012.
Huefner, Steven F. "Remedying Election Wrongs." *Harvard Journal on Legislation* 44 (2007): 265–325.
Hulse, Carl. "As Pandemic Imperils Elections, Democrats Clash with Trump on Voting Changes." *New York Times*, April 8, 2020.
———. "Seeking to End Gerrymandering's Enduring Legacy." *New York Times*, January 25, 2016.
Hutzler, Alexander. "2020 was already expected to be a record year for Election-Related Lawsuits—then Coronavirus Happened." *Newsweek*, April 23, 2020.
Ingraham, Christopher. "Republicans Are So Much Better Than Democrats at Gerrymandering," *Washington Post*, June 6, 2017.
———. "7 Papers, 4 Government Inquiries, 2 News Investigations and 1 Court Ruling Proving Voter Fraud Is Mostly a Myth." *Washington Post*, July 9, 2014.
Issacharoff, Samuel. "Beyond the Discrimination Model on Voting." *Harvard Law Review* 127 (2013): 95–126.
———. "Gerrymandering and Political Cartels." *Harvard Law Review* 116 (2002): 593–648.
———. "Judging Politics: The Elusive Quest for Judicial Review of Political Fairness." *Texas Law Review* 71 (1993): 1643–1704.
Issacharoff, Samuel, and Pamela S. Karlan. "Where to Draw the Lines: Judicial Review of Political Gerrymandering." *University of Pennsylvania Law Review* 153 (2004): 541–578.
Issacharoff, Samuel, Pamela S. Karlan, Richard H. Pildes, and Nathaniel Persily. *The Law of Democracy: Legal Structure of the Political Process*, 5th ed. St. Paul, MN: Foundation, 2016.

Issacharoff, Samuel, and Richard Pildes. "Politics as Markets: Partisan Lockups of the Democratic Process." *Stanford Law Review* 50 (1998): 643–717.

Jacobi, Tonja, and Emerson H. Tiller. "Legal Doctrine and Political Control." *Journal of Law, Economics, and Organization* 23 (2007): 326–345.

Jacobson, Gary C. "The Effects of Campaign Spending in House Elections: New Evidence for Old Arguments." *American Journal of Political Science* 34 (1990): 334–362.

———. "How the Economy and Partisanship Shaped the 2012 Presidential and Congressional Elections." *Political Science Quarterly* 128, 1 (2013): 1–38.

———. *Money in Congressional Elections*. New Haven, CT: Yale University Press, 1980.

———. "Partisanship, Money, and Competition: Elections and the Transformation of Congress since the 1970s." In *Congress Reconsidered*, 11th ed., ed. Lawrence C. Dodd and Bruce I. Oppenheimer, 89–118. Washington, DC: Congressional Quarterly Press, 2017.

Jeffries, John C., Jr., and Daryl J. Levinson. "The Non-Retrogression Principle in Constitutional Law." *California Law Review* 86 (1998): 1211–1249.

Jensen, Bryan P. "*Crawford v. Marion County Election Board*: The Missed Opportunity to Remedy the Ambiguity and Unpredictability of *Burdick*." *Denver University Law Review* 86 (2009): 535–563.

Johnson, Noel. "Resurrecting Retrogression: Will Section 2 of the Voting Rights Act Revive Preclearance Nationwide?" *Duke Journal of Constitutional Law and Public Policy* 12 (2017): 1–21.

Johnson, Theodore R., and Max Feldman. "The New Voter Suppression." Brennan Center for Justice, January 16, 2020. https://www.brennancenter.org /our-work/research-reports/new-voter-suppression.

Johnson, Timothy R, Paul J. Wahlbeck, and James F. Spriggs II. "The Influence of Oral Arguments on the U.S. Supreme Court." *American Political Science Review* 100, no. 1 (2006): 99–113.

Jones, Bradley. "Most Americans Want to Limit Campaign Spending, Say Big Donors Have Greater Political Influence." Pew Research Center, May 8, 2018. https://www.pewresearch.org/fact-tank/2018/05/08/most-ameri cans-want-to-limit-campaign-spending-say-big-donors-have-greater-political -influence/.

Jones, Jeffrey M. "Democrats Hold Edge in U.S. Party Affiliation in 3rd Quarter." *Gallup News*, October 7, 2019. https://news.gallup.com/poll/267239 /democrats-hold-edge-party-affiliation-3rd-quarter.aspx.

———. "Trump Job Approval at Personal Best 49%." *Gallup News*, February 4, 2020. https://news.gallup.com/poll/284156/trump-job-approval-per sonal-best.aspx.

Jones, Mark, Renee Cross, Jim Granato, Ching-Hsing Wang, and Kwok-Wai Wan. "The Texas Voter ID Law and the 2016 Election: A Study of Harris County and Congressional District 23." University of Houston Hobby School of Public Affairs, 2017. www.uh.edu/hobby/voterid2016/voterid2016.pdf.

Kahan, Dan. "'Ideology in' or 'Cultural Cognition of' Judging: What Difference Does It Make?" *Marquette Law Review* 92, no. 3 (2009): 414–422.

Kahn, Ronald. "Institutionalized Norms and Supreme Court Decision Making: The Rehnquist Court on Privacy and Religion." In *Supreme Court Decision-Making: New Institutionalist Approaches,* ed. Cornell W. Clayton and Howard Gillman, 177–198. Chicago: University of Chicago Press, 1999.

Kam, Dar. "Former Florida GOP Leaders Say Voter Suppression Was Reason They Pushed New Election Law." *Palm Beach Post,* November 25, 2012.

Kane, John V. "Why Can't We Agree on ID? Partisanship, Perceptions of Fraud, and Public Support for Voter Identification Laws." *Public Opinion Quarterly* 81, no. 4 (2017): 943–955.

Kang, Michael S. "After *Citizens United.*" *Indiana Law Review* 44 (2010): 243–254.

———. "Gerrymandering and the Constitutional Norm against Government Partisanship." *Michigan Law Review* 116 (2017): 351–419.

———. "When Courts Won't Make Law: Partisan Gerrymandering and a Structural Approach to the Law of Democracy." *Ohio State Law Journal* 68 (2007): 1097–1120.

Kang, Michael S., and Joanna M. Shepherd. "The Long Shadow of *Bush v. Gore*: Judicial Partisanship in Election Cases." *Stanford Law Review* 68 (2016): 1411–1452.

Karlan, Pamela S. "The Rights to Vote: Some Pessimism about Formalism." *Texas Law Review* 71 (1993): 1705–1740.

———. "Section 5 Squared: Congressional Power to Extend and Amend the Voting Rights Act." *Houston Law Review* 44 (2007): 1–31.

Katel, Peter. "Voter Rights: Should Photo IDs Be Required at the Ballot Box?" *Congressional Quarterly Researcher* 22, no. 19 (2012): 451–475.

Katz, Ellen D. "Election Law's Lochnerian Turn." *Boston University Law Review* 94 (2014): 697–709.

———. "What Was Wrong with the Record?" *Election Law Journal* 12 (2013): 329–331.

Keck, Thomas M. *Judicial Politics in Polarized Times.* Chicago: University of Chicago Press, 2014.

———. "These Are the Roadblocks to the Democrats' Big Voting Rights Bill." *Washington Post,* March 7, 2019.

Keck, Thomas, and Kevin McMahon. "Why *Roe* Still Stands: Abortion Law, the Supreme Court, and the Republican Regime." *Studies in Law, Politics and Society* 70 (2015): 33–83.

Kennedy, John F. "The Shame of the States." *New York Times Magazine,* May 18, 1958.

Kersch, Ken I. *Constructing Civil Liberties: Discontinuities in the Development of American Constitutional Law.* New York: Cambridge University Press, 2004.

Kessler, Jeremy K., and David E. Pozen. "The Search for an Egalitarian First Amendment." *Columbia Law Review* 118, no. 7 (2018): 1953–2010.

Key, V. O., Jr. " A Theory of Critical Elections." *Journal of Politics* 17 (1955): 1–18.

Keyssar, Alexander. *The Right to Vote: The Contested History of Democracy in the United States,* rev. ed. New York: Basic, 2009.

Khan, Natasha, and Corbin Carson. "Comprehensive Database of U.S. Voter

Fraud Uncovers No Evidence that Photo ID Is Needed." News 21, August 12, 2012. https://votingrights.news21.com/article/election-fraud/.

Kimball, David C. "Judges Are Not Social Scientists (Yet)." *Election Law Journal* 12 (2013): 324–326.

King, Desmond S., and Rogers M. Smith. "The Last Stand? *Shelby County v. Holder*, White Political Power, and America's Racial Policy Alliances." *Du Bois Review* 13 (2016): 25–44.

King, Kimi Lynn, Jennifer Morbitt, and John Ryan. "Voting Rights and Wrongs: Federal District Court Decisions, 1965–1993." Paper presented at the annual meeting of the American Political Science Association in San Francisco, September 1996.

Klar, Rebecca. "DHS to Share Citizenship Data with Census Bureau in Wake of Court Decision." *The Hill,* January 6, 2020.

Klarman, Michael J. "*Bush v. Gore* through the Lens of Constitutional History." *California Law Review* 89 (2001): 1721–1765.

Klein, David E. "Law in Judicial Decision-Making." In *The Oxford Handbook of U.S. Judicial Behavior,* eds. Lee Epstein and Stefanie A. Lindquist, 236–252. New York: Oxford University Press, 2017.

———. *Making Law in the United States Courts of Appeals.* New York: Cambridge University Press, 2002.

Klein, David, and Gregory Mitchell, eds. *The Psychology of Judicial Decision Making.* New York: Oxford University Press, 2010.

Kogan, Vladimir, and Eric McGhee. "Redistricting and Representation: Searching for 'Fairness' between the Lines." In *Changing How America Votes,* ed. Todd Donovan, 84–99. New York: Rowman & Littlefield, 2018.

Kopko, Kyle Casimir. "The Effect of Partisanship in Election Law Judicial Decision-Making." PhD dissertation, Ohio State University, 2010.

———. "Litigant Partisan Identity and Challenges to Campaign Finance Policies: An Examination of U.S. District Court Decisions, 1971–2007." *Justice System Journal* 36, no. 3 (2015): 212–232.

———. "Partisanship Suppressed: Judicial Decision-Making in Ralph Nader's 2004 Ballot Access Litigation." *Election Law Journal* 7, no. 4 (2008): 301–324.

Kopko, Kyle C., Sarah McKinnon Bryner, Jeffrey Budziak, Christopher J. Devine, and Steven P. Nawara. "In the Eye of the Beholder? Motivated Reasoning in Disputed Elections." *Political Behavior* 33, no. 2 (2011): 271–290.

Kousser, Morgan. "Do the Facts of Voting Rights Support Chief Justice Roberts's Opinion in *Shelby County*?" *Transatlantica* 1 (2015): 1–31.

Kowal, Michael S. "Corporate Politicking, Together: Trade Association Ties, Lobbying, and Campaign Giving." *Business and Politics* 20, no. 1 (2018): 98–131.

Kozinski Alex. "What I Ate for Breakfast, and Other Mysteries of Judicial Decision Making." In *Judges on Judging: Views from the Bench,* 2nd ed., ed. David M. O'Brien, 76–81. Washington, DC: Congressional Quarterly Press, 2004.

Krasno, Jonathan S., and Donald Philip Green. "Preempting Quality Challengers in House Elections." *Journal of Politics* 50 (1988): 920–936.

Krehbiel, Keith. "Supreme Court Appointments as a Move–the–Median Game." *American Journal of Political Science* 51 (2007): 231–240.

Kritzer, Herbert M. "The Impact of *Bush v. Gore* on Public Perceptions and Knowledge of the Supreme Court." *Judicature* 85, no. 1 (2001): 32–38.

Kruse, Kevin M. *White Flight: Atlanta and the Making of Modern Conservatism.* Princeton, NJ: Princeton University Press, 2007.

Kuhner, Timothy. "The Market Metaphor, Radicalized: How a Capitalist Theology Trumped Democracy." *Election Law Journal* 16, no. 1 (2017): 96–131.

Kunda, Ziva. "The Case for Motivated Reasoning." *Psychological Bulletin* 108, no. 3 (1990): 480–498.

Kurlowski, Drew. *Rules Matter: Election Law Revealed.* St. Paul, MN: West Academic Publishing, 2019.

Kurtzleben, Danielle. "Rural Voters Played a Big Part in Helping Trump Defeat Clinton." National Public Radio, November 14, 2016. https://www.npr.org/2016/11/14/501737150/rural-voters-played-a-big-part-in-helping-trump-defeat-clinton.

Lain, Corinna Barrett. "Upside-Down Judicial Review." *Georgetown Law Journal* 101 (2012): 113–183.

Lakier, Genevieve. "Imagining an Antisubordinating First Amendment." *Columbia Law Review* 118, no. 7 (2018): 2117–2160.

Landis, J. Richard, and Gary G. Koch. "The Measurement of Observer Agreement for Categorical Data." *Biometrics* 33 (1977): 159–174.

Lang, Mary Jo. "The Importance of Being Narrowly Tailored: A Call for Strict Scrutiny for a Fundamental Right in *Crawford v. Marion County Election Board.*" *Nebraska Law Review* 88 (2009): 582–611.

Langvardt, Kyle. "A Model of First Amendment Decision-Making at a Divided Court." *Tennessee Law Review* 84 (2017): 833–891.

La Raja, Raymond J. "The Court's Campaign Finance Jurisprudence and Its Impact on the Electoral Process." SCOTUSblog, November 8, 2011. https://www.scotusblog.com/community/the-court's-campaign-finance-jurisprudence-and-its-impact-on-the-electoral-process/.

La Raja, Raymond J., and Brian Schaffner. *Campaign Finance and Political Polarization: When Purists Prevail.* Ann Arbor: University of Michigan Press, 2015.

———. "The Effects of Campaign Finance Spending Bans on Electoral Outcomes: Evidence from the States about the Potential Impact of *Citizens United v. FEC.*" *Electoral Studies* 33 (2014): 102–114.

Lassiter, Matthew D. *The Silent Majority: Suburban Politics in the Sunbelt South.* Princeton, NJ: Princeton University Press, 2006.

Lauderdale, Benjamin E., and Tom S. Clark. "The Supreme Court's Many Median Justices." *American Political Science Review* 106, no. 4 (2012): 847–866.

Law, Sylvia A. "In the Name of Federalism: The Supreme Court's Assault on Democracy and Civil Rights." *University of Cincinnati Law Review* 70 (2002): 367–432.

Lax, Jeffrey R. "The New Judicial Politics of Legal Doctrine." *Annual Review of Political Science* 14 (2011): 131–157.

Layman, Geoffrey C., and Thomas M. Carsey. "Party Polarization and 'Conflict

Extension' in the American Electorate." *American Journal of Political Science* 46, no. 4 (2002): 786–802.

Leadership Conference Education Fund. "Warning Signs: The Potential Impact of *Shelby County v. Holder* on the 2016 General Election." June 2016. http:// civilrightsdocs.info/pdf/reports/2016-Voting-Rights-Report-FOR-WEB .pdf.

Leavenworth, Stuart. "Gerrymandering Hurts Cities Such as Elk Grove." *Sacramento Bee*, February 21, 2010.

LeBlanc, Paul. "Federal Judge Denies Bid to Undo Georgia Voter Purge." *CNN Politics*, December 28, 2019. https://www.cnn.com/2019/12/27/politics /georgia-voters-inactive-judge/index.html.

Lee, Francis E., and Bruce I. Oppenheimer. *Sizing Up the Senate: The Unequal Consequences of Equal Representation.* Chicago: University of Chicago Press, 1999.

Lemieux, Scott. "John Roberts Has Been Trying to Gut the Voting Rights Act for Decades." *The Week*, August 3, 2015. https://theweek.com/articles /568963/john-roberts-been-trying-gut-voting-rights-act-decades.

———. "Justice Kennedy's Retirement Cements His Legacy as an Enabler of Trump's Pro-Business, Racist, Anti-Woman Agenda." NBC News, June 27, 2018. https://www.nbcnews.com/think/opinion/justice-kennedy-s-retire ment-cements-his-legacy-enabler-trump-s-ncna887106.

———. "Republicans' Coup de Grace on Voting Rights?" *The Week*, December 15, 2015. http://theweek.com/articles/593609/republicans-coup-de-grace -voting-rights.

———. "Trump's Plan to Make Voters Older, Wealthier and Whiter." Reuters, July 12, 2017. https://www.reuters.com/article/us-lemieux-voting-com mentary/commentary-trumps-plan-to-make-voters-older-wealthier-and -whiter-idUSKBN19X28H.

———. "'Wholly without Merit': The 10th Anniversary of *Bush v. Gore.*" *Lawyers, Guns & Money* (blog), December 13, 2010. http://www.lawyersgunsmon eyblog.com/2010/12/wholly-without-merit-the-10th-anniversary-of-bush-v -gore.

Levick, Richard. "SCOTUS, for Now, Largely Chooses to Punt on Partisan Gerrymandering." *Forbes*, June 19, 2018.

Levinson, Sanford. *Our Undemocratic Constitution: Where the Constitution Goes Wrong (And How We the People Can Correct It).* New York: Oxford University Press, 2008.

———. "Return of Legal Realism." *Nation*, December 22, 2000.

Levinson, Sanford, and Jack M. Balkin. *Democracy and Dysfunction.* Chicago: University of Chicago Press, 2019.

Levitsky, Steven, and Daniel Ziblatt. *How Democracies Die.* New York: Crown, 2018.

Levitt, Justin. "A Comprehensive Investigation of Voter Impersonation Finds 31 Credible Incidents Out of One Billion Ballots Cast." *Washington Post*, August 6, 2014.

———. "Intent Is Enough: Invidious Partisanship in Redistricting." *William and Mary Law Review* 59 (2017): 1993–2051.

———. "Litigation in the 2010 Cycle." All About Redistricting (website), 2018. http://redistricting.lls.edu/cases.php.

———. "New State Voting Laws: Barriers to the Ballot?" Statement before Subcommittee on Constitution, Civil Rights and Human Rights of the Committee on the Judiciary, US Senate, 112th Cong., 1st session, September 8, 2011.

———. "The Partisanship Spectrum." *William and Mary Law Review* 55 (2014): 1787–1868.

———. "Professor Justin Levitt's Guide to Drawing the Lines." All About Redistricting (website), 2017. http://redistricting.lls.edu/.

———. "The Truth about Voter Fraud." Brennan Center for Justice, 2007. https://www.brennancenter.org/sites/defalt/files/legacy/The%20Truth%20About%20Voter%20Fraud.pdf.

Levy, Jacob T. "Democracy for Republicans: Simple Voting Rules for a Complex World." Niskanen Center, February 20, 2019.

Lewis, Simon, and Julia Harte. "Chaotic Wisconsin Election Signals Virus-Related Voting Battles Ahead." Reuters, April 8, 2020. https://www.reuters.com/article/us-usa-election-voting-rights-insight/chaotic-wisconsin-election-signals-virus-related-voting-battles-ahead-idUSKCN21R01L.

Li, Quan, Michael J. Pomante II, and Scot Schraufnagel. "Cost of Voting in the American States." *Election Law Journal* 17, no. 3 (2018): 234–247.

Lichtblau, Eric. "Long Battle by Foes of Campaign Finance Rules Shifts Landscape." *New York Times*, October 15, 2015.

Lieb, David A. "AP: GOP Won More Seats in 2018 than Suggested by Vote Share." AP News, March 21, 2019.

Liebelson, Dana. "The Supreme Court Gutted the Voting Rights Act. What Happened Next in These 8 States Will Not Shock You." *Mother Jones*, April 8, 2014.

Lindgren, Eric, and Priscilla Southwell. "The Effect of Redistricting Commissions on Electoral Competitiveness in U.S. House Elections, 2002–2010." *Journal of Law and Politics* 6, no. 2 (2013): 13–18.

Liptak, Adam. "How Conservatives Weaponized the First Amendment." *New York Times*, June 30, 2018.

Litman, Leah M. "Inventing Equal Sovereignty." *Michigan Law Review* 114 (2016): 1207–1273.

Lloyd, Randall D. "Separating Partisanship from Party in Judicial Research: Reapportionment in the U.S. District Courts." *American Political Science Review* 89, no. 2 (1995): 413–420.

Lopez, Tomas. "*Shelby County*: One Year Later." Brennan Center for Justice, June 24, 2014. http://www.brennancenter.org/analysis/shelby-county-one-year-later.

Lovell, George I. *Legislative Deferrals: Statutory Ambiguity, Judicial Power, and American Democracy.* New York: Cambridge University Press, 2003.

Lowenstein, Daniel H. "*Vieth*'s Gap: Has the Supreme Court Gone from Bad to Worse on Partisan Gerrymandering?" *Cornell Journal of Law and Public Policy* 14 (2005): 367–395.

Lowenstein, Daniel H., and Jonathan Steinberg. "The Quest for Legislative Districting in the Public Interest: Elusive or Illusory?" *UCLA Law Review* 33 (1985) 1–75.

Lublin, David. *The Paradox of Representation: Racial Gerrymandering and Minority Interests in Congress.* Princeton, NJ: Princeton University Press, 1997.

Maltzman, Forrest, James F. Spriggs II, and Paul J. Wahlbeck. *Crafting Law on the Supreme Court: The Collegial Game.* New York: Cambridge University Press, 2000.

Mann, Thomas E., and Norman J. Ornstein. "Let's Just Say It: The Republicans Are the Problem." *Washington Post,* April 27, 2012.

Martin, Andrew, and Kevin Quinn. "Dynamic Ideal Point Estimation via Markov Chain Monte Carlo for the U.S. Supreme Court, 1953–1999." *Political Analysis* 10, no. 2 (2002): 134–153.

Martinez, Jessica, and Gregory A. Smith, "How the Faithful Voted: A Preliminary 2016 Analysis." Pew Research Center, November 9, 2016.

Marvit, Moshe Z. "For 60 Years, This Powerful Conservative Group Has Worked to Crush Labor." *Nation,* July 5, 2018.

Masket, Seth E., Jonathan Winburn, and Gerald C. Wright. "The Gerrymanderers Are Coming! Legislative Redistricting Won't Affect Competition or Polarization Much, No Matter Who Does It." *Political Science and Politics* 45, no. 1 (2012): 39–43.

Maveety, Nancy. *Picking Judges.* New Brunswick, NJ: Transaction, 2016.

May, Gary. *Bending toward Justice: The Voting Rights Act and the Transformation of American Democracy.* New York: Basic, 2013.

McCann, Michael W. *Rights at Work: Pay Equity Reform and the Politics of Legal Mobilization.* Chicago: University of Chicago Press, 1994.

McCarthy, Justin. "Four in Five Americans Support Voter ID Laws, Early Voting." *Gallup News,* August 22, 2016. https://news.gallup.com/poll/194741/four-five-americans-support-voter-laws-early-voting.aspx.

McCarty, Nolan, Keith T. Poole, and Howard Rosenthal. *Polarized America: The Dance of Ideology and Unequal Riches.* Cambridge, MA: MIT Press, 2006.

McCloskey, Robert G. "The Supreme Court, 1961 Term—Foreword: The Reapportionment Case." *Harvard Law Review* 76 (1962): 54–222.

McConnell, Michael. "The Redistricting Cases: Original Mistakes and Current Consequences." *Harvard Journal of Law and Public Policy* 24 (2000): 103–118.

McCready, Dan. "Voter Fraud Is Part of the G.O.P. Playbook." *New York Times,* April 24, 2020.

McCubbins, Mathew D., and Thomas Schwartz. "Congress, the Courts, and Public Policy: Consequences of the One Man, One Vote Rule." *American Journal of Political Science* 32, no. 2 (1988): 388–415.

McDonald, Michael. "The 2010 Midterm Elections: Signs and Portents for the Decennial Redistricting. *Political Science and Politics* 44, no. 2 (2011): 311–315.

McDonald, Michael D., and Robin E. Best. "Unfair Partisan Gerrymanders in Politics and Law: A Diagnostic Applied to Six Cases." *Election Law Journal* 14, no. 4 (2015): 312–330.

McElwee, Sean. "The GOP's Stunning Election Advantage." *Salon*, December 5, 2015.

McGann, Anthony J., Charles Anthony Smith, Michael Latner, and Alex Keena. *Gerrymandering in America: The House of Representatives, the Supreme Court, and the Future of Popular Sovereignty*. New York: Cambridge University Press, 2016.

McGhee, Eric. "Measuring Partisan Bias in Single-Member District Electoral Systems." *Legislative Studies Quarterly* 39, no. 1 (2014): 55–85.

McGuane, Matthew J. "*Crawford v. Marion County Election Board*: The Disenfranchised Must Wait." *University of Miami Law Review* 64 (2009): 713–734.

McKee, Seth C. "Majority Black Districts, Republican Ascendancy, and Party Competition in the South, 1988–2000." *American Review of Politics* 23 (2002): 123–139.

———. "Politics Is Local: State Legislator Voting on Restrictive Voter Identification Legislation." *Research and Politics* 2 (2015): 1–7.

McKenzie, Mark Jonathan. "Beyond Partisanship? An Analysis of Judicial Decisions on Redistricting in State Supreme Courts." Paper presented at the annual meeting of the Midwest Political Science Association, Chicago, April 2010.

———. "The Influence of Partisanship, Ideology, and the Law on Redistricting Decisions in the Federal Courts." *Political Research Quarterly* 65, no. 4 (2012): 799–813.

McMahon, Kevin J. "The Justices Decide: Analyzing Attitudes, Politics and the Law (reviewing Bailey and Maltzman, *The Constrained Court*, Stephen Engel, *American Politicians Confront the Court*, and Pacelle, Curry and Marshall's *Decision Making by the Supreme Court*)." *Tulsa Law Review* 48 (2012): 265–274.

———. *Nixon's Court: His Challenge to Judicial Liberalism and Its Political Consequences*. Chicago: University of Chicago Press, 2011.

———. *Reconsidering Roosevelt on Race: How the Presidency Paved the Road to* Brown. Chicago: University of Chicago Press, 2004.

———. "Will the Supreme Court Still 'Seldom Stray Very Far?': Regime Politics in a Polarized America." *Chicago-Kent Law Review* 93 (2018): 343–371.

Mellnik, Ted, and Kate Rabinowitz. "Where a Citizenship Question Could Cause the Census to Miss Millions of Hispanics—and Why That's a Big Deal." *Washington Post*, June 6, 2019.

Mencimer, Stephanie. "Conservatives Say They Want Another Antonin Scalia. They Really Want Another Sam Alito." *Mother Jones*, May/June 2016.

Miceli, Thomas J., and Metin M. Cosgel. "Reputation and Judicial Decision-Making." *Journal of Law, Economics and Organization* 23 (1994): 31–51.

Milbank, Dana. "An Explosion Is Coming." *Washington Post*, June 29, 2018.

Miles, Thomas J., and Cass R. Sunstein. "The New Legal Realism." *University of Chicago Law Review* 75 (2008): 831–851.

———. "The Real World of Arbitrariness Review." *University of Chicago Law Review* 75 (2008): 761–814.

Minnite, Lorraine C. *The Myth of Voter Fraud*. Ithaca, NY: Cornell University Press, 2010.

———. "Voter Identification Laws: The Controversy over Voter Fraud." In *Law and Elections Politics: The Rules of the Game*, 2nd ed., ed. Matthew J. Streb, 88–133. New York: Routledge, 2013.

"The Minority Majority: America's Electoral System Gives the Republicans Advantages over Democrats." *Economist*, July 12, 2018.

Moraski, Byron J., and Charles R. Shipan. "The Politics of Supreme Court Nominations: A Theory of Institutional Constraints and Choices." *American Journal of Political Science* 43 (1999): 1069–1095.

Mudde, Cas. "The 2014 Hungarian Parliamentary Elections, or How to Craft a Constitutional Majority." *Washington Post*, April 14, 2014.

Mulroy, Steven. *Rethinking U.S. Election Law: Unskewing the System.* Northampton, MA: Edward Elgar, 2018.

Murphy, Walter. *Elements of Judicial Strategy.* Chicago: University of Chicago Press, 1964.

Mutch, Robert E. *Buying the Vote: A History of Campaign Finance Reform.* New York: Oxford University Press, 2014.

Mycoff, Jason D., Michael W. Wagner, and David C. Wilson. "The Empirical Effects of Voter-ID Laws: Present or Absent?" *PS: Political Science and Politics* 42 (2009): 121–126.

Nackenoff, Carol. "What Became of Fundamental Rights? Of Voter IDs and Voting Rights." Paper presented at the "Constitutional Schmooze" at the University of Maryland, February 2014. https://digitalcomons.law.umaryland.edu/schmooze_papers/195/.

Nagel, Stuart. "Multiple Correlation of Judicial Backgrounds and Decisions." *Florida State University Law Review* 2 (1974): 258–280.

———. "Political Party Affiliation and Judges' Decisions." *Political Science Review* 55 (1961): 843–850.

Najmabadi, Shannon. "Meet the Math Professor Who's Fighting Gerrymandering with Geometry." *Chronicle of Higher Education*, February 22, 2017.

National Association for the Advancement of Colored People Legal Defense and Educational Fund. "Democracy Diminished: State and Local Threats to Voting Post-*Shelby County, Alabama v. Holder.*" 2016. https://www.naacpldf.org/wp-content/uploads/Democracy-Diminished-State-and-Local-Threats-to-Voting-Post-Shelby-County-Alabama-v.-Holder.pdf.

National Conference of State Legislatures. "Campaign Finance Legislation Database/2015 Onward." May 7, 2019. http://www.ncsl.org/research/elections-and-campaigns/campaign-finance-database-2015-onward.aspx.

———. "*Citizens United* and the States." July 21, 2016. http://www.ncsl.org/research/elections-and-campaigns/citizens-united-and-the-states.aspx.

———. "Redistricting Commissions." January 9, 2020. https://www.ncsl.org/research/redistricting/2009-redistricting-commissions-table.aspx.

———. "Redistricting Criteria." April 23, 2019. http://www.ncsl.org/research/redistricting/redistricting-criteria.aspx.

———. "Redistricting Legislation Database: 2018 Onward." April 30, 2019. http://www.ncsl.org/research/redistricting/redistricting-legislation-database.aspx.

———. "2015 Redistricting Legislation." December 30, 2015. http://www.ncsl
.org/research/redistricting/2015-redistricting-legislation.aspx.

———. "Voter Identification Requirements/Voter ID Laws." January 17, 2019.
http://www.ncsl.org/research/elections-and-campaigns/voter-id.aspx.

Neiheisel, Jacob R., and Rich Horner, "Voter Identification Requirements and
Aggregate Turnout in the U.S.: How Campaigns Offset the Costs of Turning out When Voting Is Made More Difficult." *Election Law Journal* 18, no. 3
(2019): 227–242.

Nelson, Kjersten R., and Eve M. Ringsmuth. "Departures from the Court: The
Political Landscape and Institutional Constraints." *American Politics Research*
37 (2009): 486–507.

Nemacheck, Christine L. *Strategic Selection: Presidential Nomination of Supreme
Court Justices from Herbert Hoover through George W. Bush.* Charlottesville: University of Virginia Press, 2007.

Newkirk, Vann R., II. "The Department of Justice Stands by Texas's Voter ID
Law." *Atlantic,* July 8, 2017.

———. "How Redistricting Became a Technological Arms Race." *Atlantic,* October 28, 2017.

New York Times Editorial Board. "Kris Kobach's Voting Sham Gets Exposed in
Court." *New York Times,* March 17, 2018.

Nichols, John. "'*Janus*' Was Decided by Conservative Judicial Activists Who Are
Legislating from the Bench." *Nation,* June 27, 2018.

Nixon, David C., and J. David Haskin. "Judicial Retirement Strategies—The
Judge's Role in Influencing Party Control of the Appellate Courts." *American
Political Quarterly* 28 (2000): 458–489.

Norpoth, Helmut, and Jeffrey A. Segal. "Popular Influence on Supreme Court
Decisions: Comment." *American Political Science Review* 88 (1994) 711–716.

Obama, Barack. "The *Citizens United* Decision Was Wrong." Press release, January 21, 2015. https://www.whitehouse.gov/the-press-office/2015/01/21
/statement-president.

Office of Legal Policy, US Department of Justice. "Guidelines on Constitutional
Litigation." 1988.

Office of Legal Policy, US Department of Justice, Report to the Attorney General. "The Constitution in the Year 2000: Choices Ahead in Constitutional
Interpretation." 1988.

Oreskes, Benjamin. "Clinton Pledges Constitutional Amendment to Overturn
Citizens United Ruling." *Politico,* July 16, 2016.

O'Rourke, Timothy. *The Impact of Reapportionment.* New Brunswick, NJ: Transaction, 1980.

Owens, Ryan J., and Justin P. Wedeking. "Justices and Legal Clarity: Analyzing
the Complexity of U.S. Supreme Court Opinions." *Law and Society Review* 45
(2011): 1027–1061.

Pacelle, Richard L., Jr. *The Transformation of the Supreme Court's Agenda: From the
New Deal to the Reagan Administration.* Boulder, CO: Westview, 1991.

Pacelle, Richard L., Jr., Brett W. Curry, and Bryan W. Marshall. *Decision Making
by the Supreme Court.* New York: Cambridge University Press, 2011.

Parker, Kim, Juliana Menasce, Anna Brown Horowitz, Richard Fry, D'Vera Cohn, and Ruth Igielnik. "What Unites and Divides Urban, Suburban and Rural Communities." Pew Research Center, May 22, 2018. https://www .pewsocialtrends.org/2018/05/22/demographic-and-economic-trends-in -urban-suburban-and-rural-communities/.

Pastor, Robert A., Robert Santos, Alison Prevost, and Vassia Stoilov. "Voting and ID Requirements: A Survey of Registered Voters in Three States." *American Review of Public Administration* 40 (2010): 461–481.

Peppers, Todd C., and Christopher Zorn. "Law Clerk Influence on Supreme Court Decision Making: An Empirical Assessment." *DePaul Law Review* 58, no. 1 (2008): 51–77.

Peress, Michael, and Yangzi Zhao. "How Many Seats in Congress Is Control of Redistricting Worth?" *Legislative Studies Quarterly* 45 (2020).

Peretti, Terri. "Constructing the State Action Doctrine, 1940–1990." *Law and Social Inquiry* 35 (2010): 273–310.

———. "Democracy-Assisting Judicial Review and the Challenge of Partisan Polarization." *Utah Law Review* (2014): 843–866.

———. *In Defense of a Political Court.* Princeton, NJ: Princeton University Press, 1999.

———. "Judicial Partisanship in Voter Identification Litigation." *Election Law Journal* 15 (2016): 214–231.

———. "Where Have All the Politicians Gone? Recruiting for the Modern Supreme Court." *Judicature* 91, no. 3 (2007): 112–122.

Peretti, Terri, and Alan Rozzi. "Modern Departures from the Supreme Court: Party, Pensions, or Power?" *Quinnipiac Law Review* 30 (2011): 131–161.

Persily, Nathaniel. "The Court's Campaign Finance Jurisprudence and Its Impact on the Electoral Process." SCOTUSblog, November 8, 2011. https:// www.scotusblog.com/community/the-court's-campaign-finance-jurispru dence-and-its-impact-on-the-electoral-process/.

———. "Reply: In Defense of Foxes Guarding Henhouses: The Case for Judicial Acquiescence to Incumbent Protecting Activities." *Harvard Law Review* 116 (2002): 649–683.

———. "When Judges Carve Democracies: A Primer on Court-Drawn Redistricting Plans." *George Washington University Law Review* 73 (2005): 1701–1739.

Peterson, Jordan Carr. "The Mask of Neutrality: Judicial Partisan Calculation and Legislative Redistricting." *Law and Policy* 41, no. 3 (2019): 336–359.

Petrocik, John R., and Scott W. Desposato. "The Partisan Consequences of Majority-Minority Redistricting in the South, 1991 and 1994." *Journal of Politics* 60 (1998): 613–633.

Pettys, Todd E. "Free Expression, In-Group Bias, and the Court's Conservatives: A Critique of the Epstein-Parker-Segal Study." *Buffalo Law Review* 63, no. 1 (2015): 1–83.

Pew Research Center. "In U.S., Decline of Christianity Continues at Rapid Pace." October 17, 2019. https://www.pewforum.org/2019/10/17/in-u-s -decline-of-christianity-continues-at-rapid-pace/.

———. "U.S. Public Becoming Less Religious." November 3, 2015. http://www.pewforum.org/2015/11/03/u-s-public-becoming-less-religious/.

Pickerill, J. Mitchell, and Cornell W. Clayton. "The Rehnquist Court and the Political Dynamics of Federalism." *Perspectives on Politics* 2 (2004): 233–248.

Pierre, Robert E. "Botched Name Purge Denied Some the Right to Vote." *Washington Post*, May 31, 2001.

Pildes, Richard H. "The Court's Campaign Finance Jurisprudence and Its Impact on the Electoral Process." SCOTUSblog, November 8, 2011. https://www.scotusblog.com/community/the-court's-campaign-finance-jurisprudence-and-its-impact-on-the-electoral-process/.

———. "Is Voting-Rights Law Now at War with Itself? Social Science and Voting Rights in the 2000s." *North Carolina Law Review* 80 (2002): 1517–1573.

———. "Political Avoidance, Constitutional Theory, and the VRA." *Yale Law Journal Pocket Part* 117 (2007): 148. http://yalelawjournal.org/forum/political-avoidance-constitutional-theory-and-the-vra.

———. "Romanticizing Democracy, Political Fragmentation, and the Decline of American Government." *Yale Law Journal* 124 (2014): 804–852.

———. "What Does the Court's Decision Mean?" *Election Law Journal* 12 (2013): 317–318.

Pinello, Daniel R. "Linking Party to Judicial Ideology in American Courts: A Meta-Analysis." *Justice System Journal* 20, no. 3 (1999): 219–254.

Pippinger, Nathan. "John Roberts and the Shifting Politics of Race." *Democracy: The Alcove*, October 27, 2016.

Plunkitt, Senator George W. "Tammany's Plans Outlined." *Good Government* 21, no. 1 (1904): 15.

"Political Nonprofits (Dark Money)." OpenSecrets.org, Center for Responsive Politics. https://www.opensecrets.org/outsidespending/nonprof_summ.php (accessed February 11, 2020).

Polsby, Daniel D., and Robert D. Popper. "The Third Criterion: Compactness as a Procedural Safeguard against Partisan Gerrymandering." *Yale Law and Policy Review* 9, no. 2 (1991): 301–353.

Posner, Eric A. "Does Political Bias in the Judiciary Matter: Implications of Judicial Bias Studies for Legal and Constitutional Reform." *University of Chicago Law Review* 85 (2008): 853–883.

Posner, Richard A. *Overcoming Law*. Cambridge, MA: Harvard University Press, 1995.

———. "The Voting Rights Act Ruling Is about the Conservative Imagination." *Slate*, June 26, 2013.

———. "What Do Judges and Justices Maximize? (The Same Thing Everybody Else Does)." *Supreme Court Economic Review* 3 (1993): 1–41.

Post, Robert C. *Citizens Divided: Campaign Finance Reform and the Constitution*. Cambridge, MA: Harvard University Press, 2014.

———. "Justice William J. Brennan and the Warren Court." *Constitutional Commentary* 8 (1991): 11–25.

Pound, Roscoe. "Liberty of Contract." *Yale Law Journal* 18 (1909): 454–487.

Powe, Lucas A., Jr. *The Warren Court and American Politics*. Cambridge, MA: Harvard University Press, 2002.

———. "The Warren Court and the Political Process." In *The American Congress: The Building of Democracy*, ed. Julian E. Zelizer, 548–556. New York: Houghton Mifflin, 2004.

Pritchett, C. Herman. *The Roosevelt Court: A Study in Judicial Politics and Values, 1937–47*. New York: Macmillan, 1948.

Purdy, Jedediah. "That We Are Underlings: The Real Problems in Disciplining Political Spending and the First Amendment." *Constitutional Commentary* 30 (2015): 391–402.

Rachlinski, Jeffrey J., Sheri Lynn Johnson, Andrew J. Wistrich, and Chris Guthrie. "Does Unconscious Racial Bias Affect Trial Judges?" *Notre Dame Law Review* 84 (2009): 1195–1246.

Rainey, Rebecca, and Ian Kullgren. "1 Year after *Janus*, Unions Are Flush." *Politico*, May 17, 2020.

Ramji-Nogales, Jaya, Andres I. Schoenholtz, and Phillip G. Schrag. "Refugee Roulette: Disparities in Asylum Adjudication." *Stanford Law Review* 60 (2007): 295–411.

Rasmussen Reports. "Voters Want IDs at the Polls, Don't See Them as Discriminatory." *Rasmussen Reports*, October 3, 2018.

Replogle, Ron. "The Scope of Representation-Reinforcing Judicial Review." *Columbia Law Review* 92, no. 6 (1992): 1592–1624.

Revesz, Richard L. "Environmental Regulation, Ideology, and the D.C. Circuit." *Virginia Law Review* 83 (1997): 1717–1772.

Reynolds, Molly E. "Republicans in Congress Got a 'Seats Bonus' This Election (Again)." *Brookings Institution FixGov* (blog), November 22, 2016. https://www.brookings.edu/blog/fixgov/2016/11/22/gop-seats-bonus-in-congress/.

Rhodes, Jesse H. *Ballot Blocked: The Political Erosion of the Voting Rights Act*. Palo Alto, CA: Stanford University Press, 2017.

Richards, Mark J., and Herbert M. Kritzer. "Jurisprudential Regimes in Supreme Court Decision Making." *American Political Science Review* 96, no. 2 (2002): 305–320.

Richman, Jesse T., Gulshan A. Chattha, and David C. Earnest. "Do Non-citizens Vote in U.S. Elections?" *Electoral Studies* 36 (2014): 149–157.

Rocha, Rene R., and Tetsuya Matsubayashi. "The Politics of Race and Voter ID Laws in the States: The Return of Jim Crow?" *Political Research Quarterly* 67, no. 3 (2014): 666–679.

Rodden, Jonathan. *Why Cities Lose: Political Geography and the Representation of the Left*. New York: Basic, 2009.

Rodden, Jonathan, and Jowei Chen. "Unintentional Gerrymandering: Political Geography and Electoral Bias in Legislatures." *Quarterly Journal of Political Science* 8 (2013): 239–269.

Rodriguez, Victor Andres. "Section 5 of the Voting Rights Act of 1965 after *Boerne*: The Beginning of the End of Preclearance?" *California Law Review* 91, no. 3 (2003): 769–826.

Rogowski, Jon C., and Cathy J. Cohen. "The Racial Impact of Voter Identification Laws in the 2012 Election." Black Youth Project, November 2015. black youthproject.com/wp-content/uploads/2015/11/voter_id_after_2008 .pdf.

Rohde, David W., and Harold J. Spaeth. *Supreme Court Decision Making.* San Francisco: W. H. Freeman, 1976.

Roper Center. "How Groups Voted 2016." 2016. https://ropercenter.cornell .edu/polls/us-elections/how-groups-voted/groups-voted-2016/.

Rosen, Jeffrey. "'Give Us the Ballot,' by Ari Berman." *New York Times/Sunday Book Review,* August 25, 2015.

———. *The Most Democratic Branch: How the Courts Serve America.* New York: Oxford University Press, 2006.

Rosenberg, Gerald N. *The Hollow Hope: Can Courts Bring About Social Change?,* 2nd ed. Chicago: University of Chicago Press, 2008.

Ross, Bertrall L., II. "Paths of Resistance to Our Imperial First Amendment." Review of *Citizens Divided: Campaign Finance Reform and the Constitution,* by Robert C. Post. *Michigan Law Review* 113 (2015): 917–942.

Rove, Karl. "The GOP Targets State Legislatures: He Who Controls Redistricting Can Control Congress." *Wall Street Journal,* March 3, 2010.

———. "The National Battle for Redistricting." *Republican State Leadership Committee News,* September 5, 2019. https://rslc.gop/news/2019/09/05/the -national-battle-for-redistricting/.

Rowland, C. K., and Robert A. Carp. *Politics and Judgment in Federal District Courts.* Lawrence: University Press of Kansas, 1996.

Rubin, Jennifer. "GOP Autopsy Report Goes Bold." *Washington Post,* March 18, 2013.

Rush, Mark. "*Shelby County v. Holder*: A Case of Judicial *Hubris* or a Clash of Ancient Principles?" *Election Law Journal* 12, no. 3 (2013): 322–323.

Rutenberg, Jim. "A Dream Undone: Inside the 50-Year Campaign to Roll Back the Voting Rights Act." *New York Times Magazine,* July 29, 2015.

———. "Nine Years Ago, Republicans Favored Voting Rights. What Happened?" *New York Times Magazine,* August 12, 2015.

Salamone, Michael F. *Perceptions of a Polarized Court: How Division among Justices Shapes the Supreme Court's Public Image.* Philadelphia: Temple University Press, 2018.

Salisbury, Robert H., and Michael MacKuen. "On the Study of Party Realignment." *Journal of Politics* 43, no. 2 (1981): 523–530.

Savage, David G., and Henry Weinstein. "Right to Vote Led Justices to 5–4 Ruling." *Los Angeles Times,* December 14, 2000.

Schanzenbach, Max M., and Emerson H. Tiller. "Reviewing the Sentencing Guidelines: Judicial Politics, Empirical Evidence, and Reform." *University of Chicago Law Review* 75 (2008): 715–760.

Scheiber, Noam. "Supreme Court Labor Decision Wasn't Just a Loss for Unions." *New York Times,* July 1, 2018.

Scheppele, Kim Lane. "Hungary and the End of Politics." *Nation,* May 6, 2014.

———. "Legal but Not Fair: Viktor Orban's New Supermajority." *Conscience of a Liberal* (blog), April 13, 2014.

Schickler, Eric. *Racial Realignment: The Transformation of American Liberalism, 1932–1965.* Princeton, NJ: Princeton University Press, 2016.

Schmidhauser, John R. "The Justices of the Supreme Court: A Collective Portrait." *Midwest Journal of Political Science* 3 (1959): 1–57.

Schneider, Elena. "The Biggest Threat to the GOP Majority No One's Talking About." *Politico*, September 14, 2018.

Schubert, Glendon, ed. *Judicial Decision-Making.* New York: Free Press, 1963.

———. *The Judicial Mind.* Chicago: Northwestern University Press, 1965.

———. *The Judicial Mind Revisited: Psychometric Analysis of Supreme Court Ideology.* San Francisco: W. H. Freeman, 1974.

———. *Quantitative Analysis of Judicial Behavior.* Glencoe, IL: Free Press, 1959.

———. "The 1960 Term of the Supreme Court." *American Journal of Political Science* 56, no. 1 (1962): 90–107.

Schuck, Peter. "The Thickest Thicket: Partisan Gerrymandering and Judicial Regulation of Politics." *Columbia Law Review* 87, no. 7 (1987): 1325–1384.

Schultz, David A. "Less Than Fundamental: The Myth of Voter Fraud and the Coming of the Second Great Disenfranchisement." *William Mitchell Law Review* 34 (2008): 483–532.

———. "Regulating the Political Thicket: Congress, the Courts, and State Reapportionment Commissions." *Charleston Law Review* 3 (2008):109–145.

Schwartz, Herman. "The Public Doesn't Support Restrictive Voter ID Laws, but Many New Ones Will Be in Force in 2016." Reuters, December 8, 2015. https://blogs.reuters.com/great-debate/2015/12/08/the-public-does-not -support-voter-id-laws-but-many-new-ones-will-be-in-force-in-2016/.

Seabrook, Nicholas R. *Drawing the Lines: Constraints on Partisan Gerrymandering in U.S. Politics.* Ithaca, NY: Cornell University Press, 2017.

Segal, Jeffrey A., Charles M. Cameron, and Albert D. Cover. "A Spatial Model of Roll Call Voting: Senators, Constituents, Presidents, and Interest Groups in Supreme Court Confirmations." *American Journal of Political Science* 36, no. 1 (1992): 96–121.

Segal, Jeffrey A., and Albert Cover. "Ideological Values and the Votes of U.S. Supreme Court Justices." *American Political Science Review* 83, no. 2 (1989): 557–565.

Segal, Jeffrey A., and Harold J. Spaeth. *The Supreme Court and the Attitudinal Model.* New York: Cambridge University Press, 1993.

———. *The Supreme Court and the Attitudinal Model Revisited.* New York: Cambridge University Press, 2002.

Semuels, Alana. "Is This the End of Public-Sector Unions in America?" *Atlantic*, June 27, 2018.

Shanor, Amanda. "The New *Lochner*." *Wisconsin Law Review* 2016 (2016): 133–206.

Shapiro, Martin M. "The Constitution and Economic Rights." In *Essays on the Constitution of the United States*, ed. M. Judd Harmon, 74–98. Port Washington, NY: Kennikat, 1978.

———. "Gerrymandering, Unfairness, and the Supreme Court." *UCLA Law Review* 33 (1985): 227–256.

———. "The Supreme Court: From Warren to Burger." In *The New American Political System,* ed. Anthony King, 179–211. Washington, DC: American Enterprise Institute, 1978.

Shotts, Kenneth W. "Does Racial Redistricting Cause Conservative Policy Outcomes? Policy Preferences of Southern Representatives in the 1980s and 1990s." *Journal of Politics* 65, 1 (2003): 216–226.

———. "The Effect of Majority-Minority Mandates on Partisan Gerrymandering." *American Journal of Political Science* 45, no. 1 (2001): 120–135.

Siddiqui, Sabrina. "Democrats Got Millions More Votes—so How Did Republicans Win the Senate?" *Guardian,* November 8, 2018.

Sides, John, and Eric McGhee. "Redistricting Didn't Win Republicans the House." *Washington Post,* February 17, 2013.

Siegel, Neil S. "The Distinctive Role of Justice Samuel Alito: From a Politics of Restoration to a Politics of Dissent." *Yale Law Journal Forum* 126 (2016): 164–177.

Silver, Nate. "Measuring the Effects of Voter Identification Laws." *New York Times,* July 15, 2012.

Sindler, Allan P. "*Baker v. Carr:* How to 'Sear the Conscience' of Legislators." *Yale Law Journal* 72 (1962): 23–38.

Sisk, Gregory C., Michael Heise, and Andrew P. Morris. "Searching for the Soul of Judicial Decision Making: An Empirical Study of Religious Freedom Decisions." *Ohio State Law Journal* 65 (2004): 491–614.

Skelley, Geoffrey, and Kyle Kondik. "2018 Governors: The Battle Lines for Drawing the Lines." *Sabato's Crystal Ball,* February 23, 2017. http://crystalball.centerforpolitics.org/crystalball/articles/2018-governors-the-battle-lines-for-drawing-the-lines/.

Skowronek, Stephen. *The Politics Presidents Make: Leadership from John Adams to Bill Clinton.* Cambridge, MA: Harvard University Press, 1997.

———. *Presidential Leadership in Political Time: Reprise and Reappraisal,* 2nd ed. Lawrence: University Press of Kansas, 2011.

———. *Presidential Leadership in Political Time,* 3rd ed. Lawrence: University Press of Kansas, 2020.

Smith, Charles Anthony, and Christopher Shortell. "The Suits That Counted: The Judicialization of Presidential Elections." *Election Law Journal* 6, no. 3 (2007): 251–265.

Smith, J. Douglas. *On Democracy's Doorstep: The Inside Story of How the Supreme Court Brought 'One Person, One Vote' to the United States.* New York: Hill & Wang, 2014.

Smith, Melissa, and Larry Powell, *Dark Money, Super PACs, and the 2012 Election.* New York: Lexington, 2013.

Smith, Michael A. "Minority Representation and Majority-Minority Districts after *Shaw v. Reno:* Legal Challenges, Empirical Evidence and Alternate Approaches." *Politics and Policy* 29 (2001): 239–263.

Smith, Robert Ellis, and Richard Sobel. "Demands for Voter Identification Require a Constitutional Standard of Reasonable Suspicion of Illegal Activity." *PS: Political Science and Politics* 42, no. 1 (2009): 103–105.

Smooth, Wendy. "Gendering Redistricting: Race, Gender, and the New South-ern Strategy." Paper presented at the annual meeting of the National Conference of Black Political Scientists (NCOBPS), 2016. https://ssrn.co /abstract=2684927.

Sobel, Richard. "The High Cost of 'Free' Photo Voter Identification Cards." Charles Hamilton Houston Institute for Race and Justice, Harvard Law School, 2014. https://today.law.harvard.edu/wp-content/uploads/2014 /06/FullReportVoterIDJune20141.pdf.

Solum, Lawrence. "I'm Gonna Get High, High, High, or Deconstructing the Up-Down Distinction Revisited." Legal Theory Blog, May 4, 2003. http://lso lum.typepad.com/legaltheory/2003/05/im_gonna_get_hi.html.

———. "The Positive Foundations of Formalism: False Necessity and American Legal Realism." Harvard Law Review 120 (2014): 2464–2497.

Songer, Donald R. "Consensual and Nonconsensual Decisions in Unanimous Opinions of the United States Courts of Appeals." American Journal of Politi-cal Science 26 (1982): 225–239.

Songer, Donald R., and Sue Davis. "The Impact of Party and Region on Voting Decisions in the United States Courts of Appeals, 1955–1986." Western Politi-cal Quarterly 43 (1990): 317–334.

Southworth, Ann. "The Consequences of Citizens United: What Do the Lawyers Say?" Chicago-Kent Law Review 93 (2018): 525–560.

———. "Elements of the Support Structure for Campaign Finance Litigation in the Roberts Court." Law and Social Inquiry 43, no. 2 (2018): 319–359.

Spaeth, Harold J. "An Analysis of Judicial Attitudes in the Labor Relations Deci-sions of the Warren Court." Journal of Politics 25 (1963): 290–311.

———. "An Approach to the Study of Attitudinal Differences as an Aspect of Judicial Behavior." Midwest Journal of Political Science 5 (1961): 165–180.

———. Supreme Court Policy Making: Explanation and Prediction. San Francisco: W. H. Freeman, 1979.

Spaeth, Harold J., Lee Epstein, Andrew D. Martin, Jeffrey A. Segal, Theodore J. Ruger, and Sara C. Benesh. Supreme Court Database, Version 2018 Release 01. http://supremecourtdatabase.org (accessed April 22, 2019).

Spaeth, Harold J., David M. Meltz, Gregory J. Rathjen, Michael V. Haselswerdt. "Is Justice Blind: An Empirical Investigation of a Normative Ideal." Law and Society Review 7, no. 1 (1972): 119–138.

Spaeth, Harold J., and Douglas R. Parker. "Effects of Attitude toward Situa-tion upon Attitude toward Object." Journal of Psychology 73, no. 2 (1969): 173–182.

Sparks, Grace. "The Majority of Americans Tend to Agree with Democrats on Top Issues, Polling Shows." CNN, April 7, 2019. https://www.cnn.com/2019 /04/07/politcis/democratic-positions-majority/index.html.

Spriggs, James F., and Paul J. Wahlbeck. "Calling It Quits: Strategic Retirement on the Federal Courts of Appeals, 1893–1991." Political Research Quarterly 48 (1995): 573–597.

Squire, Peverill. "Politics and Personal Factors in Retirement from the United States Supreme Court." Political Behavior 10 (1988): 180–190.

Staudt, Nancy C. "Modeling Standing." *New York University Law Review* 79 (2004): 612–684.

Stephanopoulos, Nicholas O. "Aligning Campaign Finance Law." *Virginia Law Review* 101 (2015): 1425–1500.

———. "The Causes and Consequences of Gerrymandering." *William and Mary Law Review* 59 (2018): 2115–2149.

———. "Lessons from Litigating for Reform." *Election Law Journal* 16, no. 2 (2017): 230–236.

———. "Our Electoral Exceptionalism." *University of Chicago Law Review* 80 (2013): 769–858.

Stephanopoulos, Nicholas, and Eric McGhee. "Partisan Gerrymandering and the Efficiency Gap." *University of Chicago Law Review* 82 (2015): 831–900.

Stern, Mark Joseph. "The Supreme Court Punted on Partisan Gerrymandering. The Fight to Kill It Is Far from Over." *Slate,* June 18, 2018.

Stewart III, Charles. "Voter ID: Who Has Them? Who Shows Them?" *Oklahoma Law Review* 66 (2013): 21–52.

Stewart III, Charles, Stephen Ansolabehere, and Nathaniel Persily. "Revisiting Public Opinion on Voter Identification and Voter Fraud in an Era of Increasing Partisan Polarization." *Stanford Law Review* 68 (2016): 1455–1489.

Stokes, Donald E. "Minority Representation and the Tradeoffs in Legislative Redistricting." In *Race and Representation,* ed. Georgia A. Persons, 27–34. New Brunswick, NJ: Transaction, 1997.

Stone, Geoffrey R. "*Citizens United* and Conservative Judicial Activism." *University of Illinois Law Review* 2012, no. 2 (2012): 485–500.

Stoughton, Kathleen M. "A New Approach to Voter ID Challenges: Section 2 of the Voting Rights Act." *George Washington Law Review* 81, no. 1 (2013): 292–320.

Strauss, David A. "Modernization and Representation Reinforcement: An Essay in Memory of John Hart Ely." *Stanford Law Review* 57 (2004): 761–778.

Sundquist, James L. *Dynamics of the Party System.* Washington, DC: Brookings Institution Press, 1973.

Sunstein, Cass R. *The Partial Constitution.* Cambridge, MA: Harvard University Press, 1993.

———. "Second Amendment Minimalism: *Heller* as *Griswold.*" *Harvard Law Review* 122 (2008): 246–274.

Sunstein, Cass R., and Thomas J. Miles. "Depoliticizing Administrative Law." *Duke Law Journal* 58 (2009): 2193–2230.

Sunstein, Cass R., David Schkade, Lisa M. Ellman, and Andres Sawicki. *Are Judges Political? An Empirical Analysis of the Federal Judiciary.* Washington, DC: Brookings Institution Press, 2006.

Swain, Carol M. *Black Faces, Black Interests: The Representation of African Americans in Congress.* Cambridge, MA: Harvard University Press, 1993.

Tamanaha, Brian Z. *Realistic Socio-Legal Theory: Pragmatism and a Social Theory of Law.* New York: Oxford University Press, 1999.

Tang, Aaron. "Life after *Janus.*" *Columbia Law Review* 119, no. 3 (2019): 677–762.

Tate, C. Neal. "Personal Attribute Models of the Voting Behavior of U.S. Supreme Court Justices' Liberalism in Civil Liberties and Economics Decisions, 1946–1978." *American Political Science Review* 75, no. 2 (1981): 355–367.

Tate, C. Neal, and Roger Handberg. "Time Binding and Theory Building in Personal Attribute Models of Supreme Court Voting Behavior, 1916–88." *American Journal of Political Science* 35 (1991): 460–480.

Tate, Katherine. *From Protest to Politics: The New Black Voters in American Elections.* Cambridge, MA: Harvard University Press, 1993.

Teles, Steven M. *Rise of the Conservative Movement: The Battle for Control of the Law.* Princeton, NJ: Princeton University Press, 2008.

TerBeek, Calvin. "The Constitution as Political Program: The Republican Party and Originalism, 1977–1988." Paper presented at the annual meeting of the Midwest Political Science Association, Chicago, April 2019.

———. "Dog Whistling, the Color-Blind Jurisprudential Regime, and the Constitutional Politics of Race." *Constitutional Commentary* 30 (2014): 169–192.

———. "Originalist Scholarship and Conservative Politics: Review of *A Republic, If You Can Keep It,* by Neil Gorsuch, and *Originalism's Promise: A Natural Law Account of the American Constitution,* by Lee J. Strang." *New Rambler Review,* October 9, 2019.

Thompson, Daniel M., Jennifer Wu, Jesse Yoder, and Andrew B. Hall. "The Neutral Partisan Effects of Vote-by-Mail: Evidence from County-Level Roll-Outs." Unpublished manuscript, Democracy and Polarization Lab, Stanford University, April 25, 2020. http://www.andrewbenjaminhall.com/Thompson_et_al_VBM.pdf.

Timm, Jane C., and Adam Edelman. "Illegal Voting? Not Much in Kobach's Home State." NBC News, July 19, 2017.

Tokaji, Daniel P. "Early Returns on Election Reform: Discretion, Disenfranchisement, and the Help America Vote Act." *George Washington Law Review* 73 (2005): 1206–1253.

———. "The New Vote Denial: Where Election Reform Meets the Voting Rights Act." *South Carolina Law Review* 57 (2006): 689–732.

———. "Responding to *Shelby County*: A Grand Election Bargain." *Harvard Law and Policy Review* 8 (2014): 71–108.

———. "Restricting Race-Conscious Redistricting." *Regulatory Review,* July 31, 2017.

———. "The Story of *Shaw v. Reno*: Representation and Raceblindness." In *Race Law Stories,* ed. Rachel F. Moran and Devon Wayne Carbado, 497–539. St. Paul, MN: Foundation, 2008.

———. "Voter Registration and Election Reform." *William and Mary Bill of Rights Journal* 17, no. 2 (2008): 453–506.

Tolson, Franita. "Congressional Authority to Protect Voting Rights after *Shelby County* and *Arizona Inter Tribal.*" *Election Law Journal* 13 (2014): 322–335.

Toobin, Jeffrey. "Holder v. Roberts." *New Yorker,* February 17, 2014.

———. "Money Unlimited." *New Yorker,* May 21, 2012.

"Top Election Spenders." OpenSecrets.org, Center for Responsive Politics.

https://www.opensecrets.org/dark-money/top-election-spenders (accessed February 11, 2020).

Totenberg, Nina. "Whose Term Was It? A Look Back at the Supreme Court." *National Public Radio*, July 5, 2013. https://www.npr.org/2013/07/05/198708325/whose-term-was-it-a-look-back-at-the-supreme-court.

"Trump Picked Kavanaugh. How Will He Change the Supreme Court?" *Politico Magazine*, July 9, 2018.

Tushnet, Mark. *A Court Divided: The Rehnquist Court and the Future of Constitutional Law*. New York: W. W. Norton, 2006.

Tyson, Alec, and Shiva Maniam. "Behind Trump's Victory: Divisions by Race, Gender, Education." Pew Research Center, November 9, 2016. https://www.pewresearch.org/fact-tank/2016/11/09/behind-trumps-victory-divisions-by-race-gender-education/.

Ulmer, S. Sidney. "The Political Party Variable in the Michigan Supreme Court." *Journal of Public Law* 11 (1962): 352–362.

———. "Supreme Court Behavior and Civil Rights." *Western Political Quarterly* 13, no. 2 (1960): 288–311.

Urribarri, Raul Sanchez. "Politicization of the Latin American Judiciary via Informal Connections." In *Legitimacy, Legal Development and Change*, ed. David K. Linnan, 307–322. Surrey, UK: Ashgate, 2012.

US Elections Assistance Commission. Election Crimes: An Initial Review and Recommendations for Future Study, 2006. www.eac.gov/clearinghouse/docs/reportsandsurveys2006electioncrimes.pdf/.

US Government Accountability Office. "Elections: Issues Related to State Voter Identification Laws." Report to Congressional Requesters, September 2014. https://www.gao.gov/assets/670/665966.pdf.

Valelly, Rick. "*Shelby* and the Sisyphean Struggle for Black Disenfranchisement." 2014. http://digitalcommons.law.umaryland.edu/cgi/viewcontent.cgi?article=1175&context=schmooze_papers.

Valentino, Nicholas A., and Fabian G. Neuner. "Why the Sky Didn't Fall: Mobilizing Anger in Reaction to Voter ID Laws." *Political Psychology* 38, no. 2 (2017): 331–350.

Vandewalker, Ian, and Keith Gunnar Bentele. "Vulnerability in Numbers: Racial Composition of the Electorate, Voter Suppression, and the Voting Rights Act." *Harvard Latino Law Review* 18 (2015): 99–150.

Vercellotti, Timothy, and David Andersen. "Voter-Identification Requirements and the Learning Curve." *PS: Political Science and Politics* 42 (2009): 117–120.

Viebeck, Elise, Amy Gardner, and Michael Scherer. "Trump, GOP Challenge Efforts to Make Voting Easier Amid Coronavirus Pandemic." *Washington Post*, April 4, 2020.

Vining, Richard L., Jr. "Politics, Pragmatism, and Departures from the U.S. Courts of Appeals, 1954–2004." *Social Science Quarterly* 90, no. 4 (2009): 834–853.

Volokh, Alexander. "Choosing Interpretive Methods: A Positive Theory of Judges and Everyone Else." *New York University Law Review* 83 (2008): 769–846.

Vose, Clement E. *Caucasians Only: The Supreme Court, the NAACP, and the Restrictive Covenant Cases.* Berkeley: University of California Press, 1959.

Wald, Patricia M. "A Response to Tiller and Cross." *Columbia Law Review* 99, no. 1 (1999): 235–261.

Waldman, Michael. "An Alarming Day for Democracy." *Politico,* July 9, 2018.

Waldman, Paul. "We're Living in an Age of Minority Rule." *Washington Post,* July 13, 2018.

Walker, Thomas G., Lee Epstein, and William J. Dixon. "On the Mysterious Demise of Consensual Norms in the United States Supreme Court." *Journal of Politics* 50 (1988): 361–389.

Wang, Hanso Lo. "Deceased GOP Strategist's Daughter Makes Files Public that Republicans Wanted Sealed." National Public Radio, January 5, 2020.

Wang, Sam. "The Great Gerrymander of 2012." *New York Times,* February 2, 2013.

———. "Three Tests for Practical Evaluation of Partisan Gerrymandering." *Stanford Law Review* 68, no. 6 (2016): 1263–1321.

Wang, Tova Andrea. *The Politics of Voter Suppression: Defending and Expanding Americans' Right to Vote.* Ithaca, NY: Cornell University Press, 2012.

———. "A Rigged Report on U.S. Voting." *Washington Post,* August 30, 2007.

Ward, Artemus. *Deciding to Leave.* Albany: State University of New York Press, 2003.

Ward, Artemus, and David L. Weiden. *Sorcerers' Apprentices: 100 Years of Law Clerks at the United States Supreme Court.* New York: New York University Press, 2006.

Warren, Earl. *The Memoirs of Earl Warren.* New York: Doubleday, 1977.

Wasserman, David. "Introducing the 2017 Cook Political Report Partisan Voter Index." *Cook Political Report,* April 7, 2017.

Watkins, Eli, and Joan Biskupic. "Trump Slams Chiefs Justice after Roberts Chides the President." CNN, November 21, 2018. https://www.cnn.com /2018/11/21/politics/supreme-court-john-roberts-trump/index.html.

Waymer, Damian, and Robert L. Heath. "Black Voter Dilution, American Exceptionalism, and Racial Gerrymandering." *Journal of Black Studies* 47, no. 7 (2016): 635–658.

Weiner, Daniel I. "*Citizens United* Five Years Later." Brennan Center for Justice, January 15, 2015.

Weiser, Wendy R., and Max Feldman. "The State of Voting 2018." Brennan Center for Justice, June 5, 2018. https://www.brennancenter.org/publication /state-voting-2018.

Whitaker, Seth Warren. "State Redistricting Law: *Stephenson v. Bartlett* and the Judicial Promotion of Electoral Competition." *Virginia Law Review* 91 (2005): 203–247.

White, Ariel R., Noah L. Nathan, and Julie K. Faller. "What Do I Need to Vote? Bureaucratic Discretion and Discrimination by Local Election Officials." *American Political Science Review* 109 (2015):129–142.

Whitehouse, Senator Sheldon. "The Many Sins of *Citizens United.*" *Nation,* September 24, 2015.

Whittington, Keith E. "'Interpose Your Friendly Hand': Political Supports for the Exercise of Judicial Review by the United States Supreme Court." *American Political Science Review* 99 (2005): 583–596.

———. *The Political Foundations of Judicial Supremacy.* Princeton, NJ: Princeton University Press, 2007.

———. *Repugnant Laws: Judicial Review of Acts of Congress from the Founding to the Present.* Lawrence: University Press of Kansas, 2019.

Williams, Jackson. "Irreconcilable Principles: Law, Politics, and the Illinois Supreme Court." *Northern Illinois University Law Review* 18 (1998) 267–330.

Williams, Juan. "GOP's Voter ID Campaign Aimed at Suppressing Constitutional Rights." *The Hill*, October 15, 2012. http://thehill.com/opinion /columnists/juan-williams/261945-opinion-gops-voter-id-campaign-aimed -at-supressing-constitutional-rights.

Wilson, David C. "Public Opinion on Voter ID Laws: Strong Support, Shaky Foundation." *Huffington Post*, September 7, 2012. www.huffingtonpost .com/david-c-wilson/public-opinion-on-voter-i_b_1683873.html.

Wilson, David C., and Paul R. Brewer. "The Foundations of Public Opinion on Voter ID Laws: Political Predispositions, Racial Resentment, and Information Effects." *Public Opinion Quarterly* 77, no. 4 (2013): 962–984.

Wilson, James Q., John J. Dilulio Jr., and Meena Bose. *American Government, Brief Version*, 11th ed. Boston: Wadsworth, 2012.

Wilson, Reid. "Metro Area Populations Surge as Rural America Shrinks." *The Hill*, March 22, 2018. https://thehill.com/homenews/state-watch/379650 -metro-area-populations-surge-as-rural-america-shrinks.

Windett, Jason H., Jeffrey J. Harden, and Matthew E. K. Hall. "Estimating Dynamic Ideal Points for State Supreme Courts." *Political Analysis* 23, no. 3 (2015): 461–469.

Wines, Michael. "Critics See Efforts by Counties and Towns to Purge Minority Voters from Rolls." *New York Times*, August 1, 2016.

———. "Deceased G.O.P. Strategist's Hard Drives Reveal New Details on the Census Citizenship Question." *New York Times*, May 30, 2019.

"Wisconsin Democrat Jill Karofsky in Supreme Court Election Upset." BBC News, April 14, 2020. https://www.bbc.com/news/world-us-canada-52279608.

Wolfinger, Raymond E., and Steven J. Rosenstone. *Who Votes?* New Haven, CT: Yale University Press, 1980.

Wood, Abby K. "Campaign Finance Disclosure." *Annual Review of Law and Social Science* 14 (2018): 11–27.

Woodson, Benjamin, James L. Gibson, and Milton Lodge. "Judicial Symbols and the Link between Institutional Legitimacy and Acquiescence." Paper presented at the annual meeting of the American Political Science Association, September 2011.

Wootson, Cleve R., Jr. "Donald Trump: 'I Won the Popular Vote If You Deduct the Millions of People Who Voted Illegally.'" *Washington Post*, November 27, 2016. https://www.washingtonpost.com/news/the-fix/wp/2016/11/27 /donald-trump-i-won-the-popular-vote-if-you-deduct-the-millions-of-people -who-voted-illegally/?utm_term=.988b2c7d0486.

Wrightsman, Lawrence S. "Persuasion in the Decision Making of U.S. Supreme Court Justices." In *The Psychology of Judicial Decision Making*, ed. David Klein and Gregory Mitchell, 57–72. New York: Oxford University Press, 2010.

Yeomans, William. "Judicial Hubris." *Justice Watch*, June 25, 2013. http://afjjusticewatch.blogspot.com/2013/06/judicial-hubris.html.

Yoon, Albert. "Pensions, Politics, and Judicial Tenure: An Empirical Study of Federal Judges, 1869–2002." *American Law and Economics Review* 8 (2006): 143–180.

Yoshinaka, Antoine, and Chad Murphy. "The Paradox of Redistricting: How Partisan Mapmakers Foster Competition but Disrupt Representation." *Political Research Quarterly* 64 (2011): 435–447.

Yung, Corey Rayburn. "Beyond Ideology: An Empirical Study of Partisanship and Independence in the Federal Courts." *George Washington Law Review* 80 (2012): 505–567.

Zilis, Michael. *The Limits of Legitimacy: Dissenting Opinions, Media Coverage, and Public Responses to Supreme Court Decisions*. Ann Arbor: University of Michigan Press, 2015.

Zorn, Christopher J. W., and Steven R. Van Winkle. 2000. "A Competing Risks Model of Supreme Court Vacancies, 1789–1992." *Political Behavior* 22 (2000): 145–166.

Index